Textual Layering

Textual Layering

Contact, Historicity, Critique

EDITED BY MARIA MARGARONI,
APOSTOLOS LAMPROPOULOS,
AND CHRISTAKIS CHATZICHRISTOU

Published by Lexington Books
An imprint of The Rowman & Littlefield Publishing Group, Inc.
4501 Forbes Boulevard, Suite 200, Lanham, Maryland 20706
www.rowman.com

Unit A, Whitacre Mews, 26-34 Stannary Street, London SE11 4AB

British Library Cataloguing in Publication Information Available

Library of Congress Cataloging-in-Publication Data
The hardback edition of this book was previously catalogued by the Library of Congress
as follows:

Margaroni, Maria, editor. | Lampropoulos, Apostolos, editor. | Chatzichristou, Christakis,
editor.
Textual layering : contact, historicity, critique / edited by Maria
    Margaroni, Apostolos Lampropoulos, and Christos Hadjichristos.
Lanham : Lexington Books, 2017. | Series: Textures: philosophy /
    literature / culture | Includes bibliographical references and index.
LCCN 2016053177 (print) | LCCN 2016057245 (ebook)
LCSH: Meaning (Philosophy) | Feminist theory.
LCC B105.M4 T49 2017 (print) | LCC B105.M4 (ebook) | DDC
    121/.68--dc23
LC record available at https://lccn.loc.gov/2016053177

ISBN 9781498501330 (cloth : alk. paper)
ISBN 9781498501354 (pbk. : alk. paper)
ISBN 9781498501347 (electronic)

Printed in the United States of America

Contents

Abbreviations

A	Sophocles. *Antigone*, translated by David Grene. Pp. 177–232 in *Greek Tragedies*, vol. 1, edited by David Grene and Richmond Lattimore. Chicago: University of Chicago Press, 1991.
AC	Butler, Judith. *Antigone's Claim: Kinship between Life and Death*. New York: Columbia University Press, 2000.
AF	Derrida, Jacques. "Archive Fever: A Freudian Impression," translated by Eric Prenowitz. *Diacritics* 25, no. 2 (summer 1995), 9–63.
AO	Grosz, Elizabeth. *Architecture from the Outside: Essays on Virtual and Real Space*. Boston: MIT Press, 2001.
AT	Hereth, Michael. *Alexis de Tocqueville: Threats to Freedom in Democracy*, translated by George Bogardus. Durham, NC: Duke University Press, 1986.
B	Butler, Judith. *Bodies That Matter: On the Discursive Limits of "Sex."* New York: Routledge, 1993.
BG	Libeskind, Daniel. *Breaking Ground: Adventures in Life and Architecture*. New York: Riverhead Books, 2004.
BT	Nietzsche, Friedrich. *The Birth of Tragedy and the Case of Wagner*, translated by Walter Kaufmann. New York: Vintage, 1967.
C	Deleuze, Gilles. *Cinema 2: The Time Image*, translated by Hugh Tomlinson and Robert Galeta. Minneapolis: University of Minnesota Press, 1989.
CC	Agamben, Giorgio. *The Coming Community*, translated by Michael Hardt. Minneapolis: University of Minnesota Press, 1993.
CJ	Kant, Immanuel. *Critique of Judgment*, translated by Werner S. Pluhar. Indianapolis: Hackett Publishing, 1987.
COC	Rowe, Colin, and Fred Koetter, "Collage City." *Architectural Review* 158, no. 942 (August 1975), 66–90.
CP	Critchley, Simon. *Continental Philosophy: A Very Short Introduction*. Oxford: Oxford University Press, 2001.
CS	Kristeva, Julia. *Crisis of the ~~European~~ Subject*, translated by Susan Fairfield. New York: Other Press, 2000.
CSR	Reder, Michael. *Conversations with Salman Rushdie*. Jackson: University Press of Mississippi, 2000.
CWB	Benjamin, Walter. *The Correspondence of Walter Benjamin*, translated by Manfred R. Jacobson and Evelyn M. Jacobson, edited by Gershom Scholem and Theodor Adorno. Chicago: University of Chicago Press, 1994.
D	Derrida, Jacques. *Dissemination*, translated by Barbara Johnson. London: Athlone Press, 1981.
DE	Jay, Martin. *Downcast Eyes: The Denigration of Vision in Twentieth-Century French Thought*. Berkeley, Los Angeles and London: University of California Press, 1993.

DER   Deleuze, Gilles. *Différence et Répétition*. Paris: Presses Universitaires de France, 1993.

DI   Bakhtin, Mikhail M. *Dialogic Imagination: Four Essays*, translated by Caryl Emerson. Austin: University of Texas Press, 1982.

DL   Kristeva, Julia. *Desire in Language: A Semiotic Approach to Literature and Art*, translated by Thomas Gora, Alice Jardine, and Leon S. Roudiez. New York: Columbia University Press, 1980.

DR   Deleuze, Gilles. *Difference and Repetition*, translated by Paul Patton. New York: Columbia University Press, 1994.

EP   Agamben, Giorgio. *The End of the Poem*, translated by Daniel Heller-Roazen. Stanford: Stanford University Press, 1999.

ET   Wyschogrod, Edith. "Eating the Text, Defiling the Hands: Specters in Arnold Schoenberg's Opera *Moses and Aron*." Pp. 245–59 in *God, the Gift, and Postmodernism*, edited by John D. Caputo and Michael J. Scanlon. Bloomington: Indiana University Press, 1999.

F   Deleuze, Gilles. *Foucault*. Paris, Les Editions de Minuit, 2004.

FF   Doane, Mary Ann. *Femmes Fatales: Feminism, Film Theory, Psychoanalysis*. New York: Routledge, 1991.

FFF   Berlatsky, Erik L. *Fact, Fiction, and Fabrication: History, Narrative, and the Postmodern Real from Woolf to Rushdie*. PhD diss., University of Maryland, 2003.

FP   Kristeva, Julia. "Feminism and Psychoanalysis," interview by Elaine Hoffman Baruch. Pp. 113–21 in *Julia Kristeva: Interviews*, edited by Ross Mitchell Guberman. New York: Columbia University Press, 1996.

FS   Clément, Catherine, and Julia Kristeva. *The Feminine and the Sacred*, translated by Jane Marie Todd. New York: Columbia University Press, 2001.

FT   Cusset, François. *French Theory: How Foucault, Derrida, Deleuze & Co. Transformed the Intellectual Life of the United States*, translated by Jeff Fort with Josephine Berganza and Marion Jones. Minneapolis: Minnesota University Press, 2008.

GB   Benjamin, Walter. *Gesammelte Briefe*, 6 vols., edited by C. Gödde and H. Lonitz. Frankfurt: Suhrkamp, 1995–2000.

GS   Benjamin, Walter. *Gesammelte Schriften*, 14 vols., edited by R. Tiedemann et al. Frankfurt: Suhrkamp, 1974–1999.

GT   Butler, Judith. *Gender Trouble: Feminism and the Subversion of Identity*. New York: Routledge, 1990.

HM   Chakrabarty, Dipesh. *Habitations of Modernity*. Chicago and London: The University of Chicago Press, 2002.

HP   Kristeva, Julia. *La haine et le pardon*. Vol. 3 of *Pouvoirs et limites de la psychanalyse*. Paris: Fayard, 2005.

HS   Agamben, Giorgio. *Homo Sacer: Sovereign Power and Bare Life*, translated by Daniel Heller-Roazen. Stanford: Stanford University Press, 1998.

I   Sartre, Jean-Paul. *The Imaginary: A Phenomenological Psychology of the Imagination*, translated by Jonathan Webber. London and New York: Routledge, 2004.

IAH   Agamben, Giorgio. *Infancy and History: On the Destruction of Experience*, translated by Liz Heron. London and New York: Verso, 2007.

IDS   Buchanan, Ian, and Gregg Lambert. "Introduction." Pp. 1–15 in *Deleuze and Space*, edited by Ian Buchanan and Gregg Lambert. Edinburgh: Edinburgh University Press, 2005.

IE   Marion, Jean-Luc. *In Excess: Studies of Saturated Phenomena*. New York: Fordham University Press, 2002.

IH   Rushdie, Salman. *Imaginary Homelands*. London: Penguin Books, 1991.

IP   Agamben, Giorgio. *Idea of Prose*, translated by Michael Sullivan and Sam Whitsitt. Albany: SUNY Press, 1995.

IR   Kristeva, Julia. *Intimate Revolt*. Vol. 2 of *The Powers and Limits of Psychoanalysis*, translated by Jeanine Herman. New York: Columbia University Press, 2002.

IWS   Moran, Brendan. "An Inhumanly Wise Shame." *The European Legacy* 14, no. 5 (August 2009), 573–85.

JK   Lechte, John, and Maria Margaroni. *Julia Kristeva: Live Theory*. New York: Continuum, 2004.

KD   Müller, Bernd. *"Denn ist noch nichts geschehen." Walter Benjamins Kafka-Deutung*. Cologne: Böhlau, 1996.

KF   Ziarek, Ewa Płonowska. "Kristeva and Fanon: Revolutionary Violence and Ironic Articulation." Pp. 57–75 in *Revolt, Affect, Collectivity: The Unstable Boundaries of Kristeva's Polis*, edited by Tina Chanter and Ewa Płonowska Ziarek. Albany: SUNY Press, 2005.

KL   Gasché, Rodolphe. "Kafka's Law: In the Field of Forces between Judaism and Hellenism." *MLN* 117, no. 5 (December 2002), 971–1002.

KS   Kafka, Franz. *Kafka's Selected Stories*, translated and edited by S. Corngold. New York: W.W. Norton and Company, 2007.

LA   Watkin, William. *The Literary Agamben: Adventures in Logopoiesis*. London: Continumm, 2010.

LC   Bhabha, Homi K. *The Location of Culture*. London: Routledge Classics, 2004.

LH   Sewell, William. *Logics of History: Social Theory and Social Transformation*. Chicago: University of Chicago Press, 2005.

LK   Arendt, Hannah. *Lectures on Kant's Political Philosophy*, edited by Ronald Beiner. Chicago: University of Chicago Press, 1982.

LS   Deleuze, Gilles. *Logique du sens*. Paris: Les Editions de Minuit, 2002.

M   Badiou, Alain. *Metapolitics*, translated by Jason Barker. London: Verso, 2005.

MA   Else, Gerald F. *The Madness of Antigone*. Heidelberg: Carl Winter Universitätsverlag, 1976.

MC   Rushdie, Salman. *Midnight's Children*. London: Vintage, 1995.

ME   Bartlett, Robert. *The Making of Europe: Conquest, Colonization and Cultural Change, 950–1350*. London: Penguin, 1994.

ML   Irigaray, Luce. *Marine Lover of Friedrich Nietzsche*, translated by Gillian C. Gill. New York: Columbia University Press, 1991.

MM   Kant, Immanuel. *The Metaphysics of Morals*, translated by Mary Gregor. Cambridge: Cambridge University Press, 1991.

MRA   Henrich, Dieter. "On the Meaning of Rational Action in the State." Pp. 97–116 in *Kant and Political Philosophy: The Contemporary Legacy*, edited by Ronald Beiner and W. J. Booth. New Haven: Yale University Press, 1993.

MS1   Stiegler, Bernard. *De la misère symbolique*. Vol. 1, *L'époque hyperindustrielle*. Paris: Galilée, 2004.

MS2   Stiegler, Bernard. *De la misère symbolique*. Vol. 2, *La catastrophe du sensible*. Paris: Galilée, 2005.

MT   Hansen, Mark. "Media Theory." *Theory, Culture and Society* 23, no. 2–3 (May 2006), 297–306.

MTG   Vernant, Jean-Pierre, and Pierre Vidal-Naquet. *Myth and Tragedy in Ancient Greece*, translated by Janet Lloyd. Cambridge, MA: Zone Books, 1990.

MV   Loraux, Nicole. *The Mourning Voice: An Essay on Greek Tragedy*, translated by Elizabeth Trapnell Rawlings. Ithaca, NY: Cornell University Press, 2002.

MWC   Agamben, Giorgio. *The Man without Content*, translated by Georgia Albert. Stanford: Stanford University Press, 1999.

MWE   Agamben, Giorgio. *Means without End: Notes on Politics*, translated by Vincenzo Binetti and Cesare Casarino. Minneapolis: University of Minnesota Press, 2000.

NE   Schmitt, Carl. *The Nomos of the Earth in the International Law of the Jus Publicum Europaeum*, translated by G. L. Ulmen. New York: Telos Press, 2003.

NM   Kristeva, Julia. *New Maladies of the Soul*, translated by Ross Guberman. New York: Columbia University Press, 1995.

O   Agamben, Giorgio. *The Open: Man and Animal*, translated by Kevin Attell. Stanford: Stanford University Press, 2004.

OC   Sophocles. *Oedipus at Colonus*, translated by David Grene. Pp. 77–157 in *Sophocles*, vol. 1, edited by David Grene and Richmond Lattimore. Chicago: The University of Chicago Press, 1991.

OG   Derrida, Jacques. *Of Grammatology*, translated by Gayatri Chakravorty Spivak. Baltimore: Johns Hopkins University Press, 1976.

OGD   Benjamin, Walter. *The Origin of German Tragic Drama*, translated by John Osborne. London: Verso Books, 1998.

ON   Derrida, Jacques. *On the Name*, translated by David Wood, John P. Leavey Jr., and Ian McLeod. Stanford: Stanford University Press, 1995.

P   Agamben, Giorgio. *Profanations*, translated by Jeff Fort. New York: Zone Books, 2007.

PA   Anderson, Perry. *Passages from Antiquity to Feudalism*. London: Verso, 1978.

PB   Greenaway, Peter. *The Pillow Book*. Paris: DIS VOIR, 1996.

PD   Collin, Françoise. "The Praxis of Difference: Notes on the Tragedy of the Subject." Pp. 8–23 in *French Women Philosophers: A Contemporary Reader; Subjectivity, Identity, Alterity*, edited by Christina Howells. London and New York: Routledge, 2004.

PE   Chakrabarty, Dipesh. *Provincializing Europe: Postcolonial Thought and Historical Difference*. Princeton: Princeton University Press, 2000.

PGI   Greenaway, Peter. Interview with S. H. Abbot (1997), http://users.skynet.be/chrisrenson-makemovies/Greenaw3.htm (accessed July 28, 2011).

PH   Kristeva, Julia. *Powers of Horror: An Essay on Abjection*, translated by Leon S. Roudiez. New York: Columbia University Press, 1982.

PI   Derrida, Jacques. *Points. . . : Interviews, 1974–1994*, translated by Peggy Kamuf et al., edited by Elisabeth Weber. Stanford: Stanford University Press, 1995.

PO   Agamben, Giorgio. *Potentialities: Collected Essays in Philosophy*, translated by Daniel Heller-Roazen. Stanford: Stanford University Press, 1999.

POP   Hutcheon, Linda. *A Poetics of Postmodernism: History, Theory, Fiction*. New York: Routledge, 1988.

POW   Merleau-Ponty, Maurice. *The Prose of the World*, translated by John O'Neill. Evanston, IL: Northwestern University Press, 1973.

PP   Merleau-Ponty, Maurice. *Phenomenology of Perception*, translated by Colin Smith. London and New York: Routledge, 1996.

PPM   Bhattacharjee, Anannya. "The Public/Private Mirage: Mapping Homes and Undomesticating Violence Work in the South Asian Immigrant Community." Pp. 353–403 in *Feminist Genealogies, Colonial Legacies, Democratic Futures*, edited by M. Jacqui Alexander and Chandra Talpade Mohanty. New York: Routledge, 1997.

PS   Deleuze, Gilles. *Proust et les signes*. Paris: Quadrige/Presses Universitaires de France, 1998.

PW   Kant, Immanuel. *Political Writings*, translated by H. B. Nisbet, edited by H. S. Reiss. Cambridge: Cambridge University Press, 1970.

QP   Deleuze, Gilles, and Felix Guattari. *Qu'est-ce que la philosophie?* Paris: Les Editions de Minuit, 2000.

RA   Agamben, Giorgio. *Remnants of Auschwitz: The Witness and the Archive*, translated by Daniel Heller-Roazen. New York: Zone Books, 1999.

RI   Kristeva, Julia. *La révolte intime*. Vol. 2 of *Pouvoirs et limites de la psychanalyse*. Paris: Fayard, 1997.

RM   Libeskind, Daniel. *radix-matrix*. Munich: Prestel Verlag, 1997.

RPL   Kristeva, Julia. *Revolution in Poetic Language*, translated by Margaret Waller. New York: Columbia University Press, 1984.

RS	Kristeva, Julia. *Revolt She Said*, translated by Brian O'Keeffe. Los Angeles and New York: Semiotext(e), 2002.
S	Merleau-Ponty, Maurice. *Signes*. Paris: Gallimard, 1960.
SE	Libeskind, Daniel. *The Space of Encounter*. New York: Universe Publishing, 2000.
SH	Rushdie, Salman. *Shame*. London: Vintage, 1995.
SI	Howe, Susan. *Singularities*. Hanover, NH: Wesleyan University Press, 1990.
SIQ	Bourdieu, Pierre. *Sociology in Question*, translated by Richard Nice. London: Sage Publications, 1993.
SM	Colebrook, Claire. "The Space of Man: On the Specificity of Affect in Deleuze and Guattari." Pp. 189–206 in *Deleuze and Space*, edited by Ian Buchanan and Gregg Lambert. Edinburgh: Edinburgh University Press, 2005.
SNS	Kristeva, Julia. *The Sense and Non-Sense of Revolt*. Vol. 1 of *The Powers and Limits of Psychoanalysis*, translated by Jeanine Herman. New York: Columbia University Press, 2000.
SNT	Kortenaar, Neil ten. *Self, Nation, Text in Salman Rushdie's "Midnight's Children."* Montreal: McGill-Queen's University Press, 2004.
SOW	Irigaray, Luce. *Speculum of the Other Woman*, translated by Gillian Gill. Ithaca, NY: Cornell University Press, 1985.
SQ	Derrida, Jacques. *Sovereignties in Question*, edited by Thomas Dutoit and Outi Pasanen. New York: Fordham University Press, 2005.
SS	Debord, Guy. *The Society of the Spectacle*, translated by Donald Nicholson-Smith. New York: Zone Books, 2006.
ST	Benardete, Seth. *Sacred Transgressions: A Reading of Sophocles' "Antigone."* South Bend, IN: St. Augustine's Press, 1999.
SV	Rushdie, Salman. *The Satanic Verses*. London: Vintage, 1998.
SW	Benjamin, Walter. *Selected Writings*, 4 vols., edited by M. W. Jennings et al. Cambridge, MA: The Belknap Press of Harvard University Press, 1996–2003.
TA	Hansen, Mark. "Time of Affect, or Bearing Witness to Life." *Critical Inquiry* 30 (spring 2004), 584–626.
TE	Schor, Naomi. "This Essentialism Which Is Not One: Coming to Grips with Irigaray." Pp. 57–78 in *Engaging with Irigaray: Feminist Philosophy and Modern European Thought*, edited by Carolyn Burke, Naomi Schor and Margaret Whitford. New York: Columbia University Press, 1994.
TGS	Nietzsche, Friedrich. *The Gay Science*, translated by Walter Kaufmann. New York: Vintage Books, 1974.
THS	Irigaray, Luce. *This Sex Which Is Not One*, translated by Catherine Porter with Carolyn Burke. Ithaca, NY: Cornell University Press, 1985.
TL	Kristeva, Julia. *Tales of Love*, translated by Leon S. Roudiez. New York: Columbia University Press, 1987.
TQ	Brandt, Joan. "Julia Kristeva and the Revolutionary Politics of *Tel*

Quel." Pp. 21–36 in *Revolt, Affect, Collectivity: the Unstable Boundaries of Kristeva's Polis*, edited by Tina Chanter and Ewa Płonowska Ziarek. Albany, NY: SUNY Press, 2005.

TR   Agamben, Giorgio. *The Time That Remains: A Commentary on the Letter to the Romans*, translated by Patricia Dailey. Stanford: Stanford University Press, 2005.

TS   Kristeva, Julia. *Le temps sensible: Proust et l'expérience littéraire.* Paris: Gallimard, 1994.

TT2   Stiegler, Bernard. *La technique et le temps.* Vol. 2, *La désorientation.* Paris: Galilée, 1996.

TT3   Stiegler, Bernard. *La technique et le temps.* Vol. 3, *Le temps du cinéma et la question du mal-être.* Paris: Galilée, 2001.

VI   Merleau-Ponty, Maurice. *Le visible et l'invisible, suivi de notes de travail*, edited by Claude Lefort. Paris: Gallimard, 1971.

W   Tocqueville, Alexis de. *Writings on Empire and Slavery*, translated and edited by Jennifer Pitts. Baltimore: Johns Hopkins University Press, 2001.

WD   Derrida, Jacques. "Freud and the Scene of Writing." Pp. 196–231 in *Writing and Difference*, translated by Alan Bass. London: Routledge, 1978.

WUP   Rrenban, Monad. *Wild, Unforgettable Philosophy.* Lanham, MD: Lexington, 2005.

Acknowledgments

This book has taken a while to come to fruition. A lot of the aesthetic, textual, political, and philosophical concerns that constitute the focus of the book actually originated and were first introduced in the context of the 31st Symposium of the International Association for Philosophy and Literature (IAPL), which was held in Nicosia, Cyprus (4–9 June 2007). We would like to take this opportunity to thank the University of Cyprus for funding and hosting what turned out to be a vibrant and memorable event.

We owe a special debt to the contributors of this volume who have trusted us with their work and who, in the course of the past six years, have not lost faith in the project. We would also like to convey our deepest and most sincere thanks to Evangelos Roumeliotis for his meticulous copyediting of the essays, his professionalism, reliability, and tireless assistance, without which the book would never have been brought into completion.

Finally, our most heartfelt gratitude goes to the late Hugh J. Silverman, the philosopher whose vision has nourished (and continues to nourish) IAPL since its inception in 1976. Hugh Silverman's unwavering commitment to the critical Humanities has offered us all, at different stages of our academic life, a much sought-for refuge amidst the increasing financial, political, and other pressures that compromise thought and its life-giving, life-renewing force. The 2007 Cyprus conference on "Layering: Textual, Visual, Spatial, Temporal" (and, by extension, the present volume) was first conceived in the context of a discussion with him up on the Troodos mountain. All three of us have very fond memories of this discussion and of Hugh's smiling openness, the incredible generosity of his spirit.

Textual Layering: Contact, Historicity, Critique is dedicated to his memory.

Grateful acknowledgment is made to the following sources for permission to reproduce material previously published elsewhere: Indiana University Press for part of the introduction to *The Picture of Abjection: Film Fetish and the Nature of Difference* by Tina Chanter (2008); Open Humanities Press for chapter 8, an early version of which was first published as "Ennobled Colonialism and Counter-Revolution: The Thermidorean Thrust of Legal Positivism in Kant and Tocqueville" in *Parrhesia: Journal of Critical Philosophy* 14 (summer 2012), 36–55; Polity Press for chapter 11, a longer version of which is published in *Kristeva: Thresholds* by S. K. Keltner (2011); and Texas Tech University Press for chapter 12, a longer and significantly different version of which was published as "Rhiza Aimatoessa: On *Antigone*" in *Intertexts* 11, no. 1 (spring 2007), 1–23.

General Introduction

Textual Tradition, Body-Layering, and Nagiko's Seductions

Maria Margaroni

The term "layering" is currently used in a wide range of fields, including metaphor studies and linguistics, cybernetics, the social sciences, art, and architecture. In these contexts, the concept of "layering" functions as a paradigm for the diachronic sedimentation of information, meaning, affect, or images; the synchronic overlapping/juxtaposition of data, materials, objects, texts, photographs, compositional devices, or motifs; the methodological employment of a variety of approaches, techniques, or levels of analysis; the structural and hierarchical relationship established among individual components within a system. Irrespective of the context in which it is used and its actual function, "layering" has been invested with connotations of complexity, density and depth, mainly on the basis of the fact that the process of layering does not neutralize or cancel out the distinctness, the *marked singularity* of individual layers. More importantly, perhaps, it has been promoted as the very principle of "connection" (hence its recurrent association with the conceptual operations of metaphor) and "interconnectedness," the conviction, in other words, that everything in human life and thought is "affecting everything else."[1]

Though informed by some of the contexts above, this book employs the concept of "layering" as a convenient node where some of the key terms in what post-1960s we call the "theoretical Humanities" intersect in more or less tension. From the perspective we are adopting here, it needs to be noted that these terms (e.g., textuality, trace, memory, *différance*, spacing, the fold, intertext, the polylogue, and palimpsest, among others) have been crucial for the understanding and rethinking of three central postwar theoretical "scenes"—in Jacques Derrida's sense of the term:[2] namely, the scene of writing, the scene of history, and the (ob)scene of the (feminine-connoted) Outside. In what follows my aim is to attempt a multiple exposure of these three scenes on the rich, visually and textually layered body of Peter Greenaway's *The Pillow Book*, a 1996 film that will serve as my paradigm for the "erotics of thought" that has generated this volume.

As François Cusset defines it, the term "erotics of thought" refers to the desire that "heats up in contact with texts, whether taken whole or in fragments."[3] It, therefore, denotes not only the "flirtatious glances" of texts "moving along the sidewalks of history" (a denotation productively dramatized in part one of this volume) but also points to the subject's libidinal investment in thought (*FT*, 338), which is precisely what breathes life into texts, opening them up to the gifts and tricks of temporality. This is, indeed, why Cusset goes on to argue that this "erotics of thought" grows or diminishes "in proportion to the primary interval . . . between the emergence of writing" (as "a map of breaches" on a receptive surface; *WD*, 205) and its multiple reinscriptions, fadings, re-iterations, misprisions, expropriations, or uncanny returns. It is this historical work of the text (which all too often gets rigidified into the concept of a tradi-tion) that constitutes the main focus of the authors in part two of the volume.

There is, however, yet another interval that complicates and modulates the "erotics of thought" as the seductive contact with/of texts always exposed to the perils of history. In post-1960s Continental Philosophy and Theory this interval has consistently been associated with a certain understanding of "the feminine," posited as that in-between, interstitial site from which, to paraphrase Françoise Collin, the negative can be put to work.[4] In other words, in the context of the postmodern critique of Western metaphysics "the feminine" has repeatedly func-tioned as the space of "undoing, deconstructing, and decentring" that which is taken as an essence—be it Being, Truth, Presence, Logos, etc. (*PD*, 11). In part three of the volume the negative work of "the feminine" is called "de-layering," understood as the process that remains in force while discrete layers fold togeth-er and refold, overlap and become stratified forming tissues, networks, systems, topographies, intertexts, or polylogues; that is, following Julia Kristeva, rhyth-mical compositions that are elaborated as "more-than-a-sentence, more-than-meaning, more-than-significance."[5]

Greenaway's *The Pillow Book* is just such a polylogue, layer upon layer shaping itself in the space of this "more"; this visual, textual, conceptual excess that unworks traditional understandings of "cinema" as much as the positions of spectatorship associated with it. In *The Pillow Book* Nagiko, a Japanese-Chinese fashion-model, shares with us her quest for physical and aesthetic pleasure, a quest traced back to her early experiences as a little girl growing up in Kyoto under the adored shadow of her father, a calligrapher/writer, and in thrall to the loving voice of her aunt, who introduced Nagiko to the sensual journal of Sei Shonagon, a 10th century court lady in attendance to the Empress Sadako. Shonagon's diary, structured around lists of (elegant, splendid, incomparable, annoying . . .) "things," poetry, accounts of everyday events, and amorous ad-ventures, is the central intertext in the narration of the heroine who cherishes a strong sense of a secret bond with this remote female ancestor.[6] Shonagon's "pil-low book" is a tribute to the beauty of language, the body, and material things, which in her writing become intimately connected. It is this experience of con-nectedness that excites and captures the child-Nagiko in the context of the cere-monial inscription of her face that her father performs for her every year on her birthday: the touch of her father-calligrapher's hands on her face; the taste of ink mixed with her saliva; the red characters against her white skin; the co-eruption of speech, in its incantatory function, and the sensual materiality of writing. For Nagiko, Shonagon's distinctly feminine writing that delights in surfaces, tex-tures, colors, shapes, curves, tastes, or scents is inextricable from the more es-tablished art of calligraphy that her father teaches her to relish. Both practices form a heterogeneous but valuable textual tradition which, according to Nagiko, is in danger of extinction in the late 20th century[7] and which she consciously endeavors to preserve, precisely by opening Shonagon's amorous writing that caresses, delights in and sensually receives materiality to her father's "Godlike" practice of inscription[8] that names, blesses, approves, and claims authority over (an inevitably objectified) creaturely life.[9]

The rethinking of textual tradition in its materiality (i.e., in its bodily volume and textures, its drive-charged affect)[10] and its historical embeddedness constitutes an important aim in this collection of essays as well as a central motivation behind our decision to reinvest the concept and paradigms of "layering." Like Nagiko who dedicates herself to writing in the face of the overwhelming assault of the spectacle and the subsequent crisis of the book, the collection situates its intervention within the site of a parallel crisis: namely, the crisis of the theoretical Humanities in the face of a global economic deficit, a profit-oriented model of education, the promotion of commodified knowledge at the expense of wisdom,[11] the appropriation, finally, of liberal values such as democracy, equality, justice, etc. (the distinctive mark of the traditional Humanities) by market-oriented capitalism.[12] As Nagiko realizes, the preservation of a text-based tradition against the dominant tendencies in late 20th-century spectacle-inundated societies necessitates a renewed relation to it and a reappraisal of its most vital legacies. In his brief exposition on the distinctness of what has come to be known as "Continental Thought," Simon Critchley helps us conceptualize such a renewed relation. As he emphasizes, continental thinking defines itself precisely in terms of a concept of tradition, one understood as textual sedimentation over time as well as intertextual synchronicity produced through such practices as translation, philological commentary, critique, and hermeneutics, among others. In his analysis, what characterizes Continental Thought is "a *radical* experience of tradition" that refuses to posit cultural and textual inheritance beyond the necessity of rethinking or interrogation (*CP*, 68; original emphasis). Drawing on Edmund Husserl, Critchley demonstrates how, in Continental Thought, a practice of tradition qua sedimentation/layering is supplemented by a practice that involves both the critical engagement with the sedimented material (i.e., a process of dismantling, destructuring, or de-layering) and its reactivation (through the repetition, the recontextualization, or, indeed, the re-layering of it) (*CP*, 69). As he puts it, "one has to destroy the received and banal sense of the past in order to experience the hidden and surprising power of history" (*CP*, 72). Yet, this, he notes, entails a renewed understanding of the present; in other words, it enables a critique of the present and a historically informed praxis that aims to release its transformative potential (*CP*, 72, 74).

As I will go on to suggest, Nagiko's personal and aesthetic quest as well as Greenaway's own layered cinematic language[13] involve the reclamation of this sense of tradition which unfolds as an unsettling (at times, even violent) experience of *contact* between radically heterogeneous elements: i.e., bodies and texts, images and words, skin/page/the point of a stylus or the hair of a brush, blood and ink, ink and milk, a 10th-century Japanese court lady and a late-20th-

century fashion model, the feminine and marginalized practice of diary writing
and the art of patriarchal calligraphy, an economy of interest-oriented exchange
(exemplified, as we shall see, by the publisher and his profitable business) and a
countereconomy of erotic expenditure (which Nagiko cultivates). Layering in
the film is the visual language of this experience of contact which, as the film
progresses, comes to take on the value of an *ethics*. Through the staging of "a
visual feast around flesh and skin and words and calligraphy," a "mixture of
decorative, flat-patterned, sharply-colored, Japanese-style compositions" and a
palimpsestic overlapping of Eastern and European motifs, Greenaway confronts
us with the radical, pleasurable, disturbing, uncontrollable promiscuity that is
the distinct mark of organic life[14] and that nourishes both human thought and
imagination (*PB*, 9). What he suggests is that, if a text-based tradition can still
be preserved against the assault of the spectacle, this can only be achieved
through the reclamation of the material beauty of texts, the retrieval of their origins in the world of the senses, the return of the in-spirited Word (isolated and
privileged by a long Metaphysical tradition) to its lost home in the body:[15] "No
function of book or body is singular," Nagiko writes. "If a multiple service can
be performed. | So the inspirational air | Shares the same passageway | with salts,
words, | Sentences, Sweeteners, Paragraphs" (*PB*, 102). In *The Pillow Book*
physical love (the layering of skin on skin, the feast of eyes, tongue, and hands,
the blurring of "I" and "you," inside/outside) functions as a paradigm for this
shared passageway where "the delights of the flesh" translate into "the delights
of literature" (*PB*, 77). Love is the principle of translation itself. It becomes synonymous with unconditional openness, absolute receptivity, willing submission
to the pleasure of the beloved other. Hence the significance of Nagiko's English
lover, Jerome, who is a professional translator and who, first among all subsequent lovers, offers his body to Nagiko: "Go on. Treat me like the page of a
book. Your book" (*PB*, 67). His suicide in the course of the film is but the expected outcome of his initial self-effacing gesture for the sake of the other. It is
the necessary sacrifice that clears the way "for the next book's | sprouting" (*PB*,
102), a sacrifice which he embraces generously, wholeheartedly when he accepts
to serve as Nagiko's messenger to the publisher.[16] More importantly for the film,
his death, brought about by his swallowing of pills with "black, indelible ink," is
the epitome of Nagiko's erotic ethics, for it renders literal what can be taken as
"merely" metaphorical:[17] "Body and book are open. | Face and page. | Body and
page. | Blood and ink" (*PB*, 107).

   At the same time, the retrieval and reactivation of a distinctly textual tradition (which, as *The Pillow Book* illustrates, cannot be limited to a culture of
books)[18] are inextricable from an equally unsettling experience of *separation*. In
other words, they are predicated on the conscious practice and appreciation of
distance, understood as the critical standpoint from which evaluation can take
place and as the viewer's/reader's/writer's historical situatedness which limits
any attempt at establishing (or securing) contact, opening it to the risk of loss,
betrayal, misreading, and the possibility of a missed encounter.[19] In his influential reading of Sigmund Freud's privileged paradigm for the structure of the psy-

chical apparatus (i.e., the paradigm of "the Mystic Writing-Pad") Derrida posits this double gesture of "interruption and restoration of contact" at the heart of a concept of writing which cannot be reduced to the "external, auxiliary technique" of writing as "hypomnesis" (i.e., memory-aid), the carrier of an economy of absence and death (the absence of the speaking subject; the referent; a concrete context and interlocutor), and situated on the opposite pole of *logos* qua live, self-present, spontaneous speech (*WD*, 223, 225). Writing for Derrida, as for Nagiko, becomes synonymous with making an inscription on a more or less resistant surface. It is an act of "breaching, the tracing of a trail" which invites paradoxically both violent resistance and absolute hospitality, the renewable virginity of the receiving substance, its "unlimited receptive capacity" (*WD*, 200, 204). Writing, then, in Derrida is *technē* understood as the *play of relations* between assumed opposites: i.e., resistance and receptivity, inscription and erasure, presence and absence, legibility and illegibility, emergence and withdrawal, life and death (*WD*, 228). "The condition for writing," Derrida emphasizes, "is that there be neither a permanent contact nor an absolute break between strata" (*WD*, 226). Which is why, writing is "the *thought of the trace*" par excellence,[20] for there is no "unerasable trace" (*WD*, 230). "Traces . . . produce the space of their inscription only by acceding to the period of their erasure" (*WD*, 226).

It is this Derridean thought of the trace that permeates Greenaway's film which (in parallel with the visual language of contact the film employs through the technique of fragmenting and layering the screen)[21] unfolds, at the same time, as *play* or, in Derridean terms, as the *différance* of relations between inscription and erasure, visibility and invisibility, speech and silence, possession and loss, love and betrayal. If Nagiko's textual erotics is seductive, this is because, like a 20th-century Scheherazade, she shifts, hides, and removes layers; she manipulates gaps; plays with silences; coaxes, mocks, lures, and deceives her interlocutor/lover/reader. In seeking to preserve her father's tradition, she interrogates, re-layers and enriches it from the margins of Sei Shonagon's unique feminine style. She resolutely appropriates its authority[22] and uses it to release its force from the patriarchal, interest-oriented system that has historically controlled it. Her confrontation with the man who is simply referred to as "the publisher" is of particular interest here. If Jerome stands for love as the depropriating gesture of absolute receptivity, an ethical existence dedicated to the other, the publisher exemplifies an economy structured around power, property, and possession. As Nagiko comes to realize, he is the puppet master pulling the threads behind the scene. He is the godlike presence guiding her father's hand, prescribing her husband's choices in life and determining her lover's value as an object of exchange. He is the authorial figure who claims power over bodies as well as texts and controls their circulation, reducing their promiscuous metaphoricity to an economy, a system of exchange.[23] In contrast to everyone around her who defers to his authority, Nagiko explicitly refuses his signature on her body.[24] What is more, when she grows up, she sets out consciously to undermine his power. Combining the avenging will of Fa Mulan (the legendary Chinese heroine)[25] and the seductive wiliness of Scheherazade, Nagiko devises a plan which turns his obsessive desire for possession against him and opens his fetish-istic economy (that objectifies bodies as well as books) to an erotic and unpre-dictable flow of body/texts that intrude in his world, flatter, menace him, take him by surprise, elude, betray him, keep him in suspense, and, ultimately, hold him responsible.[26]

At the end of Nagiko's seductive game, the written word (which, throughout the film, was more or less violently shorn of its [the] body and confined within the publisher's proliferating copybooks) retrieves its original force; in other words, its incantatory, performative function. The last messenger Nagiko sends the publisher carries "The Book of the Dead" on his skin, which demands from the now resigned man to pronounce his own death sentence. If the publisher's death marks the "end of all books" (as "The Book of the Dead" suggests; *PB*, 112) it, at the same time, inaugurates the beginning of another practice of writ-ing, one which flowers from within the body, as the Bonsai tree appears to flow-er from within Jerome's body in the last scene of the film.[27] This practice of writing is uniquely singular (it *is* the writing of Nagiko Kiyohara). Yet, it is *trans*personal, for its motion is both that of organic matter (i.e., the body, na-ture . . .) and history qua the eruption of *technē*; i.e., the play of *différance* be-tween "then" and "now," the origin and its returns, one's own proper self and the inevitable movement of depropriation, "the banal sense of the past" and "the hidden," "the surprising power" of human temporality. At the film's closure, the story, as Greenaway tells us, has, indeed, "come full circle" (*PB*, 101): on her twenty-eighth birthday Nagiko is ready to write her own pillow book, exactly one thousand years after the writing of Sei Shonagon's pillow book. She has also given birth to a daughter (fathered by Jerome) whose birthday she celebrates, following her father's now renewed tradition, by repeating the ritual of facial inscription. Past and present converge at the virtual point where the circle *ap-pears to* close.

If, however, as Derrida insists, no contact is permanent but is always al-ready caught in the movement of its spacing, then the circle formed by this par-ticular configuration between past and present (the living and the dead, the 10th and the 20th centuries, tradition and its renewal) remains open to what comes from outside as its own futural possibility and cannot yet be seen. Which is why Nagiko's twelfth "Book of Birth and Beginnings" eludes both the publisher and us, the viewers. The young messenger employed by Nagiko drives by the pub-lisher's bookshop but does not stop to deliver the good tidings. Greenaway writes: "A solitary car passes in the street outside, illuminating the interior of the shop with its lights. The car radio is on, quietly playing a fifties Western 'Orien-tal' popular-song. As the car drives away, there is silence" (*PB*, 96). Like the publisher who "stares at the bookshop front-door" and "lies as still as a corpse" waiting (*PB*, 96), we can hear the new arrival—though from a distance. After the publisher's death, we can anticipate its promise in the birthday blessing Nagiko writes on her baby daughter's face and can imagine the flowering of this bless-ing ("ευλογία"/"*eulogia*" as the benevolence performed through the word) in the newly formed bond between mother and daughter. The "Book of Birth and Beginnings," however, will *not* make itself available to us. Its writing is not yet complete, perhaps. And in the process (of waiting, hoping, staring at the now empty screen), we, too, (its lovers/readers-to-be) get written.

PART ONE

THINKING WITH/
THINKING BETWEEN

Introduction to Part One

Apostolos Lampropoulos

All types of contacts between books have been part of the agenda both of traditional, philologically oriented, textual criticism and of theoretically informed studies in the broader field of literature and culture. In order to account for the complexity and multiplicity of these contacts, a number of concepts have been coined: from "intertexts" and "mosaics" to "stratifications," "rhizomes," and "folds"—to mention only a few of those that have proved to be quite popular. Similar terms abound in the humanities. Used playfully or rigorously, these terms have fashioned our ways of unpacking the various and fascinating links between textual styles, literary motifs, philosophical notions, as well as our attempts to spell out their connections with the "out there." In philosophical or literary analyses of such terms, the emphasis is variably placed on synchronies or diachronies, on the homogenization of forces or the maintaining of hybridity, on their political usefulness or on their reluctance to overtly connect with their socio-historical contexts. More often than not, concepts connoting contact speak in spatial metaphors, ranging from horizontality to verticality and from linearity to networks.

Inevitably, the perpetual invention of similar concepts problematizes, renews, and sometimes fixes our ways of *thinking with*—which is also a thinking *as a response to*—older texts. Nonetheless, as the title of this first part implies, *thinking with* can only be understood as closely related to a *thinking between,* which rejects oversimplified binaries, readymade oppositions, and easy-to-grasp comparisons. For *thinking with/thinking between* is never a thinking *between two*. It becomes, instead, a *thinking among several* or, indeed, a *thinking-without, eccentrically*; a thinking which positions itself on a periphery, on the side or along an edge. In other words, the *thinking between* performed by the essays included in this part is always still to be created. It is a driving force leading to new synergies of texts and concepts, an invitation to an extra layer that could be added above the old layers as a new rigorous reading; right in the middle of them as a destabilizing element; or even below them as an attempt to thoroughly rethink their genealogy. In this sense, *thinking with/thinking between* is an opening toward a revisited archeology or a renewed futurity, a way of describing different modes of speaking otherwise. More specifically, it can be seen as what Kristeva calls an intimate revolt responding to the society of the spectacle. It can take the form of an enrichment and expansion of the symbolic. It may give new meaning to the quest for a harmonious unity or for the eruption of conflict within unity. Or it can expand on the complicity between poetry and philosophy. These are, in fact, the axes around which the four chapters of this part are articulated, focusing on thinkers such as Kristeva, Agamben, Stiegler, Hansen, Merleau-Ponty, Deleuze, and Derrida.

The first chapter is Frances Restuccia's "Profane Mystical Practice: Resisting the Society of the Spectacle or the Society of the 'As If.'" The author departs from Kristeva's position that only by renewing ourselves can the bond with the other be forged, as well as from Agamben's idea that the messianic is our revolt. In fact, Restuccia articulates her argument around what she sees as an astonishing proximity between Kristeva's sacred and Agamben's profanation, a proximity based on the intricacies of accessing the nonverbal through discourse. The first section ("Globalizing Intimate Revolt") insists on Kristeva's distinction between religion and the sacred as the "thing without a name" lying at the crossroads between body and meaning. Given that intimacy is the most profound dimension of one's experience, intimate revolt displaces the past and translates into the dispossession of one's subjectivity leading to an "infinite recreation." It is in this way, Restuccia argues, that Kristeva attempts to replace robotic spectacular life with desiring free subjectivity, opening up the possibility for meaning to be carried into the political and civic sphere. The second section ("The Politics of the Irreparable") turns to Agamben's work referring briefly to the cannibalizing of zoë by bios and insisting on the fact that processes of desubjectification and subjectification lack foundation. It is also pointed out that messianic time is not future oriented but leads to a kind of "pleroma" instead, whereby the subject is to be situated on the caesura between potentiality and impotentiality. This leads us to Agamben's position that "what is essential is neither *that something is* (being) nor *that something is not* (nothingness), but that something is *rather* than nothingness," that is to say a "potentiality to not not-be." This potentiality is precisely what remains unrealized in the society of the spectacle or, as Restuccia terms it, in the society of the "as if." This is precisely why the chapter concludes with a concise reference to Love as "infinite recreation" and "potentiality" in both thinkers' work: "Love in Kristeva engages . . . self and non-self at the sacred intersection she privileges against the society of the spectacle's soullessness, and Love in Agamben entails being-thus in a way that pours together what the society of the spectacle puts asunder."

John Lechte's "Thinking the Image, Technics, and Embodiment: Julia Kristeva's Challenge," starts with the definition of experience as embodied time, uncovering the subject's essential finitude and mortality. Building on the thesis that narcissism is "the ego's dream of infinitude: the dream of immortality and the denegation of finitude," Lechte reminds us that the only way in which images can be passively received is in "a pathological form of narcissism." More generally, his analysis brings the different thinkers discussed together through the relation between image, temporality, consciousness, and embodiment. The second section ("Bernard Stiegler's Approach to the Image as a 'Temporal Object'") focuses on the cinematographic moment as the time of consciousness. The third section ("The Time-Image in Deleuze's Philosophy of Cinema") is concerned with Deleuze's emphasis on the durational and subjective nature of time in feature films. It also establishes a parallel between Deleuze's time-image and Kristeva's sense of a rhythmic space, which leads us to the idea that "subjectivity is the partial outcome of a cinematographic experience." The fourth section ("The Body as Interactive Art: The Work of Mark B. N. Hansen") studies the interaction between cinema and consciousness and the absence of an essentially incarnate body. In the fifth section ("The Semiotic and Sartre's Philosophy of the Image"), Lechte draws on Sartre and discusses a number of Kristevan theses, such as: images inhibit imaginary formations; art no longer has an object given that images are the repetition of the same; the image is analyzed as a thing, hence neutralized. Under these conditions, images can no longer have an impact. The mechanism of bringing an object into presence as absent, discussed by Sartre, leads us to the sixth section ("The 'Illusion of Immanence'") that analyzes how one can avoid understanding the image either as a representation or as a perception, thus how one can see the image-object as nothingness. Following Lechte, the image is a way of being in the world or an evocation. As his argument unfolds in the final section ("Kristeva and the Image"), the image is neither a thing nor a simulacrum. Instead, it needs to be perceived as that which allows the boundaries of the symbolic to be enriched and expanded.

Judith Wambacq's contribution is entitled "The Layered Being of Merleau-Ponty and the Being Layered of Deleuze: a Comparison of Two Conceptions of Immanentism on the Basis of the Notion 'Fold.'" The first section ("Merleau-Ponty's Conception of Language as Behavior") discusses Merleau-Ponty's position that language is something through which we move in the world and with which we construct relations. It also unpacks the idea that words are not *like* gestures but that they *are* gestures. So, if the meaning of gestures does not precede them but mixes them with the world they create, then for Merleau-Ponty the effort to determine the priority of nature over culture or vice versa is pointless. The second section ("Merleau-Ponty's Use of the Notion of Fold") begins with his thesis that "although it is impossible to separate expression and meaning, it is equally senseless to say that they are one and the same." In exactly the same vein, Wambacq describes reflexibility—that is to say, folding back upon something without coinciding with it—as the most intriguing characteristic of the fold. The third section ("Deleuze's Theory of Sense Being on the Border of the Thing and the Proposition") revisits two Deleuzean positions: first, the position that sense is not only the expression of the proposition, but also the attribute of the thing; second, the position that the gap between the abstract and the concrete is bridged thanks to the fact that they are both considered as two forms of the same actual. The fourth section ("Deleuze's Use of the Notion of Fold") discusses the basics of the Deleuzean approach to the fold as a nonexternal outside or a noninternal inside. If this definition of the fold is most appropriate in the context of the virtual then, more generally, the conditions of possibility are not thought to be situated outside the things they ground but inside them. That is why, in the final section ("The Fold in Merleau-Ponty and Deleuze"), the author makes clear that the two interpretations of the fold cannot be lumped together, something that explains why Deleuze criticizes Merleau-Ponty for folding too quickly. In summary, Wambacq points out that for Merleau-Ponty the fold is "the creation of a harmonious unity which is nevertheless not a self-coinciding unity," while for Deleuze the fold signifies "the infinite movement inside a violent power field." As a result, in contrast to Merleau-Ponty, Deleuze stresses "the conflict inside the unity or the immanence."

The last chapter is William Watkin's "The / Turn and the " " Pause: Agamben, Derrida, and the Stratification of Poetry." Its first section ("The Stratification of Prose and Poetry in Modern Thought") begins with a quick overview of heteroglossia in the work of Bakhtin, who sees fossilization as inherent in the concept of stratification and excludes it from his description of discursive, dialogic, and centrifugal prose. Then, Watkin turns to Merleau-Ponty's thesis that "sedimentation is not the accumulation of one creation upon another but also an integration." He concludes this section with the remark that a number of thinkers share the idea of poetry as a form of singularity, while his own approach will be based on the role of stratification in the analysis of poetry. The second section ("Agamben's Definition of Enjambment and His Call for a Stratigraphy of Poetry") throws into relief Agamben's understanding of stratification as an allegory of reading. All poetry must thus be definable as enjambment as opposed to the linearity of prose, a definition that Watkin demonstrates through a reading of Howe's "Thorow." The third section ("Derrida and the Excavation of the Fold as Site of Resistance to Philosophy") returns to Derrida's use of *entre* ("between") and *antre* ("cave") and reminds us that the hymen can be seen as the transitional moment between nonpoetry and poetry. The fact that "all poetry is definable as being verse, which . . . refers to the turning away from sense that constitutes matter or the putting of the word before the idea it may be the vehicle for expressing," allows Watkin to establish the ground on which he sees a similarity between Agamben and Derrida. In the last two sections ("Agamben and the Caesura as Poetic Thinking" and "Derrida and the Caesura as the Cut of Poetic Finitude"), Watkin focuses on Derrida's reading of Celan and speaks about the caesura not as a pause within the line but as a form of cutting off the poem-body. Watkin points out that for Derrida the caesura does not negate the poem in favor of philosophy, but seems to disjoin thought from itself. Finally, he wonders "how can poetry be what it is if projected ahead of each turn and pause is the inevitability of the last line, the non-returnable fold, the abyssal pause," to reach the conclusion that "in mining for the golden ore of singular, poetic thinking, poetry is always crushed by the sheer weight of discursive, translatable prosaic thinking as Agamben consistently describes philosophy."

Chapter 1

Profane Mystical Practice: Resisting the Society of the Spectacle or the Society of the "As If"

Frances Restuccia

For according to an intention that deeply characterizes Benjamin's thought, only where the esoteric and the everyday, the mystical and the profane, theological categories and materialistic categories are wholly identified can knowledge be truly adequate to its tasks.

G. Agamben, "Benjamin and the Demonic," *Potentialities*

In his eye-opening study *The Society of the Spectacle*, Guy Debord describes how modern society induces an enthrallment with the spectacle—images and products—rather than with human beings.[1] In a vicious cycle, our spectacle-induced isolation renders us dependent on this abusive relationship with images and products, pathetic substitutes for meaning, to assuage our loneliness. Debord, like Julia Kristeva and Giorgio Agamben, who in many ways follow in his footsteps, calls for a social critique of capitalism that never settles or stabilizes and so resists hardening into ideology. But does Debord present an effective program for thawing out the frigidity of the society of the spectacle—for treating what he diagnoses as its "generalized autism" (*SS*, 153) and restoring its disarmed "living desire" (*SS*, 45)? Debord poses psychoanalytic problems that he expects to solve via economic solutions—by catalyzing class struggle, in which he mainly puts his hope for the future.

My intent here is by no means to dismiss Debord, whose work is central to my mission of resisting the society of the spectacle. However, more promising, in my view, for sparking desire in the subject, is Kristeva's concept of intimate revolt, which entails an accessing of the *Zeitlos*, the unconscious, the abject—the very dimensions of life the society of the spectacle disavows. Her psychoanalytic approach thereby enables a sacred reclaiming of intimacy as a means of reinvigorating social relationships. "[T]he analytical experience," Kristeva proposes in *Intimate Revolt*, "leads us to the borders of thought[;] and . . . the examination of thought (what is a thought, without time, without judgment?) implies an examination of judgment, morality, and, ultimately, the social link."[2] Only by renewing ourselves can the bond with the other be forged. I want first to explicate Kristeva's psychoanalytic notion of the sacred as an antidote to the uniformity and loneliness of the society of the spectacle and then to annex Giorgio Agamben's more philosophical approach to defeating this so-called society.

We will look at points of overlap between these two contemporary theorists who have boldly taken on the formidable challenge of reviving "authentic experience" (Agamben's term, in *Infancy and History*). At least in Kristeva's case, the idea can be put even more dramatically: intimate "revolt is our mysticism" (*IR*, 4). And perhaps in Agamben's case, the phrase would be: the messianic is our revolt.

I should clarify at the outset, however, that Kristeva and Agamben have very distinct takes on "the sacred." Agamben conceives of the sacred (e.g., *homo sacer*) as banned by power to an excluded site, as completely produced and in turn suffused by power. In his "Introduction" to *Homo Sacer*, Agamben singles out "the sacredness of life" as the primary problem his book, "which was originally conceived as a response to the bloody mystifications of a new planetary order," had to "reckon with" (*HS*, 12). The trouble is that "[l]ife became sacred only through a series of rituals whose aim was precisely to separate life from its profane context" (*HS*, 66). Agamben reveals the so-called sacredness of life ("which is invoked today [naively] as an absolutely fundamental right in opposition to sovereign power") to be an original expression of "life's subjection to power over death and life's irreparable exposure in the relation of abandonment" (*HS*, 66). From the beginning of Western history, "sacred life has [had] an eminently political character," exhibiting "an essential link with the terrain on which sovereign power is founded" (*HS*, 100). Attempting to cut the tie of sacred life to this political function, Agamben advocates a folding of the expropriated "sacred" back into the dominant profane formation from which it was jettisoned. His concept of profanation entails the absorption into the center and the putting to *use* of what has been expelled as "sacred." In fact, Kristeva is also well aware of (in her terms) an anxiety-driven sacred (antithetical to the notion of the sacred she promotes) that functions for the sake of purification predicted on a dangerous exclusion of "*the impure*" or "*that which does not respect boundaries*, that which mixes structures and identities," as well as (what is often veiled in conceptions of the impure) "the domestic, corporal, maternal container."[3] Kristeva elaborates on this pernicious conception of the sacred, dedicated to banning the abject, in *Powers of Horror*. Her *preferred* concept of the sacred ironically resembles Agamben's notion of profanation—insofar as it insists that what is banned needs to be taken into account.

Despite his celebration of the profane, however, Agamben is by no means averse to what he calls "divinity." Casting a halo over our senseless society, he envisions an inclusionary profane world as "divine." Agamben asserts in *The Coming Community* that "The being-worm of the worm, the being-stone of the stone, is divine"[4] and, more broadly, that "[t]he world—insofar as it is absolutely, irreparably profane—is God" (*CC*, 90). In *Profanations*, one of his myriad definitions of "genius" is "the divinization of the person, the principle that governed and expressed his entire existence."[5] In this more recent text as well, Agamben celebrates genius as "intimacy with a zone of nonconsciousness"— "an *everyday mystical practice*, in which the ego, in a sort of special, joyous esoterism, looks on with a smile at its own undoing" (*P*, 12–13; my emphasis).

And in "Magic and Happiness," he explains his precept that "there is only one way to achieve happiness on this earth" by promoting belief in the divine (rather than the aspiration to reach it) (*P*, 21). Kristeva focuses on a similar coalescence of the mundane and the ineffable, only she calls it "sacred."

Kristeva and Agamben at times, then, seem to share a "mystical" vision of a way of life with the power to overturn the society of the spectacle. In "An Essay on the Destruction of Experience," in which Agamben urges a reacceding to infancy (a "historico-transcendental dimension" that occupies the site of "a moat between semiotic and semantic, between pure language and discourse"[6]), he asserts that "[*t*]*he ineffable is, in reality, infancy.* Experience is the *mysterion* which every individual intuits from the fact of having an infancy" (*IAH*, 58). At first this assertion may be baffling, especially since, earlier in *Infancy and History*, Agamben attacks what he refers to as "the vulgarly ineffable" (*IAH*, 4); but we must seize on the phrase "*in reality.*" It is not that Agamben rejects the idea of the ineffable but he opposes "[t]he ineffable, the un-said, [as] categories which belong exclusively to human language; far from indicating a limit of language, they express its invincible power of presupposition, the unsayable being precisely what language must presuppose in order to signify" (*IAH*, 4). Again like Kristeva, Agamben advocates an accessing of the nonverbal (living being) by discourse (speaking being). He conceptualizes and promotes such an embrace, of living being by speaking being, through his concept of infancy.

Why? For both of these theorists, the society of the spectacle has abandoned living being only to enter a meretricious world of "gross falsifications." Agamben despises capitalism for destroying the possibility of "productive activity" and for alienating language itself: "The extreme form of the expropriation of the Common is the spectacle, in other words, the politics in which we live. . . . [T]his also means that what we encounter in the spectacle is our very linguistic nature inverted."[7] Having wreaked havoc on living desire, authentic experience, living being, and language, it is the spectacle (if anything) that needs to be banned!

Globalizing Intimate Revolt

Is it certain that the model of society that privileges economic performance and technological innovation in the way that globalization handles them is always most favorable to the human person, as seemed to be the case in the era of the Industrial Revolution? If, imposed in their present form, the criteria of the marketplace and consumerism end up completely encompassing the dynamics of subjectivity, do they not risk the destruction of all those who take part in another socioeconomic system? And, beyond this, do they not, ultimately, risk their own self-destruction and the destruction of all civilization?

J. Kristeva, *Crisis of the ~~European~~ Subject*

Kristeva distinguishes between religion and the sacred. Religion, on the side of prohibition or purification of the abject, offers us "figures of consolation and of healing omnipotence" but denies sexual *jouissance* and our dependency on nature.[8] Kristeva proposes a traversal of Christianity for "free subjectivity" to flourish (*CS*, 159). On the side of free subjectivity, the sacred is the "thing without a name" (*FS*, 37). Kristeva describes it variously as an experience at the crossroads of sexuality and thought, the body and meaning—as the emergence of meaning. Linking these paradoxical locations with eroticism, she asks:

> What if the sacred were the unconscious perception the human being has of its untenable eroticism: always on the borderline between nature and culture, the animalistic and the verbal, the sensible and the nameable? What if the sacred were not the religious *need* for protection and omnipotence that institutions exploit but the jouissance of that *cleavage*—of that power/powerlessness—of that exquisite lapse? (*FS*, 26–27)

Assuming that the sacred resides at the intersection of the sensible and the nameable, where flesh becomes Word, and the emergence of meaning is thereby celebrated, then psychoanalysis itself becomes sacred. Accordingly, to Kristeva, psychoanalysis involves analytical interpretation that serves *forgiveness*—her version of which suspends judgment and instead imparts meaning through transference and countertransference. And, while the bestowing of meaning onto the subject's suffering results initially in a "dead time" in which the subject refuses the interpretation, "an elational hallucination" or "moment of *grace*" subsequently takes place "that signals . . . the analysand's rebirth" (*IR*, 36; my emphasis). The analyst forgives the analysand through a process that entails the transformation of suffering, trauma, the flesh-unarticulated into articulation, meaning, or the Word.

Kristeva's is a sacred that results in a new start—through intimate revolt. Intimacy is, to Kristeva, the most profound and singular dimension in one's experience. The Greeks termed it "soul" and defined it in relation to both the organic body and preverbal sensations—as an interiority that psychoanalysis, with its dual emphasis on affect and discourse, seeks to rehabilitate. Intimate revolt effects a metamorphosis of the subject through a turning back: the past is questioned and displaced. Through *anamnesis*, one interrogates the core of one's own very being. Kristeva's psychic revolt transpires at the "limits of the representable/thinkable/tenable" (*IR*, 7). Intimate revolt is experience with a psychical reality that puts consciousness in danger and exposes one to the pulse of being, dovetailing with the Heideggerian notion that "being is wrought by nothingness" (*IR*, 8). Subject/object borders are erased; one is assaulted by the drive.

The analysand must access Freud's *Zeitlos*—or the timeless—at the place of the unconscious especially because "psychopathological symptoms and structures," in particular new maladies of the soul generated by the emptiness of the society of the spectacle, fail "to integrate the atemporal" (*IR*, 31); and failure to plug into the timeless generates psychic trouble.[9] Necessary then is the reverse direction: the sacred act of working-through, the "insertion of nonlife into life," inscribing death into "lived actuality" (*IR*, 36). In the case of trauma, the timeless must be withdrawn "from the excitation," where it has been entombed, and made to work "at the heart of an expressible, conscious temporality" (*IR*, 38). The memory-trace persists but is spread out within the linearity of conscious memory, just as—also in opposition to the society of the spectacle's many expulsions, of the unconscious, nothingness, and death—the abject needs to be confronted and appropriated in a sacred embrace.

For this arrangement to fall into place, i.e., for the timeless to be folded into time, the analysand must journey to the end of the night and then live through separation from the analyst (or the analyst's "death") and, in turn, through the dispossession of his or her own subjectivity (as it had been, say, neurotically, perversely, or melancholically configured). The timeless is the work of death that opens "each human manifestation (act, speech, symptom) toward unconscious/prepsychical/somatic/physical continuity" (*IR*, 32). It is this intertwining of the timeless and acts, speech, and symptoms located in time, enabling the release of atemporal psychic trouble into linearity, that gives rise to a *jouissance*, which is "indispensable to keeping the psyche alive" (*IR*, 7). And insofar as the "deaths" survived maintain a presence in the analysand's renewed relation with others, this process signals a "double infinity": an "impossibility" and subsequently an "openness"—both "night and transmission" (*IR*, 40). Intimate revolt is a process of "untenable conflict" that "opens psychical life to infinite re-creation" (*IR*, 6).

In her chapter on "Fantasy and Cinema" in *Intimate Revolt*, Kristeva bears down on the process of working-through by illustrating how it can operate within the sacred space of art. For Kristeva, the psychoanalytic experience—meaning intense excursions to the end of the night, moments of grace, and acts of forgiveness—can transpire effectively outside the clinical scene. Because it is the *imaginary* that offers the most dangerous and therefore the most efficacious route to the intimate, and because the *imaginary* appears in "all its logic" and "risk" in fantasy (*IR*, 63), cinema (where, needless to say, fantasy thrives) is a potentially rich psychoanalytic site.

But film might seem to put us at the very epicenter of the society of the spectacle and therefore would appear to be anathema to Kristeva's definition of the sacred as resistance to our consumer-oriented society of image bombardment. As she points out, we are deluged with images that fail to liberate us, that stereotypically deprive us of our *imaginary* scenarios and, most alarmingly, whose phantasmatic poverty works on behalf of the abolition of psychic life. However, accessing the *Zeitlos* that most films foreclose, the "thought specular," or an "other cinema" (as Kristeva also calls it), lends itself to a primary and fragile synthesis of drives. Inasmuch as the specular is "terrifying" and "seductive," it can enable us to celebrate "our identity uncertainties and hence to locate the drive" (*IR*, 72). To access the drive and then transform it into desire through film would be to commit a sacred act enabling liberation from the controlling and deadening society of the spectacle, as it is based on instant gratification that short-circuits the dilatoriness necessary to desire.

Kristeva's category of the "thought specular" functions through lektonic traces or expressibles that put into play primary processes through tones, rhythms, colors, figures, etc. (Kristeva's semiotic). Drawing out from the specta- tor suffering that needs to be planted in representation, lektons transfigure a flat image, a denotation, into a symptom. The raw images on the screen become displacements and condensations of the spectator's psychic material—a kind of filmic dream. But, even as "the visible is the port of registry of drives" (*IR*, 69), and the thought specular certainly relies on lektons to seduce the spectator's psyche, it is ultimately not a matter of looking. The magic of the thought specu- lar is to grip us at the site of the (Lacanian) gaze. It is especially there that the specular bears the trace of the nonrepresented drive. The sensuousness of the thought-specular film lures lektonically the spectator's (timeless) trauma; in this way the spectator's psyche gets absorbed. Through a subsequent encounter with the gaze, the spectator's unconscious is initially met, massaged, and further moved—jolted—into the temporality of the film. The process is, as always with Kristeva, an intimate, interminable interplay between zones of timelessness and temporality, never one without the other, without stasis.

The "evil" of an unrepresented drive is, to Kristeva, what propels current- day abuses of globalization, which suffocate us with ready-made fantasies and shut down psychic complexity. Kristeva's intimate revolt needs to happen on the political as well as the personal level. She seeks to enrich globalization through analysis, art, dialogue, and prayer, so that it does not involve merely calculating the growth rate as well as genetic probabilities and shopping, on the one hand, and "sadomasochistic sexuality, delinquency, vandalism, and new maladies of the soul: psychosomatosis, drug addiction" (*IR*, 235), on the other. Kristeva wants to see psychoanalysis intervene in social policy. She would like especially women to play more of a role, since they "can bring a different attitude to power and meaning" (*IR*, 260) to bear against the monotony of the market, the media, and the Internet. In *The Feminine and the Sacred*, Kristeva claims that "women feel intensely" the combination of "sexuality and thought, body and meaning"; she therefore poses the question of the existence of a "specifically feminine sa- cred" (*FS*, 14). Kristeva regards the body of a woman in particular as "a strange intersection between *zōō* and *bios*, physiology and narration," flesh and Word (*FS*, 14). Being on the borderline between biology and meaning, "Kristeva's women" would seem to be in a special position to fulfill Agamben's ideal of a "form-of-life"—"a life that can never be separated from its form," "a political life in which it is never possible to isolate something such as naked life" (*MWE*, 3–4).[10]

I agree with Maria Margaroni that Kristeva conceives of the subject as split only insofar as "semiotic motility erupts from within its speaking position, de- stabilizing and rendering it inhospitable to any 'One.'"[11] Kristeva's appropria- tion of Freud's concept of Negation can help to clarify her idea of a biothanato- logical life as a mutual enfolding of subjectification and desubjectification or speaking being and living being. In *The Sense and Non-Sense of Revolt*, she explains that negation "posits and thus affirms both the *denial* of the instinctual content and the symbolic *representation* of it." This concept leads Kristeva to deduce from Freud "a model of *signifiance* that presupposes language and its instinctual substrata but grasps language and the drive through the work of the negative" (*SNS*, 56). Kristeva develops this paradoxical idea (resembling Agamben's notion of infancy) by invoking Lacan's sense of the speaking subject as "*parlêtre*"—which pun echoes Heidegger's *Dasein*, expressing the "insistence of *being* (outside-subject, outside-language) at the heart of human speech as it unfolds its negativity" (*SNS*, 58). Here Kristeva engages the "extrapsychical" insofar as she stresses reconciliation not only with oneself but with what she calls "the other of language," which is tantamount to "being," as the Greeks and German phenomenologists conceptualize it. Kristeva reads Freud as teaching us "to sexualize being" and advocates the integration of this "notion of being into the clinic" (*SNS*, 60). The psyche must be dilated to include being: this is the "highest" path to revolt and Kristeva's way of replacing robotic spectacular life with desiring free subjectivity.

It is because this Heideggerian conception of "free subjectivity" enables the "power of beginning oneself anew with the other" (*CS*, 159)—insofar as it comes with the freedom of "intimacy and mystical participation" (*CS*, 160)—that Kristeva's psychoanalytic approach has potential for social life beyond the individual subject. By keeping the psychoanalytic subject in mind, we can generate a global network that will challenge, or even stamp out, the society of the spectacle as it substitutes false objects of desire, "the stupidity of the media[,] the robotization of production[,] . . . 'new maladies of the soul'" (*CS*, 160) for the very loneliness it inflicts in the first place. Kristeva is well known by now for her assumption that engagement with the otherness, or strangeness, of oneself leads to engaging the other. Given that war against the society of the spectacle needs to be waged on a broad social scale, it must be stressed that Kristeva is concerned with an "experience of revolt" that "includes" not only "the pleasure principle" but also "the rebirth of meaning for the other" (*SNS*, 8), such a reawakening being the only thing sufficiently potent to break the fixation of today's robotized "subject" on images and products. Intimate revolt involves delving into the unconscious, with the goal of rebirth and autonomy, ultimately to facilitate "a renewed link with the other" (*IR*, 8).

In an interview conducted by John Lechte, Kristeva points to "maximum singularity" as a benefit of psychoanalysis and at the same time insists that the end of a "cure" involves "sharing": "How am I going to be able to negotiate my singularity with others." Both dimensions—singularity and otherness—comprise Kristeva's "contemporary ethic." Her politics entails, in Margaroni's words, taking "into account 'individual unhappiness' (psychic or material) and is respectful of the singularity of human lives, while working towards establishing new bonds, promoting 'a culture of "staying with"'" (*JK*, 31) that by definition removes the isolation deliberately induced by the spectacle. Kristeva is trying to put in motion a counterforce that will reconstruct a "new world order" along these lines of intimate revolt. Ideally, time will reestablish contact with the time-less, just as the timeless will be reinscribed into time. Kristeva is opening up the possibility for meaning being carried—beyond the "well-policed surface of rational consciousness" (*IR*, 25)—into the political or civic sphere, even for the incorporation of Eastern Orthodoxy's "mysticism of 'contact,'" into the international world of advanced capitalism (*CS*, 140).

The Politics of the Irreparable

> *Until a completely new politics—that is, a politics no longer founded*
> *on the* exceptio *of bare life—is at hand, every theory and every praxis*
> *will remain imprisoned and immobile, and the "beautiful day" of life*
> *will be given citizenship only either through blood and death or in the*
> *perfect senselessness to which the society of the spectacle condemns*
> *it.*
>
> G. Agamben, *Homo Sacer*

An equally alluring and compelling, though probably more fierce, contemporary critic of the society of the spectacle, Giorgio Agamben offers a philosophical approach that condemns biopower for severing zoë from bios. To Agamben, capitalist consumption removes things from "use," precluding acts of profanation, by destroying their substance, by leaving them no longer intact. In the society of the spectacle, the extreme phase of capitalism in which we reside, "everything is exhibited in its separation from itself" (*P*, 82): "now a single, multiform, ceaseless process of separation . . . assails every thing, every place, every human activity in order to divide it from itself. . . . In its extreme form, the capitalist religion realizes the pure form of separation, to the point that there is nothing left to separate." Agamben perceives the human body, sexuality, and language "now divided from themselves and placed in a separate sphere . . . where all use becomes and remains impossible. This sphere is consumption" (*P*, 81). Agamben complains that "humanity"—through biopower's full penetration of zoë in modernity, where emergency has "become the rule" (*HS*, 12)—has taken on the complete management of its animality, to the point that "humanity" is not human anymore.

Like Kristeva, in revolt, Agamben advocates, as an antidote to biopower's complete severance of zoë (natural life or "the simple fact of living common to all living beings [animals, men, or gods]") from bios ("the form or way of living proper to an individual or group" [*HS*, 1]), the dissolution of bios into zoë or, in his formulation in *Homo Sacer*: "This biopolitical body that is bare life must itself instead be transformed into the site for the constitution of a form of life that is wholly exhausted in bare life and a *bios* that is only its own *zoē*" (*HS*, 188). Zoë must become a vessel into which bios is poured: "una forma di vita tutta versata [all poured] nella nuda vita, un 'bios' che è solo la sua 'zoe.'"[12] In *Homo Sacer*, Agamben seeks to reverse the brutal and thorough politicization of zoë, the cannibalizing of zoë by bios, in part by revealing that "politics [is] already contained in *zoē* as its most precious center" (*HS*, 11).

The creative principle is yet another casualty of the biopolitical machine, as art has dovetailed with nihilism, turning into kitsch. In Agamben's words, "As long as nihilism secretly governs the course of Western history, art will not come out of its interminable twilight."[13] Agamben again overlaps with Kristeva in wanting to "restore to the poetic status of man on earth its original dimension" (*MWC*, 67). In his eyes, as in hers, people have been uprooted from their vital dwelling in language. In *The Open*, Agamben laments the fact that the "traditional historical potentialities—poetry, religion, philosophy—which from both the Hegelo-Kojevian and Heideggerian perspectives kept the historico-political destiny of peoples awake, have long since been transformed into cultural spectacles" and that, in turn, "[g]enome, global economy, and humanitarian ideology" (which manages animality), commodification, and mediatization rule the world.[14]

Caring as well, like Kristeva—who stresses the banalization and commercialization of "the seduction of eroticism" (*CS*, 145)—about the "intimacy of erotic life," Agamben notes in *The Coming Community* that it has been "refuted by pornography" (*CC*, 50). More recently, in *Profanations*, he condemns "the solitary and desperate consumption of the pornographic image" that "replaces the promise of a new use." Having been rendered unprofanable, pornography is "disgraceful—both politically and morally" (*P*, 91–92).[15]

We can approach Agamben's alternative to the society of the spectacle by way of his commentary on shame. In *Remnants of Auschwitz*, Agamben champions shame for its capacity to contemplate ruin: shame, which he defines ontologically (and not in terms of wrongdoing), occurs when the subject witnesses its own desubjectification, its "own disorder, its own oblivion as a subject."[16] As an interplay between subjectification and desubjectification, shame enables the production of invaluable testimony. Agamben claims in *Remnants of Auschwitz* that "it is precisely because the relation (or, rather, non-relation) between the living being and the speaking being has the form of shame, of being reciprocally consigned to something that *cannot be assumed by a subject*, that the *ēthos* of this disjunction can only be testimony" (*RA*, 130; my emphasis). The remnants of Auschwitz—the witnessess—are neither the ones who perished nor the ones who survived, but they are "what remains between" (*RA*, 164).

Likewise, Agamben's messianic time occupies the interval between secular and eternal times, producing a remainder. It is "neither chronological time nor the apocalyptic *eschaton*. Once again, it is a remnant, the time that remains between these two times"[17]—"*the time that time takes to come to an end*" (*TR*, 67). And insofar as Agamben's messianic time partakes of both chronos and kairos, his conception matches that of Kristeva at the intersection of temporality and the *Zeitlos*, where nothing, or no time, is cast out—or, rather, where even nothing is not cast out.

That is: Agamben refuses to "repeat the dialectic of grounding by which one thing [to use his supreme example, bare life] must be separated and effaced for human life to be assigned to subjects as a property." As he explains in *The*

Time That Remains, the "remnant" is by no means a "substantial positive residue" (*TR*, 50). Agamben repudiates the perspective that posits a foundation as "a function of a telos that is the grounding of the human being" (*RA*, 158). Processes of desubjectification and subjectification have for him "no foundation"; rather, the living being and the speaking being are linked through "an irreducible disjunction in which each term, stepping forth in the place of a remnant, can bear witness" (*RA*, 159). By opening up this place of the remnant, by thereby connecting up to what we (as subjects) cannot assume, perhaps we can generate some form of witnessing of our current status as *homines sacri* within the society of the spectacle—given that the camp serves as "the hidden paradigm of the political space of modernity" (*HS*, 123). Only by establishing such an irreducibly disjunctive site, yielding testimony, can we begin to move toward a "form-of-life" uncontaminated by power relations that entail a ban, an abandoned, abjected inclusion.

Finally, however, Agamben's philosophical vision—his idea of the new covenant or his new politics—is a post-shame, post-remnant "time" or community. "The subject of testimony is constitutively fractured" (*RA*, 151), whereas Agamben's "new creature," who embodies his "form-of-life," fully adheres to what, in shame, we are consigned to but cannot assume. Divisions such as the human/animal binarism that Agamben's wolfman, say, cuts across produce a remnant, but eventually that remnant will be superfluous, having served its purpose as an instrument of salvation: "In the end, the remnant appears as a redemptive machine allowing for the salvation of the very whole whose division and loss it had signified" (*RA*, 163).

Here Agamben takes a gigantic leap, beyond psychoanalysis, in pointing to a certain "messianic end of history or the completion of the divine *oikonomia* of salvation" (*O*, 21). In *The Time That Remains*, Agamben clinches his notion of the remnant as an "instrument" of "salvation," as what "makes salvation possible." In "the time of the now," or "messianic time," there is nothing other than the remnant," which belongs "to an unredeemable, the perception of which allows us to reach salvation." Ultimately, however, the remnant will have fulfilled its function. Agamben translates the following idea from Paul: "when God will be 'all in all,' the messianic remnant will not harbor any particular privilege and will have exhausted its meaning in losing itself in the *plērōma*" (*TR*, 56)—which, I stress, is by no means to leave political life behind. Agamben discerns a "political legacy" in the letters of Paul (*TR*, 57).

In focusing on the end of time, however, we need to be especially precise and open to a mind-boggling conception. For Agamben, the messianic is the way in which we seize hold of time, making it terminate. Agamben locates his ideal state neither in a messianic time that infinitely postpones the end (that would be to repeat Derrida's "thwarted messianism, a suspension of the messianic" [*TR*, 103]) nor at the conclusion of a linear trajectory. Messianic time is not future oriented. Rather, messianic time (the time of the remnant) leads to the "plērōma" as it signifies "each instant's relation to the messiah" (*TR*, 101). And at this point beyond time, the remnant dissolves since the binarisms of which it served as a remnant are now defunct. The present becomes "the exigency of fulfillment, what gives itself 'as an end'" (*TR*, 76)—without any gap. "[T]he messianic—the ungraspable quality of the 'now'—is the very opening through which we may seize hold of time, achieving our representation of time, making it end" (*TR*, 100). Thus:

> One can think of the halo . . . as a zone in which possibility and reality, potentiality and actuality, become indistinguishable. The being that has reached its end, that has consumed all of its possibilities, thus receives as a gift a supplemental possibility. This is that *potentia permixta actui* . . . , a fusional act, insofar as specific form or nature is not preserved in it, but mixed and dissolved in a new birth with *no residue*. This imperceptible trembling of the finite that makes its limits indeterminate and allows it to blend, to make itself whatever, is the tiny displacement that every thing must accomplish in the messianic world. Its beatitude is that of a potentiality that comes only after the act, of matter that does not remain beneath the form, but surrounds it with a halo. (*CC*, 56; my emphasis on "no residue")

Despite the major points of overlap between him and Kristeva, Agamben's philosophy is ultimately a nonpsychoanalytic conception—for one thing insofar as he favors the dissolution of the idea of "the subject" since it involves the suspension of what it is consigned to but cannot assume. Agamben ultimately favors another suspension altogether. As he writes: "To render inoperative the machine that governs our conception of man will . . . mean . . . to show the central emptiness, the hiatus that—within man—separates man and animal, and to risk ourselves in this emptiness: the suspension of the suspension" (*O*, 92). Such a plunge into the empty space between man and the animal brings to a standstill both the idea of "the subject" (giving rise to a "new creature"), then, as well as the anthropological machine that ejects animality from the human being. Agamben gestures eerily toward "something for which we perhaps have no name and which is neither animal nor man" that "settles in between nature and humanity and holds itself in the mastered relation, in the saved night" (*O*, 83). In some of the most breathtaking passages in Agamben's writing, he leaves unexpressed the "figure . . . of the life that shines in the 'saved night' of nature's (and, in particular, human nature's) eternal, unsavable survival after it has definitively bid farewell to the *logos* and to its own history" (*O*, 90).

On the question of the subject: admittedly, Agamben writes in *Remnants of Auschwitz* that "[t]o think a potentiality in act *as potentiality*, to think enunciation on the plane of *langue* is to inscribe a caesura in possibility, a caesura that divides it into a possibility and an impossibility, into a potentiality and an impotentiality; and it is to situate a subject in this very caesura." He locates this "subject" in "the disjunction between a possibility and an impossibility of speech" (*RA*, 145). But Agamben's "subject" here (he also writes) is a "possibility," "the possibility that language . . . takes place only through its possibility of not being there, its contingency" (*RA*, 146)—so that he is known for advancing a (Deleuzean) notion of subjectivity without a subject. Contingency itself takes shape as "subjectivity": as "the actual giving of a possibility," a giving that "has the form of subjectivity." Agamben presents *subjectivity* therefore "as *witness*." However, he regards "[t]estimony [as] a potentiality that becomes actual through an impotentiality of speech; it is, moreover, an impossibility that gives itself existence through a possibility of speaking"; and "[t]hese two movements," he tells us straightforwardly, "cannot be identified either with a subject or with a consciousness" (*RA*, 146). "The subject" at stake is "a field of forces," not a person who can choose or not choose (consciously or unconsciously) among certain tasks. Agamben's "subject" appears to be an abstraction—that is, potentiality as it is tantamount to impotentiality. This would explain why, in "Magic and Happiness," he asserts that "the subject of happiness is not a subject per se and does not obtain the form of a consciousness or of a conscience" (*P*, 20). Through his theorizing on shame, in other words, Agamben works toward his nameless creature, "neither animal nor man," that "holds itself in the mastered relation, in the saved night" (*O*, 83).

Ideally, there will be no identities or categories, just *being-such*—total abandonment in a world where there is no longer an agent of that ban. Agamben supports graceful conceptions of being beyond the principle of sovereignty. As an example of one such attempt, he cites Heidegger's "idea of abandonment and the *Ereignis*," where "Being itself is . . . discharged and divested of sovereignty" (*HS*, 48). Agamben calls for a "real state of exception" in which law is "confronted by life that, in a symmetrical but inverse gesture, is entirely transformed into [messianic] law." Writing plays a pivotal role in this transformation: "The absolute intelligibility of a life wholly resolved into writing corresponds to the impenetrability of a writing that, having become indecipherable, now appears as life. Only at this point do the two terms distinguished and kept united by the relation of ban (bare life and the form of law) abolish each other and enter into a new dimension" (*HS*, 55). Agamben implores us to "think the Being of abandonment beyond every idea of law," to shift out of the "paradox of sovereignty toward a politics freed from every ban" (*HS*, 59).

To grasp Agamben's coming community, we need to engage his concept of the Irreparable, his notion that "things are just as they are, in this or that mode, consigned without remedy to their way of being. States of things are irreparable whatever they may be: sad or happy, atrocious or blessed" (*CC*, 90). In other words, the Irreparable is the *thusness* of a thing, the *thusness* of the world; and insofar as the world is *thus,* it is not mere appearance—which is, needless to say, how it presents itself in the society of the spectacle. Agamben urges us to apprehend things as they are, in their being such as they are. "The root of all pure joy and sadness," he proposes, "is that the world is as it is. Joy or sadness that arises because the world is not what it seems or what we want it to be is impure or provisional" (*CC*, 91). Instead, "[t]he thus . . . finds its essence in its own being-thus" (*CC*, 93). "*Thus* means not otherwise. (This leaf is green; hence it is neither red nor yellow.) . . . [N]either this nor that, neither thus nor thus—but thus, as it is" (*CC*, 93).

It is this conception of the thusness of things and of the world that can heal "the originary fracture of being in essence and existence"—which in Agamben's vision reciprocally imply each other (*CC*, 95). In the unmistakably fractured society of the spectacle, however, shell-like things merely appear, their "essences" having been shucked. As Agamben expresses it explicitly in *The Coming Community*:

> the spectacle is nothing but the pure form of separation: When the real world is transformed into an image and images become real, the practical power of humans is separated from itself and presented as a world unto itself. In the figure of this world separated and organized by the media, in which the forms of the State and the economy are interwoven, the mercantile economy attains the status of absolute and irresponsible sovereignty over all social life. After having falsified all of production, it can now manipulate collective perception and take control of social memory and social communication, transforming them into a single spectacular commodity where everything can be called into question except the spectacle itself, which, as such, says nothing but, "What appears is good, what is good appears." (*CC*, 78–79)

In opposition to such a ruptured state of affairs, Agamben champions life "beyond both knowing and not knowing, beyond both disconcealing and concealing, beyond both being and the nothing" (*O*, 91). As he puts it in *Means without End*: "happy life" is "an absolutely profane 'sufficient life' that has reached the perfection of its own power and of its own communicability—a life over which sovereignty and right no longer have any hold" (*MWE*, 114–15).

Even Agamben's concept of "*as not*" pushes things toward the condition of their thusness, rather than opening a gap. His sense of "[t]he coming of the Messiah" is "that all things, even the subjects who contemplate it, are caught up in the *as not*, called and revoked at one and the same time" (*TR*, 41).[18] Partially explaining this paradox in *The Coming Community*, Agamben reasons that "what is essential is neither *that something is* (being) nor *that something is not* (nothingness), but that something is *rather* than nothingness." That is: Agamben adds a third term to the binarism of is/is not, which allows him (strangely in a parenthesis) to assert what is most astonishing of all: "not that something was able to be, but that it was able to not not-be" (*CC*, 104).

This third term is the crux of Agamben's theory of potentiality. That something exists is not merely "an inert fact." Instead, "a power inheres in it," a "potentiality to not not-be" (*CC*, 105). Potentiality and the impotentiality it necessarily implies close all gaps and refuse all exceptions, as the move of potentiality to actuality happens not at the expense of impotentiality but through a mere setting aside of impotentiality, tantamount in fact to a fulfillment of impotentiality, that allows it to be eternally revived in the process. Catherine Mills clarifies the threat to, and demise of, the Nothing in this enactment of potentiality: "The inauguration of happy life in which neither *zoē* nor *bios* can be isolated allows for the law in force without significance to be overcome such that the Nothing maintained by that law is eliminated and humanity reaches its own fulfillment in its immediate transparency [I would substitute "opacity" here] to itself. Happy life can be characterized as life lived in the experience of its own unity, its own potentiality of 'being-thus' (*CC*, 93)."[19] I insert "opacity" in the place of Mills's "transparency" insofar as Agamben describes Titian's lovers who have entered "a new and more blessed life, one that is neither animal nor human," in the Venetian artist's painting *Nymph and Shepherd*, as having "lost their mystery" yet as not having "become any less impenetrable" (*O*, 87).

Might we, then, call the society of the spectacle the society of the "*as if*," the society of simulacra, in which the "potentiality to not not-be" goes completely unrealized, whereas Agamben, as he writes in *The Time That Remains*, admires him "who upholds himself in the messianic vocation, [who] no longer knows the *as if*, [him who] no longer has similitudes at his disposal" (*TR*, 42)? We can deduce further that were society to shift from the "*as if*" to *thusness* or the Irreparable, it would move to a condition of Love, since to Agamben "[s]eeing something in its being-thus—irreparable, but not for that reason necessary; thus, but not for that reason contingent—is love" (*CC*, 106).

At this juncture, Agamben and Kristeva again converge, as they share a resistance to the society of the spectacle predicated on keeping alive intimacy and Love—their "cures" for biopower. Kristeva conceives of love as a form of the sacred, as it "entails passing through the nothingness of oneself as well as the nothingness of language" and "requires a certain annihilation of self, of self-consciousness" (*FS*, 35). Agamben defines his central concept of "whatever singularity" as "the Lovable": "The lover wants the loved one *with all of its predicates*, its being such as it is. The lover desires the *as* only insofar as it is *such*—this is the lover's particular fetishism" (*CC*, 2). To Agamben, love is "the experience of taking-place in a whatever singularity" (*CC*, 25).

In *Profanations*, in his opening essay "Genius," Agamben describes love again as a way of defeating a binarism or exclusion of one pole by another: "when we love someone we actually love neither his genius nor his character (and even less so his ego) but his special manner of evading both of these poles, his rapid back-and-forth between genius and character" (*P*, 17). And in *The Idea of Prose*, his idea of love maintains (in a Kristevan vein) the strangeness of the beloved, who is exposed yet opaque:

> To live in intimacy with a stranger, not in order to draw him closer, or to make him known, but rather to keep him strange, remote: unapparent—so unapparent that his name contains him entirely. And, even in discomfort, to be nothing else, day after day, than the ever open place, the unwaning light in which that one being, that thing, remains forever exposed and sealed off.[20]

Such an openness to the opacity of the beloved is fully compatible with Agamben's privileging of potentiality. He holds up passion or "*potentia passiva*," in fact, as "the most radical experience at issue in *Dasein*: a capacity that is capable not only of *potentiality* (the manners of Being that are in fact possible) but also, and above all, of *impotentiality*" (*PO*, 201). Passion would seem to exist in, if not constitute, the messianic kingdom.

Both Kristeva and Agamben combat biopower through Love insofar as biopower's "supreme ambition is to produce . . . the absolute separation of the living being and the speaking being, *zoē* and *bios*, the inhuman and the human" (*RA*, 156). Opposing such a fracture, attempting to heal it, Love in Kristeva engages (to put it simply) self and nonself at the sacred intersection she privileges against the society of the spectacle's soullessness, and Love in Agamben entails being-thus in a way that pours together what the society of the spectacle puts asunder.

Chapter 2

Thinking the Image, Technics, and Embodiment: Julia Kristeva's Challenge

John Lechte

Experience as Embodied Time

If Proust opens the way to a time that is rediscovered—to images evoked by writing—it is not through any linguistic or philosophical formalism, but through an experience of the text—through a transubstantial experience: "The term experience implies," says Julia Kristeva, "in the philosophical and hermeneutic religious tradition, a co-presence with the plenitude of Being, when it is not a fusion with God."[1] Again: "Experience unveils the subject's narcissistic incompleteness and the dramas of its individuation" (*TS*, 239). In other words, experience opens up the subject's essential finitude, or essential mortality. We note that this is said by Kristeva in the context of a discussion of the relation between the imaginary, fiction, and memory, where memory is vital for the constitution of the world of fiction and the imaginary is vital for the constitution of memory. Images produced in the fictional world, it turns out, are not representational but sensational (founded in sensations). While, on the one hand, Proust's novel could be thought as the object-source of sensation, it could also be that Proust's text activates sensations (it is interactive), that there is no sensation without activation in us, and this activation as interaction implies that the reader is no passive receptacle for the text[2]—that the textual evokes the extratextual, including the bodily domain. Thus, Kristeva writes: "Proust was building his cathedral not in hoping to communicate it to us, but to include us in an analogous experience" (*TS*, 244). If this engagement with the text as an interaction, or experience, rather than as a passive reception, spells out the subject's finitude and incompleteness (for experience reveals mortality; only God is complete and infinite), narcissism is the ego's dream of infinitude: the dream of immortality and the denegation of finitude. We recall, in Ovid's version of the fable, that Narcissus dies at the side of the pool containing his image.[3] He cannot interact with the image in the pool. Narcissus thus dies of absolute passivity—dies in the denial of the finitude that stalked him to the end. Images, though, are the lifeblood of the imaginary-memory complex. Memory cannot exist by itself, but depends on its images. Indeed, memory and images exist in what we could call a transductive[4] relation, meaning that one cannot exist without the other, that the presence of images is indicative of the presence of the memory-imaginary, that the two elements are constituted by their relation and cannot pertain outside this relation. A key implication of this is that the image is not primarily representational. We know this from the nature of the semiotic, as elaborated by Kristeva: representation would only be part of the picture when it comes to language and images. The reason is that the drives and thus the body are very much implicated, as we shall see below.[5]

The body, riven by stases and their interruption in the play of drive energy, is of course the basis of an experience that permeates the symbolic order. This bodily aspect evokes the *khôra*. The latter is "full of movement";[6] time is thus implied in the regulating movement of the drives. So, the body is formed in a movement implying time. It is not a passive pregiven entity, but is its process of evolution (it is "becoming," Nietzsche would say). This embodiment as active formation cuts across the Cartesian division of mind and body, a key point also echoed in recent discussions of technics.[7]

With regard to the semiotic, time is thus drive-based. What are the implications for the image? In order to render the image explicit in relation to the semiotic, an immanent engagement with Kristeva's position is necessary. For Kristeva herself only tends to speak explicitly of the image as a thing and not as the quintessential manifestation of the semiotic *khôra*. With a little development, however, we can perceive how the semiotic, as essentially the basis of interaction, leads to the image as interaction. Put another way: there are no images that are simply passively received other than those observed in a pathological form of narcissism. Interaction, then, is essentially time-based: it is a series of events. It is also experiential thus evoking the body. The body could only not be involved if one were to adhere to a Cartesian mind-body split. Kristeva, the like theorist of new technologies, does not subscribe to this.

My interest is in determining how Kristeva's approach to the image compares with recent accounts of the image that implicate it in technics. In this regard, I turn now to three approaches which illustrate the current state of play. Given Kristeva's ambivalence regarding technologies and the virtual, it is interesting to see the place technics might occupy in her work. These three approaches are those of Bernard Stiegler, who poses a transductive relationship between the human and the technical; Gilles Deleuze's idea of a time-image as a new rhythm of cinematic production; and Mark Hansen's thesis of "bodies in code," where the difference between the body and digital art becomes seamless. These are, it goes without saying, not the only avenues available, but they are, in my view, the most philosophically explicit in treating technics and the image, and also, indirectly, they connect with Kristeva's theoretical concerns relating to the image, time, and the body as the semiotic. What we want to explore is the degree to which Kristeva's discovery of the semiotic, particularly in relation to time and experience, can hold its own in relation to recent developments in the philosophy of technics, consciousness, and time. An important issue here concerns rethinking the Cartesian mind-body dualism such that mind and body come to form a transductive relation, much as occurs in Kristeva's symbolic-semiotic dualism. Thus, we could say that in this transductive relation the symbolic is never present without the semiotic, and vice versa.

In light of these three approaches, we will also examine Sartre's philosophy of the image and Kristeva's reading of it. I shall argue that Sartre has much to offer with regard to insights into the nature of the image, even more perhaps than Kristeva's reading is able or willing to pick up.

Bernard Stiegler's Approach to the Image as a "Temporal Object"

As a theorist of technics, Bernard Stiegler examines the role of technics in the constitution of memory and takes the domain of cinema as exemplary. Inspired by the theory of a temporal object outlined by Husserl in his analysis of melody, Stiegler proposes that film (therefore, the image) renders explicit the working of three levels of memory or retention: primary, secondary, and tertiary. In relation to cinema, tertiary memory comes into play when it is realized that what is seen on the screen is what must have taken place at some historical moment because film is part of a process of recording that Stiegler calls "orthographic," which literally means exact writing, but can be defined here as exact recording. Roland Barthes's understanding of the photograph as an emanation of (a moment of) time because of the nature of the physical process of producing a photo precisely captures the idea, Stiegler believes, of orthographic. The orthographic moment is the moment of tertiary memory (what Stiegler also calls, after Leroi-Gourhan, "epiphylogenesis"), the technical means of putting me in touch with a past, whether immediate or distant, that I have not (directly) lived. As, in addition, human memory is retentional finitude, it must rely on tertiary memory in the constitution of the self, the first key instance of this being writing. Moreover, subsequent forms of technology such as the phonogram and the camera, as orthographic instruments, reveal the selectiveness of memory: memory can be compared with the orthographic (= technical) version of events. With the repetition of hearings (of music) or viewings (of a film) the orthographic moment reveals the selectiveness of memory: one never hears or sees in exactly the same way twice. As for cinema, its time structure becomes indistinguishable from that of consciousness.

Adoption and Symbolic Misery

Hence, the cinematographic moment, like the moment of melody, corresponds to the time of consciousness. The structure of primary, secondary, and tertiary memory is as applicable to film as it is to melody—to the extent that, with regard to temporality, the two domains become interchangeable: "There is '*complete adoption*' of the time of film by the time of the spectator's consciousness."[8] And furthermore: "the characteristic of temporal objects is that the flow of their flux coincides 'point by point' [Husserl] with the flow of the flux of consciousness, for which they are the object—which means that a consciousness of the object *adopts the time* of this object: its time *is* that of the object, a *process of adoption* in relation to which the phenomenon of identification typical of

cinema becomes possible" (*TT3*, 61–62). Seen in a broader perspective, cinema—along with all media that are technologies of recording (phonogram, photography, CD)—as an instance of tertiary memory, and as such subject to the
control of the "culture industries," becomes a site of political contestation and
struggle. Because of the human's necessary *adoption* of tertiary memory—
because the human is necessarily wedded to tertiary memory—the politicization
of culture cannot be avoided.

As we shall see, Stiegler links symbolic misery (the result of marketing and
a loss of participation in the Symbolic) to the mode of "epiphylogenesis" or "tertiary retentions." For, access to memory and experience that one has not actually
lived only becomes possible through various media technologies, including images and writing (writing history). "Tertiary retentions" (= tertiary memory)
accord with Husserl's notion of imagination. In the example of a melody (an
example of a temporal object to which Stiegler refers constantly), a primary retention is an experience of a present note (the "now") which retains a trace of
the past note and anticipates the note to come (protension). Secondary retention
is the whole melody heard again in imagination after it was heard in actuality. In
short, primary retention corresponds to perception and secondary retention to
imagination. Tertiary retention—of which Husserl did not speak explicitly—is
the possibility of hearing the same melody via recording technologies such as
the phonogram and, now, the CD. Hearing the actual playing of the melody is no
longer a once-off event, as it used to be in the nineteenth century. Through tertiary memory—recording—society is put in touch with a past—with a herit-
age—which it has not lived. Through tertiary memory, community is constituted
(the *nous*, or us, as Stiegler says). It thus makes all the difference in the world as
to who has control of tertiary memory, for this is what is adopted by consciousness. Thus, we should not forget that "adoption" is part of the human attachment
to tertiary memory (= history).

Consequently, through the process of adoption, Hollywood and American
culture can come to dominate the world. Whether or not one agrees that this has
taken place, the point is to realize that it is a question of control and domination.
Critics who have failed to appreciate the significance of tertiary memory have
criticized Stiegler for this position, first, because it is thought that privileging
cinema continues the West's obsession with the sense of sight (the most "noble"
sense), and, second, because of the disembodied nature of the theory. As Mark
Hansen explains, the "fidelity" of Stiegler's argument "to Husserl's philosophy
renders it fundamentally unable to grasp the embodied basis that links together
self-affection and technical mediation."[9] David Wills has also criticized Stiegler
for privileging the cinema form of the time object because it ultimately involves
a "realist risk."[10]

With regard to Wills's and similar arguments, a "realist risk" seems trivial,
if Stiegler is correct regarding the political stakes involved. And, indeed, when
not wearing his "promotion of embodiment in digital art" hat, Hansen also
agrees with Stiegler. For he has written that "[b]y up-dating Husserl's account of
time-consciousness—and specifically his identification of musical melody as an

exemplary temporal object—Stiegler is able to demonstrate how the contemporary culture industries operate by controlling and directly capitalizing the time of consciousness itself."[11]

As illustrative of a possible approach to the image, and as a way of assessing the contemporaneity of Kristeva's approach to the image, Stiegler's work is an important point of reference because it is not limited to an ontology of technics but also engages with the effects of technics in contemporary society (maybe this is what Wills means by "realism"). In this regard, Stiegler, in the two volumes of his *De la misère symbolique* (*On Symbolic Misery*), documents the way that "hyper-industrial" society has led, for a large part of the population, to a loss of individuation and aesthetic experience, due to media techniques and marketing.[12] Aesthetic experience is understood by Stiegler as *aisthēsis*: the capacity to feel in the sense of experiences gained though all the senses (cf. *sentir*) —along with a capacity to identify with an other and thereby be the member of a community. For its part, individuation is disappearing due to a loss of participation in life governed by the symbolic. The result is symbolic misery:

> By symbolic misery, I mean the *loss of individuation* which results in the *loss of participation* in the *production of symbols*, the latter designating as much the fruits of the intellective life (concepts, ideas, theorems, knowledges) as those of the sensible life (arts, know-how, mores). And I am supposing that the present state of the general loss of individuation can only lead to a *collapse of the symbolic*, that is, to a collapse *of desire*—in other words, to the disintegration of the social properly speaking—to total war. (*MS1*, 33; Stiegler's emphasis)

Needless to say, through media and marketing, the loss of individuation and participation is adopted by the populace: it becomes part of the landscape of living in contemporary society. It entails the *"liquidation of primary narcissism"* (*MS2*, 51; Stiegler's emphasis) and, consequently, the liquidation of desire.

All of this accords with Kristeva's fears as expressed in her adherence to the idea of the "society of the spectacle." What is different is that the lack of participation mentioned earlier leads to the "distress" (*mal-être*) that occurs in the wake of the loss of a sense of community (*nous*): "Le *nous est gravement malade*" ("The '*we*' is gravely ill") (*MS1*, 123). Kristeva, albeit for different reasons, would not disagree.

The Time-Image in Deleuze's Philosophy of Cinema

Unlike Stiegler, who takes cinema time to be an extension of photographic time (time of the fixed moment), Deleuze, following Bergson, emphasizes the durational, subjective nature of time in feature films. Cinematographic time thus detaches itself from photographic time. Like Stiegler, there is nothing in Deleuze's approach to suggest that images have any meaningful existence outside their system of technical support. Durational time is, however (and this is different to Stiegler's notion), subjective and virtual, yet, by implication, outside of consciousness. For,

> [s]ubjectivity is never ours, it is time, that is, the soul or the spirit, the virtual. The actual is always objective, but the virtual is subjective: it was initially the affect, that which we experience in time; then time itself, pure virtuality which divides itself in two as affector and affected.[13]

Whereas Stiegler wants to link time to its measurement (see Stiegler's resort to the clock as constitutive of time and of making the photographic apparatus a "*clock* for seeing"),[14] Deleuze links time to quality. While time is essentially cognitive for Stiegler, for Deleuze it is sensation and affect: an experience, albeit one inscribed on the subject, if we are to believe Mark Hansen (see below). This seems to draw Deleuze closer to Kristeva's position. And there is more. For, from one angle at least, the time-image, as already mentioned, is semiotic in Kristeva's sense of a rhythmic space. Thus, according to Deleuze, the new cinema based around the time-image (which includes aspects, among others, of French New Wave and Italian Neo-Realism), as found, for example, in Bresson, Jacquot and Téchiné, and particularly in Resnais, is based on "a whole new system of rhythm, and a serial or atonal cinema, a new conception of montage" (*C*, 214). Clearly, time here is not that of Husserl's temporal object incarnate in a melody. Instead, it is time as constitutive of an emergent subjectivity (one that cannot be anticipated, only experienced), much like the subjectivity of the open system referred to by Kristeva in the opening chapter of *Tales of Love* (*TL*, 14). In this case, Deleuze argues that the rhythm of images is established not by the metaphorical or metonymic and associative procedures of conventional narrative, but through a linking of entirely independent images through irrational cuts. "Instead of one image after the other, there is one image *plus* another" (*C*, 214). The flow of images ceases to be based on metonymy and thus becomes the raw material out of which coherence has to be forged; they are not the vehicles of a prior coherence waiting to be expressed. In Deleuze's terms an encounter with such cinema changes and/or adds to circuits in the brain. Hence his much publicized quip that "the brain is a screen." Consequently, instead of a fully posited subject coming to interpret a series of cinematographic events within a pre-given interpretative framework, subjectivity is the partial outcome of a cinematographic experience.

But are we really dealing with a bodily experience of time, rather than an intellectual one? And is it not rather a one-way process, in fact, with cinema determining the brain, rather than cinema itself also being the outcome of time? Despite saying that, as subjects, we are "in time" (a notion with which Merleau-Ponty would hardly disagree), it is not clear, as far as cinema is concerned, in what sense the cinema image is in time and relates to affect and the sense in which it (as the screen) is constitutive of time. My view is that it is the latter which very much comes to the fore. But if perception is not a simple matter of reception but one of the input of affect—if it is not a matter of what is perceived being identical with the object prior to its being perceived—there is a space for a singularity to intervene, a singularity in part constituted by the drives, by the semiotic—by what is external to the screen. For Deleuze, for all intents and purposes (that is, despite "voices off"), there is no outside of the screen. Deleuze, then, tends to imply that the film as the director presents it (even as a form of "atonality") is the film as the perceiver perceives it with the result that any echo of Kristeva's semiotic is muted. Full interaction in cinema is not, in other words, Deleuze's point of departure.

On the other hand, with the time-image formed through rhythmical, nonrational breaks, the semiotic may well be Deleuze's point of arrival. For the time of the object (the nonrational break) becomes the time of the subject, in the sense that rhythm and breaks are essentially subjective, just as music is only music to the extent that it enters the body in a specific way and triggers certain effects. Semiotic cinema, like music, does not exist in itself, but only through the response of the viewer listener. It now remains to address this point in the context of Mark Hansen's work.

The Body as Interactive Art: The Work of Mark B. N. Hansen

The work of both Stiegler and Deleuze has been criticized by the innovative theorist of technics and embodiment, Mark Hansen. In an essay published in 2004, Hansen, as already noted, takes Stiegler to task, in one of five key critical points,[15] for privileging the sense of sight in his valorization of cinema as today's key temporal object. It is not just that sight plays the reductive role of *causa efficiens*, but also that the engagement with cinema becomes a one-way street: cinema impacts on consciousness without consciousness impacting on cinema. In short, consciousness is not the apparent tabula rasa implied by the process of adoption and is already historical and bodily, and thus cinema cannot function as a total model of "the contemporary technoscape" (*TA*, 601).

Deleuze, similarly, does not escape such criticism. This concerns points already evoked. Thus, when it is claimed that the "brain is a screen," this, for Hansen, implies a one-way process: from screen to brain, rather than one where there is an emergent state of affairs. As Deleuze presents it, the time-image exists, says Hansen, within a purely mental space (*TA*, 593) (rather than a bodily-mental space), so that, in fact, Deleuze's cinema of the brain contradicts the neuroscientific consensus that "thinking is constructive and emergent and that it encompasses richly embodied processes of autopoietic self-organisation" (*TA*, 593), a notion prominent of course in the work of Manturana and Varela.[16]

To see what is at stake, we consider Hansen's reference to the color videos of the artist Bill Viola (e.g., *Anima* 2000). Viola's videos are shot in normal time, then radically slowed down, so that one minute of recorded time, in the case of *Anima*, which depicts faces expressing emotions of joy, sorrow, anger, and fear, gives eighty-one minutes of playback time. The point is that the playback time tunes in with Walter Benjamin's principle, enunciated in the *Work of Art* essay, that new technologies are not only prosthetic in the sense of filling a deficit, but examples such as the telescope and microscope are also enhancements of perception able to reveal the "optical unconscious," just as Freud made manifest the psychical unconscious.[17] Viola's video, in tracking minute changes in facial expression—changes that cannot be detected by unassisted perception—shows the extent to which perception and technics are allies, not enemies. Hansen's further point is that once these minute changes are perceived, their emotional impact is more powerful than would be the case were they experienced as unassisted perception. That is, the intensity of affect is greater in the case of technologically assisted perception than it is with "normal" perception. The image, technologically assisted in a specific way, thus intensifies, rather than diminishes, experience. Of course, when speaking of emotion and affect, the body is brought in, and this is Hansen's point: images have a bodily and not just a cognitive dimension. Or rather: in their being cognitive they are also corporeal. Descartes's mind/body dualism has now been challenged, if not overcome (although not sufficiently in Stiegler or Deleuze, says Hansen).

Overcoming the mind/body dualism does not mean orienting things in favor of a preexisting material body over a virtual mind. For, in Hansen's view, there is no essentially incarnate body, only the body as experienced and thus constructed, even if this is also a material body of affect:

> What aesthetic experimentations with VR ultimately demonstrate is the capacity of new media art to accord the body new functionalities—including the extension of its capacity for self-intuition or spacing—precisely by putting it into sensorimotor correlation with new environments, or more accurately, with unprecedented configurations of information. (*TA*, 194–95)

We see that the very constitution of the body occurs through interaction: there is no body prior to interaction with an environment (this is Hansen's emergent side). It is thus an antiessentialism of the body of the most radical kind. It is a radicality largely demonstrated with respect to the context of visual digital art, although Hansen also refers to the work of Manturana and Varela in biology, which has a similar orientation.

If neither Deleuze nor Stiegler can measure up to Hansen's radical antiessentialism of the body, what of Kristeva and her concept of the semiotic? Although Merleau-Ponty is one of Hansen's references, predictably, Kristeva is not. But given that the key chapter 3 on Husserl in *Revolution in Poetic Language* (31–37) aimed to challenge fundamentally phenomenology's assumption of a preexisting, punctual subject, in favor of the semiotic "subject-in-process,"[18] the semiotic would seem to fit with Hansen's position, the differences being: a) Kristeva was thirty years in advance of Hansen, and b) unlike Hansen, Kristeva's approach is not demonstrated in a limited field such as visual digital art, where interaction is explicitly par for the course.[19] Rather, it ranges from the infant's rhythmical language (holophrastic utterances) to the art of the avant-garde: from Mallarmé to Joyce and Jackson Pollock.[20]

The Semiotic and Sartre's Philosophy of the Image

Using Hansen as a benchmark of the present state of understanding of the image and perception, where does Kristeva stand? Undoubtedly the semiotic overcomes the Cartesian mind-body dualism, and in this Kristeva is close to Hansen's position. On the other hand, despite her foray into cybernetics at the beginning of *Tales of Love* (the "open-system"), Kristeva has always been ambivalent when it comes to technics. Thus, in an interview in 1996, some time after the publication of *Le Temps sensible* in 1994, she has this to say:

> I'm one of those who think that, despite the technological era in which we live—the era of biotechnology, "cyberspace,"[21] and other gadgets which seem to radically modify the links individuals have to meaning, to their bodies and to others—a *psychic life* exists which still seems to me to be the essential value of our civilization. It is not limited to the personality but, by way of subjective experience, situates humanity in history and, beyond the history of events, in the monumental history of Being.[22]

While for Stiegler and Hansen and others, psychic life itself is supported, and even constituted, by technics (and the image also needs a technical support), Kristeva seems to argue for the complete autonomy of psychic life. Technics are there, but they are completely separate from the psyche. If writing is also a technical support for the psyche, it is so by being entirely subordinated to the structures of meaning and significance. This looks very much like technics as a means and nothing else. But what can we say of the image here? Even for Husserl it could not be understood independently of its technical support. A consciousness of images is always based around an experience that I have not lived; that is why Husserl was led to sideline the image in his analyses (*TT2*, 220). The "already there" is "essentially composed of non-lived recollections conserved as consciousnesses of images" (*TT2*, 249).

In this vein, I would like, now, to talk about the way that Kristeva's conception of image ultimately links it to the drives, sensation, and affect. To confirm this, we need to take a detour along the route of various concepts of the image. Here, were it not dominated by a notion of mimesis, Plato's *Timaeus* could be our starting point.[23] For right where Kristeva finds support for her notion of *khôra* (52c), we find the following passage: "For an image, since the reality after which it is modeled does not belong to it, must be inferred to be in another [that is in space], grasping existence in some way or other, or it could not be at all" (52c). In Kristeva's hands, *khôra*, as a "rhythmical space," seems remote from any form of the image. So as to broaden and deepen our discussion here, we turn to Sartre's philosophy of the image in his book, *The Imaginary*, and to Kristeva's reading of it.[24]

If Sartre shows what the image was and still could be, Kristeva shows that, post-Sartre, the image takes on a political significance in the "society of the spectacle" in the following ways:

The spectacle is a society of the image where everyone is flooded by images made into things (*la choisification*) (from television and elsewhere), and this stifles revolt, not only ideologically so that image-clichés and image-stereotypes dominate, but psychically, too, because, being standardized, the bevy of images inhibits imaginary formations, such as fantasy and the self as difference or singularity.

Second, art no longer has an object, which was the image, because images no longer signify, having become nothing other than a dull repetition of the same.

Third, when the image is analyzed, it is often as a thing: its effect is therefore neutralized.

Fourth, images have ceased to have an impact (whether this be symbolic or affective). The most horrific scenes fail to jangle the average nerves as traditional interdictions and moral precepts fade into the past (this is the Didier complex).[25] Nihilism dominates. To *speak of* suffering is not to manifest suffering. Further, a fantasy structure does not come into operation because fantasy is the penetration of images by passion and the drives. The analytical and symbolic surface keeps the lid firmly on the poetic infrastructure that is based in the semiotic. A violent image does not have the impact of violence.

Kristeva is concerned to introduce the element of affect (more generally, the drives) into symbolic formations and to show how the semiotic is embedded in the symbolic. This process cannot be entirely controlled by analysis, and this is what makes the semiotic problematic for certain kinds of academic study—those studies, for example, where exposition and objectification have to take precedence over rhetorical and poetic processes, or those where the noncognitive and affective, semiotic domain proves to be a challenge to conceptualization, in as much as to name the semiotic risks falsifying it. Studies of forms of art which exploit the semiotic might be an example, as might be studies dealing with emergent processes, such as the formation of subjectivity.

In Sartre, the image makes present an absent object: an object *as* absent.[26] In the "society of the spectacle" this does not happen, to the extent that the image has become a simulacrum. The image as simulacrum (= thing) is the death-knell of the imaginary, which depends on negativity for its continued existence; that is, it depends on an image as the mechanism for bringing an object into presence as absent.

The "Illusion of Immanence"

Sartre's book on the imaginary, first published in 1940, ranges over a wide area, including aspects of the experimental psychology of its day. And Kristeva notes that for this reason some parts of it are dated. In 1936, Sartre had published a book on the imagination, where the thesis of the later work was enunciated, namely: that to assume that the image is a thing—to assume that the image has physical existence like an object—is part of a popular and "naïve ontology."[27] For the image is not a thing (*chose*).[28]

A number of principles enunciated by Sartre give his thought on the image a contemporary relevance, perhaps a relevance that Kristeva herself does not fully disclose. The reason for this is that Kristeva does not spell out strongly enough the implications for a theory and an experience of the image of the principle that the image is not a thing. For example, Kristeva speaks of the difference between "mental images" and "material images," such as "photos, portraits, caricatures" (*RI*, 307). My claim would be that, for Sartre, there are no such things as "material images"; only images which are neither material nor nonmaterial, but "irreal." A reading of part of Sartre's text will make the significance of this clear.

To appreciate the force of Sartre's approach is to understand the "illusion of immanence" in relation to the nature of the image. To avoid the illusion of immanence is to avoid understanding the image either as a representation or a perception. As a representation, an image is second in relation to a primary figure: the painting of George compared to the real George. In committing the illusion of immanence (as, according to Sartre, Bergson, and Hume do), we look at the representation (painting as a thing) and compare it to the real person. In art portrait competitions, such as the Archibald prize, run by the Art Gallery of NSW in Sydney, this literally occurs: the painting and the live subject are juxtaposed and judgments are encouraged as to how successful the artist has been in capturing the true character and personality of the poser. What is happening at the level of the image, according to Sartre, has nothing to do with such a juxtaposition, whether this be real or imaginary. For the image, as a consciousness, is access to the object; it is how we encounter the object. The image, therefore, is never a thing in its own right: it is never a representation. Not even in imagination. I thus do not have a recollection image in my mind which I then compare with the real thing; for, again, access to the real thing is via the image. To think that an image in my head can be compared with the real thing is to fall into the "illusion of immanence."

In order to illustrate the point, Sartre speaks about a portrait of his friend Pierre. As an image, the portrait is the way that, for Sartre, Pierre can be present in his absence. Similarly, with the portrait of Charles VIII:

> It is him that we see not the painting, and yet we posit him as not being there: we have only encountered him "as an image" "by the intermediary" of the painting. We now see that the relation that consciousness posits in the imaging attitude, between the painting and the original subject is literally *magical* (*I*, 23; my emphasis, translation modified).

This magical element is one that Sartre believes enables a link between aspects of Western and traditional societies.

The next principle to note is that an image is not perception even though an image is the consciousness of the thing. Image and immediacy go together. The immediacy of the image is at the same time the immediacy of consciousness as conscious *of* something. The image, as the phenomenological approach tells us, is always the image *of* something.

As Kristeva noted, the image-object is a nothingness, an *objet irréel* (*RI*, 230), so that the image in a photograph has to be distinguished from its material support: the latter is objective, related to perception, while an image is subjective, related to the imaginary. In effect, does this not mean that an image is *essentially virtual*, a point which Kristeva, by implication, does not appear to accept? For, as we have said, she speaks of the difference between mental and material images, committing the error of the illusion of immanence (*RI*, 307), although she also seems to be partially correct herself in pointing out that image and thought are "consubstantial" and that "the image is neither an illustration nor support" (*RI*, 309), only to later reaffirm the initial distinction (*RI*, 312). Moreover, earlier, in a chapter focusing exclusively on the "nothingness" (negativity) of the image, Kristeva equates the society of the spectacle with the "reign of an increasingly virtual imaginary" (*RI*, 226). This is why I believe, for Kristeva, the full import of Sartre's position is not entirely appreciated. In any case, the consciousness *"imageante"* (imaging consciousness) is a nonthetic consciousness, a consciousness without an object, one that gives itself—like consciousness—immediately for what it is. In other words the image is radically transparent. It is not a matter, therefore, of engaging with the materiality of the image or its status as a representation (as Kristeva implies [*RI*, 312]), but of being entirely carried away by the image as a magical experience. Before the image in its truest form, I do not have the choice of materiality or representation—of perception or the illusion of immanence—because an image transports me totally into the world. It is the way I am in the world.

We could almost say, following Deleuze, that, for Sartre, perception is actual and objective, while the image is subjective and virtual. To further sum up what we have said up until now: images are not simulacra; they are not entities in their own right (basis of the illusion of immanence). An image of a chair is not an object. It is not a question of a simulacrum of a chair. Rather, the image gives access to the chair as a chair. An image is not a perception: thus one does not *see* an image; for the image is seeing itself (cf. *I*, 52). Media images are thus not images in Sartre's sense for two reasons: a) they primarily function as representations that can be turned into objects of contemplation and analysis, which, for Sartre, means that we are not getting to the image as image; b) the media image (and the media in general) does not really function as a medium; to be a medium means being absolutely transparent (this is the point that Stiegler fails to get across in relation to technics). To think, therefore, that it is possible to study media as an autonomous object is precisely what contributes to the effect of *choisification*. As Hansen has pointed out, it is a mistake to think that the media and/or mediation can be studied as though they were independent objects divorced from actual human communication and action (*MT*, 300). In Sartrian terms, a medium is essentially transparent, a condition of possibility of some form of activity; it is the mechanism through which the activity can become extant. Indeed, media are the becoming extant of an activity—often of the activity of communication. To study media is thus one of the most difficult things in the world. And yet, it has become so easy. Such ease is part of the Society of the Spectacle.

But what of embodiment? Is Sartre the ultimate Cartesian where cognition and volition are separated from affect and emotion? Assuredly not. And this is another reason for Kristeva being attracted to him. Thus, when Sartre talks about the impersonation of Maurice Chevalier, or of the elementary lines that evoke a human figure, there is not, first of all, a representation of Maurice Chevalier or the figure on the one hand and the real music hall personality or human being on the other. Rather the impersonation, as an image, is Maurice Chevalier, the lines *are* the human person, and this elicits an "affective reaction" (*I*, 28).

In this sense an image is an evocation. A visual sign in general is an evocation. As such, it brings what is envisaged into presence. An evocation *qua* evocation is thus entirely transparent. The sign/image of a man brings the man into presence. It matters little whether this sign is conventionalized or whether it is iconic; the effect is the same, namely, to put consciousness in touch with what is evoked independently of the evocation. The same is true of a name: it becomes an image when it renders the object present in its absence. A name/image is an evocation manifest most strongly in an incantation. In sum:

> The act of imagination, as we have just seen, is a magical act. It is an incantation destined to make the object of one's thought, the thing one desires, appear in such a way that one can take possession of it. (*I*, 125)

Sartre never mentions technics, although he does refer to a photograph of his friend Pierre. As a perception, the photo is a material object; as an image, it is the presence of Pierre in his absence. We know this. The possible place of technics is thus filled in this way: at the level of perception the material support of the image is present; the technical aspect can be present. When the image brings the object into presence as a pure transparency, the technical support disappears, in the sense that it is no longer relevant. What is important here is that technics is not on one side producing its simulacra/representations and the image/reality on the other. Instead, technics is always engaged, even with the most transparent of images. It is precisely because Sartre refuses the status of representation or simulacrum to the true image that technics is inexorably involved. This is so even though Sartre never speaks about cinema and only really speaks about photographs in passing by way of illustration. As the philosopher says: "The photo is no longer a concrete object that provides me with perception: it serves as matter for the image" (*I*, 21).

Kristeva and the Image

I consider that Kristeva's aspiration with regard to the image is similar to Sartre's: she wants to challenge the ease in which we fall into the image as a thing/simulacrum (Sartre's "naïve ontology") in the society of the spectacle. However, her language at certain points lets her down, so that it becomes difficult not to think that the issue of the image has to do with the loss of reality, that images no longer do justice to the object, to the point where the object falls away and we are left with nothing but simulacra—as though we could compare the image and the thing imaged from a third position. For Sartre, there is no such position when it comes to imaging consciousness compared with reflective consciousness.

On the other hand, no one could deny Kristeva's credentials when it comes to the body in the image: drive, affect, feeling, emotion, sensation, these are the bases of any image—of indeed, any symbolic entity to the extent that it cannot be separated from the semiotic. Kristeva shows us, too, that Proust's writing is an evocation, which she calls transubstantiation; and this means that the body (sensation, affect) and language become one. In effect, the word brings the bodily reality in Proust into presence, just as the suggestive lines of the caricature bring the person into presence. We could go further. For, in her engagement with abstract art (Rothko, Pollock), Kristeva takes up the challenge of the image's potential opacity (abstraction is also found in Bellini's colors and Giotto's blue[29]). Although she does not specify it herself, engagement with abstraction is not simply an engagement with its materiality (perception of paint on a surface). Rather, it is to become internal to the semiotic (of the work) that triggers sensation. Here, we rejoin Proust, whose text, we recall, also triggers sensations. In sum, were Kristeva to allow for it, such an encounter with the semiotic has a fundamentally virtual aspect.[30] For just as we are internal to time as necessarily virtual (any claim to a material presentation of time as such [cf. the clock] being metaphorical), so we are also necessarily internal to the force field of the semiotic. The semiotic as such is both timeless and what makes time possible, both invisible and the condition of visibility. This possibility and this condition are entirely virtual, any interpretation of it invoking the symbolic order.

Conclusion

This chapter has sought, in addressing the semiotic, to understand and evaluate the relationship of Julia Kristeva's work on the image and technics in relation to key developments in these areas as instanced by the writings of Gilles Deleuze, Bernard Stiegler, and Mark B. N. Hansen. For each of the thinkers concerned—but particularly, Stiegler and Hansen—individuality and subjectivity do not exist prior to their instantiation, be this in cinema for Deleuze, in technics for Stiegler, or in digital art for Hansen. The mode of embodiment and the play of affect (as feeling and sensibility) also traverse the writings concerned in important ways. Affect for Deleuze is manifest in a subjectivity that is never ours because it is embodied in time; for Stiegler, affect is the key element of feeling as *aisthesis* in aesthetics which makes a "we" as community possible; for Hansen, affect is fundamental to the link between the body as interaction and digital art, and as such is also fundamental to the transformation of the body. Kristeva's foray into cybernetics and autopoiesis at the beginning of *Tales of Love* (14), where love would be an open system generating transformation and renewal, places her on a plane similar to that of the more recent theorists. As Kristeva argues, love is the enactment of love. There is no a priori relation—no preexisting model, or set of conditions—to which reality does, or does not, measure up. Love, for the lovers, is a web that has no position exterior to it. This is the significance of it being inseparable from its enactment.

In a similar vein, we have seen how the semiotic, based in the drives and affect, throws attention on to what Kristeva has famously called the subject-in-process/on trial. It is the instantiation of the subject which is crucial, not an a priori model of subjectivity.

In terms of field of focus and trajectories chosen, there are significant differences between all of the thinkers concerned. Deleuze and Stiegler differ, for example, on exactly how time is instantiated in cinema, and neither Stiegler nor Deleuze take the intricate approach to digital technology and the body that Hansen takes. Nevertheless, in light of a common interest in the work of Gilbert Simondon, Deleuze, Stiegler, and Hansen are squarely within a framework that privileges emergence when it comes to the formation of subjectivity and, more precisely, individuality. Deleuze endeavors to show this in relation to cinema; Stiegler does this in relation to information technology as tertiary memory, where temporal objects are primary; Hansen, as we have seen, does it in relation to the body and digital art. In other words, each, in their own way, echo Kristeva's notion of the "subject-in-process" and love and the psyche as an open system. This, at least, is what the chapter has striven to make clear. In doing so, it has striven also to demonstrate the topicality—the relevance—of Kristeva's oeuvre with regard to the very latest thinking on subjectivity and technicity, a topic not usually associated with Kristeva. That is, through its various layers, Kristevan thought communicates with the central issues of our time, and in so doing contributes to the enrichment and expansion of the boundaries of the Symbolic—the order which, ultimately, is the very condition of possibility of embodiment and technics.

The Layered Being of Merleau-Ponty and the Being Layered of Deleuze: A Comparison of Two Conceptions of Immanentism on the Basis of the Notion "Fold"

Judith Wambacq

Categorized under the label of poststructuralism, the philosophy of Gilles Deleuze is usually not connected to the structuralist inspired thinking of Maurice Merleau-Ponty. Moreover, Deleuze explicitly distanced himself from phenomenology, and the phenomenology of Merleau-Ponty in particular. In his book *Qu' est-ce que la philosophie?* he accuses Merleau-Ponty of corrupting immanentism by creating an ontological level to which being is immanent.[1] As Deleuze is convinced that every good philosophy has to be an immanent philosophy, this critique indicates a gap between both thinkers.

And yet there are a lot of correspondences between both philosophies, more particularly with respect to the way in which they try to guarantee the immanent character of their theories. In this chapter I will examine the relation between both philosophies by concentrating on a notion they both use: the fold. Both philosophers' conceptions of language and its relation to the world—which is an immanent relation according to both—will be the frame of this discussion.

Merleau-Ponty's Conception of Language as Behavior

As it is a more or less common method in *Phenomenology of Perception*, Maurice Merleau-Ponty focuses on the psychological diseases in which a natural ability is disturbed, in order to understand man's natural use of this ability. His examination of the nature of language is thus based on the study of patients who suffer from aphasia. What is remarkable about these patients is that the words which they can hardly retrieve from their memory when asked to categorize them, are uttered without any hesitation when the practical context invites them to do so. For example, these patients might have a problem to give the name of the insect that bites humans or animals, but they shout out spontaneously "Aw, a mosquito!" at the moment when they are experiencing the bite of the insect. The problem is thus not that they do not know the word, but that they cannot use the word in an abstract manner.

Merleau-Ponty understands this as a proof that language is first of all something by which we move in the world and construct relations with it. Language is a certain intentionality: it constitutes itself as a directedness to the world, rather than being the expression of the individual's directedness to the world. It is not the means by which the individual communicates to others his relation to the world, but it is that which brings our experience of the world into being. Merleau-Ponty does not defend an instrumentalist interpretation of language, but a phenomenological one. Or in his words: "We find here, beneath the conceptual meaning of the words, an existential meaning . . . which inhabits them. . . ."[2] This is also what is caught first, when hearing or reading something. When we read the work of a philosopher for the first time for example, what is first captured is not the theoretical framework, the way in which everything is put together and placed against the background of the history of philosophy, but the philosopher's style, his way of looking at the world that is implicitly present in every explicit reasoning about the world. Merleau-Ponty describes this style as the general emotional essence that is extracted from the empirical world (*PP*, 210).

The reference to the body in the concept of emotional essence brings us to Merleau-Ponty's idea that language is a behavior and words are gestures.[3] This comparison is not metaphorical but literal: words are not *like* gestures, they *are* gestures. In what way?

According to Merleau-Ponty, gestures are not the external visibilities that accompany emotions and are grounded in these emotions. Stamping the ground with rage does not refer to anger, as if there is an extrinsic link between both, but *is* anger itself. It is the stamping itself, the experience that the earth does not respond to your stamping, that creates the divergence between the self and the other, and the aggression that is awakened by this feeling of powerlessness. In other words, the meaning of the gesture does not precede the gesture, but mixes itself with the structure of the world that is created by this gesture (*PP*, 217). The meaning of the gesture is the gesture itself; it is the way of being in the world, which is this gesture.

This example can be a little misleading however. Firstly, it suggests that there is a natural link between the emotion and the gesture that performs this emotion, and thus that gestures must be universal since our emotions are. Merleau-Ponty acknowledges, however, that a Japanese does not express anger in the same way as an Occidental: he laughs, whereas we get red and stamp. Does this mean that there only exists a contingency between the emotions and the gestures? No. We don't feel as if we could as well laugh when we're angry. In our experience, stamping *is* being angry. For us who are raised in a world where stamping is anger, this link between emotional essence and gesture has become intrinsic. Merleau-Ponty concludes that gestures are neither natural, nor cultural. The contingent or artificial relation between gestures and their meaning becomes natural when they are lived every day. It is thus senseless to try to determine the priority of nature over culture or vice versa.

Secondly, and more fundamentally, the example might suggest that—although it was said that the meaning of the gesture *is* the gesture itself—the meaning is created *in* the gesture. This is not correct: the feeling of anger or aggressive powerlessness is not something that is produced by the not yielding of the ground. In other words, it is not the case that when the emotion does not precede the gesture, that the gesture precedes the emotion. There is no causality, no "before" and "after" involved here. When a gesture, or more generally a form of behavior, is defined as a specific way of being in the world and of experiencing the world, then behavior and experience, gesture and emotion, are simultaneous. Instead of a relationship between cause and effect, there is a simultaneity, or—what is the same—an endless coming and going between the gesture and the emotion. So one could say, for example, that the stamping transforms the feeling of disagreement that I initially have into something really aggressive, into what is called anger. The gesture creates the anger. On the other hand I already must have a feeling of disagreement before I can start stamping the ground. The gesture demands an emotion in order to be launched.

Given Merleau-Ponty's understanding of gestures, what are the implications of the idea that words are gestures? If speaking is a kind of bodily behavior, and bodily behavior a positioning with respect to what surrounds us, learning to speak consists in learning what position a word can take with respect to other words, as much on the syntagmatic axe (horizontal: what is the order of words?) as on the paradigmatic axe (vertical: to which other words is this word related?). A teenager will learn the meaning of a word like "conflict" for example, by listening to the contexts in which others use the term and by trying himself to drop the word in a context he thinks is appropriate. The meaning of the word thus reveals itself through use rather than in a dictionary, and it is the knowledge of how to use a word, of what movements a word allows, that determines the meaning or sense of a word, rather than knowing its definition. Meaning is thus a positional or contextual affair.[4] In a structuralist way, Merleau-Ponty says that meaning or sense is spread out over the whole language, that it is "the total movement of speech" (*S*, 54).

That words are gestures also implies that the meaning of a word is the word itself, just like the meaning of a gesture is the gesture itself. Let us explain this by referring to an example out of Frank Baeyens's book *De ongrijpbaarheid der dingen*.[5] When a child asks his mother why she is breaking the flowers, the mother will answer that she is not breaking them but picking them in order to decorate the table. In this way, the mother does not only teach the word association "picking flowers" to the child, but she also changes the child's experience of this scene by using another, less violent word to describe what she is doing. This shows that a word is not a neutral instrument to communicate to others what you see or feel, but that your experience is also shaped by the word itself.[6] It is this endless coming and going between the experience of the world on the one hand and the language on the other hand which constitutes the meaning of a word. The meaning of a word is hence the specific experience of the world that it expresses and this experience always takes place within language.

Merleau-Ponty's Use of the Notion of Fold

In Merleau-Ponty's view it is thus impossible to make a distinction between the external order of language on the one hand and the internal order of experience, meaning or sense on the other hand. There are not two levels, but only one; there is no essential and thus original order that is separated from the secondary, non-essential order. But how does this switch from a transcendent ontology to an immanent account for the differences that do exist between expression and meaning? After all, although it is impossible to separate expression and meaning, it is equally senseless to say that they are one and the same.

The fact that, in his elaboration on language, Merleau-Ponty uses the Heideggerian notion of the fold can give us some indications as to how Merleau-Ponty would have answered the above question.[7] What is characteristic about a folded piece of paper is that the inside is made by folding the outside onto itself. There is hence no essential distinction between inside and outside; they differ without having different essences because they are both ways of the paper relating to itself. Moreover, their nonfundamental difference is never clear-cut: the outside is never completely exterior and the inside is never completely interior. Transposed to language, this means that speaking concerns the relation of existence to itself; existence never exceeds itself. Existence can relate to itself in a more expressive way or in a more silent way, although the silent experience is always shaped by language and vice versa. Language and experience are just different configurations of the same existence or being in the world.

A second interesting feature of the fold is that it installs a reflexibility—it folds back upon itself—without coinciding with itself. The upside and the downside of the folded paper will always be distinct, a bit shifted with respect to each other. Consequently, the reflexivity resulting from this reflexibility never equals a complete transparency. Hence, Merleau-Ponty talks about the nonsense of the idea of a "complete" expression or an expression in which the sign coincides with the sense. The genesis of sense is endless;[8] the process of speaking, of establishing a stance toward the world, always has to be restarted and repeated. Instead of this coincidence with itself, the existence is marked by divergencies ("écarts"),[9] fissions ("fission" [*VI*, 165, 190fn, 192, 269]), invisibilities ("invisibilités" [*VI*, 265]), and the interrogative ("l'intérrogatif" [*VI*, 139, 240]). These divergencies and invisibilities install differences that are not clear-cut distinctions; these differences are related in such a way that it is not clear what is the contribution of each party, whether this party is the inside or the outside,[10] the "I" or the other, singularity or universality,[11] creativity or tradition, nature or culture.

Deleuze's Theory of Sense Being on the Border of the Thing and the Proposition

How does Gilles Deleuze understand the meaning or sense of a word or a proposition? In *Logique du sens* Deleuze starts his examination of sense by focusing on the original linguistic interpretation of the term, to enlarge it afterward with an ontological dimension.

In linguistics the sense of a proposition is distinguished from the referent of a proposition or the level of the individual designation, as well as from the proposition itself. The proposition concerns the level of the particular style of speaking and particular opinions. The first distinction (sense-referent) explains the existence of synonyms and homonyms, and of the hermeneutic plurality of perspectives on the world. The second distinction (sense-proposition) allows to explain irony. Finally, the sense is also different from the signification of the proposition. For example, the expression "to make a mountain out of a molehill" *signifies* that one transforms a molehill into a mountain and thus blows up something, while the *sense* of it also takes into account the context with respect to which one exaggerates. Of what this context exactly consists is not really determinable, whereas the signification does allow preciseness. Signification concerns the general concepts that are inextricably bound up with words and propositions, whereas the sense is fundamentally unspeakable and forms the horizon out of which concepts are understandable. Deleuze defines the sense as the expressed ("l'exprimé") of the proposition, taking into account that the expressed is not synonymous with the explicit; the sense is the unspeakable that is expressed by the proposition. When the sense is taken as the referent of a new proposition however, it can be made explicit but not in the capacity of sense. The sense of this new proposition is again unutterable.

It is remarkable though that, according to Deleuze, the sense is not only the expressed of the *proposition*, but also the attribute of the *thing*.[12] Deleuze refers here to Spinoza's ontology in which expression is said to link substance, attributes, and modi, the three ways of the one being. According to Spinoza there is only one substance, one being from which all the beings are a part. This substance needs to be expressed in order to be known, and this is the function of the attributes; the attributes express the substance. The substance thus relies heavily on the attributes, although it cannot be reduced to the attributes. The attributes in their turn are expressed by the modi or the concrete manifestations of being. Against this background Deleuze's statement that the sense is the expressed of the proposition and the attribute of the thing, means that the thing is the expression of the sense (which Deleuze calls "event" in an ontological context[13]). The event is the attribute of the thing, which means that it is the expressed of the thing, and not the thing itself. This interpretation is confirmed by the fact that Deleuze situates the ontological sense or the event at the surface of things; as a consequence, it does not have the concreteness of the thing; it is an incorporeal layer which originates indeed from the actions and passions of bodies, but floats just above the things.[14] Strictly speaking, the event *is* not but it insists or subsists in that which exists.[15]

By defining the sense as the expressed of the proposition, as well as the expressed of the thing, or in other words, by using the relation of expression in the context of concepts as well as concrete entities, Deleuze succeeds in bringing together two sorts of being. The gap between the abstract and the concrete that characterizes any transcendentalist philosophy, between the *en soi* and the *pour soi*, is bridged here. The concrete and the abstract are considered as two forms of the same actual. Deleuze thus does justice to his principle of creating an immanent philosophy, a philosophy that refuses the classical two-worlds-ontology. It has to be mentioned however, that he introduces a new distinction: the one between the actual and the unspeakable, unformable virtual. Is this a disguised transcendentalism? Although we cannot enter here into the subtleties of the distinction between the actual and the virtual, it has to be said that the virtual forms the core of the actual such that the virtual is not something beyond the actual, and thus transcendent with respect to the actual, but something which is different from the actual but immanent to it. Deleuze uses the image of the fold in order to describe this relation of an immanent difference.

Deleuze's Use of the Notion of Fold

In his book *Le pli: Leibniz et le baroque*[16] Deleuze introduces the notion of the fold to give a new expression to the philosophy of Leibniz and to the arts and sciences of the time in which Leibniz was writing. This concept however also occurs in earlier works of Deleuze, such as *Difference and Repetition*,[17] *Proust et les signes*,[18] and *Spinoza et le problème de l'expression*.[19] In his later work, such as his book on Foucault, Deleuze uses the notion to compare Foucault's philosophy with the phenomenology of Heidegger and Merleau-Ponty. Entering into the specific contexts in which Deleuze deploys this notion would lead us too far away from the purpose of this chapter. In the light of a comparison between the philosophies of Merleau-Ponty and Deleuze, I will henceforth restrict myself to a general sketch of how Deleuze uses this term. One passage out of Deleuze's *Foucault* book will serve as starting point for the confrontation between the two thinkers.

It could be said that Deleuze uses the notion of fold mostly in contexts in which he refers to an outside which is not external—and thus, in a certain sense, part of ourselves—but at the same time not internal in the sense of something with which we are intimate. The fold thus occurs in the context of that which is always unclaimable inside the familiar and of that which is unavoidable or necessary inside the foreign. This notion of the nonexternal outside or noninternal inside is for example appropriate in the context of the virtual, being the nonrepresentational dimension inside the representational actualities, or in the context of *aiôn* as the extratemporal dimension inside the chronological time.

What exactly is the function of the fold within this nonexternal outside? The fold describes the way this nonexternal outside is structured or constituted: the outside is folded such that an inside is created that is not the inside of an intentionality; it is "an Inside that is deeper than any interior"; it is an inside that is always traversed by the outside. Or in reverse order: the inside is folded such that an outside is generated that is not the outside of the perceivable world, but an "outside [that] is more distant than any exterior."[20] The fold introduces a difference (between outside and inside) that can never be pinned down because it can be easily redone, because there is no fixed criterion to differentiate, and finally because the differentiation is not really a separation. Consequently, the fold is rather a line along which communications and changes (between inside and outside) take place, than a gap that separates. Just like Merleau-Ponty, Deleuze speaks about the endless movement inside the folded plane of immanence, about a coming and going.[21] Being a line of communication, the fold (within this nonexternal outside) can be considered as that which makes the relation between the common sense inside and outside possible (they are deduced from this nonexternal outside). Or, in other words, when actualized, the endless movement that characterizes this virtual, nonexternal outside, crystallizes in a unidirectional and less differentiated (= reduced in number of differences) movement. Applied to language, this means that every expression, every actual linguistic creation (whether it concerns a daily utterance such as "I am hungry" or an artistic expression such as a poem) is made possible by the transformation of the virtual which endlessly folds back upon itself, into a well-defined, or rather determinate difference. The ever-changing and unspeakable difference of the fold is hardened into a well-cut distinction.

In summary, the concept of the fold allows Deleuze to think the relation between unity and multiplicity. It explains the existence of differences that do not corrupt the unity of being, and the existence of conditions of possibility that are not situated outside the things they ground, but inside them. The fold allows Deleuze to conceive of a world that is in a constant change, without having to situate the motor of this change in some static, transcendent, divine principle; the motor is this world. We are hence familiar with it, although we do not know it.

The Fold in Merleau-Ponty and Deleuze

It is clear that both authors use the image of the fold to describe the non-fundamental difference between the outside and the inside (for example, between behavior and emotions, the other and the self, the cultural and the natural, the proposition and the sense, etc.). Neither Merleau-Ponty nor Deleuze believe in an outside that is radically different from, and thus completely outside, the inside. Their difference is neither determinate nor final but is, on the contrary, always in the process of making. This implies that a complete capture of the inside by the outside, the so-called coincidence or transparency, is impossible. The process of interpretation is endless.

Yet, the two interpretations of the fold cannot be lumped together. In his book, *Foucault*, Deleuze, through the voice of Foucault, accuses Merleau-Ponty of folding too quickly and too easily (*F*, 117–21). What does he mean by this? And is it at all possible to consider this critique from a Foucaultian point of view as Deleuze's own critique of Merleau-Ponty?

Let us begin with the last question. The authors that Deleuze discusses in his monographs (Nietzsche, Bergson, Hume, Leibniz, Spinoza, Kant, and Foucault) are, one by one, philosophers he adores and from whom he takes concepts. However, he always adapts these concepts to his own philosophical needs and interests. It is hence very difficult to say where the interpretation of the discussed author ends and where Deleuze's own theorization begins. Deleuze himself describes his philosophical practice as buggery, as sneaking behind an author and producing an offspring which is recognizably his, yet also monstrous and different. Moreover, numerous studies have indicated the resemblances in the fundamental orientations of Deleuze's and Foucault's thought. Both Foucault and Deleuze plead for a different thinking, which they both understand as a thinking that relates itself to the outside without wanting to familiarize it. They both favor a special kind of positivism and they are both inspired by Nietzsche.[22] Given all these elements, we can conclude that, although it would go too far to consider Deleuze's statements on the philosophy of Foucault as statements about his own philosophy, at least Deleuze cannot be disagreeing with "Foucault's" critique on Merleau-Ponty.

What does Foucault(-Deleuze) mean when he criticizes Merleau-Ponty for folding too quickly? Just like Merleau-Ponty, Foucault(-Deleuze) objects to the reduction of phenomenology to intentionality. More specifically, neither Merleau-Ponty nor Foucault(-Deleuze) consider words and things as expressions of an intentional subject. Statements ("énoncés") and visibilities are not directed toward something, they are not related to a thing, but only refer to a language or a language-being in the former case, and light or a light-being in the latter. As we discussed earlier, Merleau-Ponty is convinced that sense or meaning is spread out over the whole language and that language is a folding back upon itself of existence. In the case of the visibilities, which is beyond the scope of this text, he understands this folding as a chiasm between seeing and being seen. The fact that seeing always requires a being seen is the condition of possibility of our access to the outside world. According to Merleau-Ponty however, the fold is not only the fundamental structure of language and vision, but also of the relation between them: speaking is being folded onto the seeing and vice versa.[23] The fold structures the whole existence.

Foucault(-Deleuze) situates the fold elsewhere. In contrast to Merleau-Ponty, Foucault(-Deleuze) distinguishes two other levels that precede the level of formed statements and visibilities (or the level of the "savoir" in Foucault's philosophy). The first is the unformed level of "pouvoir," of relations of forces, which is in its turn preceded by the level of the outside ("dehors"). According to Foucault(-Deleuze), it is only on this last level that the folding takes place. The folding is thus a question of undetermined and contingently interacting forces, and not of statements and visibilities. Translated into Deleuzian terms: the fold has to be situated on the level of the virtual and not of the actual.

Foucault(-Deleuze)'s account of Merleau-Ponty's position is not really correct. As we have seen, Merleau-Ponty considers the fold as a structure of existence, and existence does not only consist of formed statements and visibilities, but also of invisibilities. These invisibilities are not possible visibilities because they are for example hidden or undiscovered—that would still subsume them under the range of the visibilities—but fundamental invisibilities. No visible can ever fill in for this invisible because the invisible is that which makes the visible possible. As such, Merleau-Ponty's invisibility has a lot of resemblances with Foucault's outside and Deleuze's virtual.[24] However, the other critique of Foucault(-Deleuze) —that Merleau-Ponty would fold too easily—does reveal a clear difference between the two conceptions of the fold. According to Merleau-Ponty, the fold makes possible a reflexivity that, although it is not a transparency, it allows communication with others and thus constitutes a society. As such it is a harmonious structure. For Foucault(-Deleuze) on the contrary, the fold indicates a violent or discordant relation. The folding is not an activity of gearing harmoniously one thing to another, but a pushing and pulling, a fight between different forces. As such, it is more about the movement of folding than about the result of the folding. From the perspective of Foucault and Deleuze, Merleau-Ponty's conception of the fold is too peaceful[25] and too static.

In summary, we could say that Merleau-Ponty understands the fold as the creation of a harmonious unity which is nevertheless not a self-coinciding unity—it is a layered being—, whereas Deleuze considers the fold as the infinite movement inside a violent power field. Hence, Deleuze does not emphasize the noun but the verb: it is not about *a layered being* but about *being layered*. He does not so much stress the unity but the differences and the conflict inside this unity or immanence.

Chapter 4

The / Turn and the " " Pause: Agamben, Derrida, and the Stratification of Poetry

William Watkin

The Stratification of Prose and Poetry in Modern Thought

It is the early 1930s and Mikhail Bakhtin is laying the foundations of his influential conception of prosaic heteroglossia. In doing so in the essay "Discourse in the Novel," he invokes the metaphor of stratification. Carving out a strong contrast between novelistic prose and poetry he makes use of a philosophical mainstay, poetic unity. The novel, he argues, does not merely reject the unity and uniqueness of poetic, centripetal language but "makes of the internal stratification of language, of its social heteroglossia and variety of individual voices in it, the prerequisite for authentic novelistic prose."[1] It is an influential tropic choice. Bakhtin chips away at it as the essay progresses, always in dialectical opposition to poetry. Poetry, he explains, cannot bear the "intentions and accents of other people," and so in a totalitarian fashion refuses them entry into language. In contrast, the ever-hospitable novelist "welcomes the heteroglossia and language diversity of the literary and extraliterary. . . . It is in fact out of this stratification of language . . . that he constructs his style" (*DI*, 298). And it is out of the metaphor of stratification that much twentieth century aesthetics has constructed the idea of prose, based on a fundamental belief that prose is composed of various different layers, while poetry is marked by a seamless unity.[2]

While we all now take for granted the idea that the novel at its best presents a complex layering of social, psychological, and linguistic forces, stratification as a metaphor is not necessarily a sound wager when it comes to Bakhtin's definition of prose. Obviously, he is invoking the nongeological use of the term to refer to the different social levels of complex societies. Yet this does not excuse his confusion over what constitutes stratification and where it is to be unearthed. The tangled location of centrifugal speech through which the dialogic word must pass is a vibrant, three-dimensional arena described memorably as "a dialogically agitated and tension-filled environment of alien words, value judgments and accents" (*DI*, 276). The word is variously compelled to "weave in and out of complex interrelationships" or to "break across" the environment, but never to delve, quarry, or burrow. So that although more than once Bakhtin refers to how heterogeneous linguistic entities are laid down into, we presume, strata, he never demands that the word itself dig. The prose word is not archaeological, although

49

always exposed to the history of a language in a way poetry, being atemporal, never can be. Heteroglossia as Bakhtin conceives of it, cannot submit to the ossification indeed fossilization inherent in the conception of stratification, for this speaks too much with the dead accents of unified, centripetal poetry. Rather, the prose writer, compelled to travel under the pull of the centrifugal, "moves out across the zone of stratification, confronting a multitude of routes, roads, and paths that have been laid down by social consciousness" (*DI*, 278). Being thus occupied, the novelist has no time to stop and dig.

Clearly Bakhtin had not quite thought out his metaphoric layers in establishing stratification as a descriptive network for discursive, dialogic, and centrifugal prose. Yet the image is powerful enough to return years later in Merleau-Ponty's *The Prose of the World* where he talks of sedimented language in strictly Bakhtinian terms as "the language the reader brings with him."[3] Developing the metaphor later he declares: "In the art of prose, words carry the speaker and the listener into a common universe by drawing both towards a new signification through their power to designate in excess of their accepted definition or the usual signification that is deposited in them" (*POW*, 87). Here, Merleau-Ponty seems to close the circle of Bakhtin's spatiodynamic confusion of moving across, yet also somehow through, a stratified zone which however the word never tunnels into, by revealing that inventive prose takes us beyond the sediment of historical significations deposited in the language of the subject by history. Thus he is able to conclude that "sedimentation is not the accumulation of one creation upon another but also an integration." Clearly utilizing Husserlian temporality as any good phenomenologist must, sedimentation consists of a step into a future which will then retrace historically those steps as being the "experience of the same truth in which they will be grounded" (*POW*, 100). Thus stratification submits to the classic protention-retention formulation of phenomenology as a whole.

Given the qualities assumed by modern aesthetics to be inherent to singular poetry, a theory of poetic stratification is harder to trace within the canon of modern aesthetics. Since Kant's equation of the beautiful to that of the finitude without purpose of natural beauty, and Hegel's commitment to aesthetic autonomy and unity, the role of singularity within art and the status of poetry as the archetypal art form means that a definition of poetry as unified and unique has become carved in stone. Heidegger hardly helps. His pronouncement that prosaic thinking "cuts furrows into the soil of Being," while asserting that to the poet "the word appears as the mysterious wonder,"[4] seems to perpetuate the same old dialectic of prose being of the ground, sedimented, and worldly and of poetry being of itself, hermetic, and other-worldly.

However, certainly since Mallarmé's *Un Coup de Dés*, modern and postmodern poetics has been marked by a profoundly stratified formalism. From the clear strata of the various strands in Mallarmé's masterpiece, grammatologically marked using simple typographical variance, through the great stratified works of modernism such as Pound's *Cantos* and Williams's *Paterson*, to the recent palimpsest texts of American poet Susan Howe, the much vaunted nontranslatable and thus singular language of poetry has committed itself to a graphical stratification not merely equal to that of prose but indeed unavailable, on the whole, to prose.[5] Meanwhile, although nearly all—if not all—contemporary philosophers of poetry are devotees of a post-Heideggerian idea of poetry in its singularity providing access to the truth of being as with-held from view, all such devotees of "poetic thinking," as both Heidegger and Badiou call it,[6] are also inheritors of a post-Mallarmean poetics. In particular, those thinkers who try to demonstrate poetic thinking through attention to the significance of the sensuousness of the poetic text (which, in the end, all must do to safeguard poetic uniqueness/difference), increasingly attempt to retain the idea of poetry as singular.[7] Yet, at the same time they end up demonstrating that poetry's linear, space-framed format is made up of sediments and strata. The most marked engagement with a singular, yet stratified, poetics is to be located on the faultlines trembling between the work of Giorgio Agamben and Jacques Derrida.

Agamben's Definition of Enjambment and His Call for a Stratigraphy of Poetry

In *The End of the Poem* Agamben becomes animated at one point that the fundamental question "What does it mean for a living being to speak?"[8] has resulted in the modern age with the assumption not that language emanates from a being, but that being is a result of language. He goes on to fulminate against the means by which aesthetics has further obfuscated the issue. This clouding of truth occurs, he claims, at the very moment of the consideration of the problem between lived and poeticized experience that Heidegger's work uncovers. At the point of crisis in poetry when the work of art reneges on any primordial wager to try to fuse with life, instead of taking up its own form as its future subject matter—the fundamental issue of the relationship between life and language—philosophy refuses to step out onto the plateau of truth. Instead, this terrain, as he calls it, is as if covered with a veneer of bad thinking.

> It is of this terrain that a summary stratigraphy should first of all be drawn. Excavation work in the direction indicated here is almost entirely lacking. . . . [W]hat ought to be the most proper site of the poetic work appears instead as a vast field partially submerged in psychological swampland, out of which imposing ruins and theological torsos occasionally rise. (*EP*, 77)

Like Bakhtin, Agamben is attracted to the potential of stratification as an allegory of reading. Indeed, his sympathy for the term reaches such a level that he can invent the discipline of stratigraphy or the writing out of layers. Such a stratigraphy is partially identifiable throughout Agamben's work as he tries to drain what I assume to be the swamp of modernity. He wishes, in other words, to return art back to life and solve the question as to what it means for a living being to speak.[9]

In defining early on in his career poetry as the tension between sound and sense resultant from the opposition of a metric limit to a semantic one, Agamben makes the highly contentious yet convincing claim that, therefore, all poetry must be definable as enjambment. At the same time as establishing enjambment as the meta-prosodic feature of poetry he concedes: "Enjambment thus thematically marks the 'rupture' between metrical pause and syntactic pause that . . . also characterizes caesura, if to a minor degree" (*EP*, 77). While enjambment is by far the most important theme here, taken together, this duality of line and space lays the ground work for something that could be called the stratigraphy of poetic layering which one finds mapped out in Mallarmé, Howe, and others as I have already suggested.

Let us take Howe's "Thorow" from the aptly named *Singularities* as progressively, projectively, and pedagogically exemplary in this regard. The poem begins with a title, "Thorow," to be read as "through" referring to the search for a "through passage" across the waterways of the Adirondacks by European settlers. This is the ostensible theme of the poem: how to recapture the lost language and culture of the native Americans as spectral palimpsest through a critical, archival, and archeological rereading of the signifiers that are laid on top of the lake in so many layers of plasticized consumerism. The title sits atop an image it appears to be caption of and captive to. Said image shows an arcing river enframing three trees below. Above the waterway is an arrow facing left. Here the linearity of alphabetical languages that reaches its apotheosis, if Agamben is to be believed, in poetic enjambment, is highlighted by its negation under the sign of the tabular simultaneity of the image, which of course does not develop sequentially along one dimension but occurs in an instant within a framed two-dimensionality. The specific image here, however, makes use of the three key elements of the very linearity it seems to exceed. These are linear directionality (the arrow), unit articulation (three trees), and boustrophedonic or folded flow (the river seems both to reveal the truth of poetic linearity and mock it).[10] The image is able to combine the three elements of enjambment as it unfolds in time—direction, division, and the turn—in one single instant. That said, what an image cannot do is pause, and this is to its detriment. What it gains in immediacy and dimensionality, it loses in terms of the fundamental need to interrupt flow. In foregrounding enjambment therefore as necessary precondition to caesuric interruption, Agamben implicitly agrees with Hegel that it is poetry's combination of image and textual field that marks it out as the art of all arts. A point which I assume Howe is also in agreement with, not only because the poem then abandons the image in favor of language, but also because Howe herself gave up being a visual artist to commit herself to poetry.

As the poem progresses it takes us upstream, against the grain or flow in the direction indicated by the arrow. We travel in other words from prose back to poetry against the directionality of Western languages which head ever eastwards. Of all forms of grammatology, it is poetry's urge to travel east or right to the point of its turn west against itself that marks it out as the source of singularity. "Thorow" as it moves left to right across each page of an east tending book, also moves west back to the source of poetry as such by systematically presenting and dispensing with all that precedes it: image and prose. The next section of the work, which is untitled, begins with narrative, descriptive, stratified prose through its application of a critical taxonomy of contemporary American topography as the poet describes the debased environs of the once idyllic Lake George: "There are two Laundromats, the inevitable Macdonald's, a Howard Johnson . . . a Dairy Mart, a Donut-land, and a four-star Ramada Inn."[11] This prose then becomes "poeticized" in the next section, "Narrative in Non-Narrative," as it fragments revealing that strata, contrary to the assumption of Bakhtin and others, often do not sit comfortable and can shift and buckle beneath our feet: "Interior assembling of forces underneath earth's eyes. Yes, she, the Strange, excluded from formalism. I heard poems inhabited by voices" (*SI*, 41). The shore of the lake seems now to tremble.

The poem "as such" begins a couple of pages later with the couplet: "Go on the Scout they say | They will go near Swegachey" (*SI*, 43). The next thirteen pages consist of one to two short lyrics per page, floating in the middle of page space as it has come to be called. The final of these abounds with images of the overlay of topography and typography which presents and performs the theme of the poem, how a territory is colonized by naming as a form of violence and how these historico-linguistic sediments sit uneasily atop one another. Poetry here, being singular, linear, interruptive, and nonprosaic, is able to approach the specters of violence locked into the icy landscape of the lake in winter, but in the end is as much a product of the violence of the West as any other discursive form. If poetry is able to take us "back west" to the source of the lake's origins in the names and language of a lost people, it abandons us, as it were, at the mouth of the cave unable to travel any further back, the surge of water burbling somewhere inside, behind, below . . . to our left. The final words of this section propose, therefore, after a slow passage from image, through prose and poeticized prose to poetry, a leap beyond poetry. No longer able to travel through a grammatological or temporal linearity, the poem expands into the atemporal space of ecstasy:

I pick my compass to pieces

Dark here in the driftings
in the spaces of the drifting

Complicity battling redemption

(*SI*, 55)

It was not simply Western European names that conquered these already occupied places, it would seem, but also their arrangement in lines and their relation to space: the very fact of their being a written language as such. The next three pages attempt therefore to exit the complicity of grammatological linearity with a series of famous Susan Howe palimpsests wherein lines are written over other lines, turned upside down, placed at a diagonal and so on as she tries to extricate herself from Western writing without succumbing to an idyll of pure orality. After this typographical and sometimes orthographic tempestuousness, the last page seems a place of beatific calm as we arrive amidst the floating world of a series of signifiers that Agamben might struggle to identify as either glossolalic, semiotic pure coincidences of sound and sense, or xenoglossic, obvious grammatically coherent syntaxes which we simply don't know the meaning of yet:[12]

anthen	uplispeth	endend	
adamap	blue wov	thefthe	
folled	floted	keen	

(*SI*, 59)

These drift in the middle of the page combining the three modes of signification the poem up to this juncture investigates: tabular simultaneous image, alinear stratified narrative/descriptive prose, and lineated poetic enjambment. In this locale, one might even term it a poetic *khôra* of sorts projecting into later debates with the work of Derrida, the three elements of the poem come together critically but also illustratively and explain the relationship between enjambment, caesura, and the enclosed poem body as basis of its singularity. A poem, Agamben argues, breaks the linearization of Western thought-writing, what Derrida calls grammatology, at a moment insignificant to the development or perpetuation of meaning. This is the enjambment that prose does not allow and which marks poetry out as singular in foregrounding the sensuous over the supersensuous (unnecessary pause for breath that interrupts the poem's sense). Yet at the same time as the poetic line flows and turns at its limit point, it is also subject internally to interruptions or caesurae, pauses which arrest semiotic flow and allow for mid-way, ecstatic semantic self-reflection. Finally the two elements, flow and interruption, are mapped out across a forward and backward or east and west flowing entity whose semiotic regularities are projective in that they recur, and yet whose semantic instabilities are retentive or cataphoric in that one must often reread or read backwards to understand where the poem is progressing. These three combine together to form the stratification of singularity within the poem, enjambment, caesura, and what Agamben tends to call rhythmic structure or the forward-interruption-backward, flow-continuum that makes up the whole poem body (a structure he inherits, as did Merleau-Ponty, from Husserl).[13]

As we can see Howe's work overlays these three different spatialities, line, pause, and field, first progressively as image (continuum), prose (line), and poetry (space). And then on this last page she suspends "words" in such a way that all three elements are presented separate and yet together, surely the definition of strata. There are lines here but their flow is undermined by the excessive gaps between words which suggest the words are autonomous of the convenience of linear presentation. There is a syntax facilitated by spacing caesurae but the words themselves do not cohere into a sense unit and the gaps between suggest concatenating division rather than a pause for coherent thought linkage. Finally, there is a field of continuum, the page, but the elements do not cohere into a single rhythmic entity but rather levitate together in a mood of mutual disdain coupled with accepting compossibility. There is, therefore, no better representation of the fact that poetry is not univocal and closed but stratified through and through, and yet that the stratification of poetry is indeed singular, than Susan Howe's completion of the Mallarmean project on the final page of "Thorow."

Indeed it was hubristic of Bakhtin to ever suggest otherwise. Stratification belongs with poetry in the first instance; prose is merely borrowing it. The very fact of enjambment reveals graphically the layer upon layer of lines that build up to make the entity called the poem. It would seem that rather than being born seamless and whole, all poetry is the accumulation of matter. All poetry is stratified. The interjection of space into the line through the use of caesura reveals an intrinsic need for differential gaps in language for stratification to be attained. While the turn of the line allows for the buildup of the poem's layers, it is the gaps between and within the lines that allow for the marking out of these layers for the eye to see. The pauses in poetry, in fact, are the graphic element of any theory of poetic stratigraphy so that although enjambment and caesura are radically dissimilar in Agamben's work, they come together to create poetic stratigraphy without ever synthesizing or succumbing to some order of transcendent *Aufhebung*. As in Howe, they hang together in a neutral, receptive, imprintable between-space.

I am digging here, trying to free from the swamp the art of stratigraphy that Agamben neglects to shape in any concrete fashion. The turn in the line defines poetry as layered, in stark opposition to the alinearity of prose. Similarly the pauses in poetry, at the end of the line, in the middle of lines, and the parergon or frame of space which surrounds the poem forming its structural body, facilitate, indeed graphically inscribe, the realization that poetry is not born seamless and unique. Rather, it is the sedimented formal accumulation of decisions or tensions existing between what Agamben repeatedly terms, after Benveniste, the semiotic materiality of the work and the poet's semantic aims.[14]

Derrida and the Excavation of the Fold as Site of Resistance to Philosophy

In "The Double Session" Derrida tries to formulate a terminology sufficient for the definition of the irresolvable nature of between-ness. Inspired by the poetry of Mallarmé he unearths the figure of the hymen or material sheet which, he argues, marks out, impossibly, an immaterial blankness which is the dividing point between presence and absence. Obviously, this division bores deep into the core of Western metaphysics but when Derrida states that it also constitutes the "space of writing,"[15] it is also clear how central the hymen is to his development of deconstruction. The importance of the hymen is hard to overstate, therefore, and as Derrida begins to tirelessly excavate the many etymological and homophonic potentialities for defining the idea of the between, we find ourselves terminologically on the rocks as we struggle in vain to set in stone the categorical law of poetic stratification. The French for between, *entre*, promotes Derrida to think also of its homophone "*Antre*: Cave, natural grotto, deep dark cavern," obviously a reference to Plato and the roots of Western philosophy in caves. Inspired by this petrological association Derrida then proceeds to lay out the following, geological, ruminations:

> The *interval* of the *entre*, the in-between of the hymen: one might be tempted to visualize these as the hollow or bed of a valley (*vallis*) without which there would be no mountains, like the sacred vale between the two flanks of the Parnassus, the dwelling place of the Muses and the site of poetry. (*D*, 212)

There is clearly something going on between great philosophers, poetry, and rocks. Apart from the fact that caves are the result of various strata that have been eroded to different degrees, such caverns are also provocative, dark in-between spaces for thought. A cave is burrowed, like the hymen, in between absence and presence. It is a demarcated absence brought about by a surrounding frame of presence. In this way the Platonic cave of philosophy is the very opposite of poetry, which is surely made present, as Derrida argues, by the parergonality of space around matter, not the other way around.[16] The hymen, become cave or *khōra* here, is then further transformed into the very valley or transitional moment between nonpoetry and poetry, the valley of Parnassus itself.[17] The hymen, constantly transformed under extreme geological and homophonic pressures, comes to relate for Derrida the in-between of presence/absence to the very undecidability of the poetic word which he then goes on to consider under the guise of the Mallarmean fold.

While Derrida unearths a different, more sublime and yet also troglodytic stratification to the swampland of Agamben, its source remains the same. The Hymen exists in the form of its folding over, presenting itself in "The Double Session" as the nonpresent spacing between presence and absence, difference and sameness, blankness and inscription, that modern philosophy has termed poetry as a shorthand for what might otherwise be etched as, modifying Hegel somewhat, the sensuous *presentiment* of the idea in the form of a material singularity that is not however, reducible to the totalization or valorization of immanent materiality as such. Such a presentiment is the sense of sense as an impending future event that is also confirmed as such after the event, where the occurrence of the idea confirms the presentiment was indeed a projection into actualization and not merely unfocused, Deleuzian *Stimmung* as such. Singularity therefore is the projected precondition of the idea as feeling or expectation that the idea will arrive followed by the retrospective confirmation that the event occurred confirming a form of enframing or Heideggerian *Gestell* onto what was previously just indistinct mood (as yet unattuned *Stimmung*). This predictive, retroactively confirmed, precondition is the projective folding structure, Derrida uses the figure of the fan, usually termed the event. The relation of event to singularity can be felt across the work of Derrida, Deleuze, Badiou, and Nancy in particular (Agamben too of course). Such a folding is another name for the turning of poetry Agamben brings to the fore with his theory of enjambment. To summarize this rather dense nexus of ideas, all poetry is definable as being verse, which, as the name suggests, refers to the turning away from sense that constitutes matter or the putting of the word before the idea it may be the vehicle for expressing.

Folding, in Derrida, seems to fill in the blanks left by Agamben's teasing call for a stratigraphic poetics. Where Agamben is reticent, Derrida is always fulsome as he acknowledges that "if there were no fold, or if the fold had a limit somewhere—a limit other than itself as a mark, margin, or march (threshold, limit, or border)—there would be no text" (*D*, 270). A remark which sets off an endless process of the folding of folds that allows for this folding without limits. This appears as an observation so vital that he goes on to admit: "If literature . . . is engaged in this fold of a fold, then it is not a mere subsection of foldedness: it can give its name to anything that resists within a given history, the pure and simple abolishing of the fold" (*D*, 270).

Literature, for which one always reads poetry in the Western philosophic tradition, is defined here as the name given to anything which resists the abolition of the fold. Poetry, therefore, is for Derrida exactly the same entity as it is for Agamben. For both men poetry is the very activity of the layering of lines through an imposed break, or fold if you prefer—what Agamben calls enjambment.[18] This is a stratificatory process wherein that which would abolish folding through an imposed limit, discursive prose, is resisted. Yet there is a terrible irony to this agreement between two great thinkers of poetry as a modality of stratified folding, for in the very passage where Agamben calls for stratigraphy, he goes on to condemn Deconstruction for obstructing such a procedure. Speaking of tendencies in what he confusingly terms modern criticism, then aesthetics, then formal criticism, before finally revealing he is speaking of a certain and partial view of deconstructive literary criticism, he declares: "the primodiality of *logos* thus quickly becomes a primacy of the signifier and the letter, and the origin reveals itself as trace. (It is here that the deconstructionist factory establishes its residence)" (*EP*, 77). Then again, is it not often the case that when two great continental plates meet, they tend to rub up against each other with great force, causing the ground to tremble, to quake?

-- fold here --

Agamben and the Caesura as Poetic Thinking

In *Idea of Prose* Agamben considers the problem of poetry and prose from the perspective, not of the inevitable inundation of prose into the suspensive tensions of poetry, but the means by which thought can find a space within the rhythmical seamlessness of the poem. In the brief essay "The Idea of Caesura," speaking of the Italian poet Sandro Penna, he remarks on the "breaking action of the caesura" (*IP*, 43). This is represented by the couplet from Penna "I go towards the river on a horse | which when I think a little a little stops." Invoking an ancient European exegetical tradition which takes the horse to represent the "sound and vocal element of language" (*IP*, 43), Agamben creates one of his many allegories. Here the horse is the voice or the word as utterance. This allows Agamben to note that "For the poet, the element that arrests the metrical impetus of the voice, the caesura of verse, is thought" (*IP*, 43). Thought within the context of the line, however, is not the same as the thinking of philosophy one finds at the line's limits. Rather, this thought is another, more fundamental mode of thinking. As he says in caesuric cadence: "The rhythmic transport that gives the verse its impetus is empty, is only the transport of itself. And it is this emptiness which, as *pure word*, the caesura—for a little—thinks, holds in suspense, while for an instant the horse of poetry is stopped" (*IP*, 44).

As has been the case ever since Agamben's earliest comments on this issue in *Infancy and History* and *Language and Death*, the transport of expression is the "infantile" voice of language as such, a pre-differential and pre-trace language. This conception of the "pure word" of vocalic transport is a language that is previous to the imposition of scission in Western metaphysical conceptions of language since the Greeks. Juxtaposing human, predivided language to that of animals Agamben notes that it is because humans must learn language, must have a linguistic infancy, that they fail to realize their existence depends on a language that can best be described as "immediate mediation" (*PO*, 47). Such a language is available for expression but is inexpressive of any particular thing. It is in this manner the potential for sense within the sensuous medium of language as such.

Agamben variously describes such a language as medium, tablet, stanza, gesture, potentiality, singularity, idea of prose, and voice across his various attempts to render this conception of a supportive medium for expression that does not succumb to the divisions imposed upon it by metaphysics. These divisions include, significantly, the difference between language and voice, between signifier and signified, animal and human, and poetry and prose. The role of poetry here is, via its material semiotic singularity, to open up a greater proximity to a vision of a pure language as such, due to its dependence on a material singularity which is expressive but of nothing in particular.

That said, Agamben does not valorize poetry but, as we saw, in fact criticizes it for succumbing to the same metaphysics of negativity and scission apropos the voice. So that while enjambment brings one closer to an idea of language as pure, inexpressive medium for thought, it is in fact the caesura or ecstatic interruption of the semiotic that facilitates said thinking. In this way the caesura is closest to Agamben's idea of language as mediality/communicability (the potential to communicate without communicating any particular thing) first because it interrupts the semiotics of the line and disallows the valorization of a pure, material immanence, second because it acts as a means of making visible the semiotics of poetry, third because it allows a space for thought in the midst of the semiotic that is not pre-designated, pre-supposed or in any way predicated either on particularity or differential scission, and finally fourth, as he argues in *The Time that Remains*, because it interrupts the *telos-eschaton* sequential temporality of the line introducing a vertical, disruptive, and yet still internalized temporality which he calls *kairatic* time.[19]

This final point is key here as it is this verticality within the line that defines the combination of enjambment and caesura into a rhythmic unit or projective retention that Agamben defines as poetic rhythm. Rhythm, like indistinction or potentiality, is one of the means Agamben proposes for an access to language as such as a future channel for in-differential thinking. Such a language is the limit point of the whole of Agamben's messianic attempt to return philosophy back to the question of the relationship between language and life. Similarly, thought here is not semantic discourse, prose as we have come to see it, but a much more poetic idea of thinking. If the voice in the poem is transport as such, the interruption of pure transport by thought is simply a moment wherein thinking is able to think the pure word without the imposed differentiation of word and world that so troubles the end of the line.

Derrida and the Caesura as the Cut of Poetic Finitude

Derrida is the great modern thinker of space, spacing, gaps, and, therefore, pauses. While there is much to say on this topic and indeed much that has been said, naturally I would wish to focus and indeed finish here on what Derrida has to say specifically about the agency of the caesura in poetic thinking. Derrida's great texts on the caesura collected in *Sovereignties in Question* all concern the poetry of Celan. In what is the Rosetta stone for the whole collection, "Shibboleth," Derrida addresses the paradox of the singularity of dating in Celan as a quasi-metaphysical term for literature and most specifically poetry. The date is both singular, a mark, and of course immediately general, a re-mark. As such it encapsulates the complex, oscillating dynamic of literary singularity which Derrida defines as both inventive and immediately conventional.

Early on Derrida describes Celan's famously elliptical poetic form as "discrete, discontinuous, caesured,"[20] before adding that for Celan, and thus by implication the whole of twentieth century poetics, "caesura is the law" (*SQ*, 4). Throughout Derrida's work on Celan he uses the term caesura as a synonym for the activity of discontinuity or cutting within a textual body leading up to the powerful statement: "Ellipsis and caesura and the cut-off breath no doubt designate here, as always in Celan, that which, in the body and in the rhythm of the poem, seems most *decisive*. A *decision*, as its name indicates, always appears *as* interruption, it decides *inasmuch* as it is a cut that tears" (*SQ*, 69–70). This double signification, that the caesura is a form of cutting off in both text *and* body— a highly poetic thing to observe—solidifies toward the end of the essay into one single statement about the relationship of the caesura to a circumcised text:

> The circumcised word is *above all* written, at once incised and excised in a body, which may be the body of a language and which in any case always binds the body to language: word that is entered into, wounded in order to be what it is, word that is cut into, written because cut into, caesured in its origin, with the poem. (*SQ*, 62)

Derrida's interest rests here on the role of the caesura not so much as a pause within the line than as a cutting off of the poem body. It is, indeed, the last caesura or caesura as textual finitude that he repeatedly finds himself sifting through like an ever-hopeful prospector.

If poetry is definable as that which resists the cutting off of verse by the re-marking of semantic prose, something both Derrida and Agamben argue, does not poetry have built into it always the seeds of its own destruction? If poetry resists that which would abolish the fold, surely it is incorrect to name this prohibitive agency discursive prose? At the moment that poetry imposes the cut, it itself abolishes itself to some future moment wherein the folding line of poetry must cease. There are certainly echoes of this potentiality when Derrida considers the importance of cutting for the very finitude of the poetic body, enacted by the paradoxical placement of the last line in a Celan poem: "The last line happens, however, to be dissociated and separated by the abyssal duration of a blank silence, like a disjointed aphorism" (*SQ*, 148).

Derrida's comments read alongside Agamben's own ruminations lead us to the following, troubling conclusion. That which defines poetry, the turn and the pause, laid down on top of each other in sediments producing a grammatological stratification, at the tip or edge of its being transforms poetry into the poem body at the very moment that poetry ceases to be what it is. The turn of the last verse suffers no return, and the pause beneath that line, not just beneath it but above, to each side and conceptually, if not grammatologically, at its very core, is no longer a pause but an abyss, its temporality becomes ruined by a sudden metamorphosis into space under extreme pressure. In a sense, therefore, Hegel was right. Poetry comes into its being due to its propensity for self-negation. The sensible presentation of the idea, in Hegel's version of events, negates the essence of poetry, its sensuousness, in favor of transport up and out to a higher plane: thought as such.

Yet both Derrida and Agamben lack Hegel's vaunting, speculative confidence. As Derrida says here, the last line does not negate the poem in favor of philosophy, but rather seems to disjoin thought from itself. The aphorism remains incomplete and we are suspended above a chasm which we do not have the means to traverse. What do we do now? Poetry's singularity resides in the fact that it combats that which resists the fold, philosophy in other words. Yet poetic sensuous singularity, the stratification of turns and pauses, is not the sensible presentation of the idea but a sensuous presentiment of poetry's own self-ruination. Every turn, each pause begs the question: what happens when the last line comes? If poetry is that which resists that which resists the fold, how can poetry be what it is if projected ahead of each turn and pause is the inevitability of the last line, the nonreturnable fold, the abyssal pause?

[please pause here]

As you may recall, Agamben intemperately denies Derrida the possibility of participation in stratigraphy in a gesture of exclusion not dissimilar to that of Plato in *The Republic* when he denies poets access to his totalitarian city-state. It is well known why, as Agamben never lets an opportunity pass to criticize, fairly or unfairly depending on one's allegiances, the Derridean archi-trace as leaving language mute and unable to speak its purity as such. But here is there not another motive? Is it not possible that Derrida is repeatedly turned away from Agamben's Academy of Stratigraphy not because of his formulation of the trace of *différance*, an idea fundamentally at odds with Agamben's own conception of language as immediate mediality, but because Derrida's ideas on folding, caesura, cutting, and the end of the poem bear an uncanny resemblance to Agamben's own considerations of the crisis inherent in all poetry? Perhaps it is not difference, diaphora, dialectic that divides the two thinkers, but indifference, similarity, compossibility, thrown together as they are by the disastrous abyss that opens up before their thinking when faced with the collapse of the plateau of stratified poetry down a bottomless cliff.

A crisis is both a turn and a pause, a turning point and/or a decision made. Yet the crisis in question here is in fact the very crisis of crisis defined as the inevitability that at some point poetry must end and be overwhelmed by generalized, prosaic meaning. Speaking in a quasi-metaphysical manner reminiscent of Derrida's development of the terminologies of hymen, fold, and caesura, Agamben says of Mallarmé's "The Swan":

> The disorder of the last verse is an index of the structural relevance to the economy of the poem of the event I have called "the end of the poem." As if the poem as a formal structure would not end and could not end . . . since the end would imply a poetic impossibility: the exact coincidence of sound and sense. At the point in which sound is about to be ruined in the abyss of sense, the poem looks for shelter in suspending its own end. (*EP*, 113)

For both thinkers, therefore, the very reliance of the poetic turn on the interposition of the pause is simultaneously the source of poetry's being and its inevitable collapse. At the moment of the poem's last turn, Agamben argues here, its strongest and most illimitable pause, the poem is unable to return poetry back to its singularity, either as an Agambenesque tension between poetry and prose, or a Derridean resistance to that which would abolish the fold. Poetry is cut off by the very agencies of turn and pause that define its singularity.

This would seem to be an earth-shattering event for poetry. The parergon which surrounds it is not, as we assumed, space. This is a false border. Instead, all poetry is totally encapsulated by prose. In this fashion, poetry resembles not so much a cave as a cave-in. In mining for the golden ore of singular, poetic thinking, poetry is always crushed by the sheer weight of discursive, translatable prosaic thinking as Agamben consistently describes philosophy. If we accept the contention to be found also in Derrida that prose and philosophy are synonymous in that philosophy has always, at least until Heidegger, been written in a discourse that resists the fold, then there is always ever so much more philosophy than there is poetry. An avalanche of philosophy has consistently, over millennia, rained down on poetry, pummeling its multilayered singularity into a compressed, hermetic nugget of self-sufficiency: the univocal closed body of the poem. Yet break open the pebble with something sharp tipped, as poets and thinkers of our age have consistently attempted—it is hard work so do not forget to take plenty of breaks—and gleaming inside is the bejewelled sediment of an aphorism.

> There is ever so much more philosophy than there is poetry but
> without this little poetry, there would be no philosophy at all.

------------------------------------- cut here ---

PART TWO

DISPLACED PASTS, EMERGING TOPOGRAPHIES

Introduction to Part Two

Apostolos Lampropoulos

Contemporary art history, architecture theory and museum studies have, more often than not, discussed the intertwinedness of space and memory. Issues that have repeatedly been addressed in this context include: processes of monumentalization; manipulations of remembering and forgetting, as well as of memory and amnesia; the production of multiple narratives and a politicization of all narrativizations of the past; history-making through uses of space and multiple cartographies of the past. A recurring pattern of memory studies has been the tension between the depth and obscurity of the past on the one hand (its ungraspability and unknowability), and the continuous effort to discover, explore, and narrativize it on the other. Every time this tension is discussed, it sheds new light on the rhetorical, indeed, fictional nature of historiography and on its limits as a record of the past. In other words, it makes us more alert to the ways in which historiography does or does not establish some kind of empathy with the archive, developing a kind of free indirect speech. It is not surprising that alternative historiographies either of the past (such as museums or monuments) or of the future (for instance, political and ideological manifestos) can open up even more controversial debates, from the (im-)possibility to speak about the experience of the Holocaust and represent it in fragments or traces, to the ways in which patterns that relate to tyranny and colonialism might be reproduced in democratic constitutional projects. The second part of the volume follows precisely in this direction. It studies the memory-politics involved in the design of iconic buildings. It seeks to activate untold myths as the *materia prima* of a storytelling to come. It approaches personal or personalized narratives as a form of micro-history and aims to develop a renewable and perpetually critical way of thinking as the basis of a resistance to different forms of oligarchy. This part is also based on a varied corpus: Libeskind, Grosz, and Marion; Benjamin and his readings of Kafka; Rushdie; Kant, Tocqueville, and Schmitt. Despite their different focus and concerns, all four texts reflect on possible ways in which one can respond to a past under reconsideration, sometimes including the emergence of a new topography such as the construction of a building or the delimitation of a territory. In this context, architecture is described as a response to a particular conception of the past, a strategy for producing spaces that renegotiate the past. Second, an infinitely unfamiliar upper past is thought to be the only one that is excluded from the mythic present or from the present as myth. Third, Rushdie's version of halal history and its manipulations of the private past helps us appreciate the line dividing intimate experience from the public or collective past. Fourth, the implicit fidelity to some of the darkest versions of the past such as colonialism is thought to encourage intellectual conformism and to exorcise futurity through the foreclosure of revolution. In all these cases, the attempt to relayer the past gives birth to a *topos* that is neither a utopia nor a dystopia, but rather a field of an always new criticality.

Michael Beehler's "Layering and Extending: Architecture's Traumatic Work of Mourning" begins with the thesis that *iconic* buildings (i.e., buildings that are exemplary of their architect's way of organizing space such as Wright's Fallingwater and Gehry's Bilbao Museum), reflect an experience of excess in built space. In the first section ("Virtuality and Architectural Excess"), Beehler discusses Elizabeth Grosz's *Architecture from the Outside* and her definition of the virtual not as opposite to the real but as the potential of the real to be other than itself. As this definition invests the actual with the trace of futurity, excessiveness in architecture is "abundance" and "potential for proliferation," calling on us to rethink architecture as a deterritorializing expenditure and gift. The second section ("Architecture as Saturated Phenomenon") is articulated around Jean-Luc Marion's *In Excess* and his position that both the idol and the icon are "saturated phenomena" rendering excess explicit. If visibility is possible only via the reduction of saturating excess to something that is simply seen, then visibility is never complete. And if the painting only gives the visible, then it is only in the museum that it exposes itself as the "potential sum of all that which all have seen, see and will see." Where the idol stops the gaze, the icon leads it toward the "unenvisageable," that is the other's human face or a counterintentionality. On this reading, a façade kills the look of the other, because only a face can look at us and Rothko is the painter par excellence that underscores the "death of the human" to which painting has always contributed. The third section ("Moses, Aaron, and Architectural Trauma") focuses on Schoenberg's unfinished opera *Moses and Aaron*, in order to reflect on the unrepresentability of the Absolute, which "*as such* shouldn't have need of the façades that archive it by layering built idol upon built idol." In the final section ("Architecture and the Work of Mourning"), the author turns to Libeskind and his thesis that the "living face" only becomes visible through a prosthesis of the photographic image. This offers Libeskind the possibility to design his buildings beyond the pure visibility and the archival violence of the façade. It also explains why Libeskind sees his Jewish Museum in Berlin as a response to Schoenberg's/Moses's call for an unmediated word. If, as Beehler argues, "the Void cannot a-void the traumatic tension between the face and the façade," Libeskind's buildings cannot avoid repeating the very trauma they recall.

Brendan Moran's "The 'Forgotten' as Epic *Vorwelt*" is a study of the Benjaminian notion of "preworld" or "prehistory." In his readings of Kafka, Benjamin sees the experience of *Vorwelt* as an oblique preconditioning by natural history that is neither entirely discernible nor entirely controllable. In his own reading of Benjamin's Kafka, Moran understands the epic as the familiar in oneself. Interestingly, the familiar in this context emerges as the strange which defies its inclusion in human conceptions. The first section ("Vorwelt") discusses the ambiguity of the term *Vorwelt*, identifying it both with myth and with freedom from myth. It also stresses the fact that Benjamin commends a silence on behalf of the incommunicable and the unrecognizable against any attempted usurping of it by processes of communication and recognition. Yet, even if redemption by myth inevitably entails a deviation from its orders and hierarchies, one can never entirely isolate one's experience from one's entanglement with myth. The second section (*"Vorwelt* and Memory") insists on *Vorwelt* as the epic forgotten. In Benjamin's "Storyteller," epic memory is the cornerstone of one's ability to explore, remember, experience uninhibitedly. In this sense, the rise of the novel-form would be both the loss of a type of recollection (*Erinnerung*), the passing on of happenings from generation to generation, and the emergence of remembrance (*Eingedenken*) as the isolated focus on one hero. This vanishing of a form of storytelling gives rise to a "new beauty." Nevertheless imperfect reminders of epic life can still surface: abbreviated names such as Josef K. can be recalled as forgotten or as ultimately not conscious. In the last section ("Redemptive Forgotten"), Moran reflects on the primacy and potential influence of the interhuman on natural history. He insists on the fact that Kafka's and Benjamin's gesture is attentiveness to people, creatures, and feelings. Therefore, interhumanity becomes mythic as an exercise of exclusion, because the strangeness of one's own body connects one not only to other humans but also to all creatures. If, then, the all-encompassing *Vorwelt* suspends myths of exclusion, it is, according to Moran, the basis of interhumanity and redemption comes as an experience somehow free from guilt-contexts or moral-legal orders that might otherwise dominate us.

In the chapter entitled "*Halal* History and Existential Meaning in Salman Rushdie's Early Fiction," Adnan Mahmutovic defines *halal* history as a "critique of ideologically sanitized historiography by dominant power [leaving] out the definition of the opposite/positive historiography as a counterideological narrative." He attempts to tackle the complexities of *halal* history in the context of Rushdie's *Midnight's Children* focusing on the character of Saleem. The author wonders whether *halal* history, read within the postmodern critique of historiography, loses its critical edge, and whether it undermines the proliferation of subaltern stories. The first section ("Existential Meaning and History") discusses Rushdie's position that interest in religious existential practices arises from the fact that the secular world has probably failed to provide alternative meanings. Attention is paid to the fact that Saleem produces himself as a narrative (rather than merely as a narrator) as well as to the fact that his consciousness of traditional narrative forms is crucial. Claiming that he conveys the undaunted in his insistence on a freedom of expression, Saleem thinks of history writing less as a political stance and much more as a revealing of intimate aspects of private life. This position transforms *halal* history into a "metaphor for all vile historiography regardless of ideology." The short second section ("Private versus Public and *Haram* versus *Halal*") explains why, while selection and censure are common practices in history writing, neither *halal* (the private sphere) nor *haram* (its opposite) are prescribed for historiography. Given that *halal* pertains to historiography in general, the section closes with the question of whether *haram* history is a form of truth surrounding the subaltern, the unholy, and the marginal. The final section ("Ideal Historiography") reminds us that Rushdie's fiction has often been read as a critique of ideology and a "speaking of the suppressed truths." This coincides with Rushdie's view about the novel being the most dangerous of art forms and as fiction par excellence. Consequently, Saleem's conception of *halal* history opens up layers of meaning to a dialectical movement so that each layer palimpsests the former, that is why the dialectics of exclusion and inclusion in *halal* history oscillate between inheritance and production. Following Mahmutovic, "if *halal* history means history cleansed of unbefitting events, then all the 'micro' histories of the subaltern often excluded from the public versions are *halal* as well, that is, ideologically sanitized," hence the significance, according to Mahmutovic, of the novel qua (dangerous) fiction. As he concludes, "let there be stories, all false, cooked up, but all free floating, and as such equally meaningless and infinitely meaningful as well."

The final chapter, written by Marios Constantinou, is entitled "Tactical Reason: Philosophy and the Colonial Question." The introductory section ("Quid Juris? Prolegomena to the Kantian Drama of Sovereignty") clarifies that the author engages with law as posited and enacted. His aim here is to deal with the paradox of an enthusiasm for social reform, human dignity, and liberty that remains dogmatically attached to the existing legality, thus unveiling sympathies with counterrevolution, censorship, and colonialism. Constantinou argues that tyranny, illegitimacy, immorality, colonialism, censorship, and cretinism occur as "Thermidorian aberrations," which he understands as the "strictly immanent effect of exhausted capacities." The second section ("Legal Positivism and the Normative Contradictions of Imperial Anticolonialism: Kant after Schmitt") begins with Kant's remark that the legitimacy of European states is grounded on the premise of an armed confrontation between *hostes aequaliter justi*. Questioning this position, Schmitt trades upon antinomies of imperial favoritism as well as on the constitutional condominium which rationalizes land acquisition. The third section ("The Thermidorian Closure of Kant's Legal Positivism") sees in Kant the quintessential ambivalence of modernity between the will to revolution and constitution, interrogation of the law and unquestioning conformity to its rule, the quest for truth and the pursuit of profit. If all this betrays a profound fear of the plebeian multitude, it is easy to understand why the republican constitution cannot contain any provision that would entitle any jurisdiction within a state "to resist the supreme commander in case he should violate the law of the constitutions, and so limit him." For Constantinou, Kant's legal positivism is predisposed to adjust the faculty of practical reason to raison d'état and to turn over political judgment to the juridical imperium of the Thermidorian apparatus. Consequently, once the revolution prevails, Kant prescribes obedience to the new revolutionary legality. The fourth section ("Methodological Digression: *L'Histoire Évenementielle* and the Sociological Thermidor") proposes as a point of reference not "the great model of language and signs, but that of war and battle." The final section ("Tocqueville's Thermidorian Positivism and its Discontents: The Moral Calculus of Ennobled Colonialism") returns to the Thermidorian pathology that renders principled politics unintelligible and anticolonial revolt unthinkable. Through a reading of Tocqueville, Constantinou criticizes the subtraction of political audacity from municipal liberty. He concludes that, by embracing both right and non-right, the new spirit of imperialism fixates itself pragmatically to the *no thing* as its object, becoming therefore a virtual impossibility.

Chapter 5

Layering and Extending:
Architecture's Traumatic Work
of Mourning

Michael Beehler

I want to begin by citing two questions and a comment, each having to do with a certain excess in architecture and with an architectural experience of trauma and mourning.

First, from theorist Elizabeth Grosz: "How can one design in such a way as to bring out the virtualities of building and of the real itself?"[1] Second, from phenomenologist Jean-Luc Marion: "How does one keep the closeness with [a] depth of 'human drama' if one wants to remain an artist assigned to flat forms, to the flat screen of the painting and the enframing of the idol?"[2] And finally, a comment from architect Daniel Libeskind, whose work is central to this chapter: "Architecture is like the plow, turning up time, revealing its invisible layers on the surface."[3]

We talk often today about *iconic* buildings—Wright's Fallingwater, for example, or Gehry's Bilbao Museum—buildings that are readily identifiable as exemplary of their architect's style or ways of organizing space. But with this city of icons as background,[4] we can engage the notion of architecture as icon in a somewhat more profound fashion. It is toward this engagement that the above writers direct us, focusing as they do upon an ideally *iconic* architecture that should serve to direct our gaze beyond its concrete façade, toward what these thinkers variously characterize as the *virtual*, the *face*, or the *invisible*. The *iconicity* of architecture, then, would reflect a certain experience of excess in built space, one that, in ways I will here explore through these writers and through Libeskind's built and unbuilt projects, repeatedly reenacts the unresolvable *question* of idolatry—of the prosthetic substitute, the question highlighted by the story of Moses, Aaron, and the golden calf—and the traumatic work of mourning.

Virtuality and Architectural Excess

Elizabeth Grosz's provocative little book, *Architecture from the Outside: Essays on Virtual and Real Space*, lays out a Deleuzian theory of excess that highlights *virtuality* as the key component of both nature and architecture. For Grosz, the virtual is not the opposite of the real. Rather, *virtuality* is precisely the potential of the real to be other than itself—a kind of potential for continual self-

71

overcoming that crosses the actual with the trace of futurity. She argues, for example, that nature itself "must be understood in the rich and productive openness attributed to it by Darwin and evolutionary theory, by Nietzsche, Deleuze, or Simondon, as force, as production . . . as a continuous opening up to the unexpected, as relations of dissonance, resonance, and consonance as much as relations of substance or identity" (*AO*, 98). Relying on Deleuze's reading of Bergson, she concludes that the virtual is *in* the real as an excess that "*requires* the actual to diverge, to differentiate itself. . . . The virtual is the realm of productivity, of functioning otherwise than its plan or blueprint, functioning in excess of design and intention" (*AO*, 130). And it is the structure of the blueprint and its excess that connects the virtualities of nature to the similar virtualities of architecture.

For just as in nature, excessiveness in architecture is defined by Grosz as an "abundance" or a "potential for proliferation," an "unassimilable residue" that "outstrips and finds no stable place . . . within systematicity itself" (*AO*, 151–53). As a kind of architectural *différance*, it precedes and exceeds every built structure—architectural, natural, or intellectual—as its condition of possibility and of impossibility. Grosz finds this excessiveness in the works of Bataille, where it is the dynamite that demolishes the phallic control of all monumental architecture, and in Irigaray, where it is more of a productive force: an unruly femininity that reminds us that "any notion of order, system, community, knowledge, and control . . . especially those involved in the architectural project . . . entails a notion of excess, expenditure, and loss that can be closely associated with those elements of femininity and of woman that serve to distinguish women as irreducible to and not exhausted in the masculine and the patriarchal" (*AO*, 156–57). This excess that both *is* and *is not* architecture, because it takes (its) place as architecture's virtual other(s), calls on us to begin to rethink architecture not within a restricted economy of containment—a logic of place understood as "container, limit, locus, and foundation" (*AO*, 161)—but as an economy of deterritorializing expenditure and of the *gift*. For Grosz, this economy of the gift is explicitly the gift of an architecture that is "always in excess of function, practicality, mere housing or shelter": an architecture *in excess* that functions not as "finished object but rather as spatial process, open to whatever use it may be put to in an indeterminate future, not as a container of solids but as a facilitator of flows" and a producer of "future desires" (*AO*, 165). Such an architecture would respond to the ethical charge to welcome the virtual stranger, to open itself to the strange virtualities of futures "in which the present can no longer recognize itself" (*AO*, 166). But the challenge remains: "how can one design in such a way as to bring out the virtualities of building and of the real itself?" (*AO*, 88).

Architecture as Saturated Phenomenon

The ethical charge Grosz lays at the feet of architecture, connected as it is to themes of excess and gift, resonates clearly in the phenomenology of Jean-Luc

Marion, whose works continually explore the phenomena of visibility, revelation, and giftedness. His thinking on the idol and the icon is well known and particularly relevant here, and its long history doesn't need additional rehearsing at this moment. Rather, I want to look at how, in his 2001 book *In Excess*, Marion deploys both the idol and the icon as examples of what he calls the "saturated phenomenon," and at how this particular phenomenon relates to architecture.

The "saturated phenomenon" is key to understanding Marion's reenvisioning of the phenomenological project and all he has to say about the possibility of a phenomenon in general. In a nutshell, the saturated phenomenon gives us a certain experience of *excess*, an experience in which our intentional concepts are overwhelmed by an excess of intuition, almost like a photographic plate that is overexposed, its conceptual image rendered invisible because of a saturating excess of light. "Here," Marion writes, "it is a question of the excess . . . of intuition over the concept, of the saturated phenomenon and of its givenness outside the norm" (*IE*, xxi). Almost like the virtualities Grosz speaks about in architectural terms, phenomena in Marion come to visibility and consciousness only thanks to and along with this invisible background of excess. His work continually responds to the question he poses in the foreword to *In Excess*: "Do phenomena always appear according to the calm adequation in them of intuition with one or several significations, or following a deficit measured from one or the other? Or instead"—and here is where Marion takes his stand—"do not some among them—paradoxes—appear thanks to (or in spite of) an irreducible excess of intuition over all the concepts and all the significations one would assign to them?" (*IE*, xxi). The paradoxes in which this excess is made explicit are what he calls saturated phenomena.

Phenomena in general come to visibility only via the reduction of this saturating excess to something simply *seen*. As an instrument of this phenomenological reduction, the painter plays an exemplary role for Marion, functioning as the resisting medium or the screen against which the purely given—the unseen, saturating excess of givenness—crushes itself, generating *at once* its own phenomenalization *and* the phenomenalization of the painter's receiving consciousness, his or her *self*, what Marion calls *l'adonné*. And this constitutive reduction leads Marion to a phenomenological theory of art. "The painter," he argues, "renders visible as a phenomenon what no one had ever seen before, because he or she manages . . . to resist the given enough to get it to show *itself*—and then in a phenomenon accessible to all. A great painter never invents anything, as if the given were missing; he or she suffers on the contrary a resistance to this excess, to the point of making it render its visibility" (*IE*, 51). Thus although in ordinary experience visibility is never complete—we can see, for example, only one side of a building at any given time, and thus what presents itself does so only along with a certain invisible appresentation—within the frame of the painting *there is nothing but the visible*, because painting "reduces the object to the presentable in it, in excluding the [invisible remainder of the] appresentable," and thus "in containing in its frame the mad energy of the visible, the painting reduces what gives itself to what shows itself—under the regime of the idol" (*IE*, 63, 68). The painting *gives nothing but the visible*: "nothing is still to be seen that is not already presented" in the painting, which "excludes absence and deception from the look" (*IE*, 66). The painting captivates our sight, taking it prisoner and fixing our look on itself, without the possibility of remainder, and this look-without-excess is the very definition, in Marion, of the phenomenon of the idol. But because the painting never gives itself once and for all, exclusively to a *single* observer or a *single* look, because it must be "reseen in order to appear," it "offers us a saturated phenomenon": it "demands that the origins of the look are multiplied: mine [in the many times I go to resee it], but still those of all the other possible spectators" (*IE*, 71). Only when housed in the architectural and social space of a museum does the painting expose itself as the "potential sum of all that which all have seen, see, and will see there" and open an "arena of space and time to all the contemplations that it gives rise to" (*IE*, 72). This excessive multiplication of looks—the painting's temporality or "eventmentality," as Marion puts it—constitutes the "radiance of the painting" experienced as saturated phenomenon.

But as pure phenomenological reduction, the idol or the painting is by definition a limited and limiting experience, a necessary crushing of what gives itself onto the flat plane of what shows itself: of givenness *in excess* of all vision to the reduced frame of visibility. Captivating our gaze and fixing it on itself, the painting leads the gaze nowhere else, and thus it normally cannot function as the other of Marion's key images of saturated phenomena: the icon which, "contrary to the idol," according to Robyn Horner, "allows the visible to become saturated by the invisible, without the invisible being reduced in any way to the visible." Where the idol stops the gaze, referring it to nothing other than the idol itself and giving us nothing *but* the visible, the icon leads the gaze elsewhere, toward an invisible that is for Marion "unenvisageable" and "represented in the visible only insofar as the visible constantly refers to what is other than itself."[5] Following Levinas here, Marion argues that the prime exemplar of this unenvisageable is the human face that "arises [as] a counter-intentionality that does not manifest itself in becoming visible but in addressing its look to me" (*IE*, 78). The face, then, is iconic, the saturated phenomenon par excellence, the paradoxical phenomenon in which there is *nothing to be seen* because it "holds itself back" from the flattening façade of the idol, the painting, and the gaze: it can only manifest itself, Marion writes, "according to an epiphany irreducible to vision." The face "does not appear" *as such*, but rather "manifests itself by the responsibility that it inspires in me," a responsibility lodged in the "silent statement of the imperative 'Thou shalt not kill (me)!'" (*IE*, 78). We experience the idol or the painting by *looking at it*, but in the experience of the icon or the face we find ourselves *looked back at* by a gaze that calls us and that precedes and exceeds every intention. Where excess in Grosz is a matter of the virtual realities of architecture, in Marion (pace Levinas) that excess is the unenvisageable look of the other's face.

And it is by coming face to face with the *face*—by artistically trying to do justice to it—that the question of architecture is most profoundly opened in Marion, the question I referenced earlier: "How does one keep the closeness with [a] depth of 'human drama' if one wants to remain an artist assigned to flat forms, to the flat screen of the painting and the enframing of the idol?" (*IE*, 79). This is first of all a painterly question, the one lived out most keenly, for Marion, by Mark Rothko, but it is there framed in distinctly architectural terms that oppose the architectural figure of the façade to the face. For here is the difficulty: if painting "exercises the phenomenological function of reducing what gives itself to what shows itself . . . if it operates this reduction in bringing back all the visible to the pure and simple plane-ness of the surface, it must end inevitably in the façade," the flat plane that "cancels all depth" in a disfiguration of the face (*IE*, 76). The façade *kills* the look of the other, for only a face can look at us. The painting thus *builds*—and has built *into* it *as* phenomenological reduction *itself*—a trauma that forces the painter (here Rothko) to make an ethical decision: "the façade forbids us to paint the face, and therefore it is necessary to choose between either killing the face in enframing it in the flatness of the painting and putting it to death in the idol, or 'mutilating' oneself as a painter and giving up producing the face directly in visibility" (*IE*, 78). Rothko, according to Marion, chooses the latter, eschewing the "idolatry of the visible" while at the same time underscoring the "death of the human" to which painting has always contributed, "whether only in taking pleasure in rendering [that death] visible, or even in assuming as a matter of principle that one could no more paint the human than death, as a corpse or prostituted" (*IE*, 79). As Rothko himself writes, "'[a]ll art has to do with the intimations of mortality,'" and it is Rothko's attentiveness to the death of the *face in the façade,* or of the *other in a built or painted space,* that highlights for Marion the "equilibrium Rothko imposes on himself": "simultaneously, visibility reduced to the pure seen on the plane and attention to what intimates death"—that is to say, the "face of the other person" (*IE*, 80). For Marion, this *ethical tension* is built into what has come to be called the Rothko Chapel in Houston, Texas, which houses the canvases from the 1960s that allude to themselves as sites of a traumatic mourning for the face whose murder they both archive and repeat: "The Chapel," Marion writes, "only deploys the crushing and magisterial symphony of its browns, purples, and blacks [the floating color-bands of Rothko's paintings] in order to exemplify the tension, or even the freely assumed contraction, between the façade and the face, the idol and the icon" (*IE*, 80). The Chapel gives place to this ethical tension, fixing in stone the traumatic experience of architecture as saturated phenomenon, architecture *in excess* of itself as simultaneously the idolatrous façade that gives death *and* the icon that proscribes this murderous gift.

Moses, Aaron, and Architectural Trauma

The traumatic experience of architecture is, of course, one of the oldest stories around.[6] For my purposes here—and in order to lead us to a consideration of trauma and mourning in the works of the architect Daniel Libeskind—I want to briefly recall the story of Moses and Aaron, a story of architectural trauma Libeskind cites as inspiration for his Berlin Jewish Museum. Arnold Schoenberg's unfinished opera *Moses and Aaron* retells this classic tale of the tension between the face and the façade. As Edith Wyschogrod reads it, the opera represents Schoenberg's obsession with the question posed by this story of God's unrepresentable word and of the concrete tablets and golden calf—the built representatives—that supplement and supplant it: with, that is to say, the "gap between theophany and inscription . . . [or] between the idol as physical artifact and writing"—arguing finally for the "necessity of mediation," the traumatic "translation of the Absolute into perceptually available content, even if such translation attenuates the power of the unrepresentable."[7] The fatal repetition of this mediating translation is precisely the "archive fever" Derrida examines in his essay of the same name, where his analysis of Freud and Yerushalmi zeroes in on the "whole question of the relation between the event of the religious revelation (*Offenbarung*) and a revealability (*Offenbarkeit*), a possibility of manifestation, the prior thought of what opens toward the arrival or toward the coming of such an event."[8] Derrida begins this essay by asking himself "what is the moment *proper* to the archive, if there is such a thing, the instant of archivization strictly speaking," and concludes that it is *not* the "so-called live or spontaneous memory" but rather a "prosthetic experience of the technical substrate" (*AF*, 22). This is the experience lived out by Moses and Aaron, where Moses's revelation *depends on* Aaron's techniques of "revealability," of the written and built prostheses of the tablets and the calf that make it into a "perceptually available content" while simultaneously attenuating its "power." It is the unavoidable *necessity* of this traumatic, archival moment that is repeated in Rothko's Chapel, in Marion's exploration of the phenomenological reduction of the face to the façade, and in Grosz's look at the collapse of architecture's virtualities into the concrete reality of the built site.

Schoenberg's opera can be read as consistent with a Schopenhauerian idealism that sustains the pure unrepresentability of the Absolute, of God's face, and an indictment of mediation and the built image, of the façade or the archive that claims to emplace or to *re*-place the unrepresentable. But by linking Schoenberg to Adorno, Wyschogrod identifies the deeper tension in the opera, one that finds *Moses and Aaron* "talking back" to this idealism, radically questioning it by "break[ing] into the claims of the Absolute's unrepresentability" (*ET*, 257). The "necessity of mediation" is affirmed, according to Wyschogrod, not just by Aaron who, in Schoenberg's version of *Exodus*, 32:19, points out to Moses that his tablets are no less images than Aaron's own idolatrously prosthetic golden calf ("'They're images also, just part of the whole idea'"), but by Moses himself, who responds to this observation by smashing the tablets in despair: "'Then I smash to pieces both these tablets, | And I shall ask him [God] to withdraw the task given to me'" (*ET*, 257). The Absolute *as such* shouldn't have need of the façades that archive it by layering built idol upon built idol, but in Schoenberg's opera it does, irreducibly, and this traumatic necessity haunts the idealism of the face of God, or of the (unrepresentable) face of the other, with a kind of archive fever I will characterize as architectural, tied as it is in Libeskind to an understanding of building as traumatic, prosthetic *re*-placement, or as a work of mourning.

Architecture and the Work of Mourning

Every painting must end "inevitably in the façade" that murders the face: this is
the trauma of painting to which Marion claims Rothko is most attentive (*IE*, 76).
But this is not necessarily the case for architect Libeskind, who argues that
buildings "don't have just façades but faces that turn either toward us or away."[9]
It has become somewhat of a universal parlor game to ridicule Libeskind, whose
work (see the plan for the 1,776-foot high "Freedom Tower" on the site of the
World Trade Center, or the supermall at the Las Vegas City Centre complex)
can sometimes descend to the level of kitschy sentimentality or crass commer-
cialism. And yet in his best work, both written and built, there is an attentiveness
to the tension between face and façade every bit as profound as the one Marion
finds in Rothko. For if Libeskind wants to assert that buildings are a matter of
both the façade and the face, both idolatrous visibility and *something other*, then
architecture may in fact underscore Rothko's comment that *all* art "'has to do
with the intimations of mortality'": that it is always, at some level, a work of
mourning.

His discussion of the face in his otherwise self-serving autobiography
Breaking Ground (whose subtitle could be "why the mess the World Trade Center site has become is *not my fault*") parallels Marion's similar rereading of
Levinas on this figure. For the "living face" for Libeskind is not visible *as such*,
but *becomes* visible only via a kind of phenomenological reduction accomplished by the prosthesis of the photographic image. He writes, "I have to admit
that the only way I can *really* see a face is to take its image from a photograph
and commit it to memory." But what is remembered here is not the face per se—
not a "so-called live or spontaneous memory" (*AF*, 22)—but "nothing more"
than "light exposed, chemically, on a plane": in short, nothing more than the
prosthetic façade that gives us nothing *other* than the purely seen that intimates
mortality by participating in the face's murder (*BG, 106*). In this manner,
memory is a work of mourning in the Derridian sense: the "attempt, always
doomed to fail . . . to incorporate, interiorize, introject, subjectivize the other in
me," and hence the experience of the double obligation in which "I must and I
must not take the other into myself."[10] For in Libeskind as in Marion, the "living
face is something entirely different" than the façade that archives it, and this
difference has to do with the gaze that looks back at me: "The fact is," he explains, "when you regard a face, what you're really looking at is *what that face
is looking at* . . . You look at something, and even if it's inanimate, it looks back
at you" (*BG*, 106). Libeskind's desire is to build buildings that would be in Marion's sense *iconic*, that would *gaze back at us* with an excess going beyond the
pure visibility and the archival violence of the façade.

This is why Libeskind continually describes architecture as the "proof of
things invisible." In his Humbolt University Prize lecture of this title, for example, he argues that the "power of building is . . . more than meets the eye," that it

is the "nonthematized, the twilight, the marginal event" that "communicates that only the superfluous, the transcendent, the ineffable is allied to us" (*SE*, 148). It promises, in other words, to bring us face to face with what *exceeds the archival violence of the eye and the façade*: with, he writes, the "uniqueness of a human face" (*SE*, 149). Architecture understood as *iconic* would thus for Libeskind function "like the plow, turning up time, revealing its invisible layers on the surface," disclosing the face that looks back at us *in excess of* the façade of the visible, "turning up" invisible layers of lines—"[l]ines of history and of events; lines of experience and of the look; lines of drawing and of construction"—all "vectors" referring us to the *unrepresentable itself*, to what Libeskind here calls "the unsubsided" (*SE*, 149). In this, he seems to most closely ally himself with the Schopenhauerian idealism of Schoenberg's Moses, rather than with his brother builder Aaron, the architect of the idolatrous prosthesis and the trauma of faithful mourning. As Wyschogrod suggests, Schoenberg may have left his opera incomplete because the tension about which both Moses and Aaron sing and talk—the tension between the face and the façade, the icon and the idol— *can never be resolved but only repeated.* But Libeskind sees his Berlin Jewish Museum *not* as the *extension* of this irreducible undecidability, but rather as the "not-musical fulfillment" of Moses's final speech, the *architectural answer to* his call for the unmediated word (*SE*, 26). Thus he designed his building to be the prosthetic substitute for the opera's missing third act: "In its stone walls, in the final space of the Void, the characters of the opera would sing silently. And in the end, their voices would be heard through the echoing footsteps of the visi- tors" (*BG*, 93). Experienced as *icon* or as *saturated phenomenon*, the unmediat- ed, façade-less void in the museum promises an answer to the *question of the idol and the trauma of mourning* posed both by Rothko's Chapel and by Schoenberg's *Moses and Aaron*. It promises to reclaim the "spiritual" or, as Libeskind writes about another of his projects, the provocatively titled *Mourn- ing*, to "embody the invisible" (*SE*, 91): to be, that is to say, the concrete archive that *remembers and memorializes* what exceeds the façade of the visible—the excessive face that *is* phenomenological *excess*—without being, itself, another golden calf.

But the Berlin Jewish Museum, when it finally opened, did so *as* the re- opening of the question of compromise and mediation—and of the museum as *prosthesis*—its Void promised to answer. And that question was emphasized by Derrida in his discussion of the uncompromising faith the architect put in his wounded building. Noting that what Libeskind does is to "withhold or subtract this void" from the political and economic forces that enabled the Museum to be built at all, Derrida nevertheless asks an *anxious* question about compromise. "My question," he explains, "ha[s] to do, not so much with what [Libeskind] thinks or what he does, but with the discourse, the word, the logic, and the grammar he *has to use* in order to make his project understandable in a peda- gogy or in texts, given the general philosophical and cultural context in which he *has to convince* us and the powers that be in Berlin. *He has to compromise*" (my italics).[11] In short, Libeskind, according to Derrida, sees the Void as a space protected from the compromises and mediations that would *fill it with visible idols*. Thus protected, it can maintain its "true" status as the iconic embodiment of the invisible: as pure *eventmentality* or *saturated phenomenon*. But when Derrida probes Libeskind about the negotiations he had to enter into in order to build this *iconic* space, he points toward the *absolute necessity of mediating compromise* and to the void as the "fragile" site not only of the excessive face but also of its "always possible deterioration or misinterpretation" *(RM, 115).* Libeskind wants to be Moses, but—like Moses himself—he *cannot avoid being Aaron*, building a kind of architectural golden calf, for what Schoenberg has Moses discover about his tablets—that they are "images also"—Derrida would also have Libeskind learn about his building: that "even your void has [a] visibility" that compromises its *iconicity* and risks again the face's murder *(RM, 114).*

Thus the Void cannot a-void—and in fact reenacts and *extends*—the traumatic tension between the face and the façade: the "prosthetic experience of the technical substrate" that is played out here as an *architectural* fever *(AF, 22).* And this is the building's *constitutive* tension, its *becoming-idol* that, as *icon*, it may (always already) be. It is a risk *at work* in Libeskind's architecture, which for Derrida depends on this foundational risk. For if the architect could be "sure" that his work "would never be altered"—if it could be finally protected from idolatrous visibility, if it could be *counted on* to be (only and forever) the iconic embodiment of the "invisible" and not the site of its idolatrous deterioration—then it would not *work*, it would not "be a work" per se *(RM, 115).* "[For] a work," Derrida tells Libeskind, "has to be left beyond your life, left exposed to manipulation or reinterpretation. That is why you build. The fragility itself is part of the possibility of the work" *(RM, 115).* In the tension of the work, the face—the *unenvisageable* or the *unsubsided* to which the work or museum as icon or saturated phenomenon pledges its faithfulness—finds itself *worked over* by the necessity of mediation and by a fatal deterioration—a *becoming-idol*—it proscribes but cannot avoid.

Libeskind's most powerful buildings, then, can be seen as complex sites of "trauma and memory," of a mourning that, like Derrida's archive, not only *remembers and memorializes* the "overwhelming emptiness created when a community is wiped out," when the face(s) of millions are *erased*, but that *reenacts* that erasure, making it happen *again (BG, 12).* For like all mourning—*especially* that which seeks to do justice to the murdered face—they cannot avoid repeating the very trauma they recall—the trauma that *de*-faces the face, that wipes it out via the phenomenological reduction, extending that deterioration in another revealed visibility, another architectural golden calf that, in the face's place, constructs the overwhelming emptiness of the prosthesis, or the idolatrous deathmask. As Derrida has taught us, *faithful* mourning of the other's face "must fail *to succeed/by succeeding* (it fails, precisely, if it succeeds! It fails because of success!)" *(PI, 321).* The *iconicity* of architecture, then, solicits the experience of this impossible mourning that *must fail* (if it is) to succeed, and vice versa. And this is the trauma of building. Fated to an archival or *architectural* fever, destined to design buildings that can never *innocently* embody the face, doomed to *both* the idealism of Moses *and* the golden calf of Aaron, Libeskind's works, like Rothko's paintings, have much to do with "intimations of mortality": never concretely *answering*, but rather fatally rebuilding and *extending into the future* the unresolvable question of the face and the façade in a mourning that can only, ever, recite its own unfaithful idolatry.

Chapter 6

The "Forgotten" as Epic *Vorwelt*

Brendan Moran

Each individual is the complete course of evolution still.
Jeder Einzelne ist die ganze Linie der Entwicklung noch.
            F. Nietzsche, *Nachgelassene Fragmente*

In his writings on Franz Kafka, Walter Benjamin often remarks on the "*Vorwelt*" of the human being. This "*Vorwelt*"—literally "preworld," usually translated in English as "prehistory"—is considered effective in every human being. As a force effective in all humans, the *Vorwelt* could be characterized as *epic*. Whereas some notions of "epic" pertain to the condition of a tribe, people, or nation, Benjamin's Kafka is epic in eliciting a force that is the "*Vorwelt*" of all human beings. Kafka's figures are epic in emitting something constant in their confrontation with forces that would constrain them.[1] The *Vorwelt* could be this epic force that slows constraint. For Benjamin, Kafka even manages to interject an "epic pace" in the conveyance of breathtaking speed (*SW*2, 815, translation modified/*GS*II:2, 437). This epic capacity to slow is also detected by Benjamin in Brecht's epic theatre, specifically in its gesture that interrupts those acting (*SW*4, 305–7/*GS*II:2, 535–39). If there is no epic wisdom or counsel in any traditional sense (*CWB*, 565; *SW*3, 326/*GB*6, 112), there remains an epic interruptive force of the *Vorwelt*. The determinacy of this epic *Vorwelt* is ultimately indeterminate. Epic experience as *Vorwelt* is oblique preconditioning by natural history, oblique preconditioning by nature that is neither entirely discernible nor entirely controllable. This is a preconditioning from which humans are inextricable, but in relation to which humans are not entirely conscious. In the latter indeterminacy, the *Vorwelt* is determinant. *Epic* experience, the experience somehow common to all, acutely does *not* fit into human lives. Whereas traditional epic involves an integrated common experience, the epic in Benjamin's Kafka seems to be the common experience that is disorienting. Unlike the situation apparently assumed in traditional epic, this common experience is unintegrated: it cannot offer or receive counsel. Nothing can be said to dispel entirely the strangeness of this experience—the strangeness to any life that could be construed as a life to be lived. As Bernd Müller puts it, there emerges the "gesture" that is experienced or effective in "ordinary" people and yet is "'epic' . . . in its spatial and temporal inappropriateness (*Unangemessenheit*)."[2] The "epic" in us is familiar, but it is familiar only as strange.

This common—epic—disorientation frees experience from myth, which is an oppressive or repressive account of experience. In the mythic account, experience is treated as somehow subordinate to human consciousness of fate. As an opening to the mysterious experience that eludes mythic containment, the epic disorientation is our common freedom from myth. Such epic disorientation of consciousness is suggested by Benjamin's reference to the *Vorwelt* as "the forgotten" (*das Vergessene*). For some readers, as will be elaborated in this chapter, the term "forgotten" seems to suggest that this prehistory is simply there to be overcome, that it is itself a mythic force to be remembered in a way that would render it no longer determinant. This characterization of the *Vorwelt* as mythic is not a characterization that Benjamin usually makes, although his analyses of Kafka are not unambiguous on this point. Benjamin's ambiguity, his self-contradiction in this regard will be discussed soon below.

The focus of this chapter, however, will be on respects in which Benjamin's Kafka writings present the *Vorwelt* as a dimension that is premythic, a dimension that defies attempts to capture or contain it in human constructions or conceptions. This epic experience, this experience common to all, can be remembered only as "forgotten," as ultimately not conscious. In this regard, Benjamin's Kafka writings tend to accord with some of his other writings. In his essay on Proust, the term "forgetting" (*Vergessen*) more clearly refers to a determinant force that can be remembered only as ultimately not conscious; the forgetting cannot be entirely overcome or rendered conscious (*SW*2, 238/*GS*II:1, 311). Benjamin keeps his work on Kafka largely separate from that on Proust. The latter work has been mentioned here in passing for its comparatively clear characterization of our common experience as the irretrievably "forgotten," as not capable of being retrieved entirely for consciousness.

This chapter will be concentrated largely on Benjamin's Kafka writings (and will refer to some of his other writings only for brief elaboration or clarification). In part one, consideration will be given to the aforementioned ambiguity or contradiction whereby Benjamin sometimes identifies the *Vorwelt* with myth and sometimes discusses it as freedom from myth. In part two, there will be discussion of respects in which his remarks could be considered to propose that the *Vorwelt* can be remembered as the epic forgotten. Finally, in part three, consideration will be given to the objection that disregard of the alleged primacy, and the potential influence, of the interhuman over natural history ensues from Benjamin's efforts to remember the *Vorwelt* as forgotten. In this objection, the interhuman is taken to involve human relations that precede, and remain ineradicable from, any supposed experience of the primacy of nature. The principal question in part three will be whether remembering the primacy of the *Vorwelt* as forgotten discounts the interhuman in experience.

Vorwelt

As mentioned above, some have proposed that Benjamin's texts on Kafka identify the *Vorwelt* exclusively with myth. Beatrice Hanssen refers to "Kafka's depiction of a mythical primeval world (*Vorwelt*)."[3] Michael Jennings remarks that Benjamin's 1934 essay, "Franz Kafka: On the Tenth Anniversary of His Death," concerns Kafka's "intimate knowledge of humanity's 'mythical prehistory.'"[4] Bernd Müller's study includes a reference to "the mythic ensnarement resulting from the 'forgetting' [dem 'Vergessen' geschuldeten mythischen Verstrickung]" (*KD*, 216). In an article in 2002 on Benjamin and Kafka, Marc Sagnol refers to *Vorwelt*—"un prémonde"—as "un monde mythique,"[5] although he remarks—in a more recent essay—that Benjamin considers the wind blowing in Kafka's works to be "from 'the primitive world' preceding myth."[6] As will be suggested below, many (albeit not all) relevant formulations by Benjamin do indeed characterize the mythic as forgetting the forgotten, forgetting the *Vorwelt*. Insofar as he criticizes the mythic for disregard of the *Vorwelt*, Benjamin distinguishes myth from the *Vorwelt*.

If Benjamin's works have themselves contributed to interpretative confusions on this topic, such confusions presumably often arise from his contradictory remarks on *Vorwelt* (particularly in some of his adaptations of writings by Johann Jakob Bachofen).[7] It is perhaps not so surprising, therefore, that one commentary on Benjamin's Kafka readings, on the one hand, seems to depict the *Vorwelt* in certain respects as nonmythic or premythic,[8] but on the other hand also refers to "the prehistoric world of myth" and makes other statements equating prehistory (*Vorwelt*) and myth (*KL*, 995, 990). This latter identification of *Vorwelt* and myth seems to follow partly from an insistence (which is not Benjamin's) that muteness and namelessness constitute myth (*KL*, 978, 996–97).

Such an insistence is expressly a carryover from a reading of Benjamin's 1922 essay on Goethe's *Elective Affinities*. In that work, there is indeed a notion of mythic muteness and namelessness but this is not an equation of *all* muteness and namelessness with myth. The muteness of the characters in Goethe's novel is their surrender to existing morality as fate. This surrender to fate tends to be the muteness that Benjamin's essay criticizes (*SW*1, 305, 327, 336, 343/*GSI*:1, 134, 163, 176, 185); the criticism converges with his criticism of a complacent silence in works by Adalbert Stifter (*SW*1, 112/*GSII*:2, 609–10; *SW*1, 343/*GSI*:1, 185). In the *Elective Affinities* essay, such complacent silence is contrasted with the protest of silence against usurpation by moral-legal order (*SW*1, 341/*GSI*:1, 182). In his 1916 essay on language and in his *Trauerspielbuch* too, Benjamin commends a silence on behalf of the incommunicable and the unrecognizable; this is a silence against attempted usurping by communication and recognition (*SW*1, 72–73/*GSII*:1, 155; *OGD*, 224–25/*GSI*:1, 398). A "moving deed," Benjamin says in a letter, has a correlate in the word that descends into and ascends from innermost muteness (*CWB*, 80/*GB*1, 327). Such muteness and namelessness are free from, and able to survive, myth.[9] The latter muteness and namelessness register a freedom from complete submission to moral-legal order—that is, a freedom from precisely the submission that Benjamin often characterizes as constitutive of the mythic. Kafka's Odysseus thus not only confronts silent sirens but resists their fateful allure by silencing their silence (*SW*, 799/*GSII*:2, 415–16).[10] Such freedom from mythic constraint will be elaborated below as a freedom impelled by the *Vorwelt*.

To reiterate: Benjamin's writings on Kafka occasionally are inconsistent concerning the relationship of myth and *Vorwelt*, and this inconsistency is particularly evident in some adaptations of Bachofen.[11]

The complication can be illustrated by a couple of Benjamin's preparatory notes (partly made in a letter) that show his occasional tendency to portray, at least implicitly, the *Vorwelt* as itself mythic. One of these notes refers to the swamp world, which is a notion adapted from Bachofen and elsewhere identified by Benjamin as the *Vorwelt*. The "power" of the swamp world, as might be expected from what has been said above, "lies in its state of being forgotten [*Vergessenheit*]." Yet this note refers to Kafka's works as though they are independent of the swamp world—that is, independent of the forgotten, the *Vorwelt*. Whereas the swamp world is portrayed as shameless, Kafka's works show shame; Kafka's works are "a victory of shame over the theological posing of questions" (*GSII:3*, 1213). In this formulation, Benjamin praises Kafka's shame about, and against, too direct theologizing, and he distinguishes Kafka's praiseworthy shame from the shamelessness of the swamp-world, the *Vorwelt*.[12] It is not entirely clear that Benjamin is saying this (we are dealing here with point-form notes), but it is possible that he is saying something along these lines. Of further possible relevance in this regard is a remark that there is an "infinite amount of hope" for the pupils or students in Kafka's work; this remark is accompanied by the seemingly pointed comment that the students do not belong to "'the hetaeric world'" (*GSII:3*, 1246; *CWB*, 453/*GB4*, 479/*GSII:3*, 1166).[13] Overall in his work on Kafka, Benjamin adapts Bachofen's notion of the "hetaeric" world (a world of concubinage or communal marriage) to refer to the "natural" and "the swamp world" in which Kafka's novels "play" (*GSII:3*, 1192).[14] Whereas such references seem to portray the swamp world as opposed to myth, there is—in the aforementioned statement on pupils or students—an infinite amount of hope for the pupils or students apparently because they do *not* belong to this swamp world. In summary, the implication of such statements seems to be that both the hope placed in shame opposed to the shameless swamp world, as well as the hope placed in the students who do not belong to the swamp world, is hope placed outside the *Vorwelt*.

Benjamin's Kafka essay of 1934 also could seem to disparage the *Vorwelt* (the obliquely preconditioning prehistory), albeit while also showing the opposed tendency (which, as noted, will be the tendency largely developed in this chapter). Benjamin contends that the forces of the *Vorwelt* demanded a great deal in Kafka's work of creation. We cannot determine, Benjamin claims, exactly the names under which Kafka found these forces appearing to him, for "[c]ertain is only" that Kafka "did not get his bearings among them" and "did not know them." Yet "the prehistoric world [*Vorwelt*] held up to" Kafka a "mirror" in "the form [*Gestalt*] of guilt," which meant that "he merely saw the future in the form [*Gestalt*] of the court [*des Gerichtes*]" (*SW2*, 807; translation modified/*GSII:2*, 427). It is not clear that the latter statement is an association of the *Vorwelt* with mythic guilt, guilt induced by oppressive or repressive constrictions.[15] If it may be read that way, perhaps the same could be said (although that too is not clear) for a later comment in the essay, a comment about the spool-like figure who intrudes obliquely upon the father of the family: in Kafka's work, "the most singular bastard which the prehistoric world has begotten with guilt is Odradek" (*SW2*, 810; translation modified/*GS*II:2, 431).

Even this last comment (with regard to Kafka's story "The Worry of the Father of the Family") might be construed, however, to belong at least partly to a discussion of a kind of guilt or obligation to the *Vorwelt*—an obligation involving opposition to mythic guilt, to the ostensible clarities of closed interpretative frameworks (*SW2*, 811/*GS*II:2, 432). Odradek is a "bastard," and thus already a transgression of familial myth. In this sense, the *Vorwelt* might include Odradek as intrusion upon the mythic endeavors of the father of the family, the *Hausvater*, to overcome or disregard the *Vorwelt*.[16] This reading of Odradek may exclude or strain other parts of Benjamin's reading of Odradek, but there seem to be some aspects of Benjamin's reading, which suggest that Odradek is a perpetually disturbing element undermining mythic claims to contain or overcome it.

Correlatively, and notwithstanding some statements associating the *Vorwelt* with what might be considered mythic guilt, Kafka's works are also read by Benjamin as recalling *Vorwelt* against myth, against confinement by guilt-contexts of the living, against confinement by moral-legal orders. In a relevant passage of the 1934 essay, Benjamin remarks that the "world of myth," the world concerned with hierarchies, "is incomparably younger than Kafka's world." It could be inferred that the world of myth is incomparably younger than the *Vorwelt*. Kafka recalls the *Vorwelt*, recalls this "forgetting" or lack of consciousness, against any forgetting of this forgetting, against any myth that is supposed to redeem us from this world, "Kafka's world" (*SW* 2, 799/*GS*II:2, 415).

In the passage just cited (from the 1934 essay), stating that Kafka's world is older than myth, Benjamin says the following: "Von Ordnungen und Hierarchien zu sprechen, ist hier nicht möglich. Die Welt des Mythos, die das nahelegt, ist hier unvergleichlich jünger als Kafkas Welt, der schon der Mythos die Erlösung versprochen hat" (*GS*II:2, 415). The world of myth brings to mind or wants to convey ("die das nahelegt") the speaking of orders or hierarchies ("[v]on Ordnungen und Hierarchien zu sprechen"). Orders and hierarchies are brought upon us by the myth promising redemption to or from Kafka's world. The world of myth is incomparably younger than Kafka's world ("[d]ie Welt des Mythos, die das nahelegt, ist hier unvergleichlich jünger als Kafkas Welt"), whereas Kafka's world resists this offer of redemption by myth and is itself redemptive in the figures that deviate from orders and hierarchies of myth.[17] It will be proposed below that, by seeming incomplete, distorted, disfigured, or not-ready in relation to myth, such figures emerge as outbreaks of the *Vorwelt*, which myth was supposed to overcome. These outbreaks emerge to offset the dominance of myth. *Vorwelt* will thus be presented both as preceding, and as ongoing release from, myth—that is, as preceding, and as ongoing release from, conscious constriction of experience. *Vorwelt* is always already before the world of myth, even though—as will be elaborated below—we cannot entirely isolate our experience of it from our entanglement in myth.

Vorwelt and Memory

Memory of epic experience, of our irrevocably shared experience, is discussed in Benjamin's oft-cited essay on "The Storyteller" (1936). Adapting the ancient Greek notion for which Mnemosyne, the rememberer, is the muse of what is (and indeed the so-called mother of the muses), Benjamin's "Storyteller" essay characterizes memory (*Gedächtnis*) as the epic faculty, which is a faculty that speaks to collective memory and can be effective in any memory. Epic memory is the ability to explore, to remember, to experience uninhibitedly and— supposedly on this basis—to speak credibly to all experience. Solely on the basis of such epic memory could storytelling also plausibly be the recollection (*Erinnerung*) passing "happenings on from generation to generation." The emergence of the novel-form indicates both a loss of such recollection and a rise of remembrance (*Eingedenken*) as the isolated focus on one hero, one struggle. Correlative to this development is the decline of tradition as something that can compellingly counsel (*SW*3, 154–55, 145–46 respectively/*GS*II:2, 453–54, 441– 42 respectively; also see *SW*2, 299–300/*GS*III, 230–31). Epic experience (the experience common to all) and counsel have diverged from one another. There is next to nothing that can be said to counsel epic experience, which cannot be integrated into tradition.

Benjamin thus disagrees with Scholem's notion of Kafka's writings as a prospect for revival of a *specifically* Judaic teaching or of some notion of holy scripture,[18] and he incurs criticism by Werner Kraft of his emphasis on the lack of doctrine or teaching (as well as his alleged lack of messianic hope) (*GS*II:3, 1168–69).[19] Regarding the prospect of teachings or counsel, Benjamin increasingly emphasizes that Kafka performs failure (*SW*3, 326–27/*GB*6, 113). Such emphasis on failure has also been criticized from the perspective of Deleuze and Guattari whereby Benjamin is said to invoke a transcendental law in relation to which there must be failure.[20] Yet Benjamin considers the failure, the disintegration, of tradition to be a potential liberation of memory, of any memory.

The "Storyteller" essay thus includes the notion that a "new beauty" may be felt with the very vanishing of traditional storytelling (*SW*3, 146/*GS*II:2, 442). Readers of the "Storyteller" essay often regard this feeling as nostalgia. Aside from whatever there may be of such feeling, Benjamin is possibly also suggesting that the feeling of beauty in the loss may give rise to a new epic form.[21] This would involve a shared—an epic—feeling of liberation from traditional counsel. In the 1920s and 1930s, he addresses certain literary works—by Kafka, Graf, Brecht, and others—as entering a new dynamic with epic memory.[22] In a fragment published in 1933, Benjamin associates the healing power of "storytelling" with swimming into "an ocean of happy forgetfulness [*glücklicher Vergessenheit*]" (*SW*2, 724–25/*GS*IV:1, 430).

In his Kafka essay from 1934, Benjamin accordingly contends that Kafka's "technique . . . as storyteller" conveys the past as an inescapable disorder that is both overwhelmingly powerful and yet also overwhelmingly inaccessible (*SW*2,

809/*GS*II:2, 429). As Benjamin puts it in one of his many little notes on Kafka, an inexhaustible "past" "presents itself as teaching [*die Lehre*], as wisdom [*die Weisheit*]" (*GS*II:3, 1205). *This* teaching, *this* wisdom, overwhelms; this past is not appropriated by any tradition. In his long letter of June 1938 to Scholem, Benjamin famously remarks that Kafka's work *presents* (*stellt . . . dar*) "a sickening of tradition" (*SW*3, 326/*GB* 6, 112). This could be considered a sickening in relation to what the 1934 essay already calls *Vorwelt*, the prehistorical forces that may appear within historical (*weltliche*) forces (*Gewalten*) (*SW*2, 807/*GS*II:2, 426–27), but do so as elements rendering the historical forces ultimately, and mysteriously, inaccessible to us (*SW*2, 797, 807, 809/*GS*II:2, 412, 426–27, 429). In a letter of August 1934 to Scholem, Benjamin thus refers to this *Vorwelt* as Kafka's "secret present" (*geheime Gegenwart*) (*CWB,* 453/*GB*4, 478/*GS*II:3, 1165).[23] This secret is ultimately untellable. It may be (as is said in notes written for the 1934 essay) that Kafka "feels" the pressure posed by "the listener . . . to the storyteller: to know counsel [Rat zu wissen]." Insofar as "storytelling penetrates Kafka," however, Kafka simply performs that he does not have counsel, that he cannot counsel. His storytelling "attitude" (*Haltung*), insofar as it exists, is only that of someone "who has the hopeless to say [der das Hoffnungslose zu sagen hat]" (*GS*II:2, 1216).[24]

Saying the hopeless attests, however, to a hope in storytelling. In his aforementioned *Elective Affinities* essay, for instance, Benjamin portrays Goethe as (somewhat unwittingly) entering the "attitude [*Haltung*] of the storyteller" in portrayals of those who have no hope (*SW*1, 355; translation modified/*GS*:1, 200). In this case, storytelling has catastrophe show itself where it would otherwise be disregarded, would otherwise simply be lived. In "experience [*Erfahrung*]" (354; translation modified/199), there emerges a "feeling" of hope so that "the sense of the occurrence" is fulfilled (355; translation modified/200), the sense that has long been obliterated in "lived experience [*Erlebnis*]" (354/199). *Erfahrung* enters the occurrence to show the hopelessness of *Erlebnis*. In *Elective Affinities*, the hopelessness is of people in love who somehow sacrifice experience to marital law and convention. The hope of the storyteller, the hope of *Erfahrung*, enters Goethe's novel in a way that shows the hopelessness of those characters who simply live without hope. Hence, Benjamin's well-known remark that hope is given to us for the sake of the hopeless (356/201).

It may accordingly be a slight overstatement of Benjamin's view to say that no "storyteller" is discernible in Kafka's prose, that "[w]e see only what those acting see—and that is little."[25] The gesture or technique of storytelling remains effective as a break of sorts with tradition, a performance of tradition and of ourselves as hopelessly conformist. In his very early writings, Benjamin refers to an ideallessness in contemporary youth that attests to youth's honesty (*GS*II:1, 44, 47). Perhaps not dissimilarly, Kafka allegedly remarks, as cited by Benjamin in the 1934 essay and elsewhere, that there is "'plenty of hope, an infinite amount of hope—but not for us'" (*SW*2, 798/*GS*II:2, 413–14, and see: *GS*II:3, 1218, 1246, 1262).[26] We can be recognized as hopeless in having closed off an appreciable memory of experience that cannot be exploited in appropriative orders.

In the 1934 essay, Benjamin notes the remark by Willy Haas that Jehovah's "'most profound characteristic'" is "'an infallible memory' ['ein untrügliches Gedächtnis'] (*SW*2, 809; translation modified/*GS*II:2, 429).[27] The distinctness of this memory from a merely human memory would seem to be that it is entirely free of what Benjamin elsewhere calls the "guilt-context of the living" (*SW*1, 204/*GS*II:1, 175), the lived experience absorbed by moral-legal order. Insofar as we humans even try, we have trouble committing ourselves to remembering what is not at least potentially exploitable in specific moral-legal contexts. Further adapting Haas's remarks, Benjamin's 1934 essay proposes that "'the most sacred . . . act of ritual is the extinguishing of sins from the book of memory [*des Gedächtnisses*]'" (*SW*2, 809; translation modified/*GS*II:2, 429).[28] This may seem to suggest that the most sacred is opposed to memory. That to which the most sacred is opposed is, however, only a certain kind of remembering: the remembering that confines itself to parameters set by moral-legal order. Life irreducible to such parameters can be regarded as, in contrast, God's memory or remembrance (*Gedenken*), which is suggested by Benjamin in his translation essay of 1921 (*SW*1, 254/*GS*IV:1, 10). Remarking in his notes for the 1934 Kafka essay that "the word 'God,' does not appear in Kafka's writings," Benjamin contends that interpreting these writings in a very directly theological way would be a little like putting a Kleist novella into catchy rhyme (*GS*II:3, 1214).[29] If there is God's memory contributing to the extinction of "sins" from the book of memory, if there is memory that in any way releases us from our appropriative guilt-contexts, this memory manifests itself in a distorted way. It can just seem foolish to recall experience outside appropriative guilt contexts. Such foolishness is an instance of our distorted memory of experience unabsorbed by appropriative guilt contexts. As such distortion, those seeming fools in specific guilt-contexts emerge as imperfect reminders of the epic life, the most determinant shared life, which we—at most—remember as "forgotten," as otherwise not conscious for us.[30]

Perhaps for the sake of such distortion that registers the otherwise forgotten forgotten, the author's name under the title of this chapter, or indeed the names of Benjamin and Kafka on their writings, should not be there in so stale a form of authorial identification. (Benjamin did, of course, sometimes use pseudonyms beyond what was required by anti-Semitic or other kinds of censorship.) The authors' proper names are most obviously there as devices for participating in social systems of identification and in systems of artistic, academic, or "intellectual" branding. There may be no other compelling justification besides such complicity with myth. The notion of the transcendental ego, to which many enamored of the *properly* named subject refer, is "mythology" and, with regard to its suppressive character, "the same as every other recognition-mythology [*Erkenntnismythologie*]" (*SW*1, 103; translation modified/*GS*II:1, 161). That at least was the view expressed in Benjamin's essay of 1917–18 on the program of the coming philosophy. In notes on Kafka, Benjamin refers to the "mumbled K," and remarks that names, such as Josef K., are "compressions of the contents of

Kafka's memory [Verdichtungen seiner Gedächtnisinhalte]" (GSII:3, 1196). Among the many possible translations of *Verdichtung*—in addition to "compression"—are "condensing," "intensification," and "heightening." Abbreviated names, such as Josef K., could be condensings, intensifications, heightenings, compressions resulting from memory of the experience, the determinant natural prehistory, which can only be recalled as forgotten, as ultimately not conscious. With such names, this memory may emerge against the proud, conscious subject that might be implied by untruncated, unabbreviated names.

Such distortion of name, like the foolish distortion mentioned already, is a correlate of distorted memory of the forgotten, a distortion detected by Benjamin in other aspects of Kafka's works as well. There is the aforementioned Odradek, whom we remember as "distorted." The bug in "The Metamorphosis" is remembered as a distortion of the transcendental subject, and of the familial mythology, Gregor Samsa. Among other distortions in Kafka's cast of figures, there is "the big animal, half-lamb, half-kitten." These "figures [*Figuren*]" are associated by Benjamin with "the prototype" of "distortion," the "hunchback"—"the little hunchbacked man," who appears in a children's verse and arises in a variety of ways in Benjamin's writings (*SW*2, 811; translation modified/*GS*II:2, 431–32).[31] However reluctantly, Kafka remembers distortion in relation to myth. The nurse Leni has a web between some fingers, suggesting to Benjamin that she—like some other figures in Kafka's writings—is a swamp creature. Benjamin proposes that the past of Frieda in *The Castle* "leads back into the dark womb of the depth where a pairing happens 'whose disorderly voluptuousness,' to quote Bachofen, 'is hated by the pure powers of heavenly light and which justifies the term, used by Arnobius, *luteae voluptates* [dirty voluptuousness]'" (809/429).[32] The assistants in Kafka's works are also portrayed—according to Benjamin—as "unfinished beings, who are therefore especially close to the womb of nature" (GSII:3, 1212).[33] The formulation "womb of nature" is indicative of Benjamin's occasionally maternal terminology for the *Vorwelt*, which is remembered only in distortions. These are distortions, for they are not pure representations of anything; they are also distortions as images that myth deems unfinished.[34]

The forgotten forgotten, the unconscious unconscious, is remembered in images that somehow withdraw from myth and thereby open the possibility of attentiveness to the natural history that myth does not make conscious. In *The Trial*, a transformation into becoming forgotten has "already begun" in the very retiring chief clerk whose hands move like bird's wings (GSII:3, 1201).[35] No non-human animals appear as such in *The Trial* (GSII:3, 1191), but Benjamin finds "suggestive" (*beziehungsvoll*) the "world" that Kafka elsewhere creates by wrapping his own thoughts in those of nonhuman animals. These animals live "in the bowels of the earth, like rats or moles, or at least, like the bug in *Metamorphosis*, on the floor, crept away [*verkrochen*] into its crevices and cracks." In some ways, these animals elude the hierarchies in which they are considered lowly. This elusive lowliness speaks, moreover, to those who are—in one way or another—excluded by law and thus maintain, however unwillingly, a kind of ignorance in relation to it. Only such "*Verkrochenheit*," such having crept away, seems to Kafka "appropriate for the isolated members of his generation and of his environment who are ignorant of the law" (*GS*II:3, 1204). In this context, the feeling of being somehow removed in relation to law is a feeling of being removed from myth, of which law is a pinnacle instance. The feeling of remembering the otherwise forgotten *forgotten* is a feeling of having crept away, a feeling of *Verkrochenheit*, in which a kind of ignorance provides a peculiar freedom—however fragile—in relation to law and, more broadly, in relation to myth.

Redemptive Forgotten

In Benjamin's rendering, Kafka pays special attention to the feeling of having crept away, the feeling that seems distorted—perhaps even ugly—by mythic standards. An attempt has been made elsewhere to formulate disagreements with the aspect of Benjamin's messianism that asserts, nonetheless, an independence from creaturely life and envisions the elimination, by slight adjustment, of the creaturely distortions (*SW*2, 811/*GS*II:2, 432).[36] There are, however, objections proposing that the messianic could be more elicited by Kafka and by Benjamin to prevail over the creaturely, over the *Vorwelt*. Rosenzweig has thus been praised for portraying "the miracle of revelation" as "constituted not simply by an inscrutable semantic power underlying the creaturely existence of humans— by our signifying stress—but also by our capacity to 'unfold' this stress through *acts of neighbor-love*, something that perhaps lay beyond the boundaries of" the Kafkaean "imagination."[37] Among readers influenced by Rosenzweig and Levinas, there often arises such regret about an alleged lack of interhuman emphases in Benjamin's dissemination of the impersonal.[38] The tenor of such objections is poignantly given by a passage of *Totality and Infinity*, a passage directed against Heideggerian ontology. Levinas's "establishing" of the "primacy of the ethical" concerns the "relationship of human to human" as "an irreducible structure upon which all the other structures rest (and in particular all those which seem to put us primordially in contact with an impersonal sublimity, aesthetic or ontological)." Levinas accordingly adds: "Everything that cannot be reduced to an interhuman relation represents not the superior form but the forever primitive form of religion."[39]

Bruno Tackels praises Benjamin for his "mot magistral," "primitive." That word actually comes from the French translation by Maurice de Gandillac, who renders "*Vorwelt*" as "époque primitive" in his translation of a passage in Benjamin's Kafka essay.[40] If the Kafkaean and Benjaminian gesture involves something like the so-called primitive, the gesture is attentiveness to people, creatures, feelings, and entities somehow excluded by interhuman myth. Interhumanity becomes mythic insofar as it is an exercise of exclusion. Associated by Benjamin with oblivion (*Vergessenheit*) (*GS*II:3, 1213; *SW*2, 810– 11/*GS*II:2, 431), Odradek in some respects emerges as an antidote to forgetting the excluded, which includes the disregarded *Vorwelt*. Odradek is—like "the forgotten"—elusive; Odradek registers that the *Vorwelt* has "voices" (*Stimmen*).

In its independence of us, its survival of us, the "forgotten" makes Odradek's laugh sound "'something like the rustling in fallen leaves'" and makes it "'a laugh such as one can produce without lungs'" (*GS*II:3, 1214–15).[41] Such sound of nonhuman—even nonlunged—nature can also be heard from our own bodies, which bear this ultimately unfathomable prehistory that emerges not least as our deaths (*SW*2, 815/*GS*II:2, 436–37; *GS*II:3, 1217). There need not, moreover, be disagreement here with the view suggesting that this "creaturely life" in Benjamin's Kafka is not nature in isolation but rather "natural history." As noted above, however, natural history involves the *Vorwelt* as determinant of humans but neither entirely discernible nor entirely controllable by humans. If the natural is not extricable from the historical, therefore, this does not necessarily entail that the natural—the aforementioned *Vorwelt* or creaturely force—is simply a by-product of excitations of power.[42] For Benjamin's Kafka, excitations of power exist to control the *Vorwelt*; they are emotions stirred by our wish to control, and thereby find a kind of release from, the *Vorwelt*. They are, in other words, much more a response to the *Vorwelt* than the *Vorwelt* could be a response to them, even if our sense of the *Vorwelt* is always mediated by sociohistorical factors. The *Vorwelt* and sociopolitical structures are undoubtedly intertwined to the point where we cannot entirely distinguish the *Vorwelt* from sociohistorical influences. This does not require, however, that we relinquish the idea of a dimension or force that is epic, universal, in its independence of mythic influences, which treat sociohistorical constructions as though they are all-encompassing. We do not have to relinquish the idea of epic independence even if we never live or entirely express this epic independence. To relinquish this idea of a nature independent of us is to relinquish each other, to turn away from our sole irrevocable community. Benjamin's ontological gesture—if it may be called thus—is not the Heideggerian one in which, at least according to Levinas's worry, the others are forgotten in the gesture of Being. For Benjamin's Kafkaean "attentiveness" (*SW*2, 811/*GS*II:2, 432), the strangeness of my own body (810/431), the natural prehistory in it, connects me not only to other humans but to all creatures (811/432; *GS*II :3, 1214), including nonhuman animals from whom Kafka did not tire of "hearing the forgotten" (*SW*2, 810; translation modified/*GS*II:2, 430). The *Vorwelt*, in which all and everything participate, suspends myths of exclusion.

For Benjamin, "the redeeming" accordingly inheres in Kafka's portrayals of distortion or disfigurement. The distortions of space and time distort mythic space and time. They disturb our myth-laden perceptual world (*GS*II:3, 1196, 1239–40; *SW*2, 812/*GS*II:2, 433). The transformation, however slight it might sometimes be, is considered by Benjamin to be very much needed in a world in which we often conduct ourselves as though our moral-legal orders are all and everything, as though we live—as he puts it—in a thousand year empire (*GS*II:3, 1200). Performance of failure in relation to myth can emerge, therefore, as preparation of "the new constitution of humankind, the new ear for new laws and the new regard for new relations," and the performance can do this precisely "in the dregs and in the lowest level of creations, among the rats, dung-beetles, and moles" (*GS*II:3, 1196).[43] The possibility of this emergent community of the ostensibly lost is the hope that Benjamin gleans too from Kafka's clumsy, awkward, and yet often content figures, who seem incomplete by mythic standards (*SW*2, 798–99/*GS*II:2, 415). Against the definiteness of mythic standards, Kafka's gesture echoes an incomprehensibility that can occasion potentially interminable interpretation (*GS*II:3, 1229; *SW*2, 802/*GS*II:2, 420). To acknowledge—against myth—that there is no conclusive reading is a way to pay respect to one another, to ourselves, and indeed to all else.

At a period in his life, an acquaintance of Benjamin reportedly "felt quite well. He settled [*erledigte*] little and considered nothing as settled [*erledigt*]." In this period, the acquaintance liked to recall a story containing "the enigmatic instruction 'Don't forget the best'" (*SW*2, 591; translation modified/*GS*IV:1, 407). Benjamin's 1934 Kafka essay also cites the saying "*Vergiß das Beste nicht!*" ("Don't forget the best!"). This could be rendered as *Don't forget the forgotten*, for the forgotten—as irretrievable for consciousness—"always" involves "the best"; "it involves the possibility of redemption [*Erlösung*]" (*SW*2, 813/*GS*II:2, 434).[44] The forgotten, the unconscious, involves the best, the possibility of redemption, for that possibility is what we do not remember ever living; it is our experience that we have never "lived." Redemption, the best, is our experience somehow free from guilt-contexts or moral-legal orders that might otherwise dominate us. We respect the best, including the best in each other, when we regard nothing as settled. Recalling this best *requires* that we regard nothing as settled, least of all any questions concerning the best. Not to keep all unsettled is to transform into myth our relations with each other, with ourselves, and with whatever we call nature.

We could consider ourselves reminded of the unconscious forgotten any time that we forget something; such events could become reminders that loosen our attachment to the conscious, which is myth insofar as it instills submission by excluding regard for what cannot be consciously retrieved. In his 1934 essay, Benjamin remarks: "Everything forgotten mingles with the forgotten of the prehistoric world [*Vorwelt*], and with this forgotten of the prehistoric world everything forgotten enters into innumerable, uncertain, changing connections to ever new monstrous products [*Ausgeburten*]." This oblivion, this condition of being forgotten, this *Vergessenheit*, "is the receptacle [*Behältnis*] out of which the inexhaustible in-between world in Kafka's stories [*Geschichten*] presses toward the light" (*SW*2, 810–11; translation modified/*GS*II:2, 430).[45] Kafka's world is *in-between*, for the outbreaks are not direct manifestations of the *Vorwelt*; they are oblique reminders of it, which are monstrous or strange simply in coming from what is—at least on any explicit level—excluded from the moral-legal.

Once moral-legal orders assert parameters, we have a capacity for studied release from such parameters. Admittedly, the 1934 Kafka essay states that "a tempest . . . blows from forgetting, and study is a cavalry attack against it [ein Ritt, der dagegen angeht]" (*SW*2, 814/*GS*II:2, 436).[46] The studying could thereby seem opposed to the forgotten, but another reading would be that study is opposed by Benjamin to forgetting the forgotten. In "On the Concept of History"

(1940), the storm pushing forward is indeed opposed to the angel's backward-looking studious gaze. The angel turns its back to the future, but its wings are still caught in the forward blowing storm. The angel looks, however, at the pile of wreckage that the storm called progress leaves in its wake (*SW*4, 392/*GS*I:2, 697–98). Each storm—the storm mentioned in Benjamin's texts on Kafka and the storm in his "theses" on history—is a storm oriented by forgetting (not least forgetting the wreckage of history). Both storms seem distinct, nonetheless, from the storm that blows from the *Vorwelt*, for the *Vorwelt* disrupts the complacency of history by reminding it of all it has forgotten. Benjamin claims there is—in Kafka's work—the same wind blowing that Kafka says propels the boat of the hunter Gracchus. This is the wind from "'the nethermost regions of death,'" the wind that "so often blows from the prehistoric world [*Vorwelt*] in Kafka's works" (*SW*2, 815/*GS*II:2, 436).[47] Benjamin quotes Plutarch referring to two primary essences and two opposing forces—one pushing straight ahead and the other turning around and driving back (*SW*2, 815/*GS*II:2, 437).[48] The force turning around, and driving back, is study. Study considers, and is impelled by, the *Vorwelt* that is disregarded by the forward-moving storm, which is myth.[49]

In its independence from sociohistorical myth, the *Vorwelt* registers—albeit in the aforementioned distorted ways—as deviations that happen in people, non-human animals, and other entities. These dissonances may be studied in non-compliance with Adorno's preferences that Benjamin's work about Kafka become more "*durchdialektisiert*" to facilitate an overcoming of conceptual *Unfertigkeit*, unclosedness or unfinishedness, concerning the relationship of "*Urgeschichte und Moderne*" (primal history and modernity) (*GS*II:3, 1175, 1178). The dissonances could also be considered one basis on which Benjamin's work on Kafka seems to defy expectations brought to them by Brecht (*GS*II:3, 1165, and 1252–55) and others.[50] That Benjamin's writings on Kafka do not yield to expectations of greater conceptual bravura or of other kinds of bravura is often ultimately the recalcitrant memory of our sole inextinguishable common, the unmythic *Vorwelt*. Myth shows itself to be myth in its denial of, or disregard for, this unincorporated "forgotten," this unincorporated *Vorwelt*, that—for Benjamin—is integral to Kafka's world and is our shared, our epic, world.

Chapter 7

Halal History and Existential Meaning in Salman Rushdie's Early Fiction

Adnan Mahmutovic

The issue of *halal* history is both simple and complex in *Midnight's Children*. The phrase is above all associated with the crucial question of censure, which has dominated Salman Rushdie's fiction and essays ever since his first attempts at journalism and drama in Pakistan, prior to his turbulent novelistic career in Europe. Rushdie has indeed become a symbol of the struggle against state censorship of public opinion, historiography, and especially art. In Daniel Pipes's account, Rushdie's works have been experienced as both the forbidden fruit and vicious imperialist propaganda, not least in the countries to which he has devoted his greatest attention, India and Pakistan.[1] *Halal* history as the bearing metaphor for censorship is at first sight culture specific, because the idea of *halal* belongs to the Islamic regulations of existence. However, Rushdie lets its general meaning flow over to include the secular history of modern nation-states as well. The reason for this lies in the idea that ideologically produced and maintained meaning constitutes the ground for censorship. Meaning, which is a part of the diffuse power of ideology, governs everyday discrimination between social phenomena, that is, the practice of inclusion/exclusion.

Even today, twenty years after the immense international turbulence against Rushdie's expression, and demands on censorship under the threat of death sentence, one meets with similar stipulations to discrimination and censure. The real state of affairs within particular communities in relation to censorship is often overshadowed by impulsive as well as calculated violent actions against anything offensive to that which is most meaningful for any particular community. Though not on the scale of events of *The Satanic Verses* affair,[2] the riots against the publication of the infamous Danish caricatures of Muhammad serve in the media as further emphasis on Muslim bigotry and staunch fundamentalism. This is the perfect contrast to the incessantly lauded Western liberalism. Although all manner of fundamentalism has escalated in modern nation-states since the time of Rushdie's first publications, as he states in a TV interview with Bill Moyers (CNBC), the West still stands for intellectual enlightenment and progress as opposed to reactionary Eastern countries. Open hostilities toward the Danish cartoons serve to put a vital intellectual debate into the background. These riots overshadow the bulk of Muslims who wish to express their concern with the racist ideology in some cartoons as well as to point out that satire itself does not merely elicit liberated laughter, but in turn produces censorious laughter as well. The major point equally overlooked by many Muslims and European commentators is the fact that there is no blasphemy in Islam. This is of course a disputed issue among Muslim scholars, but the only blasphemy the Qur'an explicitly forbids is against other people's beliefs and objects of worship, thus rendering the infamous destruction of the Buddha statues anti-Islamic.[3]

The aversion to offensive art, violent and instinctive as it has been, also clashes with the Islamic aversion to fetishism of images and person cults. As Rushdie himself asks, how is it possible to blaspheme against Muhammad whose life struggle was against person cults?[4] People who counter the offensive art with violence obscure the possible ideological coloring and the censorious ground of such art, and turn it into symbols of freedom, thus producing an either/or dichotomy. The publishing of the blasphemous fiction or cartoons does not become a matter of editorial intellectual choice, but a question of giving in to fear or publishing them in sheer spite. The censorship defeats its purpose by turning obscure and local drawings into agents of nearly global proportions. What is important is that the debaters as well as rioters are intent on protecting the power and sanctity of their existential structures, in particular their meaning. Indeed, despite his anticensorship principles, Rushdie once made an exception in the case of the Sandinista in his *Jaguar Smile*.[5] He still maintains that editorial inclusion/exclusion is necessary but on intellectual and aesthetic grounds. He has welcomed the censure of both satirical literature and film that exploited his predicament under the threat of the *fatwa*.

With this in mind, I will go back to analyze Rushdie's first and only use of the term *halal* history in the beginning of the 1980s. I claim that in *Midnight's Children* Rushdie's argument against censorship through a creative use of a term from Islamic tradition bites its own tail like the metaphorical Ouroboros snake. *Halal* history is a critique of ideologically sanitized historiography by dominant power, but it leaves out the definition of the opposite/positive historiography as a counterideological narrative. Read along with the postmodern critique of historiography, the concept of *halal* history loses its critical edge, and, in the final analysis, even seems to undermine the proliferation of subaltern histories.

Existential Meaning and History

Rushdie has argued that the reason behind the renewed interest in religious existential meanings and practices lies in the failure of the secular world to provide alternate meanings, which are as crucial as the solutions to the material conditions of the so-called Third World nations in the wake of Global Capitalism (*IH*, 388). Partly influenced by Rushdie, Homi K. Bhabha has proposed that "minoritarian affiliations or solidarities arise in response to the failures and limits of democratic representation, creating new modes of agency, new strategies of recognition, new forms of political and symbolic representation."[6]

Midnight's Children stages a desperate, albeit satirized, existential quest for an authentic existential meaning, which will tie Saleem's chaotic life together, that is, help him select and place only relevant events into his life history, but his particular life is "mysteriously handcuffed to history, my destinies indissolubly chained to those of my country."[7] Being handcuffed to history manifests as attempted synchronicity between macrocosmic activities in the subcontinent and the micro level of the family or individual.[8] Saleem's troubled oscillation between the private and the public spheres is directly caused by the meaning he received from Jawaharlal Nehru, "your life . . . will be, in a sense, the mirror of our own" (*MC*, 238). It is not solely the amusing "accident" of midnight birth that binds Saleem to the history of India, but Nehru's political interpretation of it. This allegorical and yet also existential meaning forces Saleem to assume the reality of *the* national history that totalizes heterogeneous multitudes. Saleem adjusts his life to the official history, which "operates on a grander scale than any individual" and therefore takes "a good deal longer to stitch it back together and mop up the mess." The progress of Indian history is also tied to the negotiation of the meaning of the nation. This abstract totality is exposed to a process of imagination and reimagination.

Even as a group, "the children of midnight were also the children *of the time*: fathered, you understand, by history" (*MC*, 118). To be the child of the time is to reflect the era, to capture the essence of its history, or perhaps to reflect that which Sartre described as "some powerful unitary force revealing itself behind History like the will of God."[9] One could argue that Saleem articulates his meaning in terms of the Sartrean paradox of singular-universal:

> I am the sum total of everything that went before me of all I have been seen done, of anything done-to-me. I am anything that happens after I've gone which would not have happened if I had not come. I am everyone everything whose *being-in-the-world* affected was affected by mine. Nor am I particularly exceptional in this matter; each "I," every one of the now-six-hundred-million-plus of us, contains a similar multitude. (*MC*, 383)

There is an implied dispersion of multitudes, which are then held together by an enormous web of history.[10] Since the "nation" is itself an allegory, as Timothy Brennan shows, Saleem is an allegory of an allegory.[11] To escape this doubling, Saleem struggles to find material links between him and the real peoples of the subcontinent. Yet, to be a material manifestation of an allegory is incommensurate with his historicism, and is more understandable in terms of something like being an avatar, a Vishnu incarnation. At the same time as it gives meaning to Saleem's life, this allegory signals a suspension of meaning. As Lloyd Spencer explains, allegoricity is "symptomatic of a significant loss of a sense of genuine, immediately accessible, *imminent* meaning. Allegories, even those which proclaim the stability and fullness of meaning in the (hierarchized) universe can thus be seen as deconstructing themselves."[12]

Saleem's grappling with allegory implies a critique of existential meaning, especially when the meaning of each singular is rhetorically tied to the overarching national life and politics. Yet, Saleem also shows that no matter how much we deconstruct existential meaning and its ideological ties, this does not necessarily rid one of its influence. Saleem's desperation seems to reflect Friedrich Nietzsche's claim: "man would sooner have the void for his purpose than be void of purpose."[13] Nietzsche seems to suggest here that the need for meaning is inherited, that it is a part of the social paradigms into which one is born, or, in Saleem's phrase, "fallen."

It is due to his desire to prove that he allegorizes Indian history that Saleem attempts to preserve or "pickle" this history. The pickling of meaning becomes a form of dredging of the past. As he endeavors to preserve his meaning, he produces himself as narrative, something made in and as a work of art. He draws attention to his own narrative strategies.[14] His consciousness of traditional narrative forms is crucial. He has to decide what narrative form(s) to employ, yet he is aware that each will in its own way affect the result. For instance, the epic form produces an epic hero. He opts for the novel form, which has potentiality to comprise a range of other narrative forms: autobiography, history, the epic, romance, realist and surrealist narrative.

Saleem's meaning obliges him to conform to the Indian history, yet at the same time he claims the public history is purged of all elements that could be unsettling to the ideological powers that shape it. Saleem then sets on a quest for the total, unabridged version of history, which must contain all the peculiarities of private individual lives. A large part of his project consists in removing the sacred veil from the private sphere. Aware of his author position, he finds it necessary to caution potential readers against reading only chosen parts of his story and skipping others: "there are so many stories to tell, too many, such an excess of intertwined lives events miracles places rumors, so dense a commingling of the improbable and mundane! I have been a swallower of lives; and to know me, just the one of me, you'll have to swallow the lot as well" (*MC*, 9). Since he is an indiscriminate swallower of lives, the reader must be equally voracious: "I repeat for the last time: to understand me, you'll have to swallow the world" (*MC*, 383).[15] For this reason, early in the narrative, Saleem uses the word "halal" in what can strike a reader informed in Islamic discourse as incorrect, or even an unlawful use of the word that *Oxford English Dictionary* in the first instance translates as "lawful":

> Family history, of course, has its proper dietary laws. One is supposed to swallow and digest only the permitted parts of it, the *halal* portions of the past, drained of their redness, their blood. Unfortunately, this makes stories less juicy; so I am about to become the first and only member of my family to flout the *laws of halal*. Letting no blood escape from the body of the tale, I arrive at the unspeakable part; and, undaunted, press on. What happened in August 1945? (*MC*, 59; my emphasis)[16]

Saleem claims he conveys *the unspeakable*. He is *undaunted* in his insistence on a freedom of expression, and even the right to expose the ugly truth. Yet, in the case of history, it is not an expression of a political stance—which he indeed often avoids due to his fear of parental and communal reactions—but the posthumous revealing of scandals about his closest relatives. In another place, Saleem conceals details about the magical children with the excuse that he must respect their privacy.

The insistence on the culture-specific use of *halal* rather than *censure* is crucial. *Halal* evokes practices tied to Islamic beliefs and laws. *Halal* (حلال), a Semitic (Arabic) adjective denoting that which is permissible,[17] is mostly connected to dietary laws in Islamic religious practices. The meaning of *halal* is defined by its opposite *haram* (حرم, prohibited and sacred), which only implies things explicitly forbidden in the Qur'an. For example, one can say that the private sphere is *haram*, sacred and protected from the prying public eyes.

Saleem expands the idea of *halal* history and uses it as the metaphor for all vile historiography regardless of ideology. For instance, Saleem's adopted son Aadam is born at the moment of Emergency when Indira Gandhi silences the opposition. Consequently the boy is entirely mute. Saleem both offers a critique of a specific culture of censorship, which he locates in Pakistan, and opens the idea that history can be censored on the basis of existential meaning, which is that particular meaning which serves as a guiding principle of his identity and action. As Claude Lévi-Strauss expressed it, "in so far as history aspires to meaning, it is doomed to select regions, periods, groups of men, and individuals in these groups and to make them stand out as discontinuous figures, against a continuity barely good enough to be used as a backdrop."[18] "Censorship" can imply any ideology and does not immediately evoke the existential mechanics behind particular acts of exclusion in the way *halal* does.

Private versus Public and *Haram* versus *Halal*

Having connected history to bodily functions,[19] it appears perfectly logical for Saleem to apply *halal* to historiography even though basic Islamic sources do not contain such usage. Selection and censure are regular practices in all history writing, but the heavy criteria of *halal* and *haram* are not prescribed for historiography. The passage that evokes *halal* draws particular attention to the private/public dichotomy. Here lies the second connection to Islam, in which the private sphere is *haram* in the sense of being sacred and protected from the intrusion of the public eye. For this reason, Saleem can claim to do *haram* (the taboo) by revealing family shame. He focuses on the sixth and ninth of August, which correspond to the world-historical dates when the atomic bombs were dropped on Hiroshima and Nagasaki. On the first date his sister *fell* ill, and on the second her father *dropped* the "bomb-shell," that is, the news that his daughter's marriage is unconsummated after two years (*MC*, 61). The conflict (narrative blood) of the chapter "Under the Carpet" is the literal lack of Mumtaz's blood. More importantly, Mumtaz's marital virginity is a blown up version of Aadam's own first nuptial night. When the public demanded that Aadam present a bloodstained sheet as the proof of Naseem's chastity, Aadam stained it with red sanitizing Mercurochrome (*MC*, 30–31).[20] Aadam sanitizes or *halalizes* his family history for fear of public shame. Saleem divulges Aadam's sleight of hand and turns the private into public. The lack and/or falseness of blood disrupt the idea of the sacred privacy of family upon which the larger structures of the nation and class are built. The undermining of the meaning of real blood points to the fact that blood has always been used metaphorically to strengthen social ties. Saleem draws a parallel to the official history, which is purged of the subversive elements. Here, the sanitizing of history produces the real blood of genocide. Even the metaphor of the sheet inscribed in blood, as Kortenaar claims, is "a literalization of the common metaphor of history written in blood," which is the elimination of the disturbing subaltern elements with different existential make-ups (*SNT*, 35).

Saleem's existential meaning, being-national-allegory, makes him public, like Indira Gandhi in the saying "Indira is India, India is Indira." Saleem stresses that the private histories are always molded in order to meet the demands of the public life. The public history is then censured again in official historiography, which could be seen as the narrative that propounds the idea of "lack" and "inadequacy" of the subaltern vis-à-vis European models of history writing, as Dipesh Chakrabarty maintains. Since Saleem is from an Islamic family, he knows that the words *halal* and *haram* apply to the split between the private (sacred) and the public spheres, which are not exclusively Western concepts, as outlined in Chakrabarty's work.[21] Although Islam prescribes no laws for historiography, except for the demand on truthfulness, there are rules that protect the private/sacred sphere of one's family from the prying eyes of the public, which Saleem observes when protecting the identities of the midnight's children. Yet, the split between the private and the public in modern India is informed by the European model, which prescribes a different classification and division. In the secular model, things religious and mythical should keep to the private sphere and not interfere with state politics. However, this seems impossible if one understands religion as a major shaping factor of everyday lives. As Chakrabarty claims, "action involves emotion, memories, tastes, feelings, will, and values—and these things have histories over which we have much less control than we have over our consciously thought out philosophies."[22] Structures of existential meaning, in this analysis, permeate each of these factors.

Saleem's aversion to vile censure begs the crucial question about the possibility of a more open form that can hold multitudes like his mind or his famous spittoon that holds all kinds of spit. I would call it *haram* history. Is *haram* history then devoid of ideology, or perhaps informed by a more progressive and positive ideology in terms of Stuart Mill, that is, a form of public rhetoric that can comprise diverse political and cultural representations as discursive and dialogical exchange? By flouting the laws of Aadam's *halalized* history, Saleem disturbs the private/public distinction and makes *haram* history. Further, to read such a history is in a sense to do something *haram*, because the reader participates in the taboo. Yet, the part that Saleem omits is his own right in Islam to reveal or censure his personal history as he chooses. His supposed flouting of the laws of *halal* is a turn of phrase whose aim is to make the narrative appear more controversial, juicy, and thrilling than it is. Exposing his family in order to make a large claim about a culture of censure and a critique of Islam per se, Saleem does not reveal the fact that no Islamic source (of dogma) provides instructions about any of the social practices that he treats negatively, and that he is ultimately critiquing a specific communal tradition (though not specific to Islamic communities only). Similarly, the critique of the riots based on the theft of the prophet's hair is on a par with Qur'anic critique of person cults and fetishism, rather than a critique of Islam, as it might appear on the first reading. This, however, is a less juicy truth.

Saleem never uses the term *haram* as if he really is subscribing to the Islamic prescription that only God can state what is *haram*. Instead he employs fictional rhetoric to evoke the idea of *haram* history. He is quite vague about what exactly this might consist in, which he takes as his artistic privilege to evoke but not to elaborate on. A close analysis yields two potential answers. Anti-*halal* history is either the sum of all neglected subaltern histories, formed with some type of existential authenticity in mind, de-ideologised, antidogmatic, open to a plurality of meaning. Alternatively, it is fiction, which is always assumed to be inferior to scientific and sacred narratives. If the bloodlessness of *halal* history pertains to historiography in general, is the blood that is retained in *haram* history a form of truth about the subaltern, forbidden, unholy, and marginal? The excluded histories have over the centuries belonged to minorities such as slaves, convicts, women, the working class, children, gays, etc.

Ideal Historiography

To speak about censored history is to evoke the notion of historical truth and representation. Saleem's ideal historiography is suggestive of openness to the plurality of existence and of being artistic and imaginative in character. Rushdie's fiction has often been analyzed in terms of postmodernism, which to Linda Hutcheon entails the conscious use of inherited ways of understanding the world and humanity in order "to question, but not to resolve."[23] Postmodern fiction juxtaposes different ideologically produced and maintained meanings that (in)-form self-understanding. It reveals their historical contingency and deprives inherited meanings of universality. A narrative such as *Midnight's Children* displays "the stubborn assertion and equally insistent undermining of both individuality and universality" (*POP*, 190). It does not offer resolutions and new dogmas. It does not propound ideologies. Instead, it seeks to heighten the *awareness* of ideological structures that have become part of everyday life to the extent of being naturalized. For instance, the principle of "shame" in *Shame* is part of the basic existential structures: "shame is like everything else; live with it for long enough, and it becomes part of the furniture."[24] This immediately begs the question about the possibility of reconciling the ideas that fiction too is ideologically influenced and that it undermines ideology.

For Hutcheon, postmodern fiction often takes the shape of "historiographic metafiction," which is an artistic reworking of recorded histories. This model seeks to show that both "history" and "fiction" are historical, ideologically loaded forms (*POP*, 105). Ideology is here understood as "a general process of pro-duction of meaning" (*POP*, 178). Historiographic metafiction uncovers the ideo-logical production of meaning, and emphasizes its historical contingency instead of embracing universal validity.

Postmodern readings such as Sabrina Hassumani's also advocate the idea that history is ultimately nothing but narrative.[25] However, although we know Rushdie's history as narrative, it seems impossible to talk about it only in terms of textuality. We can hardly claim that for Rushdie, who felt history in the mak-ing through his *fatwa*, history is mere narrative. The *fatwa* was a political reac-tion to Rushdie's *haram* history. That history can only be known (in the less dogmatic sense of *known*) through various narrative strategies, does not mean that anything goes. Rushdie shows this by writing diverse errata to *Midnight's Children*. The reason for this is exactly the indecision as to what constitutes the alternative *haram* history. To write errata seems to me to either denounce post-modern readings or an unequivocal submission to the official, ideologically purged and shaped *halal* history. It is to deny that the ironic remarks in the novel about the events that never *officially* happened, such as massacres in the Indo-Pakistani war, lose their value, because the point is exactly, even for a postmod-ern reader, that the novel makes a claim that these really happened, and are not a matter of subjective truth. The ironic twist turns the tables and seems to imply something like the bloody/non-*halalized* historical truth. Any other reading eras-es the point of the critique of ideology, and renders the novel vapid even in the postmodern sense.

The reason I claim that for Rushdie, and his character Saleem, history is not a mere narrative comes forth through his famous literalization of dead meta-phors. If overtly metaphoric language draws attention to art/fiction/artifice and supports the stress on history as narrative, the literalization of dead/stiff meta-phors is a narratological device that breaks the assumed spell of language and indexes into the world. This literalization is a gesture of what Mieke Bal calls "Qur'anic semiotics."[26] It is not a fundamentalist gesture, but an antidogmatic, antifundamentalist gesture of ideological sedimentation of meaning. Literali-zation of dead metaphors is an index into the reality as experienced by a particu-lar community. Literalization potentially hints at the ideological processes em-ployed to sediment or make *halal* certain meanings and erase or palimpsest other.

In *Midnight's Children*, there is hardly a dead metaphor that is not made literal. It is significant, for instance, that this strategy dominates the chapter enti-tled "Under the Carpet," where Saleem evokes *halal* history. Indeed, Rushdie has argued, "[i]n my own writing, I have tried to bring things out from under various carpets."[27] The forbidden truth of his sister's unconsummated marriage takes place under the carpet, in the family cellar.

Since Saleem is the allegory of the *secular* India, he seeks to explain mate-rial causes behind the development of officially sanctioned history. Indeed, since his meaning is Nehru's gift, Saleem omits the period 1919–1942 characterized by Gandhi's National Movement, which as Erik Strand claims, enabled political criticism of materialism and rejection of standard notions of modernity and progress.[28] An ideal history, for Saleem is inclusive and enriching. The i*ncorporation* entailed in ideal history is optimally a movement away from transformation according to a master code, which homogenizes historical phenomena, that which Chakrabarty terms History1. Rather, such history should carry the sense of experience like that of tasting. Saleem does not only embrace the new secular meanings and the historicist vision of the world, but incorporates History2s, the histories not solely informed by the ideas of capital, abstract, and real labor, etc. History2s signify a plurality of lived, intimate histories. As Rushdie has argued, "[i]f one is to attempt to honestly describe reality as it is experienced by religious people, for whom God is no symbol but an everyday fact, the conventions of what is called realism are quite inadequate . . . a form must be created which allows the miraculous and the mundane to coexist at the same level" (*IH*, 376).[29] This form seems to be the novel, which like Saleem's spittoon can contain a multitude of personal fluids. It accumulates and preserves memories, which are to Saleem the fluctuating ground for history: "O talismanic spittoon! O beauteous lost receptacle of memories as well as spittle juice" (*MC*, 448). Indeed, there is potential irony in Saleem's examples of his and his family's effects on history and vice versa. As the ominous midnight of Independence approaches, Nehru delivers a monumental speech: "A moment . . . which comes but rarely in history, when we step out from the old to the new; when an age ends" (*MC*, 116). This historically specific moment brims with significance that will determine the development of future history. When Nehru proclaims, "We end today a period of ill-fortune," Saleem's father Ahmed drops a chair on his foot and breaks his toe (*MC*, 117). The breaking of Ahmed's toe will never enter the official history, of course. Yet, in Saleem's version it is indeed significant, if only as an amusing literary device which contrasts the solemnity of Nehru's speech and gives original flavor to history. On a metaphorical level, the events are compatible, suggesting that the end of one historical misfortune is the beginning of another.

Saleem flaunts his mere will toward inclusion as a positive, albeit utopian drive. This basic ethical assumption is demonstrated through the inclusion of his archenemy Shiva. Yet, in fiction, Shiva serves as the antagonistic force (narrative blood), which defines Saleem as a "wannabe" hero, be it epic or mock-epic, individualist or communalist. Saleem's history is inextricably fictional. Not in the sense of being an utter fabrication, but in the sense of being a work of art, a creative recounting of the official history that lifts up the real flavors of life, and therefore tells more truth than for instance the statistics about the massive migration of Muslims to Pakistan. If all history writing entails a form of discrimination, exclusion/inclusion, with the same token the fictive imagination is not worse, but not better either. Yet, Saleem posits fiction as genuine criticism of the official, imposed truths, and thus an opening onto a more genuine truth. Nandini Bhattacharya claims: "stories, though factually incorrect, are conceptually true and therefore intrinsically threatening to the dictator who wishes to control the bodies and minds of people."[30] As Chakrabarty puts it, the "telling of a story, whether biographical or fictional, this works on the principle of the irreplaceable social rather than the general abstract social of the law or theory. . . . This is what makes narrative a political force in a sphere that law or theory can never reach" (*HM*, 113). Indeed, a truthful history, according to Saleem, might be found in fiction: "*Truth*, for me, was . . . hidden inside the stories Mary Pereira told me" (*MC*, 79). For him, the fictional space is by default more open, and more dialogical, that is, it allows for proliferation rather than sedimentation of meaning.

Saleem is not giving an account of what really happened in India, but constructs a fictional India juxtaposing his history to any other history in terms of "historiographic metafiction."[31] He contrasts his narrative to the history of Pakistan, which is the epitome of *halal* history because it is in a sense Islamic history, in which *halal* has its provenance. The same claim recurs in *Shame*:

> It is well known that the term "Pakistan," an acronym, was originally thought up in England by a group of Muslim intellectuals. . . . [I]t was a word born in exile which then went East, was borne-across and trans-lated, and imposed itself on history; a returning migrant, settling down on partitioned land, forming a palimpsest on the past. A palimpsest obscures what lies beneath. To build Pakistan it was necessary to cover up Indian history, to deny that Indian centuries lay just beneath the surface of Pakistani Standard Time. The past was rewritten. . . . It is possible to see the subsequent history of Pakistan as a duel between two layers of time, the obscured world forcing its way back through what-had-been-imposed. It is the true desire of every artist to impose his or her vision on the world. . . . I, too, like all migrants, am a fantasist. I build imaginary countries and try to impose them on the ones that exist. I, too, face the problem of history: what to retain, what to dump. (*SH*, 87)

The narrative juxtaposes two exercises in imagination, one political and one artistic. At surface they seem equaled to one another, in that they are both fictions and equally censorious. The narrative irony accrues the artistic imagination a greater value, because the political imagination establishes ideological power relations, whereas the artistic one undermines them. Hutcheon indeed argues that postmodern fiction "also reminds us, by its very paradoxes, that awareness of ideology is as much an ideological stand as common-sense lack of awareness of it" (*POP*, 180). Still, this awareness and self-critical position sets it apart from other art forms and movements. This setting-apart is directedness toward some form of historical truth, indeed different, but still a teleological enterprise. As Rushdie has argued, "the speaking of suppressed truths is one of the great possibilities of the novel, and it is perhaps the main reason why the novel becomes the most dangerous of art forms in all countries where people, governments, are trying to distort the truth" (*CSR*, viii). If all fiction is set upon de-sedimentation of intellect, Rushdie contradicts himself when criticizing V. S. Naipaul's travelogues in Pakistan: "The trouble is that it's a highly selective truth, a novelist's truth masquerading as objective reality" (*IH*, 374).

In *Midnight's Children*, although Saleem's narrative is fiction, there is still a differentiation between truth and lie. Though not true in the epistemological sense, as Kortenaar shows, "fictions retain a sense of other possibilities, while lies deceive by denying that the world could be imagined differently" (*SNT*, 42). In other words, Saleem deems the world insufficiently imagined. The supreme fiction is supposed to work against the entropy of meaning. Saleem's narrative, which indeed assumes a very private confessional tone, seems to be a combination of the Western, bourgeois, internalized narrative and "Indian lust for allegory" (*MC*, 96). Chakrabarty shows that in the Indian context the forms such as the novel and autobiography tended to be overtly public histories, lacking intimate, private details (*PE*, 35). Wanting to be public seems to be the question of wanting to matter, to mean something beyond the narrow private sphere.[32]

Having defined his narrative in contrast to *halal* history, Saleem suspects that readers may not "swallow" his all-inclusiveness assertion. Therefore, he frequently confesses he has lied or distorted the facts. At one point he blames it on the faulty nature of memory: "Memory's truth. . . . It selects, eliminates, alters, exaggerates, minimizes, glorifies, and vilifies also; but in the end it creates its own reality . . . and no sane human being ever trusts someone else's version more than his own" (*MC*, 211). The notion of "memory's fault" has been another hallmark of postmodern historiographic metafiction: "I swore to tell it all. . . . But how can I. . . . I'm tearing myself apart, can't even agree with myself, talking arguing like a wild fellow, cracking up, memory . . . plunging into chasms . . . only fragments remain, none of it makes sense any more!—But I mustn't presume to judge . . . sense-and-nonsense is no longer for me to evaluate" (*MC*, 422). Weakness of memory cannot be helped, but in Saleem's eyes this excuse does not pertain to *halal* history. In the case of the Qur'an, Saleem is ready to stress the lack of vile intentions (unlike in Pakistan and India): "Abubakr and the others tried to remember the correct sequence, but they didn't have good memory" (*MC*, 82). In *The Satanic Verses*, which is in part an artistic rewriting of the beginning of Islamic history, we find the opposite claim. Mahound (Muhammad) rushes to erase the untoward event of the satanic verses from the public "record for ever and ever, so that they will survive in just one or two unreliable collections of old traditions and orthodox interpreters will try to unwrite their story" (*SV*, 123). Since Holy Scriptures and secular historiographies are opposed to fiction, in *The Satanic Verses*, Salman the Persian renounces the superiority of any scripture over his poetic imagination. Rushdie evokes the privileged status of poets in pre-Islamic, polytheistic society: "Poets stand on boxes and disclaim while pilgrims throw coins at their feet." In this scene, an established poet Abu Simbel speaks to the emerging poet Baal "'You like the taste of *blood*,' he says. The boy shrugs. 'A *poet's work*,' he answers. 'To name the unnameable, to point at frauds, to take sides, start arguments, shape the world and stop it from going to sleep.' And if rivers of *blood* flow from the cuts his verses inflict, then they will *nourish* him. He is the satirist, Baal" (*SV*, 97; my emphasis). Here poets struggle for truth and against stagnation of intellectual discourse, the sleep of reason. Islam, on the other hand, distinguishes between poets who speak the truth and those who use fancy poetic rhetoric to seduce people to throw coins at their feet.[33]

In *Midnight's Children*, Saleem both questions the supremacy of historical epistemology in a postmodern fashion and propounds the value of fiction, which is teleologically oriented toward establishing meaning as well.[34] Even if the goal of fiction is questioning, it still has a *telos* of anticipated meaning that directs censoring. For Hutcheon, this should not be the case in postmodern fiction, which resembles Saleem's spittoon, in which a multitude of personal bodily fluids mix but neither dominates the other. The spittoon is like Saleem's novel, or Saleem's consciousness, a form that contains multitudes: "the last object connecting me to my more tangible, historically-verifiable past" (*MC*, 432).

For Erik L. Berlatsky, Rushdie wished to write what "Henry James would call the 'loose, baggy monsters' of fiction."[35] Indeed,

> Rushdie's invention of the Hummingbird and his Convocation illustrates the broader truth of the historical marginalization of moderate Islam. . . . [E]ven if not all coordinates of the legend of Abdullah and his Convocation are historically accurate, they nevertheless keep alive the truth of the historical and contemporary existence of a substantial part of the Islamic community that is not ardently anti-Hindu or anti-India, as the two have become increasingly conflated in contemporary political rhetoric. (*FFF*, 362)

Indeed, the form of the novel too is oriented toward selecting values, meanings, and ideologies. Hutcheon argues that the postmodern questioning and situating of inherited meanings is indeed "to acknowledge the ideology of the subject and to suggest alternate notions of subjectivity" (*POP*, 159). Yet, the explicit undermining of the subject position also has the opposite effect. The narrator is trusted much more than some putatively omniscient voice, as we can see from several reviews of *Midnight's Children* in the USA and the UK. Kortenaar has shown that whenever the narrative highlights a mistake, the rhetoric of fallibility and proposed will-to-honesty serves to "forestall criticism" and induce the listener/reader to believe the rest (*SNT*, 237). Saleem confesses:

> How I persuaded them—by rhetoric, by questioning their judgment and invoking their beliefs in just as incredible things. Apparitions, phantoms, mirages, sleight-of-hand, the seeming form of things: all these are parts of Maya. . . . Brahma's dream. . . . Chutney and oratory, theology and curiosity: these are the things that saved me. And one more—call it education, or class-origins. . . my "brought-up." By my show of erudition and by the purity of my accents, I shamed them into feeling unworthy of judging me. . . . It's a dangerous business to try and impose one's view of things on others. (*MC*, 211–12)

By evoking all the usual persuasion devices (theology, rhetoric, education, and class) without elaborating on how they are employed, Saleem flaunts his awareness of the traditional systems of persuasion. At the same time as he says that he has used theological or Marxist rhetoric, he implies that he has done no such thing, or rather that he does not believe in it. Negating different forms of rhetoric, Saleem does not outline exactly what his own metarhetoric may be, but only hints at it. This metarhetoric is supposedly also antirhetorical, anti-ideological, and as such it is proposed as more ethical.

If Saleem's conscience forces him to admit to every distortion, then everything else he has not pointed out as errors must be correct, the lawful, *halal* truth of his life. Still, Saleem likes "cutting up history to suit [his] nefarious purposes" (*MC*, 259), and "rearranging history" (*MC*, 260). The word "nefarious" here is positive. Saleem's narration is nefarious because it is an egoistic enterprise, which serves to underpin his existential meaning. He claims that imposing views is dangerous, but he insists on the readers "swallowing" his entire narrative. Saleem includes all the "juicy" details, yet nevertheless cuts a great deal. By opposing his own attitude of "refusing to censor [his] past" (*MC*, 316) to the negative *halal* history, he draws attention away from the fact that his narrative might be produced merely to entertain. His awareness of his potential readership is enormous, which forces him to include juicy, exotic bits to keep the reader thrilled in the way "serpents dramatized [his] speech" (*MC*, 413). The narrative thrill makes this praised autocriticism more transparent so that "what actually happened is less important than what the author can manage to persuade his audience to believe" (*MC*, 270–71). Like in the passage from *Shame*, by evoking the vileness of Pakistan's ideological mixing with history, Saleem tones down the negativity of his own censures: "my story does indeed end in fantasy. . . . I have been only the humblest of jugglers-with-facts . . . in a country where truth is what is instructed to be, reality quite literally ceases to exist so that anything becomes possible" (*MC*, 326).

Hutcheon points out that Saleem "would like to reduce history to autobiography, to reduce India to his own consciousness" (*POP*, 162), and since he constantly fails, he thus "contests the [Cartesian] *cogito*" as the origin of meaning (*POP*, 164). This is still an apologetic stance on the art of postmodernism, whose supposed openness accrues it greater value. Ideologically informed or not, the desire to inclusion of plural singularities is better than exclusion. John J. Su evokes Lukács to claim that "the moment of failure in the novel is 'the moment of value.' By drawing attention to its own inability to achieve the aesthetic totality of epic, the novel can convey 'a true totality of life. . . . Thus, the novel's supposed failure of representation makes it possible to perceive the world in terms of its multiplicity, not homogeneity.'"[36] For Saleem, such would be a positive *telos* sheltered in the novel form. His metaphor of *halal* history demonstrates the character of an artwork to open up layers of meaning to a dialectical movement, which furthermore potentially produces new meanings that will or will not palimpsest the former. By being unfaithful, or rather doing something non-*halal*, Saleem emphasizes certain structures of meaning, inheritance, and production, which are bound to the mechanisms of inclusion and exclusion in (hi)story writing. Though Saleem propounds *haram* fiction, he cannot avoid establishing historiographic metafiction's own *halal*. Saleem's "urge to encapsulate the whole of reality" (*MC*, 75), an idealist illusion governed by his existential meaning, renders him "prepared to distort everything—to re-write the whole history of [his] times purely in order to place [himself] in a central role" (*MC*, 166). To be an allegory is to be inscribed into the world of poetic meaning, to live poetically.

In *Poetry, Language, Thought*, Heidegger explains, "the art work is . . . a thing that is made, but it says something other than the mere thing itself is, *allo agoreuei. The work makes public something other than itself . . . it is an allegory*. In the work of art something other is brought together with the thing that is made."[37] This inexplicit "something other" is a form of truth, though not truth as *fact*, but rather truth as authentic meaning. Saleem's allegorical historiography seems to convey some hidden truth.[38] Yet, as Chakrabarty has argued, "'[p]oetically, man dwells . . . '—true, but within the poetry lies the poison of inescapable prejudice, all the more unrecognizable because it comes disguised as value" (*HM*, 137). Although Saleem claims that ideally "art must be beyond categories" (*MC*, 45), he shows that fiction too indeed has its *halal* and *haram*. Saleem's idealization of (postmodern) fiction is not ideology-free and *haram* history. It conceals, as I have pointed out, misguided critiques, critiques made obscure and perhaps deliberately ambiguous even in those instances where no such ambiguity seems to have any but purely ideological reasons.

If Saleem's historiographic metafiction undermines the understanding of history as a grand, all-comprehensive narrative, it shows that censure is inevitable and even necessary if the historical narrative is to make any sense instead of resembling the faceless crowd from the novel. The question is, what is the value of subaltern histories if historical truth-value, that is, the *haram* blood, is not valued more than the official sanitized history? The final crux is, if *halal* history means history cleansed of unbefitting events, then all the "micro" histories of the subaltern often excluded from the public versions are *halal* as well, that is, ideologically sanitized. Left undeveloped and merely evocative, the metaphorization of *halal* and its implicit opposite *haram* oversimplifies on liberal grounds. The novelistic discourse, taken at its face value, obscures the possible value and positive reinterpretation of traditional theological implications for both existentialist and materialist critiques of ideology and modern cultural fundamentalism. This is exactly what happened in the event of the Danish cartoons. The strong ideological forces of both the Islamic and liberal fundamentalists obscured exactly the possibility of critique of ideology, social dogma, and the very material conditions that play a major role in the entire conflict.[39]

It seems as if Rushdie's excess of metafictional awareness of ideological workings actually stifles the dialogical character that Benjamin ascribed to the genre of the novel. In fact, Rushdie censors by inclusion, excludes through inclusion, and creates strange *halal* novels, in which all the elements that are impure and inedible are included, but their inedibility is accentuated. In the end, the moral lesson seems to be nothing but, let there be stories, all false, cooked up, but all free floating, and as such equally meaningless and infinitely meaningful as well.

Chapter 8

Tactical Reason:
Philosophy and the Colonial Question

Marios Constantinou

Quid Juris? Prolegomena to the Kantian Drama of Sovereignty

> *"I am no traitor's uncle; and that word 'grace'*
> *in an ungracious mouth is but profane.*
> *Why have those banisht and forbidden legs*
> *Dared to touch a dust of England's ground?. . .*
> *Why have they dared . . . to march*
> *frighting her pale-faced villages with war*
> *And ostentation of despised arms?*
> *Why foolish boy, the King is left behind*
> *And in my loyal bossom lies his power"*
>> Duke of York to Henry Bolingbroke, thereafter Henry IV,
>> in W. Shakespeare's *King Richard II*, Act II, Scene III

> *"Great Duke of Lancaster . . .*
> *Ascend his Throne, descending now from him*
> *And long live Henry, fourth of that name!"*
>> Duke of York to Henry IV, Act IV, Scene I

The conceptual core of positivism, regardless of its historical forms and astonishing varieties, may be defined by a stubborn adherence to established facts. What, in fact, happens, however, is that facts are objectified by the positivist impulse to establish certainty about them. My use of the term in this essay extends beyond its original sense which indicates a situation of observation, experiment, and deduction of law and may be traced back to Francis Bacon and Auguste Comte. Moreover, it addresses a geopolitical and constitutional context outside the range of logical empiricism whose formal foundations were laid by the Vienna Circle in the 1920s and 1930s. In other words, I am not concerned with the logical structure of legal propositions but with law as *posited* and *enacted.* In this case, I am interested in the intellectual authority it elicits and the speculative justifications propounded in its name. What is implicated in this is, I will argue, a passionate zeal for the preservation of order which incorporates the censorious outlook of the counter-Enlightenment. In fact, this paradoxical pattern tends to repeat itself. Auguste Comte, himself the high priest and popularizer of Positivism who grew up in the aftermath of the French Revolution and lived through its utmost consequences, reached the point at the end to advocate a new ceremonial religion of humanity with its own clergy conducting its mysteries. What I will try to unpack is precisely this paradoxical symptom which manifests an enthusiasm for social reform, human dignity, liberty, eternal peace, etc., while, at the same time, being dogmatically attached to the disciplinary apparatus of existing legality, thus introducing uncanny rationalizations which invalidate any supposed claims of reason.

What this points to is an obstinate will to preserve what is given or posited as *law and order* without, however, arriving at this conclusion by reasoning (which would be the logical outcome of the spirit of Enlightenment and its professed outlook as the Age of Reason). Instead, it betrays incomprehensible sympathies with the spirit of counterrevolution, appeals without hesitation to censorship, and justifies colonialism. Regardless of the differences between Immanuel Kant and Alexis de Tocqueville, this is more or less a shared assumption which is animated by what Alain Badiou calls "Thermidorian subjectivity." Thermidor is the name of that month of the French revolutionary calendar which extends from mid-July to mid-August. It describes a tempered sequence of supposed social and political moderation during which, however, Georges Couthon, Robespierre, and Saint-Just were guillotined. This Thermidorian figure who "rescues" the revolution by terminating it, who renounces his revolutionary enthusiasm and retails his political capacity to the order of proprietors "is more persistently French than our admirable insurrections," Badiou argues.[1] This Thermidorian shift, I would further claim, designates positivism as the condition of *law and order*. More to the point, positivism in this essay is addressed broadly in terms of its legal and political sense, especially as it is typified by Montesquieu, accepted pragmatically by Kant and acted upon by Tocqueville.

For instance, Tocqueville explains in volume two of *Democracy in America* (chapter 21) why the state form of a democratic society is incompatible with revolutionary breaks that depose the existing legality. Insofar as revolutions threaten the existing legal structures of property and trade as the mainstays of democracy, citizens will be disinclined to take the risk. Tocqueville elucidates the sociological underpinnings of legal positivism as follows: "Daily they change, alter, and renew things of secondary importance, but they are very careful not to touch fundamentals. They love change, but they are afraid of revolutions. Although Americans are constantly modifying or repealing some of their laws, they are far from showing any revolutionary passions."[2] In the same vein, Kant defended legal continuity, while Montesquieu was more interested in the enduring spirit of positive law rather than the subject of justice.

One major shortcoming of either positivist theories of law or political theories of freedom is that they fail to account for the expedient, makeshift, and opportunistic reduction of law and politics, respectively. This tacticist bearing of law, as well as the diplomatic and maneuverable quality of conventional politics, point to an inherent aporia attending any theoretical endeavor to insulate them from possible distortions and instrumental appropriations which are immanent in the process of their exhaustion. Politics, law, morality, and peace as Kantian ends in themselves are constantly exposed to the possibility of being inverted to their opposite. Tyranny, illegitimacy, immorality, colonialism, censorship, and cretinism are not merely possible outcomes of an end in itself distorted unexpectedly or unintentionally in the process. Rather, as Alain Badiou argues, these Thermidorian aberrations are the strictly immanent effect of exhausted capacities.[3] The transition from a presumed private opinion to a publicly coordinated judgment by spectators is not necessarily immune to influence or unhampered by partiality, fear, loyalism, and prejudgment.

Kant's watchfulness against civil dissension overshadows inconsistently both his defense of the French Revolution as well as his professed anti-colonialism. But it also discharges an air of smugness, unscrupulous legalism, and even opportunism characteristic of the free rider. With all the necessary changes made, Kant's attitude appears to reflect the neuter grace of the Duke of York in Shakespeare's *King Richard II*.[4] The latter's is not simply a paradigmatic embodiment of the inviolability of sovereignty. It is also an undeviating fidelity to its continuity, to the divine right of the law not only to overrule any other right (including that of rebellion) but to outweigh all other duties (including the affective loyalty between relatives) as well. In a striking anticipation of the Kantian subjectivity as a positivist predicate of legal sovereignty, the Duke of York does certainly reflect on the limits of his patience to endure the suffering of wrong and disgrace, yet what takes precedence at the end is nothing else than "fair sequence and succession" (104). In addressing King Richard, he counsels that wrongful seizure of rights will "pluck a thousand dangers on your head, you lose a thousand well-disposed hearts, and prick my tender patience to those thoughts, which honor and allegiance cannot think" (Act II, Scene I, 179–82). However, the farthest this Kantian intuition can go is a ministerial acknowledgment of the critical situation of revolt: "Well, well, I see the issue of these arms; I cannot mend it . . . because my power is weak . . . but if I could . . . I would attach you all and make you stoop unto the sovereign mercy of the King. But since I cannot, be it known to you, I do remain as neuter. So fare you well." (Act II, Scene III, 151–58); "or it may be I will go with you: but yet I'll pause; For I am loth to break our country's laws. Nor friends, nor foes, to me welcome you are: things past redress are now with me past care" (Act II, Scene III, 168–71).

Shakespeare through the Duke of York stagecrafts the drama of sovereignty and its continuity in a way which fully anticipates the Kantian emphasis on the sanctity of obedience and dutifulness. So much so that, after the enthronement of Henry IV, not only is the Duke of York disposed to absolve the new authority of any offences, not only is he cunningly prudent to become an advocate of its legality, but he rushes, moreover, to report his son to the King, exposing thus his plot to restore Richard to his former seat: "Thou fond mad woman, wilt thou conceal this dark conspiracy? A dozen of them here have ta'en the sacrament, And interchangeably set down their hands, to kill the King of Oxford. . . . Away fond woman! Were he twenty times my son, I would appeach him" (Act V, Scene II, 99–106). This scene, which also dramatizes inexorably the affective stakes of sovereignty, received by Kant an honorable place and an outstanding treat-

ment, becoming, that is, the foundation stone of his constitutional theory of legality. In discussing the relationship of theory to practice in political right, Kant
qualifies his conclusion with the following critical caveat: "There is no *casus
necessitatis* except where duties, i.e., an *absolute duty* and another which, however pressing, is nevertheless *relative* come into conflict. For instance, it might
be necessary for someone to betray someone else, even if their relationship were
that of father and son, in order to preserve the state from catastrophe. This preservation of the state from evil is an absolute duty, while the preservation of the
individual is merely a relative duty. . . . The first person might denounce the
second to the authorities with the utmost unwillingness, compelled only by
(moral) necessity."[5]

In thinking beyond the Kantian logic of state security, of pacification, and
the exaltation of a strictly regulated publicity within the existing limits of constitutional and cultural legality, I would argue that love of public freedom without
the love of a truth capable of puncturing the inexorable propaganda of fixed
opinion and the operational influence of police, cannot motivate any inquiry into
the foundations of a persisting political order.

In this sense, a positivist, self-referential logic of politics calls our attention
to a philosophical lacuna. For instance, Clément Rosset demonstrates this self-
referential logic by adducing the following hypothesis: there comes a moment
when the evidentiary ground of an argument recedes impotent, stumbling on the
thing itself which can be validated only by itself. At this very moment all delib-
eration ends and philosophy is interrupted ingloriously: *adveniente re, cessat
argumentum.*[6] That is, philosophy torn between the real and its double, between
rationalization and the unthought. My contention is that Clément Rosset's reasoning encapsulates in condensed form both Kant's controversial defense of the
French Revolution, which arbitrarily terminates any further inquiry about the
event itself on positivist grounds, but also Tocqueville's equivocal anticolonialism, which was consistent with French imperialism. In my view, both share
a profound ambivalence on the issues of revolution, constitution, and the colonial question. Consequently, the deficient treatment of these issues corrupts judgment, depriving it of any moral or legal foundation.

In light of this perspective I proceed by rethinking Carl Schmitt's reading of
Kant in *The Nomos of the Earth*,[7] which, despite its self-serving interest and
evident opportunism, remains self-defeatingly revealing beyond the critic's intention. Moreover, I argue that, although Kant appears as a reticent but astute
spectator of the revolution, his Thermidorian defense of legality at the expense
of justice reflects his wavering attitude on the colonial question.[8] Finally, despite
differences, there also appear striking similarities with the subsequent dilemmas
faced by Alexis de Tocqueville. These, I argue, make better sense if we integrate
them in the mindset, the institutional practices, and the foreign policy inaugurated by what Badiou designates as the "Thermidorian subjectivity."

This is then a critical sequence of reflections on how philosophical reason
accommodates itself almost sociologically to time than to truth. What I suggest
is a rethinking of the Thermidorian condition which induces a reduction of rea-

son to the prevailing opinion of an expedient rationalism. This process will hopefully disclose what all postcolonial peoples know as a plain fact of survival; namely, that the prevailing consensus over the necessity of the civilizing process of imperialism is not simply an embarrassment to the inquiring reason; it is in itself a Thermidorian backlash against the very possibility of thought. Unavoidably any anti-imperialist opening of thought takes the form of an inquisitive hubris.

Legal Positivism and the Normative Contradictions of Imperial Anticolonialism: Kant after Schmitt

In addressing the insoluble aporias and deeper limits of peace-making as an imperial craft, it is advisable to reckon with Kant's anticolonialism and its paradoxes. At first sight, anticolonialism is the Kantian vocation par excellence. Consider, for instance, the following unequivocal statement:

> If we compare with this ultimate end (i.e., the public law regulating relations between nations) the inhospitable conduct of the civilized states of our continent, especially the commercial states, the injustice which they display in visiting foreign countries and peoples which in their case is the same as conquering them, seems appallingly great. America, the negro countries, the spice islands, the Cape, etc. were looked upon at the time of their discovery as ownerless territories; for the native inhabitants were counted as nothing. In East India foreign troops were brought in under the pretext of merely setting up trading posts. This led to oppression of the natives, incitement of the various Indian states to widespread wars, famine, insurrection, treachery, and the whole litany of evils which can afflict the human race.
>
> China and Japan, having had experience of such guests, have wisely placed restrictions on them. China permits contact with her territories but no entrance into them, while Japan only allows contact with a single European people, the Dutch, although they are still segregated from the native community like prisoners. The worst thing about all this is that the commercial states do not even benefit by their violence, for all their trading companies are on the point of collapse. The sugar islands, that stronghold of the cruellest and most calculated slavery, do not yield any real profit. They serve only the indirect (and not entirely laudable) purpose of training sailors for warships, thereby aiding the prosecution of wars in Europe. And all this is the work of powers who make endless ado about their piety and who wish to be considered as chosen believers while they live on the fruits of inequity. (*PW*, 106–7)

Yet, this pious advocacy for an anti-imperialist Enlightenment makes room for contradictory prescriptions regarding perpetual peace such as the following:

> But man (or an individual nation) in a mere state of nature robs me of any such security and injures me by virtue of this very state in which he coexists with

me. He may not have injured me actively (*facto*), but he does injure me by the very lawlessness of his state (*statu iniusto*), for he is a permanent threat to me, and I can require him either to enter into a common lawful state along with me or to move away from my vicinity. (*PW*, 98)

Kant's reasoning proceeds from the premises of a state legality which identifies the force of civilization with constitutional sovereignty vis-à-vis lawless, stateless, and hence "uncivil" societies founded solely on ethos and virtue which, as of necessity, have to be coerced out of the threatening state of nature. In this sense, Kant's legal philosophy brings to a conclusion a line of reasoning typical of the humanistic jurisprudence of the 16th century which prescribes maxims of justice applicable only to public wars, involving sovereign belligerents who are mutually recognized as equals. This nondiscriminatory concept of a public war involving just enemies based on parity, hence entailing a just war on both sides—*bellum utrimque justum*—establishes the essence of *hostis* upon the principle of *aequalitas*.

In other words, the legitimacy of European state wars was grounded on the premise of an armed confrontation between *hostes aequaliter justi*. These, according to Alberico Gentili were predicated on sovereignty (as *ordo ordinans*, ordering order) and not on the justice or injustice of the reasons for war offered by either side (*NE*, 156–59). A non-state war, therefore, was considered nonpublic, i.e., it did not correspond to state legality, hence its illegitimacy.

In consequence, revolutionaries, robbers, pirates, etc., were not considered *justi hostes* (just enemies) but mere objects to be rendered harmless and/or prosecuted as criminals (*NE*, 153). That was the core concept which regulated the *jus publicum Europaeum*. Kant appended a conspicuous maxim to the concept of *justus hostis* which, although implied by the *jus publicum Europaeum*, was not elaborately conceptualized in terms of discriminatory war: "There are no limits to the rights of a state against an *unjust enemy* (no limits with respect to quantity or degree, though there are limits with respect to quality); that is to say, an injured state may not use any means whatever but may use those means that are allowable to any degree that it is able to in order to maintain what belongs to it."[9] This criminalization of the nonsovereign as *hostis injustus* obtained operational status in the 20th century which countenanced total wars of annihilation. Kant's identification of the *hostis injustus* with the criminal, despite cautious prescriptions, counsels of prudence, and alarmist provisos, makes allowances for discriminatory wars and crusades as a legal method of eliminating effectively the enemy.

Consider also the following fragment from Kant's oversubtle reasoning. Triumphant constitutional states

are not called upon to divide the territory (of the vanquished) among themselves and to force the state, as it were, to disappear from earth, since that would be an injustice against its people, which cannot lose its original right to unite itself into a Commonwealth, *though it can be coerced to adopt a new constitution that by its nature* will be unfavorable to the inclination for war. (*MM*, 155, par. 60; my emphasis)

Kant does not specify whether the imposed constitution is meant to forestall anticolonial war. Yet, the degree and intensity of coercion implied by such constitutional engineering pertains only to protectorates. Such method remains as equivocal and obscure as is the concrete specification of the *hostis injustus*. Kant provides paradoxical answers which, not surprisingly, can be interpreted in any direction at will. The nebulous ground regarding the status of land appropriation, colonial constitutionalism, and the unjust enemy can be further ascertained if we follow closely Kant's reasoning, framed as it is by the contradictions of imperialist legality which it attempts to accommodate. In discussing the right of state after colonial war, Kant concedes that

> [A] defeated state or its subjects do not lose their civil freedom through the conquest of their country. . . . A colony or a province is a people that indeed has its own constitution, its own legislation, and its own land, on which those who belong to another state are only foreigners, even though this other state has supreme executive authority over the colony or province. The state having that executive authority is called the mother state, and the daughter state, though ruled by it, still governs itself (by its own parliament, possibly with a viceroy presiding over it) (*civitas hybrida*). (*MM*, 154–55, par. 58)

Despite all due hesitation and benevolent discretion with regard to the legitimacy of constitutional legality under colonial guardianship, Kant's reasoning cannot rationalize away the pastoral logic[10] of imperial trusteeship as a method of extracting spatial surplus value. This kind of protectoral constitution-making by the curators of international law anticipates the fate of condominia that was to be decided by the 19th- and 20th-century treaty legality. Moreover, this form of imperial legality reduced colonies into daughter states, client states, etc. It marked the beginnings of a geopolitical species of biopower exercised by the caretakers of modernity cum trustees of international law. The distinction itself between mother and daughter states already implies colonial bonds and constitutional patronage within the unfolding family romance of imperialism.

A vivid illustration of such an underlying biopolitical mandate attendant on Kantian exceptions to the rule of justice could be the case of the second Preliminary Article of a Perpetual Peace between states. This postulates that no independent state, large or small, may be acquired by another state by inheritance, exchange, purchase or gift: "For a state, unlike the ground on which it is based, is not a possession (*patrimonium*). It is a society of men, which no one other than itself can command or dispose of. To terminate its existence as a moral personality and make it into a commodity contradicts the idea of the original contract without which the rights of people are unthinkable." However, Kant qualifies this with the following caveat: "in the case of the second article, the prohibition relates only to the mode of acquisition, which is to be forbidden henceforth, but not to the present state of political possessions. For although this present state is not backed up by the requisite legal authority, it was considered lawful in *the public opinion* of every state at the time of the putative acquisition" (*PW*, 97). Although these irregularities are not considered by Kant as an exception to the rule of justice, he does concede that they "allow some subjective latitude according to the circumstances in which they are applied (*leges latae*)" (*PW*, 97).

In order to elucidate this oddity it is advisable to bring into play Kant's disquisition on property right in *The Metaphysics of Morals*. Articles 14 and 16 corroborate in pedestrian fashion Carl Schmitt's alarming assertion that "the History of International Law is a history of land appropriation, land occupation, embargoes, and blockades as a constitutive process for every commonwealth and empire" (*NE*, 48). Of course, it is more than a reasonable probability that Schmitt's animus and motive is to provide those sufficient grounds of legitimation that will absolve Nazi philosophy of any perceivable charges regarding expansionist claims. It is plausible that Schmitt's *nomomachy* petitions the recognition of Nazism within the sanctionable technicalities of a strictly state legality, namely, an *aequalitas hostium* (equality of enemies) that will yield Hitler and National Socialism a status of *justus hostis*. Despite Kant's fear that the exception eventually becomes a rule, Schmitt is able to trade upon the former's antinomies of imperial favoritism as well as on his inconsistent qualification of the odd concept of constitutional condominium which sequentially rationalizes land acquisition. Kant writes:

> There can be two complete owners of one and the same thing, without its being both mine and yours in common; they may only be possessors in common of what belongs to only one of them as his. This happens when one of the so-called joint owners (*condomini*) has only full possession without use, while the other has all the use of the thing along with possession of it. So the one who has full possession without use *(dominus directus)* only restricts the other *(dominus utilis)* to some continual performance without thereby limiting his use of the thing. (*MM*, 90, par. 17)[11]

We may recall that for Kant *possession* of *territory* (according to the second preliminary article of perpetual peace) is compatible with his pacifist imperium, unlike the *state* itself which *cannot be possessed*, therefore enjoying conditional constitutional autonomy (which certainly can be revoked by the *condomini*, according to circumstances). Thus, the constitutive process of land appropriation is not just tacitly assumed but precedes explicitly any legal order. These maxims produce the constitutional logic of colonial *condominia* in terms of world ordering cum biopolitical adjustment, not immeasurably far off from the 20th-century racial geopolitics espoused by Schmitt's *Grossraumtheorie*, i.e., the transition from small space (*Kleinraum*) to large spatial spheres (*Grossraum*). Land acquisition, therefore, along with the relative autonomy of colonial states, becomes the condition of possibility for the peace-building of the federal imperium. Protectorship in this *Grossraum* sense of geopolitical discipline (i.e., protection, security, custody, guardianship) specifies a juridical condition that conjoins reformist superpower politics with the right to discipline within an inexorable spatial logic of influence. Imperialism re-places to all purposes and intents universality with an apparatus of influence. The protectorate, then, is what is disposed by the spatial economy of the imperial apparatus. It is simply the terminal disposition of the spatial logic of governmentality. In other words, even a protectorate striving to assert its quasi-stateness, needs first to be induced as a biopolitical inscription in the disciplinary continuum of spatial spheres of influence. There is nothing outside this spatial apparatus[12] of security and juridical governmentality except the ungovernable counterpoint of anticolonial revolution.

The Thermidorian Closure of Kant's Legal Positivism

Schmitt's contribution as a reader of Kant is, in my view, not so much his assertion about the urgency and intensity of the political. What emerges amorphously from Schmitt's reading is Kant's preoccupation with rescuing the political from the state of nature in the context of a reformist biopolitical imperium. This very gesture, however, seems to defeat the purpose insofar as republican reformism achieves the political by doing away with it, i.e., by transforming itself into Thermidorian imperialism which neutralizes any probing into its origins. Schmitt's contribution lies precisely in the foregrounding of the decisionistic nature of pastoral imperialism which overshadows Kant's republican thought. Schmitt as a reader of Kant enables one to trace the state of exception in the self-exemption of reason, although Schmitt does not pursue this any further. Kant, however, is alert to this disquieting homology which voids claims to rationality of all pretension. In the sixth proposition of the "Idea for a Universal History with a Cosmopolitan Purpose" Kant is undeceiving:

> And even though as a rational creature, he desires a law to impose limits on the freedom of all, he is still misled by his self-seeking animal inclinations into exempting himself from the law where he can. He thus requires a master to break his self-will and force him to obey a universally valid will under which everyone can be free. But where is he to find such a master? Nowhere else but in the human species. But this master will also be an animal who needs a master. . . . Nothing straight can be constructed from such warped wood as that which man is made of. Nature only requires that we should approximate the idea. (*PW*, 46–47)

But even an approximation of the idea is hard to attain because any reckoning with the *pouvoir constitué* (constituted power) presupposes, according to Kant, prior accomplishments, skill, and goodwill, factors which are not easily found in conjunction, except after numerous and unsuccessful attempts. The answer which Kant provides to the question of mastery and sovereignty in terms of self-exemption, goes at the heart of modernity's intractable tension between founding origins and normativity.[13]

Neither pole is explainable by referring one to the other. Constitutional founding typifies the originary character of modernity and foregrounds the interrogative gesture of critique as integral to beginnings. This alone explains the persistence of the political through the impossibility of terminating sustained inquiries regarding origins without at the same time violating truth procedures and fidelity to modernity's revolutionary event, in Badiou's sense. But even in accordance with Kantian protocols of reason, any suspension of the principle of investigation would be a self-incurred error closing off the possibility of further critical enlightenment. The paradox of proscribing inquiry lies in modernity's self-awareness that its beginnings may grow into an affliction of messy complications, restive dilemmas, and unruly "passions for the real." Thus, closure remains an ever present temptation.

Yet, however modern this interdiction is, in its Kantian version, it embodies an archetypical anxiety which perennially haunts the Platonic thought about law and politics. After having experienced a terminal disappointment at Syracuse, Plato writes down no less than twelve books of *Laws*, still in search for a pliable tyrant but also for an ideal state which, he thought, would be a synthesis of the legal codes of Sparta, Crete, and Athens. What is surprisingly missing from Plato's probing in the *Laws* is not the dialogical form (although the Cretan Clinias and the Spartan Megillus are rather uninspiring listeners) but Socrates himself and in particular the method of *Socratic inquiry*. The *Laws* maintain the dialogical form but eliminate dialectical investigation per se which opposed both the unpatriotic sophistic that criticized all being and nonbeing, as well as communitarian ignorance and imprudence.

The *Laws* do not simply override the Socratic method, they rather reject it wholesale in what appears to be one of the most astonishing and tragic inversions in the history of philosophy. This overturning of tables takes place fifty years after the writing of *Gorgias*, of *Phaedo* (whose dramatic setting is Socrates in prison), and the thrilling speech in *Apology*. Thus, Socrates was delivered to posterity as the leading philosopher of thought and justice, executed in the name of an abject fidelity to law. Only that Plato came to adopt the standpoint of his accusers, thus ceding the good life of the just and the beautiful to the order of legal instruction.

On the verge of this inglorious counterevent which amounts to the self-effacement of philosophy, Plato (in the name of the Athenian stranger) states the following: "For in your case (your laws being wisely framed) one of the best of your laws will be that which enjoins that none of the youth shall inquire which laws are wrong and which right, but all shall declare in unison, with one mouth and one voice, that all are rightly established by divine enactment, and shall turn a deaf ear to any one who says otherwise" (*Laws*, Book 1, 634e).[14] Of course, Plato suggests a combined method of lawmaking which tempers compulsion with persuasion. Only that this labor comes through a quite rudimental and uncomplicated manner. In order to enhance consent, Plato introduces a prelude to each legal statement. By prefacing each enactment with a proem, i.e., an introductory discourse predisposing citizens to obedience, Plato expects to avert any inquisitive hubris regarding the origins of law (*Laws*, Book 4, 722–23). Hence legal enactment is not only the state's jurisdiction; it is also invested with an inscrutable authority. In this positivist sense, late Plato abandons the ideal of a new Republic in favor of the second best rule of law. Evidence of Plato's positivist default is also present in his seventh *Epistle* where he urges not only the youth but also the intellectual of sense (*dianooumenon emfrona*) not to interfere with city affairs, even when he disapproves of certain policies or when he finds that the city itself is ill-governed. Because all this is "*mataios erein*," fruitless speech which leads to a pointless death (*Epistle* VII, 331c–d). But rather than this being a political withdrawal from the cacophonous and unprincipled logomachy of the marketplace, it is meant by Plato to be a cynical act of deference to expediency and the deceptive imperium of raison d'état.

My argument is that there are strong resonances of this Platonic uneasiness and even cynicism in Kant's perspective on the French Revolution. Being a reluctant enthusiast of the French Revolution, and by virtue of this improbable confounding of law and affect, Kant comes to embody the quintessential ambivalence of modernity between the will to revolution and constitution, interrogation of the law and unquestioning conformity to its rule, the quest for truth and the pursuit of profit, politics and property. In his extensive general remark "On the Effects with Regard to Rights That Follow from the Nature of the Civil Union," Kant warns austerely (and with strikingly Platonic overtones) about procedures of sustained agitation: "A people should not inquire with any practical aim in view into the origin of the supreme authority to which it is subject; that is a subject ought not to rationalize for the sake of action about the origin of this authority, as a right that can still be called into question (*ius controversum*) with regard to the obedience he owes to it" (*MM*, 129–30). For a people already subject to constitutional law such a sequence of inquiries into origins which keeps the dialectic of truth and knowledge from rigidifying "are pointless and, moreover, threaten a state with danger." It is evident that the constitution of modernity engenders a logic of origins not in terms of causality but in terms of novelty which thrusts the executive rationality of the state into crisis.

Kant's distrust of origins betrays a profound fear of the plebeian multitude. The latter is viewed as a source of happiness which can be accomplished only in a state of nature, not in a civil state. Hence it is considered as a factor of disorder. He treats origins as entirely deceptive. By driving the normative pole of modernity against its originary foundations, Kant forecloses any critical investigation of the sources of legality:

If a subject, having pondered over the ultimate origin of the ruling authority, wanted to resist this authority, he would be punished, got rid of, or expelled (as the outlaw, *exlex*) in accordance with the laws of this authority, that is, with every right. A law that is so holy (inviolable) that is already a crime even to call it in doubt in a practical way, and to suspend its effect for a moment, is thought as if it must have arisen not from men but from the highest, flawless lawgiver;

that is what the saying "all authority is from God" means. This saying is not an assertion about the historical basis of the civil constitution; instead it sets forth an Idea as a *practical principle of reason*: the principle that the presently existing legislative authority ought to be obeyed, whatever its origin. (*MM*, 130)

Over and again, we come across a divine economy of authority, with God being figured as an apparatus. Due to the insufficiency of human virtue, existing legality be that revolutionary or counterrevolutionary is thus sanctified irrespective of origins. Whether constitutional monarchy or parliamentary oligarchy, it remains inessential for the utility of sovereignty. The apparatus of positive legality cum divine economy is above regimes. In this sense, Kant constitutionalizes the necessity of the apparatus as a disposition of rationality. That reflective judgment is assigned to a public authority which branches out into the legislature and the executive does not entail any limit to sovereignty whatsoever. For the republican constitution, according to Kant, cannot contain any provision that would entitle any sectional authority or jurisdiction within a state "to resist the supreme commander in case he should violate the law of the constitution, and so limit him" (*MM*, 130). Hence the supposedly moderating function of a constitution intended to limit the sovereign command is an absurdity for Kant because the act of containing sovereignty belongs to *prudence*, not *right*. It follows that people should restrain the task of politics to the mode of government by representation, a task which is incomparably more beneficial in Kant's view than investigating the sources of sovereignty. Kant is alarmed at the randomness of origin myths. Inexplicable and miraculous as they are, they become resources of a plebeian fantasmagoria, spectral meaning, and fanaticism.

On the other hand, judgment as the augmented rationality of the executive estate is posited as an antipopulist antidote. This prescription was devised as a remedy for plebeian adventurism, i.e., modernity's delusionary obsession with the realization of origins and the initiation of new beginnings. Yet, in the end it undermined the very principle of publicness. Kant's distrust of the revolutionary public of the commons echoes the intensity which engulfed the French Revolution, i.e., a split between the Jacobin appeal to the people as the grounding source for further originary action and the Thermidorian terror which effectively terminated the revolution as a political sequence.

In sum, the Thermidorian apparatus reduced law to the protection of property, security, and peace with universality relegated entirely to a secondary concern (*M*, 129). Boissy d'Anglas, the quintessential Thermidorian, according to Badiou, invokes the pacifying power of law as a medium for suppressing revolutionary movements in the supposedly "sleepy colonies." The three maxims of Thermidorian legality (which in modified and amended version figure in Kant's "Doctrine of Right" and "Perpetual Peace") stipulate firstly that the colonies belong to France precisely because of landownership there. Secondly, Law compels pacification of the anticolonial movement because it threatens *property*. Thirdly, direct administrative control of the colonies is desirable because the security of the French Republic is at stake (*M*, 131).

My argument is that when all is said and done, and despite extenuating circumstances, Kant's legal positivism is already strategically predisposed to compromise the principle of publicity, to adjust the faculty of practical reason to raison d'état, and to turn over political judgment to the juridical imperium of the Thermidorian apparatus. Thus, the *sensus communis* unravels under the exception revealing the *sensus privatus* cum Thermidorian providence: "the head of state has only rights against his subjects and no duties (that he can be coerced to fulfill). Moreover, even if the organ of the head of state, the ruler, proceeds contrary to law, for example, if he goes against the law of equality in assigning the burden of the state in matters of taxation, recruiting, and so forth, subjects may indeed oppose this by complaints but not by resistance" (*MM*, 130).

Expectedly, Kant proscribes the right to revolution and by implication any right to resistance: "for a people to be authorized to resist, there would have to be a public law permitting it to resist, (that is) a provision that makes the people by one and the same judgment sovereign over the ruler," which is self-contradictory because "the people wants to be the judge in its own suit" (*MM*, 130). Insofar as obedience to prevailing law takes precedence and overrules all other obligations, revolution can never be sanctioned on sufficient rational grounds or be defended in the name of just causes. However imperfect a sovereign is, he ought to subsist since regime law is a sacrosanct embodiment of reason. Positive law is upheld not by subordinating morality to politics but by reference to the divine rights of rulership, however autocratic they are.[16]

We should recall that the French monarchy rested on the prescription of a constitutional paradox. A presumably absolute monarchy could not encroach on the existing body of rights and immunities enshrined by a medieval constitution without imperiling its rule. Given the impotence of the king to levy higher taxes, he proceeded undoubtedly in accordance with constitutional protocols by convening the Estates General, the nearest thing to a representative institution at the time. By assuming the mandate of reform from the sovereign, however, the Estates General triggered the formation of parties and soon afterward it claimed sovereignty for itself, i.e., advocating representation of all Frenchmen without distinction, ending the feudal order, expropriating Church lands, terminating censorship restrictions, obliterating age-old administrative and provincial divisions, and ultimately by drafting a new constitution.

According to Kant, however, this sequence amounted to less than a revolution. As the king's act of summoning the Estates General in 1789 was practically an act of resignation and voluntary abdication of the throne, it follows that legal continuity was not disrupted. If that was a revolution then the king was the "first revolutionary" in a plausible scenario of legal change of rule in terms of continuity, despite the storming of the Bastille. And that is precisely the reason for Kant's staunch condemnation of the execution of the king. His status was an embodiment of legal continuity (*MM*, 132). A defective constitution can be amended only by the initiative of the sovereign, that is, by reform from above and not by initiative from below which amounts to revolution. Resistance is warranted only by proxy, i.e., by people's representatives and not by the people's direct involvement, "combining at will to coerce the government to take a certain course of action, so itself performing an act of executive authority" (*MM*, 133). Once the revolution prevails, however, and a new constitutional order consolidates, Kant prescribes blind obedience to the new revolutionary legality.

This explains to a great extent why Kant's oddly peculiar enthusiasm for the French Revolution remains on principle strictly confined to that of a more or less free rider's disinterested sympathy and not in the least entailing any practical assistance and solidarity. Absent of any spirited predisposition for solidarity and militant vigor, lacking, in other words, a strong motivational component, this impartial viewpoint of the spectator secures a mannerly and urbane impersonality in judgment, but entails no morally required assistance. What is important for Kant's impartialist justification of revolution is not the militant will and fidelity of revolutionaries to the realization of the latent possibilities of a situation but the retrospective viewpoint of the spectators who do not give in to the supposed fanaticism of the actors.

Kant appears to stake too much on the distinction between spectator enthusiasm and actor fanaticism. Although in fact he concedes that "any affect is blind either in the selection of its purpose or (if that were to have been given by reason) in the manner of achieving it."[17] Kant acknowledges that without the rapturous joy of enthusiasm, nothing great can be accomplished. Enthusiasm strains our forces by ideas which impart to the mind mightier and more permanent effects than impulses produced by sense. Such a moral agency cautiously animated by a well-proportioned spectator enthusiasm resonates, however, with an opportunism of sorts insofar as it remains risklessly bystanding, refraining from action, and tending the void between a singular, local decision and a universal truth until the singular can achieve to be universally predicated and postulated by an altered legality or situation. The spectator's enthusiasm, therefore, warranted as it is by a safe distance, is qualified by reason to engage in sanctioned transgressions without yielding to fanatic "delusions beyond all bounds of sensibility." Kant appears to discern between unbridled imagination and madness which he considers "a passing accident that presumably strikes even the soundest understanding on occasion" as opposed to "mania, a disease that deranges it" (*CJ*, 136). Yielding to the latter is like attributing divine purpose to nature by way of determinate rather than reflective judgment.

This is consistent with Kant's reasoned respect for the French Revolution which of course does not add up to approbating its revolutionary origin. Had he displayed fidelity to origins he would be affirming subsequent work done in the name of the event. That would also be a commitment to renaming processes carried out by interveners, who are the only ones able and willing to know if something ever had taken place. Kant is mistrustful of origins because of the fateful propensity of one generation after another to perceive themselves as a probate court authorized to authenticate a political will to origins. This, he fears, will release an ever renewable passion for perpetual rethinking and revalidation of beginnings by way of an apprenticeship in revolution. Instead, Kant aspires to channel revolutionary enthusiasm to republican reformism before the former escalates to a revolution in permanence.

It is evident that there can only be Kantian spectators, not Kantian actors. In consequence, the space of the political is purged of the dialectic between revolution and constitution, with all hopes for reform placed in the executive patriotism of the administrative staff. In this way, even a monarchy ruling without representation can qualify as republican government. Dieter Henrich commenting on Kant and "The Meaning of Rational Action in the State" argues forcefully that it is lamentable indeed to expect the general welfare and progress of humanity "through actions which Kant himself regards supremely unjust from the standpoint of reason and legality, toward which the very unfolding of progress is oriented!" (*MRA*, 110).

However, insofar as the revolution is not simply dismissed but emphatically condemned as a radical evil and fanatic derangement, one wonders whether what is involved in the privileging of the spectator is a failure of perception of the situation. Short of affective insight, a moral agent understandably can never perform acts of intervention. A duty-bound reason adopting spectator-judgment and impartial maxims affectively indifferent to the situation are sure to fail in application because of a lack of discernment. Holding universal and rational maxims at hand cannot and will not tell actors when and where people are suffering, precisely because impartial judgment may not regard the situation as presenting a political issue or moral challenge. On this issue Arendt's commentary is unerring. Impartiality as a viewpoint of framing judgments "does not tell one how to act. It does not even tell one how to apply the wisdom, found by virtue of occupying a 'general standpoint' to the particulars of political life. . . . Kant does tell one how to take others into account; he does not tell one how to combine with them in order to act" (*LK*, 44).

Learning to be an intervener may prescribe actions not considered to be options before the event, hence perceptual shifts appear necessary in order to pierce through the reified *sensus communis* which animates the existing state of the situation. This is nolens volens, an act of moral and political unbinding which extends the situation beyond the bounds of common sense. In Badiou's glossary, it subtracts itself from the representative fiction of commonsensical accounts, by revealing its discursive inconsistencies, seeking instead consistency of acts and maxims which affirm the singularity of the event.

Methodological Digression: *L'Histoire Evénémentielle* and the Sociological Thermidor

Badiou's skepticism if not hostility toward sociology's obsession with empirical regularities is not totally unwarranted. Sociological insight into the singularity of an event is a rare exception in a tradition which has been onerously subordinate to positivist mandates from its inception. At present, however, indications of such a rare accident are visible and vocal. They can be intuited by a mental opening afforded by an episode of contentious confrontation with rational choice positivism. In this dispute, William Sewell literally seizes for a moment what

Badiou calls the "unequalled intensity of existence" as an entry point into politics and subjective composition: "in most revolutions worthy of the name, the goals of the revolution, and for that matter the identities of the actors as well, are significantly transformed in the course of the revolutionary process. What makes political struggles revolutionary is that they fundamentally change the nature of the ideological and institutional alternatives available to members of the polity, and that they do so by elaborating new and surprising political and moral options."[18] Indeed, the subject, according to Badiou, "in no way pre-exists the process. The subject is absolutely nonexistent in the situation 'before' the event. We might say that it is the process of truth that induces a subject."[19]

Doubtlessly, there was no other better fit to initiate this promising encounter between sociology and philosophy than the ex-positivist William Sewell. The following outrageous remark concerning the French Revolution exposes with defiant spirit all the positivist pretensions of the sociological Thermidor: "the consequences of the rupture have only recently begun to appear and additional, perhaps surprising, consequences may yet emerge" (*LH*, 261).

The break with positivism retrieved here involves a gesture toward the event as the truth of innovation which interrupts inherited significations and intensions and not as a hard structural fact of knowledge. But this is also a gesture which guards itself against self-objectification. Epistemologically, it is a process that involves "a confrontation of form with its real limit or impasse." In other words, this site of resourceful creativity, i.e., the formlessness of the event remains internal to the means of formalization.[20] In William Sewell's evental sociology which could be renamed *sociology of truth*, events have the power to transform social causality, hence contradicting the methodological assumption that causal structures are uniform through time: "events must be assumed to be capable of changing not only the balance of causal forces operating but the very logic by which consequences follow from occurrences or circumstances" (*LH*, 101). What is suggested is that the truth implied in this possibility may not be subject to immediate meaning, despite Sewell's gracious gesture toward Hermeneutics. In fact, it comes through the hermeneutic failure of meaning and the impasse of any interest analysis whatsoever.

William Sewell, then, appears to a significant extent as resisting the re-enactment of the positivist Thermidor in sociology conceived as a restoration of the primacy of calculable interests, causality, continuity, or even meaning. In other words, he seems to be vertically opposed to sociology's founding positivist myth and its persistent fascination with master processes and teleological temporality. All this is condensed in Sewell's opposition to the rational choice paradigm which typically asserts that interest lies at the core of every subjective composition, thus rendering virtue incongruent with, and extraneous to any politics of change. Sewell courageously, indeed, contests Charles Tilly's reduction of the French Revolution into a repertoire of violent incidents which merely "accelerated already existing trends."[21] This rollback of the revolution into a continuum of violent protest arising from gradual evolutionary processes as a consequence of state centralization is of course of Tocquevillean provenance and will be addressed in the following section.

In some respect, however, Sewell also appears to be radicalizing a critical opening effected from within the positivist logic of quantitative history. For instance, Emmanuel Le Roy Ladurie,[22] a master practitioner of quantitative history, concedes that a different and more complex heuristic approach (which would restore to the event its proper status, even in quantitative and structural history) might be imagined: "to move in the opposite direction, back through time, starting from a given structure, the existence of which is well attested and empirically evident, *but the origins of which are shrouded in mystery, and to look for the initial traumatic event which may have acted as a catalyst for its emergence. The event itself would then have to be relocated always bearing in mind its aleatory features, within the structures prevailing at the time of its occurrence.*"[23] In this sense, William Sewell reiterates, in my view, Le Roy Ladurie's diagonal gesture toward *histoire événementielle*.[24] Most importantly, however, he restores to the contemporary sociological imaginary a missing inquisitive virtue and decency which concerns the trauma and perverse ironies attendant on the colonial encounter. Sewell should, thus, be duly credited for addressing this void in sociological inquiry (*LH*, 197–224).

Yet, in his engagement with Marshal Sahlins it seems that Sewell concedes too much "to anthropological structuralism as a privileged method for framing the colonial event" despite his novel formulations such as the "structure of conjunctures" and the "conjuncture of structures." My dissenting point is that colonialism cannot qualify as an event because it is radically incapable of any truth whatsoever, i.e., it cannot invoke a universal nomination of the event, but only a conjunctural manipulation of presumed substance and full particularity which are only forms of inertia and intriguing imitations. Rather, the colonial encounter is a signifier of the counterevent par excellence, as it steers through a simulacrum of truth. This is, then, what my critical supplement to Sewell's sociology of punctual change would be: a counterimperial epistemology of the event. Here I certainly receive my cue from Foucault's attempt to retrieve the event as a nodal problematic of history and especially from his enduring insight into the genealogy of relations of force that go beyond the domain of signifying structures. When faced with the challenge of colonialism and imperialism it is, I think, critically important to heed Foucault's warning not simply to transpose the emphasis from structure to the event by "locating everything on one level. . . . The problem is to distinguish among events, to differentiate the networks and levels to which they belong and to reconstitute the lines along which they are connected and engender one another." From this, however, follows that our point of reference "should not be the great model of language and signs but that of war and battle." Because, Foucault says, the defining force of history that is absolutely critical, "has the form of war rather than that of language: relations of power, not relations of meaning. History has no meaning, though this is not to say that it is absurd or incoherent. On the contrary, it is intelligible and should be susceptible of analysis down to the smallest detail—but this is in accordance with the intelligibility of struggles, of strategies, and tactics. Neither the dialectic as a logic of contradictions, nor semiotics as the structure of communication can account for the intrinsic intelligibility of conflicts. Dialectic is a way of evading the always open and hazardous reality of conflict by reducing it to a Hegelian skeleton, and 'semiology' is a way of avoiding its violent, bloody, and lethal character by reducing it to the calm Platonic form of language and dialogue."[25] This will become more evident in my treatment of Tocqueville.

Tocqueville's Thermidorian Positivism and Its Discontents: The Moral Calculus of Ennobled Colonialism

> *But now, become oppressors in their turn,*
> *Frenchmen had changed a war of self-defence*
> *For one of conquest,* losing sight *of all they had struggled for.*
>
> W. Wordsworth, Prelude

In unraveling the knot between the colonial quest of the West and its underlying positivist presumption, it is necessary to elucidate the *Thermidorian hypothesis.* The Thermidor, according to Badiou, "marks the passage from a principled and defensive Republican war to a war of rapine and conquest and the trafficking of army supplies. But above all, there are the close ties with the colonialists and slave traders" (*M*, 130). Badiou, however, conceptualizes the Thermidorian question by focusing on the political incapacitation of *virtue* and its identification with *terror.* This operation is carried out by a counterrevolutionary order consisting of the colonial lobby, financial speculators, and pillaging generals, which undertakes to couple the state to sheer interest, property, and colonial war. In other words, the Thermidorian turn signals the termination of the political sequence that was inaugurated in 1792 and lasted until 9 Thermidor 1794, effected by the state-processing of political subjectivity and its attachment to calculated interest and colonial speculation. Colonialism in this sense is coextensive with the Thermidorian order. Insofar as the center of gravity is no longer the revolutionary situation itself but the *state of the situation,* the only subjective trajectory that counts is the one which plunges in colonial speculation and situational placement: "As a subject, the Thermidorian is constitutively *in search of a place,*" Badiou argues (*M*, 133).

But, why is this Thermidorian operation in itself so important for understanding the positivist disarticulation of politics from any inventive principle, maxim or critical sequence? Because, Badiou argues, the institutionalization of the formal features of Thermidor (i.e., the self-aggrandizing activism and enterprising parliamentarism which thus effectively privatize legality) "invariably signifies the concurrent eviction of thought, specifically from the political field" (*M*, 136). Otherwise put, this persistent Thermidorian pathology renders principled politics at home unintelligible and anticolonial revolt abroad unthinkable. Both are reduced to a seriality of violent convulsions which threaten imperial grandeur and the pursuit of private enrichment.

Alexis de Tocqueville is that political and intellectual figure who (by virtue of this combination) epitomizes and sublimates the long-term consequences of the Kantian logic of imperial constitutionalism that circumscribes the moral limits, the cognitive horizon, and legal bounds of a revolutionary sequence. Like Kant, Tocqueville considered political stability indispensable for the survival and greatness of the republic, hence his opposition to constitutional change at will. Interestingly, while being a radiant illustration of the consequences of the Thermidorian dispensation, especially with regard to its imperial adventurism, Tocqueville nonetheless registered quite vocally his discontent with and despair over the state of depravity and corruption it brought about.

Let us recall that Tocqueville had forcefully argued that the French Revolution was an unnecessary and pointless bloodshed, as the Ancient Regime was heading through successive reforms in the same direction of equality and administrative centralization anyway.[26] Like Kant, Tocqueville yielded to the aftereffect of the revolution but dismissed the event itself. Unlike Kant, however, he proceeded to dissect the afflictions induced by the subsiding of the event, namely, indifference, apathy, docility, selfishness, and lack of political will which he considered to be the new civic disorders of democratic despotism. For Tocqueville equality was not a static state but a long-term process that was initiated by the *ancien régime* and culminated in the French Revolution. This process was irreversible and consistent with modernity and its democratic thrust toward the condition of equalization. Militating against it would be vain and meaningless.

Yet, Tocqueville, as the canonical and normative Thermidorian par excellence, was also fully aware of the vicious pathologies which progressed and multiplied under the new order as they undermined its legitimacy. Tocqueville was farsighted but still a desperate positivist. He admonished the disaffected dignitaries and notable families still attached to the old regime and secretly aspiring to the restoration of the Bourbon monarchy, to settle down in the new order and strive confidently to redirect its institutions from within. His vision was to rescue the aristocratic freedoms enjoyed under the old regime and reproduce them through the constitutional regulation of equality and the decentralization of authority in the postrevolutionary republic.

All the same, Tocqueville assaulted the liberal government of François Guizot who considered as its primary task precisely the pacification of a country convulsed and confused by revolutions, wars and counterrevolutions. Tocqueville was alerted to the fact that the Thermidorian long term was virtually becoming the vanishing point of politics itself. This was undermining, in his view, the republican premises of the postrevolutionary order. Being the spiritual trustee of aristocratic republicanism, Tocqueville was quick to realize that the supplanting of principles by the distribution of favors and political privileges misused for economic advantage was ultimately privatizing public life and depoliticizing the parliament itself. Thus, Tocqueville felt he was "vegetating in a shadow-boxing parliament" while "the lack of great political debates and clashes that could lead to the formation of political groupings" condemned citizens into passive franchise.[27] He thus forewarned the political class comfortably accommodated by the Thermidorian system that it was sleeping on a volcano:

"any government which sows vice will sooner or later reap revolutions."[28]

However, Tocqueville's discontent with the unfreedom of an atomizing condition of progressive equalization and its attendant self-seeking politics—which fused with Bonapartist nationalism and the empire of spoils—should not be viewed as an anti-imperialist critique of the centralized state. For instance, his vision with regard to the state form of French colonial rule in Algeria was in accord with a sufficiently strong civilian state able to subdue and tranquilize the population by manipulating nothing but interest: "it would not be very wise to believe that we can succeed in binding the natives to us by a community of usages, but we may hope to do so by building a community of interests. Already in many places this type of tie is coming into existence. . . . Everywhere the natives receive higher prices for their crops and labor because of our presence. On the other hand, our farmers willingly employ indigenous population. The European needs the native to increase the value of his land; the Arab needs the European to obtain a higher salary. Thus interest may bring together two men otherwise far apart."[29]

Tocqueville, then, was not immune to tactical as well as strategic uses of self-interest when it came to the consolidation of French colonial rule. His undertaking to synchronize liberalism with colonialism, by making both profitable to all, presupposes a Bonapartist state apparatus, i.e., a precarious balancing between corporatist interests which Tocqueville so vehemently despised as an agency of centralization inimical to liberty.

However bewildering and insoluble Tocqueville's self-contradictions[30] are, it is more than probable that he did associate the moral vitality of aristocratic liberty with the Frankish genealogy of conquest and the Germanist tradition of monarchy. The latter was aggregated in the forest assemblies by the nobility, in contrast to the absolutist monarchy that was despotic and of Romanist bourgeois inspiration.[31] The lineage of this prerogative of conquest lays open interesting elective affinities between the existential norms of Tocqueville's republican liberalism and the moral calculus of his commitment to colonialism.

Tocqueville's pledge to aristocratic liberty was not a sort of idiosyncratic inclination. In fact, this singular form of egalitarian liberty was the sustaining force behind the imperial drive of medieval Germanism which laid the social and political foundations of the making of Europe. In particular, Tacitus early on had thoughtfully considered the constitution of Germanic peoples and the structure of their kingship, emphasizing the fact that their kings were elected (although noble by birth) and that consequently they exercised no absolute arbitrary power. If there ever was an invariable of *Germanentum*, that was it. Not "*Blut und Boden*" but the "union of the free," "Frank and Free." In the assembly the state-chief or king was given a hearing not because of his power to command but because his advice carried weight: "if a proposal displeases them, the people shout their dissent; if they approve, they clash their spears. To express approbation with their weapons is their most complimentary way of showing agreement. . . . On matters of minor importance only the chiefs debate; on major affairs, the whole community."[32]

This fundamental quality of the Germanic constitution which combines a combative equalitarianism with liberty, contrasts sharply with the Roman tradition. Although the constitution of the Roman Empire was identified as republican, the emperor exercised supreme authority as the chief of military command, held tribunal power, was personally inviolable, could convene the Senate and initiate legislation, had power to intervene at his discretion in the provinces, run his own treasury, he was *pontifex maximus* of the state religion, and even supervised public morals.[33] The Roman people were thus effectively reduced to the functional enslavement of breads and circuses, Roman soldiers served only for a salary, while Roman generals were flashing out their status and wealth. In contrast to this sumptuous republic of appearances and sophisticated corruption, the value system which underpinned the Germanic constitution was sustained by the nobility of honor, valor, courage, fidelity, and the esteem of peers in a folk assembly of equals. These communal enclaves of egalitarian liberty which lasted through the medieval age "were basically a Germanic inheritance, survival of the original rural systems of the forest." Likewise, the legal and constitutional system of the medieval synthesis entailed "folk justice of a popular character and a tradition of formally reciprocal obligation between rulers and ruled within a common tribal community."[34]

And yet, this folk condition of forest egalitarianism, which ensured to landlord nobility and ordinary warriors their liberty, was founded on a colonial frontier of immense peregrinations, demographic diffusion, and conquest. This expansion of pioneering colonial aristocracies through conquest determined not only the subsequent evolution of Western feudalism but also the imperial map of medieval Europe through the creation of overseas crusader states and colonial societies. The preexistent imperial structure of invader communities directed by a colonial thrust from the Frankish north, generated "a slow process of fusion, integrating both Germanic and Roman elements into a new synthesis that was to supersede both of them" (*PA*, 122). Charlemagne brought this process to maturity and completion by reviving the empire which effected the political, military, and cultural unification of the West.

The above necessary digression on the diffusion of the Frankish aristocratic diaspora throughout Europe and the Eastern Mediterranean provides, in my view, a long missing but enabling genealogical framework for the reassessment of Tocqueville's liberal-aristocratic defense of imperialism. Far from constituting an anomalous exception in the making of his intellectual profile, Tocqueville's imperialist propriety could be viewed in terms of hereditary conformity to a persistent Frankish ethos characteristic of conquest lordship. Many aspects of the aggressive dynamism and acquisitive expansionism conspicuously displayed on the Frankish frontier of conquest and colonization figure strongly in Tocqueville's writings on empire and slavery.

The "crusading tournament" of the Frankish aristocracy, which had pursued the gamble of foreign conquest and had established dynasties from Scotland to Cyprus, obeyed the logic of a forced complex of inherited conquest characteristics. That was a kind of *mentis ambitio*, a transferable birthright of the desire to rule, i.e., "a psychological striving that surpassed simple economic need."[35] But, more precisely, what really was the *differentia specifica* of this medieval type of ennobled imperialism?

In the first place, according to Bartlett, it was a process of replication rather than differentiation. In other words, this specimen of imperial expansion followed a logic of cellular multiplication of homeland norms and legal procedures rather than a core-periphery schema of hierarchical subordination of the latter to the former. Interestingly, the prime actors of the imperial system that distinguished the Middle Ages were not state formations but *consortia* of "entrepreneurial associations of Frankish knights, Latin priests, merchants, townsmen and as non-voting members, peasants" (*ME*, 307).

The standard case exemplifying such a freelance, stateless imperialism— although monarchical direction was still important—which sustained a successful expansionary movement in the eleventh and twelfth centuries, was certainly the crusading enterprise that transformed the political landscape of the Levant. For instance, the crusading consortium which conquered Cyprus and the entire Eastern Mediterranean was not driven by imperial statecraft but "by a curious assemblage of Western magnates and knights, ecclesiastics of both a papalist and an independent bent, and Italian merchants, impelled by motives as diverse as their status and origins. Contemporaries remarked how the armies of the First Crusade were 'without lord, without prince' or how they 'fought without King, without emperor'" (*ME*, 308). What was then so outstanding in this imperial formation of eclectic *consortia*? Certainly the diverse and divergent interests that constituted its drive for conquest do not carry exceptional value. Rather, it was the absence of statecraft and political masterminding. What precisely distinguished medieval colonialism was a kind of *voluntarium inter fatres*, an almost autopoetic, self-regulated lay-clerical *consortium*.

By and large, the generic features of this Frankish specimen of civic-corporatist imperialism and colonial settlement are reflectively reinforced and reclaimed by Tocqueville in the case of French Algeria. "We must count principally," Tocqueville argues, "on the free, passionate, and energetic actions of individuals" for colonial success.[36] The colonists' freedom to act is less restrained than in the mother country: "we should learn from this fact" (*W*, 91).

That is the reason Tocqueville was so opposed to the subjection of the colonial society of French Africa under a permanent state of exception: "All right. But it is still necessary to indicate in advance and permanently what the exception should consist in and where the rules apply" (*W*, 106). And yet, he goes on wondering in the typical form of an impeccable positivism which legitimizes the state of exception: "why could we not establish through law what had been founded on organic ordinances (that is those relative to the creation and the division of powers)?" (*W*, 106). In fact, he argues "I am not opposed to allowing the case of emergency to remain. This is necessary, but instead of saying that decrees made in cases of emergency must be ratified by the government, which means nothing, we must fix a time after which the decree is nullified, and not rightful law, if it is not ratified" (*W*, 106). The officialdom of the war ministry as well as the military governor of Algeria "are the least appropriate men to organize and even to imagine a colonial civil society" (*W*, 106). Insofar as the colonial society of French Africa rests on the arbitrary authority of ministerial decrees which substitute civil justice, then its foundations "rest on nothing solid."

But why is Tocqueville so forcefully emphatic on the virtues of a civil and rational colonial legality instead of simply accommodating his positivism within the circumstances of exceptional powers and summary proceedings that will eventually be naturalized? Because, he argues, we cannot confide to a military man "the work of colonization, which is our greater task" (*W*, 108). Because "what matters most when one wants to create and develop a colony quickly is to ensure that those who arrive there feel exiled as little as possible, and that they encounter, if possible, *a perfect image of their homeland.* All the colonizing peoples have done that" (*W*, 110; my emphasis). The Greeks and the Romans had sustained this municipal liberty in their colonial ventures of the past while the English gave us their own modern counterpart with the American colonies. Tocqueville envisioned the same fortune for Algeria. He, of course, forgot to mention the medieval consortium of Frankish colonialism that was almost homegrown. In all, Tocqueville appeared to be normatively committed to a model of colonialism which ought to replicate, as Bartlett argued above, rather than differentiate. In effect, he concluded that the French colony of Algeria should not be kept as a dependency but as an ideal replica of the home nation, approximating constitutional perfection as possible.

Short of this vision, however, which ran aground on the harsh realities of colonialism, Tocqueville adjusted his legal positivism to a second order civilian rule. Although that was a shorthand version, lacking much of the egalitarian splendor of the canonical Frankish model of colonialism initiated by imperial brotherhoods, Tocqueville's proposals for colonial reform retained much of its vital ethos. That may or may not be a paradox, but Tocqueville, we should be reminded, had delicately acclimatized his "precious liberties" to the state of exception of the colonial situation: "In any case, we can say in a general way that all the political liberties must be suspended in Algeria. But, for almost all the rest, I maintain that there are only advantages and no inconveniences in faithfully reproducing in Africa what exists among us" (*W*, 112). By these, Tocqueville means corporatist, intermediary bodies of manufacturing and commercial councils "not elected, but chosen by the governor allowed under certain circumstances to make their wishes known" through forms of indirect representation (*W*, 112).

The background medieval vision which contrasts with Tocqueville's watered-down colonial corporatism is of course the nobilitarian maxim of Frankish expansion: "*All colonies began as communes;* in antiquity as in our own time, they have almost all owed their birth and their development to the communal spirit" (*W*, 112; my emphasis). Hence, in order to sustain a semblance of credibility for the reflexive continuation of medieval corporatism, Tocqueville needed to call urgently and without further postponement for the reconstruction of the destroyed communal spirit of municipal power. Yet, the heterogeneity of the

Algerian population made election a disadvantage to functional colonial rule: "So do not have any elected municipal bodies. But at least have appointed ones and give back to these bodies, from whom you have nothing to fear, as they come from you and are dependent on you, the responsibility of making use of the municipality's resources. . . . An active municipal power is at the same time more necessary and less dangerous (in Algeria) than elsewhere: more necessary because a social life that does not yet exist must be created there; less dangerous because *there is no need to fear that municipal liberty will degenerate into political license*" (*W*, 113; my emphasis).

This subtraction of the political nerve of municipal liberty (which was precisely what qualified the Frankish imperium) along with Tocqueville's preparedness to sacrifice medieval immunities in the name of property, consigns his colonial agenda to the Thermidorian folder: "Who does not see that one moves to a colony to make money and not to make war?" Apparently, no one will come if they know in advance that their property will be subject to requisition "by the unlimited jurisdiction of the administrative court" (*W*, 114). In other words, Tocqueville's reformist colonialism agonizes with the discontents of the colonizers who paradoxically are dominated by their domination, as they themselves are the victims of their own instruments of colonization.[37] Tocqueville, who even considered becoming himself a colonist by purchasing land in Algeria,[38] was at great pains coping with the moral and political strains of what may be called a *self-inflicted colonialism*. What Tocqueville evidently underestimated was that the colonial apparatus of the Thermidor presupposed a certain functionalist invariant in terms of which administrative rules fused indiscriminately with legislative and executive power. This he correctly understood as a state of exception, only that the latter could only be installed as an *apparatus* of counterinsurgency and not as a *field* of competing norms and concepts of reform.[39]

But even in the case of the abolition of slavery, of which Tocqueville was a cunning and prudent advocate, the essential stake was not so much slave emancipation itself but the hegemonic and preemptive maneuver to retain the Thermidorian colonies in exchange. For this reason, Tocqueville suggested an orderly and disciplined emancipation of the slaves.[40] His proposal included not only sufficient subsidies and compensation for the plantation owners but also a training of the former slaves into "free wage labor" through the enforcement of legislation against landownership and vagabondage, i.e., moratorium on the freedoms of movement, property, and residence that would force the emancipated slaves to remain in the plantations as wage earners. These measures, Tocqueville argues, are not only "the most effective but also in reality the least oppressive of all the *exceptional measures* to which we could have recourse" (*W*, 221; my emphasis).[41]

By transplanting the pastoral ethos of slavery into capitalism, Tocqueville inaugurates in principle the first biopolitical mutation of imperialism that was destined to become the axiomatic rationality of *preventive counterinsurgency* in the second half of the panoptic 20th century. "What are we exactly doing?" Tocqueville asks and responds thus: "We are placing them artificially in the position in which the European worker finds himself naturally. Assuredly, that is no tyranny, and the man on whom only this obstacle is imposed as he leaves slavery, would not seem to have any right to complain" (*W*, 221).

That was indeed the absolute *renovatio imperii*. Nonetheless, the passage from the old empire to the new and to modernity proper was marked indelibly by the reflexive medievalization of biopower, not by the universal consciousness of a common humanity. Only one thing remains emphatically unambiguous in this shift. By embracing both *right* and *non-right*, the new spirit of imperialism fixates itself pragmatically to the *no thing* as its object. Hence, although positively existing, it becomes at the same time a virtual impossibility. A contemporary of Tocqueville in 1851, Melville charted the contours of this incalculable positivity of nothingness in literary form. Captain Ahab, of course, shall always calculate the drifting of the elusive Moby Dick, ascertaining seasons for hunting him in particular latitudes. Waged slavery, this new dreadful force of being, conjured, anatomized, and potentiated by Marx as an Epicurean swerve, fixated temporarily by Tocqueville's imperialist humanism, and imagined by Melville as an errant dread-provoking white whale, is the nothing that promises to become all by reminding Ahab of his unconscious thrownness in the deadly waters of modernity.

Epilogue

What I hope I have accomplished in this essay is to have traced the tensions and irresolvable aporias between the making of Empire, the professed liberty advocated by two outstanding connoisseurs of the French Revolution and the spurious attempts at colonization. Yet, by examining the complicity of philosophical refinement and sociological insight with the overseas distribution of land and commerce I was not simply interested in elucidating authorial intent by reference to historical context. Rather, what I attempted was to think the philosophical antinomies of the imperial mind as a critical background for rethinking a) the intricate knot binding the notions of ennobled colonialism and Enlightenment pacifism to the willpower of counterrevolution at home and b) the terminal discontinuity between revolution and empire, universal emancipation and national Thermidor. Ultimately, my principal aspiration was to think the imperial process as a Thermidorian negation of the emancipatory promise of thought.

The motivating force for this reassertion of spirit is the present situation on the island of Cyprus, indelibly marked by the long duration of interlocked histories of successive empires. The legacy of this serial imperialism on the moral and political fabric of the island has been devastating. Presently, it amounts to an intellectual servitude of sorts. Indeed, this essay was written in response to the spiritual desolation of the present, as a means of testing our intellectual nerve against the sprawling of a new volunteering empire of NGOs staffed by little biopolitical Jacobins, fanciful peacemakers, conflict-managers, political middlemen, dealers, and traffickers of the latest imperial Thermidor. Besides inventing new techniques of making a quick fortune, the intellectual contribution of the new Thermidorians begins and ends with sophistic rationalizations about the consequences of colonialism, its progressive role and civilizing mission in bringing diverse communities together, enhancing communication and understanding, ostensibly exposing the supererogatory character of anti-imperialism as the testing ground for a meticulous assessment of the critical possibilities of universality. Such rhetorical vindications of imperial overseas operations induce a postcolonial anesthesia which attends colorful (but untrue to life and politics) visions of expanding, multiethnic, porous, elusive, and precarious frontiers of empire. That these pacifist squads of opinion (sustained by ambassadorial encouragement and overseas subsidy) occasionally appeal to Kant in order to gain a minimum of philosophical respectability is both an amusingly vulgar paraphrase of the internationalist mainstream of imperialism and a terrifying sign of the new civil power of imperial purpose in our age.

PART THREE

DE-LAYERINGS
OF THE FEMININE

Introduction to Part Three

Apostolos Lampropoulos

Gender has been one of the most crucial topics of research in the human, social, and political sciences over the last decades. At the same time, it has undergone intensive theorization and has become one of the main tools of contemporary philosophical thought and cultural analysis. In more or less direct ways, gender is linked to the consecutive waves of feminism, women, body and sexuality studies, and, of course, queer theory. In this context, understanding and redefining the feminine has been a challenging task triggering heated and highly politicized debates. In addition, the feminine continues to be of crucial importance in public discourses that are linked to biopolitics. From civic rights in non-Western societies to manipulations of HIV-positive female bodies in times of crisis, a wide range of issues demand thorough analysis and a passage to one or another kind of activism. This quasi-omnipresence of the feminine has had at least two effects. On the one hand, it is no surprise that it has occasionally led to a—sometimes crude and vastly unproductive—re-essentialization of the feminine, bringing it back to the supposed truth of its biological "reality." On the other hand, the feminine has in many cases gained the status of a key concept, detached not only from the female condition and its meanings across countless different contexts, but also from gender strictly speaking. In a sense similar to what—apropos of Derrida—Carole Dely calls "the perchance of a coming of the otherwoman,"[1] this part of the volume aims to rethink the feminine as a renegotiation both of the already established layerings that make up our notions of sex, sexuality, and gender *and*, perhaps, of the very concept of layering. This double possibility is precisely what the title "De-Layerings of the Feminine" aims to reflect, also profiting from the ambiguity of the "of," which produces the feminine not merely as the object of a de-layering process but *simultaneously* as its acting instance. In any case, the feminine is seen neither as the product of an accomplished de-layering nor as pure virtuality. It is, instead, process, agent and result of a prospective, future-oriented de-layering: no simple excavation in the history of the concept, no common-discourse deconstruction of it, no call for a policy-driven activism, but an exploration of what remains to be seen and problematized. This part touches on a number of related issues: revolt-in-the-feminine as an approach to the unrepresentable; abjection and fetishism as facets of a censored feminism; rereadings of Oedipus as a way to reproblematize the basics of psychoanalysis; the figure of Antigone as a nonnatural, noncorporeal, and nonrepresentational immediacy; finally, Irigaray's feminism as a philosophical machine.

In "Kristeva's Revolt, Illusion, and the Feminine," Gertrude Postl aims to investigate how women, located at the crossroads between atheism and mystery, contribute to the enactment of revolt. The first section ("Kristeva's Concept of Revolt") clarifies a number of issues: it describes revolt as an attempt to intertwine the psychoanalytic perspective with an analysis of the cultural and political condition of the West in the late 20th century; it elaborates on the etymological connections between *revolt* and the Latin *volvere* ("curve," "entourage," "turn," and "return"); it points out that, within the context of the European artistic and cultural tradition, culture is understood in terms of critical conscience— "to think is to revolt"; finally, it reminds us of the three figures of revolt that Kristeva takes from Freud, namely revolt as transgression of a prohibition, as repetition, and as displacement and game. What is important for Postl is that, in order for revolt to take place, the construction of meaning can no longer be limited to the conscious dimension. The second section ("Femininity and Illusion") takes into account Kristeva's way of integrating bisexuality and the phallus as illusion in her description of the feminine. At the same time, it analyzes the way in which Kristeva uses atheism: i.e., in the most general sense of disbelief or even as a version of the critical questioning associated with revolt. The third part ("Revolt, Illusion, and the Feminist Project") questions the understanding that Kristeva may have treated revolt as an exclusively male enterprise. In fact, Postl analyzes this false impression by drawing our attention to the fact that Kristeva (along with Irigaray and Butler) makes an effort to unhinge and disrupt the patriarchal order by undermining it through playing along. What is more, if culture is an "exquisite mystery" in its capacity of veiling and unveiling, then this relates to the feminine's ability to explore illusion. In the same vein, masochism is important as a revolt through suffering as a result of an illusion linked to the feminine (and perhaps atheistic) exploration of the other. Finally, Postl articulates woman as the site of a number of tensions, including the tension between seductress and martyr or that between representation and the unrepresentable. She then reaches the conclusion that the revolt arising from this liminal space will contribute to a different future which may also be the future of an illusion.

Tina Chanter's "The Layering of Abjection in Relation to Fetish: Reading Kristevan Abjection as the Unthought Ground of Fetishism" takes a close look at the psychoanalytic scenario that all bodies should be reflective of male morphology and that the female body is always seen to fall short of the idealized missing penis. This leads to the first part of Chanter's reflection, namely the psychoanalytic approach to the fetish: when the masculine imaginary installs one, it invents a distraction in which it can invest libidinal energies, whereas the female body comes to represent castration anxiety for the male. This approach to the fetish often converges with the Marxist approach: the fetishism of commodities that become fossilized in the implacable demands of the market. The overall logic of fetishism has found its way, as Chanter remarks, into feminist, race, film, and cultural theory. After reminding us of the ways in which Marxist approaches often underestimate issues of gender, Chanter criticizes corrective feminist analyses claiming that they tend to reinvent new forms of marginalization. She also mentions that the language of fetishism has often gained currency in contexts that remain ignorant of the ideological commitments to which the purveyors of the term convey themselves. Moreover, Chanter believes that the prevalence of fetishism depends upon the erection and celebration of a univocal meaning and she wonders how abjection might refigure it, taking into account one's will to be inside oneself and, at the same time, remain outside oneself. Chanter goes back to Kristeva's reading of Mary Douglas and to the ways in which rituals of purification delineate the identity of communities. This appears to be the context within which "femininity" presides over inassimilable meanings. Consequently, the feminine is admitted only insofar as it can contribute productively to a society or the state, otherwise it is discarded—at least in terms of a universal logic—as incoherent, insane, and nonsensical. In the light of this, the integrity of the concept of gender needs to be resisted, because this would repudiate its vital messiness. This is why, for Chanter, abjection is needed: to undo the categories that fetishism cultivates, by erupting and taking effect in various ways. Abject moments can put imaginaries into crisis by exposing their instability and breach boundaries that are assumed to be unassailable. All in all, Chanter thinks that abjection is not merely to be suffered: it is mobile, a strategy of survival, a form of protest, a political maneuver, and an artistic endeavor.

S. K. Keltner's "Reviving Oedipus: Oedipus, Anti-Oedipus, and the Nomadic Body in Kristeva" is articulated around the position that the Oedipal subject, representative of the dialectic between desire and the law, is in crisis. The first section ("Reviving Oedipus") retraces Kristeva's analysis of the Sophoclean cycle in *Powers of Horror*. It begins from Kristeva's position that the family structure as it is formalized by Freud is an indefensible one; it then deals with her effort to address *pre-* and *trans*-Oedipal dynamics of social and familial alliances that break from the normalizing paternal figure. Keltner reminds us that abjection breaks out the very moment Oedipus discovers impurity in his own body and becomes a criminal and *pharmakos* instead of king. This abjection stages the reversal both of a class and of a sexual difference. What is more, the ambiguity between pre-Oedipal processes (the conditions of subjectivation) and trans-Oedipal ones (its ruptures) challenges social and symbolic formations of self-identity and our relations to others. The second section ("Oedipus is Dead, and We Have Killed Him") studies Kristeva's direct confrontation with Freudian Oedipal theory in *The Sense and Non-Sense of Revolt*. Keltner departs from Kristeva's summary of Oedipus as a fantasmatic organization of psychic life supposing the primacy of the phallus as a narcissistically invested organ. If phallic identification is always already a failed identification and an impossible sovereignty, then an archaic revolt can allow psychoanalytic alterity to open up a space of interlocking alterities. The third section ("Anti-Oedipus—Beyond Sexual Difference, an Incurable Stranger") focuses on Kristeva's *La haine et le pardon* where she studies Oedipus as an animating principle of the development of thought. More specifically, it sees anti-Oedipus as a criticism of Oedipus and as part of the historical formation of subjectivity. Keltner insists that Kristeva's analysis of anti-Oedipus intersects with the experiences of a modern, nomadic body. She concludes that Kristeva's Oedipus both stands for psychoanalytic normativity and challenges it. It is an archaic subject and a modern one. It is a living proof of Freud's genius and the most eminent example of his failure. Oedipus also questions a number of binaries, such as intimate and public, psychic and social, foreigner/stranger and citizen, or even German and Jew. Its radical ambiguity gives us the right to see it, as Keltner succinctly remarks, as a field of difference in need of revolt.

Kalliopi Nikolopoulou's "Tragedy as De-Layering: The Opaque Immediacy of Antigone" underscores the links between the concept of de-layering and the notions of transparency, simplicity, and immediacy; questions the opposition between the complex and the immediate and sees Sophocles's *Antigone* as the most transparent and opaque Western text exemplifying the double-edged character of the immediate. For Nikolopoulou, though discourse's reflexivity protects us from the night of the primitive, one cannot miss its inability to account for its own hidden violence each time it tries to resolve incommensurable oppositions. What Antigone can tell us when we approach her from the precarious limit that interrupts discourse, rationalizations, legitimation, and authorization, is made audible only if we appreciate the fact that she is given over to death; she is the one who is about to be not and stand against natural life. This is the basis on which Nikolopoulou opposes her reading of Antigone to Butler's: the latter does not avoid the trap of representability and remains in the service of a political agenda. Nikolopoulou finds Butler's "feminist politics" problematic mainly because its position has no antistatist elements. In the second section ("Law, Blood, and Incest"), what is at stake is the law dictating that humans are mortal and the priority of fatality as such. Antigone is the uncanniest of all violence-doers because she is someone absolutely simple and absolutely inscrutable, the artless one who is not skillful enough to dodge the death that awaits. Her law is sovereign in the sense of Bataille's concept of expenditure. It is what drives her to join the dead and go to waste. Antigone's adherence to chthonic law dictates that all dead deserve a place under the earth, as opposed to Creon's concern for the safety of the land. Similarly, her commitment to blood as a feature of mortality attests to her ethics of interrelatedness instead of state politics of exclusion. Her ungraspable simplicity is to move from kin to friend, from necessity to freedom, and from chthonic duty to responsibility. Thus, she proves herself worthy of her relatives' love as if this love could be revoked. Antigone's love for Polynices is heightened after his death because of the ordeal of his corpse, something that accentuates her relation to death, rendering any evasions impossible. In the short concluding section ("Crystal (Un)Clear"), Nikolopoulou declares that Antigone demands less explanation and more reverence not thanks to what she represents (ethical conduct *in extremis* or fearlessness) but to what she presents: namely, the secret and withdrawal. Therefore, contemporary theoretical obsession with complexity is far from the stony opacity of Antigone and her crystalline hardness.

The final chapter is Elena Tzelepis's "Metaphysical Topo*graphies* Re-layered: Critique and the Feminine." It begins by pointing out the double interpretation of Platonic mimesis in Irigaray's *This Sex Which Is Not One*: i.e., *production* on the one hand and initiation, *specularization, adequation,* and *reproduction* on the other. However, Tzelepis insists on what she sees as performative and deconstructive mimesis in Irigaray, that is to say, on its capacity to supplement, supplant, or even subvert the regulatory norms of the philosophical tradition. This sort of mimesis addresses the limits of knowability, while it obscures traditional distinctions between philosophical writing and literary devices. In the first section ("Mimesis"), the author reminds us that Irigaray's mimesis challenges the distinction between the original and the copy. She also proposes that this mimesis means engaging with the intelligibility of metaphysics in order to reappropriate the feminine. This is exactly what allows us to find ourselves impelled by Irigaray's style of thinking and reading otherwise. However, it is through maintaining the distinction between the *heteron* and the *enantion* that mimesis safeguards the sign's future appropriations from foreclosure. The second section ("Eirōneía") argues that Irigaray's mimicry of Socratic irony de-authenticates and de-normalizes regimes of truth. Her writing is both a disruption of the philosophical tradition and echoes an intimacy with it. It is a *paleonymy* emerging as a re-archiving of both the past and the future. In Elizabeth Weed's words, cited by Tzelepis, it resembles a "radical citationality." The third section ("Woman") rethinks the binary essentialism/antiessentialism and draws our attention to Irigaray's effort to discursively imitate this putative antithesis. What is "proper" to a woman is an endless errancy or a perpetual becoming. That is why Irigaray employs the word "speculum" and critically opens the scene of phallogocentric representation as it is structured by male spectatorship and the specularization of woman. The short fourth section ("Actio in distans") underlines woman's ambivalent relation to, at the same time distant from and intimate with, the performance of representation. The final section ("Philosophy's *eidolon*") wonders whether such a project of performative and deconstructive mimesis can ever succeed, and whether Irigaray manages to move away from the language that she endeavors to destabilize. Tzelepis reaches the conclusion that we can no longer read metaphysics without Irigaray's strategic layerings and mimetic revisitations. It is thanks to her affirmative deconstruction of the feminine as a phantasmatic and failed copy that the very notion of "failure" has changed.

Chapter 9

Kristeva's Revolt, Illusion, and the Feminine

Gertrude Postl

Illusion and the feminine are assigned a special status within Kristeva's concept of revolt. An account of Kristeva's understanding of revolt and her notion of the feminine as illusion will set the stage for showing how women—located at the crossroads between atheism and mystery—contribute to the enactment of revolt in a very specific way.

Kristeva's Concept of Revolt

Kristeva's concept of revolt, first developed in her 1996 *Sens et non-sens de la révolte* (*The Sense and Non-Sense of Revolt*) and further expanded on in *La révolte intime* (*Intimate Revolt*, 1997) marks a clear departure from her earlier notion of revolution from *La révolution du langage poétique* (*Revolution in Poetic Language*, 1974). While the notion of revolution focused more closely on the development of the individual speaking subject, in particular on the tension between the semiotic and the symbolic (with the investigation of the political relevance of the semiotic limited to certain formations of avant-garde literature), the concept of revolt includes the cultural-political dimension in addition to the individual development of the subject. The notion of revolt is an attempt to intertwine the psychoanalytic perspective with an analysis of the specific cultural and political condition of the West at the end of the 20th century. Rather than limiting the political implications of this analysis to certain manifestations of avant-garde literature, the notion of politics is now expanded and includes an individual as well as a social dimension. To be more specific, Kristeva approaches the notion of revolt through locating it within the context of etymology, contemporary culture, and psychoanalysis.

Etymology
Kristeva mentions the Latin verb *volvere* and refers to the meanings of "curve," "entourage," "turn," and "return" which are supplemented via the Italian influence with "circular movement," "temporal return," and "turning back." Mentioned are also "to leave," "to abjure," and to "turn away." According to Kristeva, the term "revolt" or "to revolt" was used until the 18th century in a political as well as a psychological sense, whereby the psychological sense "contains an idea of violence and excess in relation to a norm" (*SNS*, 2). The etymological traces of the related term "revolution" Kristeva develops within her analysis of time and space. There she explains that the word "revolution"—used during the

143

Middle Ages to signify change and mutation—was extended only during the 16th century to the area of politics: "the revolution of time leads to the revolution of State" (*SNS*, 3). And only during the second half of the 17th century the now dominant meanings of political conflict and social change become prevalent. But all these etymological references shall not distract from the preliminary and approximate quality of each of them: "While I encourage readers to use etymology as a deciphering tool, do not rely solely on the appearance (or image) of a word and its meaning. Go further, go elsewhere, interpret. Interpretation, as I understand it, is itself a revolt" (*SNS*, 2).

Contemporary Culture

According to Kristeva (in this point following Guy Debord's *Society of the Spectacle*), we live in a time of the image, the entertainment, the spectacle, characterized through a power vacuum and what she calls the patrimonial individual. The currently dominant order is neither totalitarianism nor fascism but the seeming anarchy of a new world order. "Signs of a new world order do exist, and if examined closely this order appears to be both normalizing and falsifiable, normalizing *but* falsifiable. . . . [T]here are no longer laws but measures . . . invisible power, nonpunitive legislation, delaying tactics, on the one hand, and media theatricalization . . . on the other" (*SNS*, 4–5). This normalizing and perverted configuration of an absence of power corresponds to an individual composed of body parts and determined through biological technologies. "The human being tends to disappear as a person with rights, since he/she is negotiated as possessing organs that are convertible into cash. . . . 'I' am, quite simply, the owner of my genetic or organo-physiological patrimony" (*SNS*, 6).

Kristeva contrasts this scenario of a power vacuum, media representation, body parts, and commodity exchange with the European tradition of art and culture as revolt, whereby "culture" is understood in terms of "critical conscience." Contemporary developments render this very tradition of culture as revolt as meaningless and not any longer applicable; a culture driven by the spectacle, by bodily fragmentation, and by concerns for cash value has no need for a critical conscience. "I would underscore that an essential aspect of the European culture of revolt and art is in peril, that the very notion of culture as revolt and of art as revolt is in peril, submerged as we are in the culture of entertainment, the culture of performance, the culture of the show. . . . If this is the case, who can revolt, and against what?" (*SNS*, 6 and 8).

Since our time is no longer a time of the revolt (repeated references to the history of May '68 are no coincidence in Kristeva's text), all we can do is to rethink the notion of revolt, to think it again, to recall its traces as they unfolded in the past, and to reappropriate it in a new way. The goal of this turning back and turning around, of this recapturing based on interpretation, of this return in order to regain, is not a unified, organized opposition to questionable cultural developments. Rather, Kristeva wants to establish an alternative "to the robotizing and spectacular society that is damaging the culture of revolt: this alternative is, quite simply, sensory intimacy" (*IR*, 5). Or, as it is called at a different place, an experience: "I think we all need an experience, by which I mean something unknown, surprise, pain, or delight and then comprehension of this impact" (*SNS*, 11). "Intimacy" in this context is to be understood in terms of privacy, inwardness, subjectivity, even soul. This type of revolt has to take the private realm, the subject, as its starting point and is thus not to be confused with political programs or organized forms of resistance. "Alongside and in addition to the culture of the image—its seduction, its swiftness, its brutality, and its frivolity— the culture of words, the narrative and the place it reserves for meditation, seems to me to offer a minimal variant of revolt. . . . [W]e will have to re-turn to the little things, tiny revolts, in order to preserve the life of the mind and of the species" (*IR*, 5).

Living in a culture where everything—from perception to desire, and to modes of expression—is regulated and turned into a variation of the spectacular and the show, preserving the life of the mind and the species become political goals; goals to be brought about through interventions and interferences on the intimate level of personal experience through "the culture of words"—"to think is to revolt."[1] Whereby, this level of personal experience becomes a matter of social concern and—strangely enough—also a concern for the species. "Revolt is indispensable, both to psychic life, and to the bonds that make society hang together" (*RS*, 38).

Psychoanalysis

According to Kristeva, Freud offers two different but related accounts of revolt: the Oedipus complex and what she calls the return of the archaic. In *Totem and Taboo* Freud explains the beginning of human civilization as the revolt of the brothers against the father over their available access to women. The father is killed, the brothers gain access to women, and the murderous act is symbolically repeated as ritual. "They replaced the dead father with the image of the father, with the totem symbol of power. . . . [G]uilt and repentance cemented the bond" (*SNS*, 12). The feelings of guilt and repentance following the murder of the father turn the original social bond between the brothers into a religious bond. "The social and/or religious link is also . . . where revolt finds its conditions of possibility" (*SNS*, 13). This religious (or spiritual) dimension of revolt Kristeva develops through her notion of the sacred, understood as transgression, as the space where the rebellion against the law (originally regulating a desire for purification) takes place. Psychoanalytic interventions but also art and literature—in that they are forms of transgression—are considered as a continuation of the sacred with other means: "art and literature are rites as well: recall that Aristotle considered them catharses (in French *purifications*)" (*SNS*, 20). And the murder of the father also regulates the brothers' relation to the feminine in a dual sense: "The brothers . . . resorb the feminine, renounce it. This feminine is the feminine of women, as objects of desire, but also the brothers' feminine, in the sense of their passive desire for the father" (*SNS*, 13). This way, repressed homosexuality (plus the commodity status of women) will become the foundation for the social contract.

The second meaning of revolt within the context of psychoanalysis is the return of the archaic, understood as the return of the invisible and inaccessible contents of the unconscious. "The word 'revolutionary' used by Freud has nothing to do with moral, much less political, revolt; it simply signifies the possibility that psychoanalysis has to access the archaic, to overturn conscious meaning" *(SNS, 15)*. Kristeva mentions three figures of the revolt which can be derived from Freud: revolt as transgression of a prohibition; revolt as repetition (working-through, working-out), and revolt as displacement and game *(SNS, 27–29)*.

To recapitulate: we are dealing with the beginning and end of culture, the beginning and end of religion. Art and literature (or representation in the broadest sense) are presented as mediators between culture and religion, as reminder, as critical conscience. But these tasks cannot be pursued in a nonculture such as ours. In order for art and literature to regain their lost position, means and ways have to be found to return them to revolt. And these means and ways can be provided only through the psychoanalytic process, be it as transgression, as working-through and working-out, or as displacement and game. The manifestations of culture can realize their potential for revolt only if they are (re)connected to the intimate as well as to the sacred, to the sensuous experience as well as to the ritual. Understood in this way, the goal of revolt is less a social upheaval or political change but a state of questioning, a form of criticism, the privacy of a sensory (or sensuous?) intimacy, of experience. Writing, language, art entail the potential of a turning, the potential to reconnect to a lost tradition of criticism which Kristeva would like to revive. But for this revival to succeed, the construction of meaning cannot any longer be limited to the conscious dimension. Rather, the cultural renderings of the individual as well as of the social life will have to take into account the hidden, the repressed, the abject, so as to lay open the undercurrents that keep the contemporary spectral nonculture in place.

Femininity and Illusion

When discussing Freud's claim in *The Future of an Illusion*, that everyone wants an illusion, Kristeva states: "Structurally . . . a woman is better placed than anyone to explore illusion" *(SNS, 106)*. In order to understand this somewhat dubious privilege of the feminine, we have to return to the early stages of psychosexual development of both sexes.

The beginning is marked for the girl as well as the boy through a period of "phallic monism" (referring to the central status of the phallus as general signifier of lack for both sexes). With the onset of the Oedipus complex, however, the developments start to differ and woman will eventually be characterized through three related "double features": a double Oedipus (Oedipus 1—referring to both sexes' phallic desire for the mother; Oedipus 2—relevant only for the girl and referring to the need to give up her desire for the mother by replacing it with a desire for the love of the father), a gap or disjunction between the sexual/sensory/excitational level and the level of signification (the inscription of the feminine subject into the phallic-signifying order), and bisexuality (resulting from the girl's ambiguous relationship to the mother: desiring her but also desiring what the mother desires, the love of the father). In that those three "double features" mark the changing facets of woman's attitude toward the phallus they are closely interconnected. As a result of this developmental structure, woman is faced with two possibilities: she either accepts the determining function of the phallus while realizing its illusory character; or she denies her bisexuality and thus also the illusory character of the phallus (*SNS*, 101). Hence the subtitle of the chapter in question: "The Feminine between Illusion and Disillusion" (*SNS*, 94). In both instances, bisexuality and the phallus as illusion are at the center of Kristeva's account of the feminine: either in a positive, affirmative sense as acceptance or in a negative or reversed version as denial.

This emphasis on bisexuality hinges, of course, upon woman's ambiguous positioning: she is always already on two continents at the same time, the phallic (which she recognizes to be an illusion) and the Minoan-Mycenean of the mother (*SNS*, 101). And while motherhood provides the woman with the possibility of an alternative to the signifying realm of the symbolic (through the child the phallus gains a real presence), she cannot escape her bisexuality and thus the illusory character of the phallus (even denying both just produces the same pattern in reverse): "[T]he phallus, because of the perception/signification dissociation, always already appears to the woman as illusory. 'Illusory' basically means that this law, this pleasure, this phallic power and, simultaneously, their lack . . . is a game. It is not that it is nothing, but it is not everything either" (*SNS*, 100). We should recall at this point that Kristeva mentions "game" as the third possible formation of revolt or "revolt culture," in addition to the archaic or sacred and the variations of the psychoanalytic process (*SNS*, 29).[2]

According to Kristeva, participating in phallic power by playing it like a game "does not necessarily lead to 'as-if' personalities or false selves" (*SNS*, 101). Rather, realizing the illusory quality of the phallic offers advantages and possibilities for women. The ongoing disjunction between the sensory and the signifying level guarantees woman access to as well as distance from the symbolic order and the alleged truth of the signifier. Although never having had any part in setting up the rules of this game, she nevertheless knows how to play them in her favor. In short, she participates in the game from a distance, without ever being fully submerged in it. "The . . . investment of this illusory phallicism . . . mobilizes the beautiful seductress: constantly made up, provocative, on parade, and just as constantly not fooled and disappointed" (*SNS*, 102). Living up to the cultural standards of femininity without ever being dominated by them, the beautiful seductress knows how to remain in control and how to stay on top of her own machinations. Kristeva's image of the beautiful seductress somehow triggers all the wishful associations with a type of superwoman who has it all and who also looks good on top of it.

The play with and the distance from the symbolic order allows woman to also live in a closer proximity to the maternal, sensory-corporeal level of pure desire and it helps her to overcome possible masochistic tendencies entailed in

the denial of the illusory character of the phallus. This proper acceptance of bisexuality in terms of a participation in the phallic game is, according to Kristeva,
characterized by an atheistic dimension (distinguished from the mystery of masochism that characterizes the denial of bisexuality). "With bisexuality understood as the resolution of female masochism, I am convinced we are touching on
the psychical spring of atheism" (*SNS*, 106). However, the atheism associated
with a proper acceptance of bisexuality is not to be confused with an antireligious attitude. Rather, Kristeva seems to use atheism in terms of a general
sense of disbelief, perhaps even the critical questioning associated with revolt,
which in turn brings it close to illusion. But she also describes it with respect to
the other: "I am not sure 'atheism' means anything more than taking the other
and exploring it" (*SNS*, 106).

In order to understand this affinity between woman and atheism we have to
look at the relationship between phallic culture and religion. As has been developed through the tale of the brothers, the act of patricide has been transformed
not only into a social but also a religious bond—in the words of Ewa Ziarek: "a
phallic cult is at the basis of religion."[3] Subsequently, the realization of the illusory character of the phallus will lead to an attitude of distance or disbelief also
with respect to religion. "I see in the psychical bisexuality of the woman not a
cult of the phallus or something beyond it, much less beneath it, but a maintenance and an estrangement of illusion as illusion. The future of an illusion?
Necessarily! . . . [A] woman is better placed than anyone to explore illusion"
(*SNS*, 106).

Knowing about the illusions of the phallic game also entails to know about
the illusory character of religion. As it turns out, woman's ambiguous status (she
inhabits two continents at the same time) and her resulting ability "to explore
illusion" not only enables her to play the "phallic game," but, as a necessary
aspect thereof, also the "religious game." Women were never part of the patricide committed through the brothers that established a social as well as a religious bond. In its contemporary rendering, this means that the beautiful seductress maintains her distance to the phallic order as well as to the religious cult
while all along being perfectly capable of participating in both. It is for this reason that the notion of atheism must not be understood in an antireligious sense
but rather as an attempt toward embracing an unavoidable illusion and making
the best out of it.

The distance and disbelief entailed in this version of the feminine (the affirmative acceptance of bisexuality) clearly awards woman a form of revolt not
accessible to those who are fully integrated in the phallic order. "Taking the
other and exploring it" (rather than excluding, expelling, or abjecting it) can be
read in terms of the questioning, critical attitude that Kristeva associates with
revolt. Whereby, this "other" can be understood as an individual as well as a
cultural other—thus the possibility of a cultural revolt (disguised as illusory
play) in terms of a critical but nonhostile investigation, an open encounter with
the other rather than an antagonizing suspicion.

As mentioned already, woman's participation in the phallic game is just one of two options. In the second possible development (the denial of both bisexuality and the illusory character of the phallus), the girl demonstrates a phallic ambition and attempts to compensate for her inherent lack; she is not satisfied with participating in a game—she wants the phallus just like the boy does. "The denial of bisexuality presents itself as a denial of the illusory. Such a denial implies identification with the phallus as such, which amounts to an identification with the man's phallic position. . . . The result of this is the female paranoiac: the boss, director, or virile lesbian, partisans of power in all its more or less dictatorial forms" (*SNS*, 102).

Contrary to the "beautiful seductress" who knows how to play with male power and how to protect herself against any possible disappointment resulting from it, the "female paranoiac" takes phallic power seriously and thus sets herself up for failure. Consequently, a masochistic component cannot be avoided when opting for the path of denial. "The phallic girl . . . makes herself more Catholic than the pope, becoming saint, martyr, and militant of a signifier whose illusory aspect all her erogenous zones are mobilized to deny" (*SNS*, 101).

If woman renounces her bisexuality, she engages in a kind of painful sensuality which ends up in hysterical depression or melancholy. She acts as if she had a phallus, while her suffering appears now as a denial of bisexuality in favor of a fantasy of "androgynous totality" (*SNS*, 105). The "phallic accomplishments" (*SNS*, 105) that are typical for this version of femininity cannot prevent the masochistic suffering that comes with it. Psychical bisexuality "remains a promised land that we must attain" (*SNS*, 105).

In other words, bisexuality as well as the phallic illusion that accompanies it, has an ongoing presence even in their denial. The two versions of femininity Kristeva offers are bound to each other and have to be read like the flipsides of the same coin. Wanting the phallus—the model of androgynous totality just discussed—is as much an illusion as is the recognition of the phallus as illusion. Both versions are intrinsically connected with each other through the presence/absence of illusion (or the acceptance/denial of bisexuality).

This bisexuality which is either accepted or denied—"not less phallic but more-than-phallic" (*SNS*, 105)—produces a strange kind of *jouissance*, which Kristeva calls mysterious. And it is the link to the mysterious which will help in the following to clarify the relation between the feminine and revolt. Both formations of the feminine seem to be suited for revolt in a different way, each offering advantages as well as disadvantages for a disruption of the phallic order: "These different articulations of the phallus offer privileges but also set traps, like every psychical structuring" (*SNS*, 102).

Revolt, Illusion, and the Feminist Project

At first glance, Kristeva seems to treat revolt as an exclusively male enterprise. While the master revolutionaries in *The Revolution of Poetic Language* were Mallarmé and Lautréamont, now in the "revolt-project" we meet Aragon, Sartre, and Barthes. The founding narrative for the beginning of culture is a tale about a horde of brothers who oppose and kill their father over their access to women. The tradition of critical questioning, of an intellectual conscience, which Kristeva would like to revive is a nearly exclusively male tradition. Her three-volume study of the philosopher Hannah Arendt, the psychoanalyst Melanie Klein, and the French writer Colette, commonly referred to as the female genius trilogy, seems to be an independent project which is not directly related to issues raised in the revolt-volumes. The word "revolt" is hardly mentioned in her analysis of the bisexuality of women. Thus, we might wonder, what exactly is the function of revolt for the feminine, and what is the function of the feminine for revolt? Which part might, then, be assigned to Kristeva's concept of revolt (if any) when considering feminist claims for social and political change?

In *The Revolution of Poetic Language* it was still possible to connect revolutionary poetic language to the ruptures of the semiotic (always associated with the body of the mother, thus the feminine) into the symbolic. The meaning of "revolt," to the contrary, is not predominantly determined through negative, destructive qualities, nor is it in any structural sense related to the maternal or the feminine.

The multiple aspects of Kristeva's concept of revolt range from the movement of turning or turning around/back, over the exposure of the unconscious and the archaic, the revival of a critical tradition in art and literature, all the way to the notions of experience and sensory intimacy. "Revolt, then, as returning/turning back/displacement/change, constitutes the profound logic of a certain culture that I would like to revive here. . . . What makes sense today is not the future . . . but revolt: that is, the questioning and displacement of the past. The future, if it exists, depends on it" (*SNS*, 5). What part are women (and the feminine) supposed to play in this "questioning and displacement of the past"?

When asked by the interviewer about women's role for revolt in *Revolt She Said*, Kristeva responds rather indignantly and doesn't seem to fully understand the motivation for the question: "As for revolt, I'm in the middle of writing a work dedicated to the feminine genius—nothing less than that. . . . No, women have a place in revolt. And I don't understand why you want me to separate men and women so unkindly" (*RS*, 94–95). Thus, given Kristeva's own commitment to a connection between women and revolt, I would like to pursue the path most obviously laid out by her: the account of the feminine as expert in illusion.

Maybe the society of the spectacle turns what seemed to have been women's downfall for too long into an asset. If Kristeva is right—and this seems difficult to contest—that our Western culture is characterized by a power vacuum, an absence of authority (no heroes, no leaders), if the spectacle and the show define public and private life, if personal identity becomes a matter of body parts, if commodities reign the world, then those beings who never had any power or authority, who always have been reduced to an image and a spectacle, who have been defined in terms of body parts and commodities all along, gain an edge over the rest. They know about the illusory character of the phallic game; but being part of it while being excluded from it at the same time enables them to "play the game" differently.

I say that woman is a stranger to the phallic order she nonetheless adheres to, if only because she is a speaking being, a being of thought and law. But she keeps a distance vis-à-vis the social order, its rules, political contracts, etc. and this makes her skeptical, potentially atheist, ironic, and, all in all, pragmatic. I'm not really in the loop, says the woman, I'm staying outside, I don't believe in it, but I play the game, and at times, better than others. (*RS*, 93)

What enables her to possibly play the game "better than others" is, of course, her status of being inside and outside the system at the same time. The dual positioning of women described above, their bisexuality, the double Oedipus, the gap between the sensory and the symbolic, and the fact that they reside on two planets at once, pay off. However, playing the game "better than others" is a questionable attribute and does not yet necessarily translate into revolt. Even worse, the possibilities Kristeva considers—the beautiful seductress on the one hand, the female paranoiac (the woman more Catholic than the pope) on the other—do not seem to offer practical role models for women any feminist would like to subscribe to. Still, if one is willing to cut through the seeming cynicism and conformism that Kristeva's suggestions entail, maybe the feminine's close proximity to illusion offers a possibility for revolt after all—"a woman is better placed than anyone to explore illusion" (*SNS*, 106).

Being positioned at a distance to the phallic order (including its religious manifestations) can be viewed as yet another form of exclusion or as a chance. The foreigners always had a crucial function for those nations they inhabited. Maybe we should look at woman as a foreigner in a familiar land. Mastering the codes without being fully immersed in them opens up a second meaning of "playing"—not only can she *play along* (if she chooses to do so), but, more importantly, she can *play with* those codes; not only can she *play the game* but she can *play with the game*. The position of distance and the skepticism, pragmatism, and irony that come with it grant her insights and forms of access not available to those who are full-fledged participants in the phallic game. Let's not forget, woman inhabits two continents not just one, making her a stranger in both but also part of both. Being positioned between the phallic and the maternal, between body and language grants a different access to the body as well as to language, to the law of the father as well as to motherhood.

The focus on the feminine's privileged access to illusion and woman's ability to play (with) the game moves Kristeva's concept of revolt close to other models of what, I would call, a feminist politics of subversion. For example, according to Luce Irigaray, woman's only possibility to speak within the context of a patriarchal linguistic order is a mimetic repetition of the masculine forms of representation. However, through the concept of "playing with mimesis," Irigaray allows for the option to make the mimetic gesture visible, thus affirming and undermining established systems of representation with the same linguistic move.[4] A comparable strategy—just more specifically geared toward the performativity of gender—can be found in Judith Butler's notions of a "parodic repetition" or "performative subversion" where elements of a given gender norm are repeated in a deviating fashion so as to reveal the seeming naturalness of a heterosexual gender identity as constructed.[5] In my reading, Kristeva's notion of the feminine as illusion and the role it plays for revolt follows a similar pattern. In all three instances, in Irigaray, Butler, and Kristeva, we find the attempt to unhinge and disrupt the given patriarchal order by undermining it through playing along.

It should be clear by now that the feminine potential for revolt, as presented by Kristeva, has nothing to do with violence or the literal overthrow of a given order. Rather (and here again resonating Irigaray and Butler) it is first and foremost directed at the level of the signifier. As Ewa Ziarek puts it: "Kristeva does not associate the feminine logic of revolt primarily with the reactivation of the Oedipal rebellion, which is sustained by phallic *jouissance* and violence. . . . This ironic play with illusion . . . opens the symbolic to ongoing transformation" (*KF*, 69).

This position of ironic distance, the foreign gaze, the familiarity with illusion clearly has an impact on all the other aspects of Kristeva's revolt. Maybe this distance enables woman to read the archaic tale of human origin differently, e.g., as yet another manifestation of an illusion. Maybe her double positioning as inside and outside of the system at once lets her see the role of the mother behind the repressed tale of the brothers' patricide or the violence done to the sisters whom this archaic account reduces to mere commodities exchanged at will. Having been excluded from art and literature, her double positioning between the body and the word may allow her to develop forms of intervention or critique by using language in a more "bodily" manner—which would include the semiotic drives and rhythms of the pre-Oedipal primary processes as Kristeva herself described them in *Revolution in Poetic Language*. And not to forget, her distance from and insights into the illusions of the phallic order bring her closer to a sensory intimacy. "The immense responsibility of women in regard to the survival of the species . . . goes hand in hand with this rehabilitation of the sensory" (*IR*, 5). This sensory intimacy, though, is not to be taken in exclusively private terms. Rather, it reveals the sensory quality of any form of linguistic signification as well as the public dimension of intimacy—as we know from the history of feminism, the personal is political. The expressions of the intimate are not opposed to the public; rather, they are manifestations of the public on the level of the immediate, embodied experience, with sexuality at the center of this very experience.

But any account of the connection between the illusions of the phallic game and revolt must remain incomplete without a brief excursion into Kristeva's understanding of mystery and the sacred. Going back to the Dionysian mysteries and the etymological roots of the word "mystery," Kristeva perceives the notion of mystery in terms of a showing and hiding, originally "of the supreme sign, the phallus" which eventually was transformed into a showing and hiding (or veiling/unveiling) of desirable objects. Often the desirability of these objects was due to the veiling/unveiling itself (*SNS*, 89). From this account, Kristeva draws a line to baroque art, in particular the use of folds in baroque sculpture. These artistic manifestations she identifies as "a kind of abstract art" which represent nothing other than "representation itself or its possible failure, namely, the cult of the unrepresentable" (*SNS*, 90). The crucial conclusion Kristeva draws from this reading is the claim that culture itself, in its capacity of veiling and unveiling, is "an exquisite mystery" and thus a revolt. "Perhaps mystery and revolt are the same thing" (*SNS*, 90).

It is at this point where I see a connection to the feminine and its ability to explore illusion. Is not the adherence to or denial of illusion a form of veiling and unveiling that places the feminine at the center of the question of representation? What is at stake in Kristeva's discussion of women's bisexuality and the feminine play with illusion (or rejection thereof) is nothing other than two possible responses to "the supreme sign, the phallus" (*SNS*, 89) and thus to possible versions of revolt. The acceptance of bisexuality and the distance to the phallic-religious order would be a revolt through playing with illusion while the masochism resulting from the desire to have the phallus would be a revolt through suffering because of an illusion.

In either case, taken together, the two formations of the feminine constitute a continuous oscillation between a veiling (illusion) and an unveiling (denial of illusion) that—either in a playful or in a masochistic attitude—pretends a phallic presence that is indicative of the operations of representation itself. The play with the phallic illusion constitutes a veiling and unveiling (of objects, of body parts, of signifiers . . .) which affirms but also disrupts and undermines the phallic order at the same time. Perhaps it is for this reason that Kristeva claims female bisexuality to be "nothing more or less than an experience of meaning *and* its gestation, language *and* its erosion, being *and* its reserve" (*SNS*, 105).

If "mystery and revolt are the same thing" (*SNS*, 90) and if revolt is considered "as sacred space" (*SNS*, 30), perhaps a line can be drawn from mystery to the sacred through the specific ways the feminine deals with representation. "The sacred . . . allows our most imperative bodily needs to access symbolic representations that could be shared and that are sometimes sublime . . . , [a] transition from the body to meaning, from the most intimate to the most binding" (*RS*, 34). In other words, revolt takes place at the transition from the body to signification, from the psychic to the law, from the intimacy of the private experience to the social realm.

The description of the sacred in terms of "balancing pleasures and sacrifice" (*RS*, 35) not only offers an account of the sacred as transgression resulting from the rebellion against the law, it may also serve as a description of the two versions of the feminine—the pleasures of the "beautiful seductress" and the sacrifices of the "female paranoiac." Revolt thus takes on a spiritual dimension of a different kind, one that has nothing to do with the religious-social bond established through the patricide of the brothers. The spirituality of this—perhaps specifically feminine version of—revolt marks the crossroads between mystery and atheism. The feminine play with illusion, read as the veiling/unveiling typical of mystery, establishes a form of representation (or aesthetic experience in the broadest sense) that allows not only for a connection between immediate bodily desire and existing modes of signification (between the unconscious and the law) but also for the (atheistic) exploration of the other. If culture itself is a mystery, a continuous interplay between a veiling and an unveiling (the play with illusion), and if "mystery and revolt are the same thing" (*SNS*, 90), then the forms of symbolic representation developed within this mysterious context will produce an aesthetic experience of revolt (art and literature) that maintains a form of critical questioning which does not bypass or subordinate the other but renders him/her an integral part of this very questioning. And it is woman or the feminine which is particularly suited to pull all these strings together in a very specific type of revolt.

Woman, being placed at the tension between accepting and denying illusion, between a veiling and an unveiling, between the seductress and the martyr, between the flesh and the word, between representation and the unrepresentable, between the individual and the community, pragmatic but caught in illusions nevertheless, might be in a more privileged position to modify "the previous conception of the sacred" (*RS*, 35). The revolt that arises out of this type of sacred space will certainly contribute to a different future—but a future which might quite possibly be the future of an illusion.

However, in times like ours, in the midst of the society of the spectacle, illusions are not any longer what they used to be either. If everything is a spectacle, a surface, an appearance, then "illusion" too takes on a different meaning. If there is no real, no original, if everything is a game, then illusion is all there is— and thus it has to be taken seriously for the "questioning and displacement of the past" (*SNS*, 5), Kristeva mentions. Maybe this is the challenge for woman: not just to play with the phallic order but to play with the illusion of the phallic order, engaging in a game of illusions without getting lost in those illusions, using the means of the spectacle in order to resignify the illusions created by the society of the spectacle, interconnecting mystery, pragmatism, and atheism, identifying neither with the seductress nor the martyr but treating both as necessary illusions and playing them thus against each other ("balancing pleasure and sacrifice"), engaging in artistic and linguistic interventions knowing that they might just add yet another layer of illusion. Or, to put it in Kristeva's own words: "I will conclude by pointing up the incommensurable psychical effort required in acceding to this psychically bisexual being that is woman, a being, one might even say, that never adheres to the illusion of being, any more than to the being of this illusion itself. And I admit that what I have said may only be illusion as well" (*SNS*, 106).

Chapter 10

The Layering of Abjection in Relation to Fetish: Reading Kristevan Abjection as the Unthought Ground of Fetishism

Tina Chanter

Fetishism involves a compensatory mechanism, fueled by a threat of otherness that cannot be integrated into one's preconceptions without altering those preconceptions. If the facts on the ground do not match up with our preconceptions, we remake history to make it fit, and this substitute reality suffices. The classic psychoanalytic scenario in terms of which the apparently infinitely malleable trope of fetishistic disavowal was originally stated concerned the expectation, based upon the assumption that all bodies should be more or less reflective of male morphology, that if there is no penis, as we had expected there to be, we simply fabricate a substitute one—hence the production of the fetish. If the mirroring function of the world around us doesn't reflect our own idea of what it should be, we manipulate the reflection until it accords to this idea. Never mind the truth of the matter, which consists of a female body that is abjected and degraded in advance, since it is always already seen to fall short of the idealized, missing penis it never had in the first place.

Fetishistic disavowal according to its psychoanalytic formulation strictly speaking involves a logic whereby the "original" state of affairs—the "fact" of the matter, which consists of the commitment to the mythologized, universal penis—is not so much obviated by the production of the fetish as coexistent with it. Castration—albeit mythical—is thereby disavowed. That is, the fetish comes to stand for a mythological penis, which was never empirically there in the first place, but which derives from the firm belief that it should have been/should be/will be (the disarmingly casual manner in which Freud fails to respect the distinct domains of past/present/future is a product, perhaps related to his thesis concerning the timelessness of the unconscious); we can hypothesize this, although the logic of the fetish does not, in fact, strictly adhere to a logic of repression, is not in fact synonymous with a logic of the unconscious, but is rather a matter of holding two incompatible theses simultaneously—or at least in a temporality of oscillation—while refusing to obey the demands of Hegelian dialectical logic, which would require that two mutually incompatible truths eventually cancel one another out, in a progression of history that might sometimes take a while to evolve, but which eventually does, and when it does, it issues in a rational world, which shows itself to be the truth of a less rational world, the

155

contradictions of which are sublated in their higher resolution—the truth of the absolute.

Marx's commodity fetishism puts a slightly different spin on this psychoanalytic narrative of the fetish. For Marx, the fetishism of commodities turns on its head the relations of social production, which become fossilized or ossified in the apparently implacable, impersonal demands of the market. So far are such processes of ossification and sclerosis allowed to proceed, that the human relationships from which market forces originally derived their energy become entirely obscured. The relation between laborer and capitalist owner, in the context of which human labor produces value, which in turn becomes represented by the uniform, abstract, monetary values that cancels all the differentiation that exists at the level of skilled labor, can now exist only as alienated. The laborer is alienated from himself, from his labor, from other laborers, and from his product, which, the chances are, he cannot afford to purchase, despite the fact that his labor is congealed in it, and from that labor the product accrues value, which, however, can now only be represented as a function of exchange value. The latter performs its own leveling effect, abolishing all the differences between an infinitely various array of products, reducing them all to their expression as quantifiable ratios of one another, to be measured according to the universal standard of gold. Herein lies the fetishization of the gold standard, itself removed from the tangible, sensuous reality of that metal that is abstracted from its material qualities and made into money, which comes in turn to be so many flickering, digitalized figures on a computer screen.

For psychoanalytic fetishism, there was no penis in the first place, except in the masculine imaginary. The powerful productivity of the masculine imaginary installs a fetish to compensate for its empirical lack, thereby inventing a distraction in which it can invest libidinal energies, and by which it can overcome the fear of castration. The female body comes to represent castration anxiety for the male, precisely due to his reluctance to concede that his presuppositions of universal phallic morphology might prove to be wrong. For commodity fetishism, what is disavowed is not the (imaginary) castration of the female, but the humanity of the worker, the human relations that underlie the logic by which profits accumulate. These relations become incapable of being represented in their social dimension, subjected as they are to ever increasing degrees of abstraction, which take on the appearance of necessity in the guise of market forces that come to drive the motor of capitalism. The lineaments of bourgeois economy take on the appearance of inevitability, and begin to dictate human behavior. We become beholden to the gods of the market, we no longer act as self-willed, we are compelled by an imperative that appears to be wholly outside us, to come from on high. The imperative is to accumulate profit, and to take all the necessary steps to avoid thinking through the cost in human misery. The market becomes the god, and the goods that are exchanged make the world go round. The false idols that circulate in the form of brand names we come to desire not for the sake of their use value, but for the cache that their labels carry. They come to rule our lives to the point that we live to buy for the sake of being seen to have purchasing power, rather than for the inherent worth of the things we fetishize.

The logic of fetishism, employed in different ways by psychoanalytic theory and Marxist theory, has found its way into feminist theory, race theory, film theory, and cultural theory. It has been exported from psychoanalytic theory to race theory, often without its purveyors attending to the complex series of translations and obfuscations that such a proliferation of layers produces. If an imaginary sexual referent is transposed into an equally imaginary racial referent, but the residue of such a transposition is left unthought, that residue is liable to recapitulate itself as a logic of abjection that haunts the newly transposed logic of fetishism.

In questioning the continued theoretical commitment to recycling the logic of disavowal, even when this fetishistic trope is used as a critical resource, or even when its production is inadvertent, I suggest that Kristeva's notion of the abject can provide critical resources. Neither object nor subject, the abject designates a domain to which those unthought, excluded others are relegated, whose borderline (non)existence secures the identity of those who occupy authoritative positions in relation to dominant discourses. Kristeva says "there are lives not sustained by *desire*, as desire is always for objects. Such lives are based on *exclusion*."[1] Abjection designates the problem of the constitutive outside, or the always improperly excluded other, that which is excluded for the sake of establishing identity as coherent. Mothers, daughters, and wives whose unpaid physical and psychic labor could not be recognized by Marxist class theory were abjected by a theory that is incapable of acknowledging the contribution of women due to its exclusive concentration on class relations and the categories of paid labor. In turn, those shadowy figures, who people the imaginary of the official story that mainstream, white, middle-class, Western feminism tells itself, function as abject. African American domestic workers, or South Asian immigrant homeworkers, render precarious the public/private distinction that has been so central to formulating mainstream feminist theory.[2] The very existence of racialized minorities who perform paid labor within the home is ignored by the representation of home as domestic space out of which (privileged, white, Western) women must migrate, and the public realm as a space of freedom and work which must be accessed. Far from being a space of liberation, as it is typically construed within Western feminist frameworks, the public realm operates in oppressive and imperialist ways for colonized peoples. The forced inclusion and incorporation of native women by U.S. governmental systems, and the imposition of U.S. citizenship on these (non)subjects, whose land and ways of life were appropriated, cannot be accounted for by the categories of mainstream feminist categories.[3] Peripheral yet facilitating, the zones that these figures occupy are ambiguous border zones that straddle the neat dichotomy between public and private, and complicate the legacy of civil rights as unambiguously liberatory.[4]

The ignorance that has allowed mainstream feminist theory to proceed in ways that are oblivious to the racialized exploitation of certain others has been explored in a variety of ways. Yet these corrective analyses systematically encounter the problem of reinventing new forms of marginalization in the very attempt to redress hegemonic relations. The invention of new others can be specified as a problem of omission—where the interests or concerns of certain marginalized groups are simply neglected or overlooked. Or it can be construed as structurally produced by the ongoing specification or inclusion of previously marginalized groups as no longer marginalized, or not-to-be-marginalized. A dynamic is set up whereby new forms of fetishization spawn new subjects who are placed in relation to abjection, new dejects. To take just one example, the imperative that South Asian women should not be marginalized by white, Western, feminist discourse, is issued with the self-consciousness that even the category "South Asian" functions hegemonically, reinventing the terms of imperialism, and privileging the experiences and reflections of some South Asians over others.[5]

The language of fetishism has gained currency, and with it the concept of disavowal has begun to circulate, often in contexts that remain ignorant of, or disown, the ideological commitments to which the purveyors of this term thereby commit themselves.[6] It is recycled with varying degrees of success, but the economic laws governing its recirculation are not in question. They are governed by masculinist and racist assumptions, the measure of which has apparently not yet been taken, given the prevalence of the language of fetishism, which takes on a universal, homogenizing symbolic value, much like the monetary value decried by Marx under the commodity form of production. An unreflective commitment to a universally fetishizing discourse recycles in a subtle but pervasive way the priority of white, heterosexist, masculinist, capitalist values, a tendency to be guarded against, especially in work that takes itself to be feminist, or presents itself as asserting the importance of race in the face of white feminists' and psychoanalytic neglect of it.

Is the univocal register in terms of which theories of fetishism establish themselves as the cultural currency of theory accidental, or does it reflect something internal to the theory itself? If the universality with which gender or race or class assert themselves as the privileged, authoritative, and autonomous terms of radical discourses mimetically reflects the dominance assumed by the discourses of patriarchy, white supremacy, or bourgeois ideology against which they are mobilized, can the tendency to produce new dominant narratives of gender, class, race, or sexuality, guard against new forms of abjection? Must each of these discourses retain a discrete, impervious focus that reinvents the hegemonic terms of the very discourses under protest in order to achieve success? Is there too much anxiety associated with confronting multiple forms of oppression at once? What could help prevent the all too frequent relapse into a false universalism that undercuts the radical intentions of apparently progressive discourses?

By casting fetishism as only a moment of an ongoing process that is implicated in the fluidity of imaginary, amorphous, invisible, excluded, unthought others, we can draw attention to the logic of abjection that grounds fetishistic discourses, a logic that such discourses utilize more or less consciously. There is an ambivalent inclusion of subjects, who are on the one hand situated outside of representation, in a mythical, indeterminate past that is mythologized as prior to civilized society, and on the other hand granted access to forms of representation that are nevertheless shaped and informed by their exclusion. Access is granted to these forms of representation only if those who are excluded acquiesce to their representation as subjects who conform to the imaginaries of dominant narratives. Articulating this logic of abjection clarifies how discourses of racism, sexism, classism, heterosexism, and nationalism are implicated in each other in ways that play off one another to produce their own internal others. At the same time, the prevalence of the trope of fetishism, a trope that has asserted itself in different ways within the discourses of Marxism and psychoanalysis, and has been imported into the discourses of feminist and race theory to create new dominant narratives, depends upon the erection and celebration of a univocal, monolithic value. While the value of fetishistic theory—whether in commodity fetishism or its psychoanalytic variant—resides in its capacity for transference across discourses, its reassertion of an apparently universal standard of value in every case marks the limits of its interpretive capacity. What needs to be problematized is the tendency of discourses that take themselves to be progressive to reinvent the universal appeal of fetishistic values, without heeding their own production of the abject. From the beginning of her work, Kristeva has been concerned with demystifying the fetish that either commodities or signs become in the processes of economic or symbolic exchange characteristic of capitalism. As Joan Brandt puts it in her exploration of Kristeva's affiliation with the journal *Tel Quel*, "[p]roductive labor . . . is essentially denied by the capitalist system, concealed by society's fetishization of the product and of the money that serves as its sign in the system of exchange. Kristeva's emphasis on textual productivity and her attempt to uncover the multiple, pre-linguistic processes that both constitute but also undermine the unity of meaning are . . . central to her own and *Tel Quel*'s critique of traditional notions of language."[7] If critics have successfully mapped the continuity in Kristeva's work between her earlier critique of fetishism from a Maoist point of view, to her later critique of consumer society (*TQ*, 34), they have focused less on the critical distance Kristeva takes on the version of fetishism Freud embraces and Lacan inherits. Kristeva turns to Freud in *Revolution in Poetic Language* for a theory of subjectivity that she finds missing in Marxism, but in what way does she rework Freudian fetishism? How are multiple sites of meaning opened up in the imaginary or semiotic processes that Freud and Lacan recuperate in the form of primary processes under the name of the paternal signifier, and in terms of fetishistic theory? Specifically, how might abjection refigure the univocal meaning enshrined in the trope of fetishism?

Kristeva has mapped out the logic of abjection by showing how the mother's body becomes the site of a defensive maneuver on the part of the child, such that all that is displeasing comes to be posited as outside the body, while all that is pleasurable comes to be contained in the body, and thus a clean and proper body is instituted as the imaginary body. This reworks Freud's understanding of the bodily ego, the boundaries of which are instituted by a defensive mechanism that does not yet conform to the phallic, fetishistic logic that sets up sexual differentiation.[8] If imaginary bodies come into being on the basis of what pleases me and what displeases me (or disgusts me), and if that pleasure is not yet calibrated in terms that privilege sexual difference, it is possible to think about the ways in which racist, classist, or nationalist imaginaries inform what, in the language of Freud's essay "Negation,"[9] I would like to be inside me, and what I would like to remain outside me. That the delineation of inside and outside remains, initially, fantasmatic, in the developmental chronology Melanie Klein maps out, and on which Kristeva draws, only serves to highlight the usefulness of the trope of abjection as having explanatory force in the sphere of political imaginaries. Abject figures become the repositories of a world in which shifting boundaries allow various dejects to mark the limits of socially acceptable, purified, civilized imaginary norms.

Everything from conventions and rituals of cleanliness and ideologies of child-care rearing, to variations in ethnic cuisines, will impact what is available to be taken into the body and what is construed as that which must be kept outside the body. Tastes and dislikes will be constructed according to cultural variation. What can be taken into the body and what must be kept out, what I separate myself from, and what I identify with, will be organized according to strictures that organize the world according to religious, cultural, and social prohibitions and taboos. This opens up the possibility of understanding how subjects construct, from infancy, a sense of themselves that draws on, for example, racist imaginaries, such as that which informs the child who, in Frantz Fanon's famous description, abjects (we could say) him with the words "Look, a Negro! . . . I'm frightened!"[10] As such, it potentially expands the compass of psychoanalytic thinking, making it possible to think the primal mapping of the body in terms of racial geographies, such as Fanon's account of the corporeal fragmentation he experiences under the gaze of the child. Critical attention has tended to focus on the fragmentation and dislocation of the body image experienced by Fanon, yet equally important is the power of the mythology that has impacted the white child's way of seeing Fanon's black skin. If a nascent theory of abjection is born in Fanon's phenomenological reworking of the mirror-stage, it remains subordinate to an overarching commitment to a fetishistic narrative by which Fanon confirms rather than displacing the normative theories of sexual difference that pervade Freudian and Lacanian psychoanalysis.[11]

Drawing on Mary Douglas, Kristeva has shown how rituals of purification help to delineate the identity of communities, and how such rituals separate what comes to be understood as human, as distinct from the animal and the spiritual. The sacred and the profane are thus distinguished according to communal frameworks that endorse a culturally and historically specific understanding of what is acceptable and what is unacceptable. The boundaries of cleanliness and uncleanliness, the boundaries of the pure and the impure, the boundaries of decorum are set up in line with culturally generated taboos. Thus *Powers of Horror* is concerned not only with the provisional boundaries the infant sets up in abjecting the mother and becoming a subject, henceforth capable of formulating a desire for objects which are now understood in contradistinction from itself as subject. It is equally concerned with the ways in which social and cultural boundaries are put in place as a defense against what henceforth is figured as defilement and impurity: dirt, menstrual taboos, excrement, sites that are constructed as disgusting and unclean. Since parental codes are constituted in the light of culturally specific norms that specify what counts as unclean and impure, the ways in which infants abject the maternal body will also be informed by cultural codes that discriminate, in Klein's language, the fantasmatic good object from the bad object.

Any discourse that claims for itself a foundational status by exempting from its orbit those it designates as other at the same time as appropriating what it can from them conforms to the logic of abjection. Whether the language of appropriation is sexist, colonialist, or imperialist, meaning and value is established through absorbing what can be assimilated, and relegating to some unthinkable region that which does not conform to the dominant values. Whether the value to be tapped is reproductive capacity, labor resources, a market for consumer products, raw materials, energy sources, or land for cultivation, the logic of appropriation consigns to prehistory that which is discarded, and designates it as an inassimilable other. Women are rendered unthinkable by patriarchy except as reproductive vessels or maternal caretakers, while the humanity of workers cannot be registered within the logic of capitalism, which acknowledges them only as labor power or consumer power. The environment is reduced to the wasteland of slag heaps, while the natives of colonized lands either are not recognized as properly human, or only become so through forced practices of assimilation.[12] Thus, there is a systematic production of waste, of that which is useless, unproductive, of that which does not conform to the logic of patriarchy, capitalism, or colonialism. At the same time there is a usurpation, exploitation, and appropriation of precisely that which is only admitted insofar as it is capable of conforming to such logics. Theoretical discourses endorse, participate in, and reinvent such dynamics, creating their own logics of marginality.

Take psychoanalysis, for example, which has the dubious merit of constructing multiple marginal figures, on the basis of their gender, sexuality, class, and race, but whose primary other is figured in terms of femininity. In their attempt to legitimate themselves, psychoanalytic narratives produce sites of excess or irrationality that are posited as exterior and anterior to their own coherence and logic. The feminine comes to stand for a mythical past, relegated to a time that predates the Oedipal narrative, the terms of which are formulated in a way that precludes the entry of the feminine, other than as masquerade. At the same time psychoanalytic constructions of femininity systematically appeal to raced others. The very possibility of representation is consonant with Oedipal identity, such that any claims to be heard outside Oedipal logic are condemned as illogical or nonsensical. The sole form of representation that is admitted as coherent is that condoned by the Oedipal narrative, which represents itself as universal only by foreclosing any interrogation of its historical and progressive privileging of masculinity, which it presents as a more advanced or civilized state than femininity, and which is therefore determinative of meaning. The Oedipal configuration thereby surreptitiously acknowledges what it repudiates. Phallic privilege comes to determine what constitutes value, the contingency of which is occluded through a conflation of the values that are instantiated by the ideal of masculinity and those that are taken as representative of humanity. A symbolic system of meaning and its values is established by way of a compensatory narrative that covers over its lack, finitude, or frailty, by positing this inadequacy as outside itself, an outside that is projected into a mythical past which comes to be associated with the feminine. Figured as a castrated—and castrating—other, femininity presides over "meanings" which, from the perspective of phallic logic are inassimilable, can only ever appear to be fragmentary, incomplete, or momentarily incandescent. Lacking, by definition, the phallic principle of completion, which is achieved precisely through the fantasmatic and prosthetic production of wholeness in the face of its threat, the feminine becomes a constitutive outside of the very discourse it both enables and from which it is exempted.

The production of the feminine as a site of excess by a masculine imaginary allows for the inclusion of those aspects that prove useful for inclusion and incorporation by a masculinist and ostensibly universalist logic. The feminine is admitted only insofar as it constitutes the raw material to be worked over and made to conform to a logic that will not admit it as excessive or different, but requires its otherness or alterity to subsist as inferior and contained. Thus, both at the material level of the reproduction of the species, and at the level of signification, the feminine is admitted only insofar as it can contribute productively to the society or the state, the ends of which are defined by an invisibly white, patriarchal capitalism. Anything that cannot be converted into assets from this point of view is discarded as incoherent, insane, nonsensical, outside the bounds of reason, as defined by a logic that is taken to be universal. To be admitted into the system as meaningful is to signify within its terms. To exceed its terms is to be dismissed as inferior or meaningless. Yet the site of conversion from non-meaning to meaning remains significant in a way that cannot be captured from the point of view of the categories in which meaning resides. How, then, can this significance be acknowledged without assuming the legitimacy of the meaning toward which the scales are tipped?

While this logic of marginality is replicated across various discourses—patriarchal, capitalist, colonialist—it is equally true that attempts to bring into question each of these discourses are liable to reproduce a similar logic internally. Feminist discourses produce their own internal others, variously marked in racial, sexual, or class terms. Whatever advances are made in the name of feminism must be balanced against the capacity of particular feminist discourses to remain critically alert to their own complicity with racist, heterosexist, and middle-class assumptions. Postcolonial discourses, unless they pay systematic attention to issues of gender, are liable to reinvent gender oppression in their efforts to formulate anticolonial, nationalist discourses. The internally differentiated logic of each meta-discourse—even apparently progressive discourses such as feminist and subaltern movements—militates against any attempt to render them completely homologous with one another. The tendency of radical politics to reproduce at another level and in a new guise the exclusionary gestures against which they are protesting, and thus to invent a new series of others in their attempt to combat the processes that have in turn hypostasized them as other, demands theoretical reflection.

Forms of self-expression are dictated according to the norms legitimated by commodity culture, so that in order to be recognized as such, even the available means of dissent have been anticipated, and conveniently packaged for consumption.[13] Needless to say, such control need not be overt or coercive, indeed, more often than not, consent is manufactured, and ideology functions in a way that assimilates potential rebels or transgressors through procedures of self-regulation.[14] Given the efficiency with which consumer-citizens produce themselves in accordance with dominant norms, subjecting themselves to and reproducing commonly recognized forms of expression, perhaps it is not surprising that even apparently progressive discourses such as feminist, antiracist, anticolonialist, anticapitalist, and LGB discourses tend to have recourse to available forms of discriminatory logic. In order to shore up their own claims to be recognized, such discourses resort, often unconsciously, to the same kind of divisive thought patterns to which they object, setting up their own internal others to be maligned, disparaged, or dehumanized. Subjects thereby replicate the structures according to which they have been marginalized, merely infusing them with new content.

In efforts to take seriously the fact that the construction of gender has relied upon an inarticulate, indeterminate notion of race, or that of race has a repressed gendered history, theorists have rendered determinate those racialized or gendered histories that had been left indeterminate. The very process of rendering determinate this indeterminacy leads to possibilities of reifying or fetishizing those marginal excluded others who have played a constitutive role in the configuration of gender or race discourses, but whose role has not been acknowledged as such, or has only been acknowledged in exclusionary ways. The logic I am pointing to goes something like this: gender, for example, is pulled from a nonconceptual background which is the messy, indeterminate life of immediacy in all its confusion (what Levinas calls the elemental) and is treated as if it made sense as a coherent, independent, abstract concept. Whether part of a patriarchal discourse or part of a feminist discourse, the apparent independence and integrity of the concept of gender needs to be resisted, because it repudiates its messy, material indeterminacy, and the impossibility of divorcing it from other terms that present themselves as if they too could be reduced to clearly definable concepts, such as race or class or sexuality. In fact, however, while appearing to leave indeterminate a host of other notions, including race, class, and sexuality—as if they remained in some murky, nonconceptual, undefined, and nondefinable flux—in order to be what it is, to have come to have the history that it has, the concept of gender constructs highly specific and determinable notions of race, class, etc. So, gender presents itself as independent, appears to leave as indeterminate all these other terms, but in an unacknowledged, covert way draws upon imaginary racist, classist, and heterosexist myths, the content of which are culturally specific and socially sanctioned.[15] Not only is there a danger of fetishizing previously excluded others, but in the process of bringing to light their abjection, in the process of giving shape to, or specifying the contours of their history and experience, as often as not new others are abjected.

Abjection, as Julia Kristeva puts it, "draws me toward the place where meaning collapses" (*PH*, 2). At the same time as threatening the current symbolic order, abjection provides the opportunity for its reworking, precisely insofar as it represents a crisis in meaning. By paying attention to abject moments, and to the moments that produce and follow them, moments in which identity appears to coagulate and cover over the fissures and cracks that help to produce it, we can contest the forces that tend to gain hegemonic power over us. The specific histories of particular individuals, and the political circumstances in terms of which identities have been shaped, together with the irreducibly singular ways in which individuals come to respond to what life presents to us, can be revealed in the fractures of the stories we tell, and are told, about others and about ourselves. Privileged moments of abjection can help to reveal the ways in which I have been unconsciously shaped by forces over which I am never in complete control. If intrinsic to the operation and elaboration of the symbolic is not only the necessity of abject positions, together with the impossibility of their complete articulation within the systems they maintain, but also the production of new abjects, it might be wise to pay attention to the logic of this operation. Abjection can figure as a site of dissolution or undoing of the categories fetishism works so hard to keep in place, by bolstering up the symbolic meaning that is always already secured in advance by a masculine imaginary, subtended by a racial imaginary, the interrogation of which psychoanalysis has foreclosed. Abject moments can erupt, and can take effect variously. Abjection "is something rejected from which one does not part" (*PH*, 4). Whether it is a matter of subjects identifying their subjectivity, or communities cementing what binds them by way of expelling that which comes to be constituted as radically other, the movement of expulsion is constitutive of subjects and communities. It is not just that there is an outside constitutive of who I am, nor merely that in order to consolidate my identity there are various exclusions that I do not so much perform as discover myself as having always already benefited from, even as I challenge them and in doing so transform them. The point is to understand the inherent mobility of such constitutive gestures, the ways in which they can turn into something else, or become other than themselves—sometimes in creatively transformative ways and sometimes in regressively defensive ways.[16]

Abjection renders problematic any assumption of the stability of boundaries separating objects and subjects. Its moral charge is neither inherently good nor inherently bad. While it is necessarily transgressive in the sense that it does not respect the fixity of boundaries between self and other, passive and active, private and public, or inside and outside, its transgressive character can be mobilized in the service of politically regressive or progressive forces. Abject moments can put into crisis imaginaries by exposing their instability. As such they can provide opportunities for reworking identificatory mechanisms. Equally, abject moments can be used to shore up identities whose stability has been threatened in the wake of breaching boundaries that might have been assumed to be unassailable.

Abjection is constitutive of the coherence and integrity of subjects and communities, such that a movement of rejection or expulsion is foundational to the identity of subjects and communities. If central to the founding of subjectivity is an expulsion that is at the same time constitutive of the other as other and the subject as subject, then subjectivity is indebted to and contingent upon a defining of boundaries that establishes the distinction between subjectivity and otherness. In this sense, that which becomes other, that which is designated other, is constitutive of subjectivity precisely in its exclusion. The very possibility of being a subject, and of distinguishing other objects and subjects from oneself, owes itself to a preliminary and tentative positing of boundaries, a demarcation or discrimination of I from not-I that marks the moment of moving beyond primary narcissism. For Kristeva, at the level of the subject the separation of the infant from the mother is paradigmatic of abjection. It is a separation that is, for the infant, at the same time a provisional institution of subjectivity through the rejection of the mother as other. Kristeva's account of the abjection of the mother marks a departure from Freud, for whom the mother is the first object-choice. It marks a departure from Lacan insofar as it rewrites the mirror phase, situating the significance of the prematurity of the infant at an earlier point of development. The mirror stage, fetishism, and castration theory have taken center stage in Lacanian film theory. Abjection offers a way of developing a new direction in film theory. Of particular interest is the way in which abjection returns to haunt the symbolic that it both founds, and from which it is rejected. If the abjection of the mother's body is a founding moment of the symbolic/social order, it is only through the order that it founds that its movement comes to be articulated. That articulation occurs in political discourse, even in purportedly liberatory discourses, in a way that establishes a metonymic chain of dejects—as raced, classed, or othered in ways that fall outside of the normative, idealized subjects that stand for the status quo.

Since for Lacan the entry into the symbolic is indissociable from castration, to be a desiring subject is to be a subject of castration. Built into castration theory, with its attendant theory of fetishism, and the transcendent role of the phallus as master signifier, is an understanding of sexual difference that positions the maternal-feminine as prior to language or presymbolic.[17] Freud attributes a lack to women, based on their failure to live up to the expectation that women, like men, have penises, a mythical castration that provokes castration anxiety. Fetishism is a defense against the threat that women thereby represent. Women are the occasion for fetishism, yet have little need of fetishism themselves, for women are always already subject to a mythical castration. This has not prevented film theory from having taken up fetishism as an interpretive strategy intended to shed light on the general experience of spectators.[18]

As a corollary of castration theory, in Freud there is a consistent, although problematic, distinction between identification as aligned with the father, and object-choice, which is aligned with the mother. In fact, Freud's introduction of the phallic phase could be read as symptomatic of his repression of maternal identification. The consequences of this extend beyond Freud's well-established failure to elaborate a theory of maternal identification. For, although less pronounced than the discourse that reads it as a defense against women's mythical castration, the trope of fetishism is also implicated in a racialized discourse. If femininity is figured as lack—the horrific, abject, unthought ground of castration anxiety—its abject status is articulated in terms of an imaginary racing of subjectivity which subtends the more overtly thematic organization of psychoanalysis by sexual differentiation. In this sense one might say that race is the real, that which stages the psychoanalytic Oedipal narrative, but which itself remains unvoiced or unrepresented by it. The impossibility of figuring the symbolic work of this racial discourse that breathes life into the psychoanalytic scenario, but which is itself strategically omitted from its theoretical recycling is reflective of a cultural imaginary that has repudiated the necessity to think through the racial tropes that help to constitute the psychoanalytic corpus. While the theoretical work that race does for the trope of fetishism is usually ejected from the terms of textual analysis, it is recuperated at the level of cultural criticism. The fetish becomes applicable to racial marginalization, but in a way that repudiates its elaboration in terms of sexual difference. Without thinking through how race and gender are implicated in one another, race theorists transfer the fetish in an exchange that takes place between the discourses of feminist theory and race theory, so that it is reflective of a universal, monolithic value, albeit reborn.

Even the construction of the maternal body as abject might be read as inseparable from the devaluation of motherhood that pervades the postindustrialist capitalist logics of modernity. In this sense, we should not take for granted that Kristeva's privileging of the maternal body as abject is innocent of the pervasive sexism that infects psychoanalytic theory, any more than we should read as neutral the taboos and cultural constructs that Douglas analyzes, including those which posit menstruation as taboo, as innocent of sexist assumptions.[19] Having said this, the import of Kristeva's reading of abjection in *Powers of Horror*—even if it derives in part from a logic that sometimes participates in, or is complicit with, the abjection of the feminine—resides in the opportunity it opens up to go beyond the privileging of the incestual and parricidal taboos of Oedipal logic, replete with the patriarchal heterosexism constitutive of that logic.

My effort here, then, has been to expose the abject layers of feminized others who subtend the discourse of fetishism in its various applications. Effeminized day laborers, or immigrant workers, whose productivity is as precarious as their day-to-day living situations are, and whose livelihood consists of seeking out subsistence level survival if they can, and whose labor supports the systems of commodity fetishism that subsume bourgeois aspirations, suffer abjection from the capitalist machine. Members of the trans community, whose sexuality is, and continues to be, abjected by the universalizing assumptions of some feminists who dogmatically adhere to the canons of sexual difference, as much as by psychoanalytic castration theory, suffer abjection. Yet, abjection is not merely to be suffered. Abjection, by its very nature, is mobile, and as such it migrates from the negative to the positive with surprising lability. Abjection can be taken up as a strategy of survival, or protest, as a political maneuver, as an artistic endeavor that refuses to adhere to the canonical ways in which aesthetics has proceeded to discriminate purity from impurity, and beauty from ugliness, all the while making certain genders, races, classes, abilities, religions, nations represent some allegedly purified, idealized version of humanity, while others come to inhabit zones of illegibility.

Chapter 11

Reviving Oedipus: Oedipus, Anti-Oedipus, and the Nomadic Body in Kristeva

S. K. Keltner

The figure of Oedipus represents one of the central points of contention between psychoanalysis, on the one hand, and recent continental and social philosophy, on the other. At stake is the legitimacy of psychoanalysis as a universal science, primarily its "discovery" of the Oedipal family at the foundation of psychic and social life. The controversy over Oedipal subjectivity is historically significant insofar as it concerns the diagnosis of the modern failings of social, cultural, and political discourses of meaning and the subsequent fragmentation of the modern subject and the social bond. The Oedipal subject, as representative of a structural relation of identification between desire and law, is in crisis. If psychoanalytic and continental social theorists agree that Oedipal identification is in crisis, they radically diverge in their evaluations of it. Whereas traditional psychoanalytic theory insists on the resolution of the Oedipal crisis via the strengthening of "the paternal function"—as the essential *need* of the modern subject—, social theorists commonly challenge identification as a repression of desire that limits new formations of meaning, subjectivity, and social-political relations.[1]

Kristeva's intervention into the discourses surrounding Oedipus challenges the psychoanalytic reliance on, as well as the philosophical rejection of Oedipus as the nuclear, foundational structure of psychic, social, and cultural formations. On the one hand, against traditional psychoanalytic and psychoanalytic-anthropological attempts to discover Oedipus at the end of analysis, be it of an individual or a culture, Kristeva insists on social and symbolic processes of meaning production that both "precede and surpass" Oedipal theory.[2] On the other hand, against attempts to write Oedipus's obituary—which is also ulti-mately an attempt to write Freud's—Kristeva redescribes Oedipus as a figure transformative of law and meaning. In what follows I retrace three key invoca-tions of Oedipus in Kristeva's oeuvre—her analysis of the Sophoclean cycle in *Powers of Horror*, her first direct confrontation with Freudian Oedipal theory in *The Sense and Non-Sense of Revolt*, and her more recent reflections on "anti-Oedipus" in *La haine et le pardon*[3]—in order to isolate her confrontation with the figure as an animating principle of the development of her thought.

Reviving Oedipus

In a 1980 interview, "Feminism and Psychoanalysis,"[4] Elaine Hoffman Baruch questions Kristeva's reliance on psychoanalytic theory in the context of the

169

technological and social transformations of the family and reproduction. Kristeva does not defend the structure of the family formalized by Freud in the Oedipal triangle of daddy-mommy-me, but rather suggests that it is becoming an
indefensible theoretical position.

Here we are in the face of a humanity whose character is completely unforesee-
able. In the present state of things, one attitude one might have, a defensive
one, would consist of saying, "There must be preserved, along a straight Freudian line, the distribution of the paternal function, on the one side, and the maternal function, on the other, so that the speaking subjects who are constructed,
psychically and not just biologically, can have the 'normality' that we think of
as theirs." And what is this normality? It is that which succeeds in getting
along, surviving, in the Oedipal triangle. This position seems to me more and
more untenable. (*FP*, 120)

Kristeva thus links psychoanalytic Oedipal theory and practice to a social and
political process of normalization in which one can only "get along" or "survive" within it. The same year that the interview was conducted, Kristeva's
Powers of Horror also appeared, and research for what was to become *Tales of
Love* was on the horizon. *Powers of Horror* already contained a critique of Oedipal theory,[5] and in *Tales of Love* she articulates what she calls *pre-* and *trans-*
Oedipal dynamics of social and familial alliances that break with the central,
normalizing paternal figure. Kristeva offers an alternative account to the psychoanalytic solution of strengthening the prohibitive paternal function constitutive of Oedipal subjectivity and insists, instead, on love as the space of an interrogation that might reveal alternative possibilities.

Though Kristeva develops pre- and trans-Oedipal dynamics that challenge
Oedipal theory, the only extended discussion of Oedipus in the 1980s occurs in
Powers of Horror, where Kristeva rereads the first two plays of Sophocles's
Oedipus cycle, *Oedipus Rex* and *Oedipus at Colonus*—a reading that prefigures
her account of amatory idealization in *Tales of Love*. Significantly, Kristeva's
reading of Oedipus takes its point of departure not from Freud, but from the
classical scholar, Jean-Pierre Vernant, coauthor of a two volume work entitled
Myth and Tragedy in Ancient Greece.[6] In two chapters devoted to Oedipus,
"Oedipus without a Complex" and "Ambiguity and Reversal: On the Enigmatic
Structure of *Oedipus Rex*," Vernant criticizes the psychoanalytic imposition of
modern Oedipal theory on Greek myth and tragedy. In the first chapter, Vernant
criticizes psychoanalytic interpretations for failing to make use of philological
and historical methods, which demonstrate, he claims, that the Oedipal complex
is not only a distortion of Greek myth and tragedy, but also of the Oedipus myth
and *Oedipus Rex* in particular. In the second chapter, Vernant develops his thesis
that "the true mainspring of the tragedy" lies not in the conflict between Oedipal
desire and a prohibitive law, but in a logic of "ambiguity and reversal" (*MTG*,
140). According to Vernant, the figure of Oedipus is sovereign and *agos* (defilement); king and *pharmakos* (scapegoat); Corinthian stranger and Theban

native; clairvoyant and blind; a dispenser of justice and a criminal; Thebes's savior and doom: "Oedipus, he who is renowned to all, the first among men, the best of mortals, the man of power, intelligence, honors, and wealth discovers himself to be the last, the most unfortunate, and the worst of men, a criminal, a defilement, an object of horror to his fellows, abhorred by the gods, reduced to a life of beggary and exile" (*MTG*, 119). The animating principle of the play is not Oedipal desire, but the ambiguity and reversal of the parts Oedipus plays, which are revealed through Oedipus's questioning of his own identity. "Who is Oedipus?" is the question that guides Oedipus to the oracle, then to Thebes, and then to his downfall—the solver of riddles is a riddle to himself. *Oedipus Rex* is socially and historically significant, according to Vernant, because it challenges the organizing social structures of power in Greece that divided the king from the people and both from the *pharmakoi*. Oedipus himself is enigmatic insofar as the social oppositions governing Greek life are revealed in his own being. Nevertheless, Vernant does not conclude that the play is thus no longer significant *for us*. At the close of his essay, Vernant asks what accounts for *Oedipus Rex*'s "fresh and perennial qualities" (*MTG*, 140)? He answers that if the logic of ambiguity and reversal is the heart of the play, it will indelibly remain open to new interpretations. But what is more, the logical schema governing the riddle of existence can have a history; that is, it is not constrained to a Greek world. He concludes, "[w]e can also understand how it is that *Oedipus Rex* has acquired new meanings as, in the course of the history of Western thought, the problem of the ambiguity of man has shifted and changed its ground while the enigma of human existence has come to be formulated in different terms from those used by the ancient Greek tragedians" (*MTG*, 140).

Kristeva's reading of *Oedipus Rex* emphasizes not the Oedipus complex of Freud, but the riddle, identified by Vernant, that operates as a logical schema of ambiguity and reversal: "The mainspring of the tragedy lies in that ambiguity" (*PH*, 84).[7] Kristeva's appropriation of Vernant's reading of the play affirms the philological and historical method of analysis, which challenges the psychoanalytic essentialization of myth and tragedy. However, she does not thereby dispense with the Freudian emphasis on the threshold of desire/affectivity and law: "prohibition and ideal are joined in a single character in order to signify that the speaking being has no space of his own but stands on a fragile threshold as if stranded on account of an impossible demarcation" (*PH*, 84–85). On the one hand, Kristeva extends and deepens the reading of Oedipus offered by Vernant in terms of the threshold of affectivity and law. On the other, she extends and deepens the Freudian account by delineating new and various configurations of the affective threshold and by interpreting Oedipus as an historical formation of psychic and social life in Greece. The implication of Kristeva's analysis is that both Vernant and Freud's analyses of Oedipus remain abstract. By developing the *affective* threshold offered by Freud (in terms of abjection, symbolic capacity, and the experience of sexual difference) and the *historical* moment offered by Vernant (social configuration of Greek society), Kristeva's reading of Oedipus inaugurates a transhistorical account of abjection from Greece to Hellenism and the Bible, and finally to modernity. Kristeva's reading of Oedipus is thus contextualized within a history of abjection, as one shape that the archaic border between the self and otherness may take, and a concern to examine, she says, "the alterations, within subjectivity, and within the very symbolic competence, implied by the confrontation with the feminine and the way in which societies code themselves in order to accompany as far as possible the speaking being on that journey" (*PH*, 58).

Kristeva thus approaches the logic of ambiguity and reversal in *Oedipus Rex* in terms of a confrontation with abjection, in which she emphasizes "the feminine" as the privileged paradigm of that encounter. She begins her analysis of Oedipus by emphasizing the elision of the feminine with the abject: "The tragic and sublime fate of Oedipus *sums up and displaces* the mythical defilement that situates impurity on the untouchable 'other side' constituted by the *other* sex, within the *corporeal border*—the thin sheet of desire—and, basically, within the mother woman—the myth of natural fullness" (*PH*, 83; first emphasis mine). Starting from Oedipus's sovereignty, abjection breaks out when Oedipus discovers impurity—the body, desire, death (i.e., abjection)—in his own being. Oedipus the (knowing, responsible, sovereign) King—a being above the law, a dispenser of justice—becomes himself the criminal and a *pharmakos*. Kristeva's analysis of this border draws out the role of sexual difference in the social distinction: "Where then lies the border, the initial phantasmatic limit that establishes the clean and proper self of the speaking and/or social being? Between man and woman? Or between mother and child? Perhaps between woman and mother? . . . At the limit, if someone personifies abjection without the assurance of purification, it is woman, 'any woman,' the 'woman as a whole'" (*PH*, 85). For Kristeva, Oedipus's ambiguity is codified in terms of sexual difference, and his embodiment of social distinctions (King and *pharmakos*) is simultaneously the collapse of sexual difference within his own being. Oedipus's abjection not only stages the ambiguity and reversal of a class difference, but of sexual difference as well.

Kristeva claims that the affective and social threshold in *Oedipus Rex*, as a crisis in the social organization of differences, sums up "the mythic variant of abjection" (*PH*, 84) in which the "solution" proceeds by means of exclusion: spatial (social) exclusion (Oedipus's exile) and visual (symbolic) exclusion (Oedipus blinds himself). By becoming "*pharmakos*" Oedipus "allows the city to be freed from defilement" (*PH*, 84), i.e., Oedipus as *pharmakos* accomplishes a social and symbolic *katharsis*. Exclusion, as a solution to the Oedipus crisis that reveals desire, death, and corporeality at the heart of Oedipus's sovereignty, both socially and symbolically constitutes the limits of civic belonging, which may be represented by the very walls of the polis (remember that Thebes's "solution" was to make Oedipus dwell just on the outside of the city's walls). The mythic and ritualistic logic of abjection in *Oedipus Rex*, however, does not determine the fate of Oedipus, as we know from *Oedipus at Colonus*—a play, Kristeva says, "that does not seem to have preoccupied Freud" (*PH*, 88): "[Oedipus] knows and bounds the mythic universe constituted by the question of (sexual) difference and preoccupied with the separation of two powers: repro-duction/production, feminine/masculine. Oedipus completes that universe by introducing it into the particularity of each individual who then unfailingly be-comes *pharmakos* and universally tragic. But for such an interiorization to take place, a transition was needed; from Thebes to Colonus, ambiguity and reversal of differences become *contract*" (*PH*, 85–86). Following *Oedipus Rex*, a whole new territory, a territory that is "completely other," becomes the ground of a new "solution" to Oedipus's abjection. *Oedipus at Colonus* stages a set of alli-ances based not on the exclusionary logic of social and sexual differences, but on the contact between those who are strangers to one another.

The opening theatrical presentation of Sophocles's *Oedipus at Colonus*[8] stages three strangers wandering on sacred ground: the blinded, maimed, and orphaned "Greek"-foreigner, Oedipus; his daughter/sister, Antigone, who guides Oedipus toward the citizenry and laws of Colonus; and a third, a man named only "A Stranger." The Stranger, *a* stranger among many other strangers, includ-ing the citizenry who Oedipus addresses as "strangers" and the exile-King The-seus, is a stranger to Oedipus and Antigone. But, Oedipus and Antigone are also unknown, and to one another. Is Oedipus father or brother to Antigone? Is he her mother's child, her grandmother's child, the generational equal of Antigone's mother, grandmother, herself? In *Oedipus at Colonus* strangeness proliferates. A fourth figure of strangeness is also staged as the stage itself, an extraterritorial or otherworldly ground: the sacred, which is personified as feminine and is ad-dressed by Oedipus, the Stranger, and the citizenry as an "inviolable" "ground" on which no one should "tread" and "none may live in," as it is possessed by "Goddesses most dreadful, the daughters of Earth and Darkness" (*OC*, verses 30–40). The Chorus tells us it is a "dwelling place [they] pass with no eyes to look, and without voice to speak, with silent guard on lips, that no words may a pious mouth sound forth" and which Oedipus has failed to revere (*OC*, verse 130). Oedipus nonetheless calls *this* place his "place of safety" (*OC*, verse 270) and "a place of hospitality for strangers" (*OC*, verse 90). The crisis of the laws governing sexual, generational, and civic differences is the very sacred ground bearing the strangers. It is on the ground of *this* place that Oedipus claims, "I am here as sacred and pious both" (*OC*, verse 280), and it is also the ground ena-bling new and alternative dynamics of social alliances to be formed.

If *Oedipus Rex* stages a mythic logic of abjection through the purificatory ritual of social and symbolic exclusion, *Oedipus at Colonus* represents, Kristeva says, a change in "the fate of abjection": "Neither excluded nor blindly other, [abjection] finds its place as his *not known* within a 'subject on the verge of death'" (*PH*, 87–88). No longer "the feminine," the other sex, abjection is "a flaw in Oedipus's impossible sovereignty, a flaw in his knowledge" (*PH*, 88). The purificatory rites at Colonus, Kristeva insists, are not simply the *exclusion* or *rejection* of self or other, as in Thebes. The purification of Oedipus's abjec-tion at Colonus takes place through the *sayings* of Oedipus: "abjection, in a Greece in the process of becoming democratic, is taken over by the one who, through speaking, recognizes himself as mortal (so much so that he leaves no

male issue) and subject to the symbolic (one will note the purely nominal handing down of his mortal jouissance to the foreigner, Theseus)" (*PH*, 88). The
"saying of abjection" as a new process of purification is clarified by Kristeva as
sublimation, in opposition to exclusion. By being mired in abjection and symbolically *repeating it*, abjection is symbolized as the conditions of a mortal, de-
sirous, corporeal being: "I am abject, that is, mortal and speaking" (*PH*, 88). For
Kristeva, *Oedipus at Colonus* stages not a sovereign Oedipus in crisis, but an
Oedipus who is a *subject*. Oedipus *is not the Law*, but subject to it. That is to
say, Oedipus's relation to law is one of estrangement, rather than possession or
embodiment. This shift in relation to law and the purificatory rites that Oedipus
undergoes also opens new formations of social binding.

Oedipus is equivalent not to his sons, who are engaged in Oedipal quarrels
over sovereignty, but to his daughters and to the exile-King, Theseus. *Oedipus
at Colonus* points to nonfamilial, non-Oedipal points of alliance that challenge
familial sexual and generational differences constitutive of Oedipus as patri-
arch/King:

- "the sons born out of Oedipus's incest will perish, while [Antigone] will survive only within another logic, that of contract or symbolic existence, as . . .
  seen in *Oedipus at Colonus*" (*PH*, 85).
- Ismene, "the daughter so often silent," "speaks in order to object to the very
  Oedipean quarrels of the sons" and she "also heralds [Oedipus's] salvation
  through the gods" (*PH*, 87).
- "*Exile*, first desired, then refused by his sons, has become *rejection* before
  being transformed, for Oedipus, into *choice* and *symbolic handing down*. For it
  is on foreign soil, and to a foreign hero, Theseus, a symbolic son, that he be-
  queaths, at the same time as his daughters, the secret of his death" (*PH*, 87).

Oedipus at Colonus thus represents a new subject. Oedipus himself, Oedipus the
Greek-wanderer in a land of foreigners, a stranger to law, embodies the capacity
to be reborn again and again: first, on a mountainside between Thebes and Corinth; second, between Corinth and Thebes; third, through an exile that saves him
from being stoned to death; and finally in the sacred place of Colonus just before
death.

Oedipus at Colonus thus presents a movement beyond "Oedipal subjectivity" and toward other modifications. Kristeva is here less concerned with the
modern Oedipal subject than she is with the sociological and anthropological
analysis of abjection in Greece. However, her analysis also serves as a challenge
to the modern Oedipal subject, contained within the very Greek texts that became so significant for Freud, as well as a development of the Freudian insight.
Kristeva's challenge is issued through a reading of sexual and generational difference constitutive of kinship structures, which points toward an insight into the
sociohistorical reality of "Oedipus" as the figure of a culture obsessed with
power. Contrary to a resolution through phallic identification (which is, for
Freud, a kinship identification proper, and which is the "solution" of Thebes),

Oedipus's fate opens a vision of nontraditional genealogical alliances based not on blood, but rather on symbolic and cultural encounters with foreigners (including his daughters who appear foreign to him), who ensure his place within a new civic formation. The whole of *Oedipus at Colonus* is organized around the question of foreign alliances that give birth not only to Oedipus's belonging to a polis, but also to kinship relations insofar as it transforms Oedipus's estranged familial relations through symbolic alliances among foreigners. Oedipus's alliance with Theseus, the foreigner-King of Colonus, makes these other (non-Oedipal) alliances possible.

The crisis in genealogical bloodline thus opens the question of the constitution of familial and social relations. Kristeva's emphasis on alliance, contract, symbolic encounters, and speech acts distinguishes the relations among Oedipus, his children, and Creon from familial blood relations and demarcates a sublimatory relation to a foreigner-King/law. The familial bond is not a given, presocial relation, but constituted through social alliances. The purificatory rites that Oedipus undergoes in *Oedipus at Colonus* reconciles him to the Greek citizenry and his daughters, but Kristeva emphasizes several differences from the identification with sovereign power: a) Oedipus's identification with the foreigner-King Theseus does not stage a battle for sovereignty; that battle is subsequently undergone by Oedipus's sons and their uncle, Creon; b) Oedipus's accomplishment of civic belonging through the alliance with foreigners is not determined by blood relations or genealogical inheritance; c) the purificatory rites do exclude impurity, but offer an alternative dynamic between purity and impurity (*katharsis* is transformed from a purification that cleanses Oedipus of corporeality, death, and desire—or more simply "the feminine"—to a *katharsis* that sublimates through a linguistic act); d) Oedipus's relation to his daughters/sisters, Antigone and Ismene, is *transformed into* familial alliances made possible by Oedipus's civic belonging. For Kristeva, the significance of the Oedipus cycle must be understood within its historical context. Sophocles's Greece is a world in which the "democratic principle begins to hold sway" and thus the relation between bloodlines and sovereignty are open to a new interpretation. At Colonus, Oedipus's familial and civic ties are dependent not upon blood, but upon a nomadism in which Oedipus is a stranger to all. The principal distinction that organizes Oedipus's civic belonging at Colonus is thus not a distinction between the state and the family, nor even sexual difference, but rather a distinction between the exile-foreigner and the state. What distinguishes Oedipus's civic belonging in *Oedipus at Colonus* from all other forms of civic belonging in the Oedipus cycle (Creon, Eteocles, Polynices) is that it is precisely *accomplished.*

The "purificatory" process announced in *Powers of Horror*, which distinguishes Oedipus as King from Oedipus as Subject, is further developed in terms of "amatory identification" in *Tales of Love*. While Kristeva does not here return to the Sophoclean cycle, her analysis of an alternative form of identification, which challenges paternal prohibition, is carried over and becomes the central occupation. Importantly, for Kristeva, social-symbolic being is not accomplished through phallic identification but is rather prepared by another form of alliance: pre- or *trans*-Oedipal identification, which Kristeva calls "direct and immediate" and "prior to sexual differentiation" (*TL*, 38). Contrary to the identificatory structure proper to Oedipalization in Freud and Lacan, Kristeva identifies another dynamic of identification with what she calls, after a close and generous reading of Freud, "the father of individual prehistory." This father, Kristeva says, has "nothing to do" with the Oedipal father of law (*SNS*, 53). In *New Maladies of the Soul*, Kristeva clarifies her notion of identification and claims to maintain the term for two reasons only: first, for its account of the internalization of a foreign entity; and second, because "the problem of identification," she says, "shifts the emphasis from the Oedipus complex . . . to another intrapsychic experience, which precedes and surpasses the Oedipus complex, and which avoids the generic labels of psychiatric 'structures'" (*NM*, 177–78). She thus insists on a pre- or trans-symbolic identification. Kristeva interprets Freud's claim that the other of this amatory identification has "the sexual features of both parents" to mean that it is prior to sexual difference. She calls it "the coagulation of the mother and her desire" (*TL*, 41). "Coagulation," recalling as it does the flow of blood, maintains a fluid ambiguity between differentiation and nondifferentiation. For Kristeva, this dynamic is an archaic identification insofar as it is prior to or disruptive of self-identity.

At the purely psychoanalytic level of Kristeva's account, the pre-Oedipal dynamics of subject constitution are *prior to* Oedipal identification. These relational dynamics are not relations of power, but primary relations to otherness. In *Tales of Love*, she calls her psychoanalytic account an "evolutionary postulate" that allows her to "elaborate *various dispositions*" that give access to the symbolic function (*TL*, 44). As a *theoretical postulate* of "subjective diachrony," psychoanalytic theory illuminates the complexity of the "fragile threshold" between meaning and being, or affect and its organization. However, Kristeva clarifies her sense of the *pre*-Oedipal as "trans"-Oedipal, i.e., threshold dynamics of meaning production that are not structurally identifiable, but processes of symbolic activity. The ambiguity between "pre-" and "trans-"Oedipal processes clarifies the "conditions" (pre-) as "ruptures" (trans-) or *trans*-formations of meaning and subjectivity. As *transformations*, such processes are open to genetic analysis. Further, they are not solely "symbolic," but "social" insofar as they challenge, simultaneously, social *and* symbolic formations of self-identity and relations to others. Kristeva's analysis of Sophocles's Oedipus in *Powers of Horror* condenses her challenge to Freudian (Oedipal) identification as process of normalization punctuated by "ruptures" transformative of social-symbolic structures and meanings. As such, Kristeva's Oedipus is "revived" insofar as she identifies within Oedipus himself pre- or trans-Oedipal dynamics constitutive of Oedipus's social-symbolic being, which remains open to transformative and trans-historical processes of meaning production.

Kristeva's reading of Oedipus in the 1980s grapples with the conditions of a subject in crisis. In this sense, though she submits Sophocles's Oedipus to an historical analysis, she also identifies a trans-historical threshold constitutive of individual, social, and symbolic life. The "fragile threshold" of the speaking being recalls the modern crisis of Meaning that situates the significance of the figure of Oedipus in contemporary thought and which is the context of Kristeva's own redescription of Oedipus in *Powers of Horror*. However, if Kristeva sought to shift the emphasis from Oedipus to "other modifications," why, sixteen years later in *The Sense and Non-Sense of Revolt*, does she return to defend Freudian Oedipal theory? If Oedipal theory is linked to a process of normalization, and Kristeva seeks to identify opportunities for transforming concrete existence from conditions in which one can only "get along" or "survive" (*FP*, 120) in the Oedipal triangle, why does Freudian Oedipal theory become an exemplary thesis of revolt? If Kristeva sought to distinguish her account of *trans*-Oedipal identification from Freudian Oedipal identification, why does she insist on returning Oedipal theory to stage center?

Oedipus Is Dead, and We Have Killed Him

In *The Sense and Non-Sense of Revolt*, Kristeva develops an account of the dynamic of meaning production constitutive of self-relation and relations to others in terms of revolt. Revolt is examined not in the register of politics, but from a psychoanalytic and literary perspective. Within Freudian psychoanalysis, Kristeva identifies two models of revolt. The first, "Oedipal revolt," recalls her account of Oedipus's "impossible sovereignty" from *Powers of Horror* and its sociohistorical location and significance. However, this time she seeks to account for the Oedipal figure of modernity and its relationship to the Greek Oedipus. "Oedipal revolt," she reminds us, has two evolutions in Freud: a) the structural organization of the psyche of the speaking being; and b) a phylogenetic hypothesis that is, she says, a "less historical than historic" speculation. Oedipal revolt is the transgressive confrontation with authority. Within the history of religion, Freud identified the repetition of a crime of parricide in multiple and various symbolic forms. In her analysis of structural Oedipus, Kristeva will draw out the importance of the historical account as a minor history. She will also infect the structural account with a second Freudian model of revolt, which she calls "archaic revolt." Archaic revolt or "return to the archaic" "overturn[s] conscious meaning" (*SNS*, 15). Revolt as "access to the archaic" is articulated in terms of time. The archaic is a "timeless temporality," "sensible time," or an "impossible temporalizing"[9] that Freud called the *Zeitlos* (lost time, or even more literally, a broken-off bit of time, a time that is "unleashed," let go). Kristeva privileges Freudian psychoanalysis for proposing a rupture of time that touches on the somatic and where, Kristeva says in *Intimate Revolt*, "being itself is heard" (*IR*, 50). The "analytical revolt," as presented by Freud, is a process at the threshold of affective heterogeneity and discourse. It is a dynamic of return to nonintegratable, or better "infinitely signifiable," heterogeneity that is articulated or given signs. Kristeva summarizes her motivating concern thus:

> It is no longer a matter of conforming to the universal (in the best of cases, eve-

ryone aspiring to the same values, human rights, for example) or asserting one's difference (ethnic, religious, sexual) as untouchable and sacred; still less of fighting one of these tendencies with the other or simply and skillfully combining them. It is a matter of pushing the need for the universal *and* the need for singularity to the limit in each individual, making this simultaneous movement the source of both thought and language. "There is meaning": this will be my universal. And "I" use the words of the tribe to inscribe my singularity. *Je est un autre* ("I is another"): this will be my difference, and "I" will express my specificity by distorting the nevertheless necessary clichés of the codes of communication and by constantly deconstructing ideas/concepts/ideologies/philosophies that "I" have inherited. The borders of philosophy and literature break down in favor of a *process* of meaning and the speaking being, meanings emitted and values received. (*SNS*, 19)

Oedipal revolt inscribes the self in the language of the social-symbolic set by transforming inherited meanings. Kristeva thus returns to defend Freudian Oedipal theory, but this time Oedipus appears not as a structure that is becoming "more and more untenable," as she claimed in her 1980 interview. There, Oedipal theory was implicated in a structural simplicity that perpetuated processes of sociohistorical normalization.

Kristeva's presentation of structural Oedipus in *The Sense and Non-Sense of Revolt* examines the significance of the phallic reference as a social-symbolic moment of subject constitution that gives access not to linguistic capacity or autonomy as such, since these, according to Kristeva's earlier development of the pre-Oedipal dynamics of bodily signification, are already rudimentally established. Rather, the phallic reference formally inscribes a relation to power and law and transforms the subject into a social subject—a subject capable of thought and capable of regulating aggressive and erotic desire in relation to itself and others. Kristeva thus insists on a thesis of *phallic monism*, regardless of whether the subject is biologically male or female, as constitutive of a subject. She summarizes Oedipus thus: "the Oedipus complex is a fantasmatic organization, essentially unconscious, because repressed, that organizes psychical life and supposes the primacy of the phallus insofar as the phallus is, on the one hand, a narcissistically and erotically invested organ and, on the other, the signifier of the lack, which makes it suited for identification with the symbolic order itself" (*SNS*, 74). The "essential fact" that Kristeva seeks to articulate is that "the phallic reference is indispensable for *both* sexes as soon as they are constituted as *subjects* of the lack and/or the representation that culminates in the capacity to *think*" (*SNS*, 75). Kristeva thus insists on the phallus as *invested* (i.e., the phallus is valued, which transforms its status as an *organ* into the status of a symbol) and on the phallus as the "signifier" of a lack (i.e., the phallus is what is *threatened* and *detachable* and thus becomes a symbol of presence/absence, a logic at the heart of significatory systems). The phallus, for Kristeva, is the co-presence of sexuality and thought: "we are neither pure biological or animal body nor pure mind, but the conjunction of drives and meaning, their mutual tension" (*FS*, 59).

The sexuality/thought copresence is further articulated as the copresence of desire and law. This is essential because "meaning" is not individual meaning, but always already *socially organized* according to law and, thereby, open to ethical critique. If the phallic reference/threat of castration *organizes* desire into acceptable and nonacceptable patterns, it also establishes the possibility and capacity of ethical critique. First, power/law is opened to challenge insofar as it institutes a *revolt*. Kristeva's revival of the phallic reference de-emphasizes the law as the submission and regulation of desire and emphasizes the fragility and traversability of power, meaning, and law. According to Kristeva, Freud did not emphasize the submission to phallic law as the optimal outcome of development or the clinic, but rather emphasized its *impossibility*. Phallic identification is always already a *failed* identification or, in the language of *Powers of Horror*, an "impossible sovereignty." Nevertheless, though Oedipus fails, "Oedipus remains a hero for the unconscious; we repress the universality and ineluctability of the Oedipal failure" (*SNS*, 76), which results in the renewal of revolt. Second, Oedipal revolt is ethical insofar as the law's mediation and traversability concerns our relations to others. Kristeva claims that the "amorous link" perhaps "consecrates both the failure of Oedipus . . . and its renewal" (*SNS*, 77). The revolt that opens thought, as well as ethical critique, as a transformation of meaning, power, and law, is significant for Kristeva insofar as it is a structural capacity resistant to normalization and capable of other forms of modification.

As *structuring yet traversable*, the Oedipal subject, who is subject to a phallic organization that can be challenged, is not necessarily a subject who vies for sovereignty, nor a subject whose ethical meaning is necessarily determined by the phallus. "[T]he phallic issue as the Oedipus presents it to us . . . cannot be the sole issue" (*SNS*, 87). There are "human organizations," Kristeva insists, "that emphasize not the ordeal of power but other modulations of the symbolic-sexual copresence. . . . The Freudian tradition has the advantage of having underscored the structuring role of Oedipus and the phallus. But it perhaps has the disadvantage of having done so without indicating forms of modification, transgression, and revolt vis-à-vis this order. In any case, we cannot speak of revolt without redefining the axis against which it is organized and elaborated in the psychical space of the speaking being" (*SNS*, 87).

Kristeva's structural account of Oedipus, again, must be understood in terms of the two *diachronic* models of revolt that Freud proposed: first, the phylogenetic account of the historical transmission of transgression against authority and, second, the archaic. First, recalling the phylogenetic account, Kristeva says that Oedipus "is linked to the destiny of the subject in our civilization" and that Oedipus is, significantly, Greek—a philosophical, knowing, tragic subject of revolt. She thus links modern Oedipus to the Greek Oedipus. However, this is not to say that Freud says "the truth of Sophocles." However, she claims that though we do not find the desiring subject in Sophocles's Oedipus, we do find its logic (*SNS*, 69), and Freud examines what he "rediscovers internalized/hidden/dreamed in the contemporary psychical experience" (*SNS*, 71). Kristeva thus offers her own phylogenetic account of Oedipus. That is, she provides a tale, a story, a *narrated* history of revolt. The second diachronic model, "archaic revolt," concerns subjective diachrony and denotes a primary, affective relation to otherness. Following the phenomenological accounts of Husserl, Heidegger, and Sartre, Kristeva calls this dynamic of revolt "absolute transcendence." Archaic revolt decenters the subject: "Far from being absolutized as the summit of a pyramid from which the other gazes at me with an implacable and severe eye, the problematic of psychoanalytic alterity opens a space of interlocking alterities. Only this interlocking of alterities can give subjectivity an infinite dimension, a dimension of creativity. For by gaining access to my other-being, I gain access to the other-being of the other, and in this plural decentering . . . [is found] a sort of advent of plural and heterogeneous psychical potentialities that make 'my' psyche a life in being" (*SNS*, 67). Therein lies the most radical revolt. Oedipus's *ethical capacity*—historical, social, a life in being with other beings—both *precedes* and *surpasses* Oedipal subjectivity. Surpassing the phallic reference is not to be elided with *renunciation*, but rather the *transformation* of the phallic reference beyond the ordeal of power, i.e., representation beyond the phallus. The dynamics Kristeva identified in the 1980s as trans-Oedipal, primarily through attention to love, is here brought into explicit relation to the dynamics that Freud identified as Oedipal. Nevertheless, Kristeva does not reserve the transformative process she unearths in the Freudian Oedipus to Oedipus alone.[10] Indeed, the process of the transformation of meaning that she identifies in Oedipal revolt is later reiterated in terms of an anti-Oedipus.

Anti-Oedipus—Beyond Sexual Difference, an Incurable Stranger

The term "anti-Oedipus" appears in at least two of Kristeva's published works: first, in *The Sense and Non-Sense of Revolt*; second, in *La haine et le pardon*. The two references are contrary to one another in their meaning. The first is contextualized within a defense of Oedipus as a modern nomadic figure of revolt. In *The Sense and Non-Sense of Revolt*, anti-Oedipus seems to consolidate Kristeva's thesis of a society of normalization. She suggests that anti-Oedipus would be an avoidance of revolt effecting the automation, homogenization of psychic life. The second, more interestingly, is contextualized within a criticism of Oedipus as a figure of the historical formation of subjectivity under conditions of nationalism. Correlatively, anti-Oedipus appears within the latter as a modern nomadic figure. In *The Feminine and the Sacred* Kristeva confesses to Clément: "It seems to me that psychoanalysis is a micro-anthropology of the depths, where ethnic and national boundaries become permeable . . . and give way to our irremediable strangeness" (*FS*, 23).

In *La haine et le pardon*, the term "anti-Oedipus" emerges within an analysis of the foreigner. In "Celanie" in *La haine et le pardon*, which originally carried the title "Paul Celan: the Celans, the pain of the nomadic body," Kristeva claims that her reading of Celan's work and his letters, "is necessarily a projection of [her] own experience of exile" and also, "thus," of "those of [her] patients" (*HP*, 581). She emphasizes three aspects of the experience of the nomadic body: first, its pain. Whereas contemporary thought is tending toward an idealization of the stranger, "the new Sesame that will open the doors of the City" (*HP*, 581–82), Kristeva recalls us to its affectivity, "an election" that is painful and "destines us" (*HP*, 582). Second, the end of psychoanalysis is not the choice of a sex, he or she; but, rather, beyond "sexual identity," "the end of analysis confronts the subject with his irremediable solitude": "I am a potential and incurable stranger" (*HP*, 584). From these two hypotheses, Kristeva thirdly "distinguishes two great categories" (*HP*, 585): the sedentary body, which she will relate to Heideggerean dwelling, and the nomadic body, which she relates to Celan, the Jewish experience, her own, and that of her patients. Of Celan, she says: "This anti-Oedipus is armed against his mother country, gashes/cuts his maternal language; he is freed of the bonds of sense and thus to those of his life, in a deicidal, radical vertigo" (*HP*, 585). But, between these two, Kristeva does not insist that the latter is a pathological variant of the former (understood structurally or historically), that what is needed is a reconciliation to the former, to dwelling on a stable earth. Rather, she asks whether the interrogation, painful as it is, leads us to an altogether different accomplishment.

Kristeva's reading of the nomadic body as one that "takes place" takes as its occasion Heidegger's comment that he, a great admirer of Celan, was ignorant of Celan's Jewishness. Though, she admits, Heidegger is the first philosopher to interrogate the radical strangenesses that fissure the twentieth century, Kristeva says she would like to think that those two, Heidegger and Celan, could not meet: "The one believes that only the return to the dwelling can save us. . . . The other, Celan, does not dwell. *He takes place* [*se tenir*, is held, stands]: for nobody, for nothing, not known by anyone, 'for you,' certainly, but 'alone'" (*HP*, 587). Celan's language "evokes a space without language, a soil without soil, de-solate, of an irremediable, unrepresentable exile" (*HP*, 587). It is "a Jewish message, that of wandering" and of a risky vigilance (*HP*, 587). And, it is in this space that Celan's poetic speech is held, stands, takes place. The "two great categories," each representative of a distinct ethos, are not opposable in the terms of traditional logic. There is not an Oedipus and an Anti-Oedipus; rather, Anti-Oedipus is what remains essential but heterogeneous to Oedipus, as negotiations of the meaning of being that are *trans*-Oedipal ethical resistances. Kristeva's analysis of Oedipus and its challenge intersects with the significance of a modern, nomadic body.[11]

Kristeva's revival of Oedipus represents something both "universal" and "social-historical." Oedipus is at once a figure of psychoanalytic normativity and a figure that challenges psychoanalytic normativity; a sacred, nomadic figure and a "deadly Greek"; an archaic subject and a modern one; the genius and the failure of Freud. Even further, Oedipus embodies, and thus challenges, metaphysical and social binaries: intimate and public; psychic and social; male and female; foreigner/stranger and citizen; even, German and Jew. Perhaps true to his appearance as both detective and criminal in Sophocles, Oedipus is a riddle, a stranger to himself—a boundary-being irreducible to a single structure, dynamic, or referent. The figure of Oedipus is thus, for Kristeva, *ambiguous*, and to such an extent that the figure seems to metamorphose into other figures radically at odds with whom Oedipus has come to represent, including most recently and surprisingly, Anti-Oedipus. Oedipus stands as a condensatory metaphor of a specific and traversable, sociohistorical field of difference in need of revolt.

Chapter 12

Tragedy as De-Layering: The Opaque Immediacy of Antigone

Kalliopi Nikolopoulou

Introductory Remarks

Layering brings to mind complexity, multiplicity, the image of something neither simple nor transparent. Thus, in trying to think through de-layering, I brushed against the notions of simplicity, transparency, and immediacy. Can we think the simple without reducing it to the simplistic? Can we see in the simple the most difficult? Why have modern theory and philosophy fetishized the complex as opposed to the immediate?[1] Looking up the linguistic associations of the complex, I came upon terms belonging to the sphere of the technic: the complex is related to networks, interfaces, and other such technological structures. Insofar as our modern mode of disclosure has been technological, it seems thus appropriate that complexity is so valued. What I hope to do in this chapter is to ask the question of whether it is possible for us moderns to reactivate simplicity in all its elemental difficulty;[2] whether it is at all possible for us to experience the simple, which also means to be derailed by its resistance to be analyzed, broken down, and explained away. The simple, I want to say, puts us most in danger. If there is one Western text that best exemplifies this double-edged character of the immediate, as the most transparent and most opaque at the same time, this is *Antigone*.[3]

My remarks here respond to a recent Antigone, that of Judith Butler. Just as the Sophoclean *Antigone* served for Butler as a locus of incitation for questions that exceed the scope of Sophocles, so Butler's text offered me, somewhat in reverse, a motive to reread *Antigone* as a guidepost toward a modern problematic. I would identify this problematic with an optimistic, profoundly untragic vein that runs at the heart of contemporary theory, and with the ethical and political consequences that such untragic thinking entails.[4] Butler's reading of the play as a critique of law's exclusion of the nonnormative family implies such an optimistic theoretical assumption according to which theory can isolate specific problems, identify their social determinations (let us note that in her case at least the determinations are invariably sociocultural), and thereupon undertake the project of improving the world. This sometimes implicit and other times explicit voluntarism of social-construction theory illustrates well the contemporary theoretical failure to understand tragic logic in general—namely, the logic of the irrational par excellence, the logic that exists beyond justification, and in which "bad things can happen to good people," so to speak. Yet I think that, despite its

183

obvious unfairness that sounds so off-putting to our modern ears, this ancient logic allows for more profound differences among human beings than social construction does; this, even when social construction, like much of contemporary theory, claims difference as one of its central concepts. Tragic logic highlights the unpredictability of human beings in the unique way each one inhabits its actions and responds to unexpected adversity. Thus, while I understand the democratic spirit of social construction when it comes to addressing the civic nature of things, I submit that tragedy offers the site where the hard question of what exceeds civic—and hence, human—determination is rehearsed. In the precinct of the tragic, we cannot claim that all relations—blood commitments, commitments of love, cries of betrayal, and so forth—can or should be leveled out.

The forgetting of tragedy is concomitant with the discursive privileging of complexity, a rationalist tendency that relegates tragedy to the night of ethical life. Martha Nussbaum writes of this narrative of alleged progress from the violence of tragic conflict to the rationality of modern thought:

> The avoidance of practical conflict . . . has frequently been thought to be a criterion of rationality for persons—just as it has frequently been thought to be a condition of rationality for a political system that it should order things so that the sincere efforts of such persons will regularly meet with success. . . . And it has become firmly entrenched in modern thought, pressed even by some who defend a "tragic view" of individual cases of practical conflict. It has profoundly colored modern criticism of ancient tragedy. For the claim is that the human being's relation to value in the world is not, or should not be, profoundly tragic: that it is, or should be, possible without culpable neglect or serious loss to cut off the risk of the typical tragic occurrence. Tragedy would then represent a primitive or benighted stage of ethical life and thought.[5]

The history of philosophy and criticism, then, progresses as a gradual distancing from this "primitive," simple state, by subjecting it to the mechanisms of self-reflexivity, of complex questioning and commentary that mediate and mitigate its threatening darkness. The reflexivity of discourse supposedly protects us from the night of the primitive, under the conceit of lifting us from the embarrassment of primitive immediacy. Needless to say, however, in drawing this equation between obscurity and immediacy, philosophy must also admit that the immediate and the simple are not in fact all that "simple." Rather than failing the test of philosophical clarity, the archaic night confronts us with the inability of reflexive thought to account for everything, least of all for its own hidden violence each time it strives to resolve incommensurable oppositions. Thus, even in its retreat from understanding, this tragic darkness yields a deeper kind of lucidity, a kind of lucidity discursive obscurantism lacks.

Hence, to understand tragedy as the process of de-layering requires a move away from discursivity and rationalization. It requires our attunement to tragedy's fundamental law, which explodes all rationalization, and which Nietzsche expressed in a paradoxical, almost oracular, formula: "All that exists is just and unjust and equally justified in both."[6] In other words, we are not always in control of what exists and, often, there is nothing we can do to improve the world at our will. I would daresay that, in fact, our very conception of the world as a project for improvement[7]—though potentially noble in its intentions—might ironically be responsible for much of the suffering it wishes to resolve. This is, after all, Creon's plight in the play. Creon's project too was the security and improvement of his city, but in the name of this project he destroyed everything dear to him and to the very civility of the city. Insofar as politics remains encased within the framework of project, capitalizing in the immanence of human agency, and refusing to engage with that exteriority tragedy calls fate and philosophy calls nature, politics will remain tragically Creonic—that is, it will remain unwittingly blind in its own rejection of tragedy.

To understand tragedy as de-layering means to peel away at the multiple layers of human project (and projection, in its psychological form as well), and return to the nature of things, to the patency of what exists—an obviousness that is no less opaque, however, than the obviousness of stone. In that she presents us with this immediate yet impenetrable nature of things (the nature of kinship, of gods and mortals, of justice, of love, and of death most of all), Antigone has become over the ages a figure of contestation in philosophical, political, and literary discourses alike. The question, however, remains: what can Antigone tell us—if anything—when we approach her not from the false self-certainty of discourse, but from that precarious limit that interrupts discourse, rationalization, legitimation, authorization, and so on? From the place near the grave? What if we start thinking of her not as a subject of interpretation to be interrogated (has she not been already interrogated enough from Creon?), but as someone who willingly approaches something terrible, as if trying to communicate to us part of its wisdom and its impossibility? What happens, if we start listening to her from that brink of exposure that lies beyond the rational layers and cunning inventions with which we regulate and protect our ordinary existence from what makes this existence possible and threatens it at the same time?

Indeed, regardless of the exhaustive treatment of the play in the philosophical and literary tradition, scholars and lay readers alike have been drawn toward this work in an original manner—not only in hoping to find something new, but in being drawn above all to Antigone herself and encountering her directly. Jacques Lacan spoke of the attention she commands in terms of fascination, a fascination that draws us toward her essence: who is she really, and what does she stand for?[8] Each time a reading begins more or less guided by these two questions and, somewhat tragically, in this sequence. "Who is she?" slides into "What does she stand for?" Slipping from presencing to representation, we forget Antigone, falling instead into the interpretive vortex of reducing her to some political representative. Antigone is (but also *is not*) what she represents. Interpretation forgets the negative copula, even in the most emphatic sense that from the start Antigone is given over to death: she is who is (about) *to be not*. It is in this sense of primordial not-being that we should be hearing her proper name—

the one who does not generate. Antigone: the name of the nameless, of the one who dies for blood ties by also standing against mere natural life.

Butler's rereading of the tragedy aspires to an original encounter, but does not avoid the trap of representability. In evoking legal rhetoric, *Antigone's Claim* is already situated within a long-standing tradition that reads the play as the quintessential example of law and literature, with Creon and Antigone representing different facets of the law. Though Butler's critique of the law problematizes this tradition, her own analysis reproduces the principal argument she critiques. Her Antigone is sought "as an example of a certain feminist impulse" (*AC*, 1), that is, in the service of a political agenda, which, no matter how carefully framed at the limits of representation, remains largely within it. Yet even this objection is merely formal on my part, and I certainly would not dwell in it, had the content of the representation been as radical as Butler intended it to be— namely, a representation of an *antistatist* feminist politics (*AC*, 1). This, however, is not the case, since Butler's analyses of Antigone's speech-acts as legal discourse place Antigone back into state politics, and cannot sustain a non-dialectical opposition between Antigone and Creon (the state) that much traditional classical scholarship has hitherto been prudent enough to sustain. But before we delve further into this issue, some words concerning the status of sexual difference in this tragedy are due.

Let it be clear at the outset that it would be absurd to argue against Antigone's significance as a woman in the play. Sophocles's every twist and turn reminds us how crucial it is that the one who dares violate the tyrant's edict is a woman. From the very start, the play makes it clear that women were expected to be submissive—an understanding Ismene exemplifies as she asks Antigone to join her in complacency—thus accentuating all the more Antigone's dissent. Creon's list of suspects too consistently refers to men, indicating that it would be unthinkable, if not "unnatural," to have a woman commit such an act of disobedience. Later on, when Creon hears the unlikely news, his anger is visibly more intensified, precisely because he feels humiliated not only as a ruler by a subject, but as a man by a woman. It is the gendered nature of this conflict that Creon impresses angrily upon his son, Haemon: "we must not let people say that a woman beat us," Creon boasts (*A*, verse 734), ordering Haemon to forget his nuptials to Antigone. As he puts it vulgarly, "there are other fields for him to plow" (*A*, verse 627). It is thus evident that the issue of sexual difference is not simply one of many themes of the plot. Accordingly, Antigone scholarship— even before feminist theories became prevalent in the academy—recognized in some way or another the vital importance of gender in the play.

To speak of sexual difference intelligibly in the context of this tragedy (something that scholarship in classics has often addressed, even though Butler self-consciously forgoes such work for the most part[9]), one has to address the particular characteristics that made of the feminine the feminine and of the masculine the masculine in the ancient tragic tradition. For instance, that women were the guardians of familial duties, cardinal among which was the tending and burial of the dead, is such a characteristic. Hegel correctly mentions it, albeit he puts it to work in the interest of his dialectical interpretative edifice: feminine duty to the chthonic gods and care of their customs belongs for Hegel to an obsolete ethical order that is successfully superseded in the passage of Spirit by the victory of state law over family customs. More recently, Nicole Loraux's *The Mourning Voice* revisits this opposition between the feminine space of mourning and the male space of civic duty, except that for her the opposition is not a matter of dialectics resolving its antagonisms through the suppression of the tragic term and its supersession by politics. Instead, in Loraux's oppositional configuration,[10] the tragic voice, which is synonymous with the female voice, raises itself as the incommensurable other of political organization; indeed, it functions as the only refuge wherein the human being can express what politics has rendered inadmissible to its discourse, and at times even explicitly illegal: the private pain that follows loss, which is also the most universally shared aspect of human experience, since both victors and vanquished are bound to undergo it at some point in this life.

It is exactly at this juncture that I consider Butler's claim regarding the "feminist politics" of Antigone problematic—not simply because it continues to render Antigone a symbol of *a* politics, but because of the *kind* of politics it evokes, which is scarcely antistatist. According to Butler, Antigone shares in Creon's legalese and "assumes the voice of the law in committing the act against the law" (*AC*, 11), thus appropriating legal rhetoric to subvert his. Beyond my interpretative disagreement with her as to the meaning of Antigone's words in her confrontation with Creon (I hear in Antigone a revelatory tone that surrenders her to the ultimate of her fate, not a legalistic game or even a defense), I think that the legalization of Antigone's character hinders the argument Butler actually tries to advance: how can Antigone become emblematic of antistatist feminism once she has been rendered Creon's subversive mirror? I am afraid that we are right back to Hegel.

It is as if the one who is all about being—Antigone, the being pure and simple—obliges us always to dislodge her, send her over to symbolization and layering. Perhaps this is one way, and an ironic one at that, to understand Hegel's notorious statement that Antigone shows woman as the "everlasting irony of the community."[11] Perhaps he saw in Antigone an irony not against any community, but against the community of scholars most of all, as she relentlessly turns them into someone like her own father/brother, the ambitious but eventually defeated investigator. For, like Oedipus, the critic must overcome his/her predecessor and solve the enigma of Antigone only to end up blinded by his/her own method. And just as the Sphinx's mystery owes mostly to the patency of her riddle, Antigone's mystery too owes to her elemental simplicity, to a peculiar obviousness in her that erects a theoretical stumbling block.

Law, Blood, and Incest

While I commend Butler's vision "to extend legitimacy to a variety of kinship forms" (*AC*, 74), reading Antigone in the service of this agenda obscures what is at stake. At stake in Sophocles is law not as juridical procedure, not even as the more primal incest taboo, but law in its most originary and necessary sense as the beginning that dictates what human beings are: mortals.

Nevertheless, concerning the necessity of Antigone's death, Butler asks: "Is her fatality a necessity? And if not, under what non-necessary conditions does her fatality come to appear as necessity?" (*AC*, 27). At issue in questioning law's necessity is not simply the specific reason behind Antigone's death, but the very ontological priority of fatality as such. This way of politicizing Antigone—namely, in the context of interrogating the limits of law, while proposing inclusion ad infinitum of the unrepresented, thus infinitizing the law—happens at the expense of the tragic. To read from the infinite extension of the law is to read rationalistically, the tragic-ironic predicament of the modern thinker, who knows rationality to be anything but beyond suspicion, but who in the name of culture must also renounce the irrational forces of tragedy. Such "cultured" posture, however, also does away with the originary law according to which human culture happens, *the law* according to which humans emerge as creators of culture, as bearers and critics of their own *laws*. To read untragically: to read outside ruin, for the law is first and foremost ruin (*atē*)—the law not simply of the tragic genre, but the law that declares tragedy to be the humans' essential disposition.

Heidegger's reading of Antigone in his *Introduction to Metaphysics* rests on this tragic principle:[12] the human attempt to respond to the terrifying knowledge of our mortality renders us makers of a world through work, but at the same time exposes us to the futility of such projects. Such works, admirable though they may be, serve as ephemeral distractions, turning the human away from the death that confronts it. (In this sense, layering is *a* name for such discursive evasion of mortality.) Heidegger recasts these poles of human resourcefulness and the power of death in the respective terms of *technē* qua human violence-doing and *dikē* qua the overwhelming sway of Being. In responding to the provocation of the overwhelming sway, human violence-doing exposes us to perdition. Perdition is not contingent upon our way of handling the situation; it cannot be avoided by a more efficacious application of *technē*. *Technē* is only a mode of contestation against the overwhelming sway that puts us irrevocably at stake.

Antigone is the uncanniest (*deinotaton*) of all violence-doers not because of what she does, as her violence hardly involves a material transformation of the world of the kinds listed in the second choral ode. She stands as the *deinotaton* because of who she is, someone absolutely simple and absolutely inscrutable at once: she is the artless one, the one without skills to dodge the death that awaits.[13] "She does not know | how to yield to trouble," says the chorus of her lack of *technē* (*A*, verses 516–17). Drawn by death alone, obeying only the law of *dikē*, she engages in the most exemplary form of violence by radicalizing the daring, and making most immediately manifest this uttermost contestation in her refusal of *technē*. Antigone does not simply bury Polynices; she does so in pursuit of her own death. To stand by the dead on the risk—or, better, the guarantee—of one's own death: this is Antigone's noninstrumental *nomos*, a law that exceeds all violence-doing by accepting and facing head-on the overwhelming sway. She thus makes sure to be caught, as if to show Creon that it is not he who catches her, but something beyond human agency, something whose force he comes to glimpse only after his own ruin. This ontological law of perdition is made explicit in the third choral ode: "For the future near and far | and the past, this law holds good: | nothing very great | comes to the life of mortal man | without ruin to accompany it" (*A*, verses 662–66).

Antigone's law has to be thought outside the register of Right, which is Creon's sphere. Her law is sovereign not in the instrumental sense of Creon, but in the Bataillean sense of excess and expenditure: she acts so as to expend herself, to join the dead, to go to waste.[14] Antigone buries her brother not because of any "laws," written or unwritten; she is the source of her own law, or we could say, law comes to show itself through her being. In simply existing as she does, she illuminates for us the primordial law of being exposed. This is the meaning behind the a-chronological temporality Antigone ascribes to her law in front of Creon: "*They* [the laws] are not of today and yesterday; | they live forever; none knows when first they were" (*A*, verses 500–501). Antigone is not a solipsist who cannot abide by the laws of others—the laws of the state—but rather shows in her autonomy the true heteronomy of the law that exists before every lawmaker: to exist is to be perpetually confronted with and claimed by the corpse of Polynices.

With this understanding of law that exceeds both social convention and primal taboo, I turn to the issues of blood and incest. Blood does not have to be thought only as a marker of biological determinism; it also serves as a marker of singular contingency, namely, as an ethical figure. Blood ties mark the accidental, in that one cannot choose one's bloodline; thus, to act ethically to the kin means also to do so because that kin is simply another human being, not necessarily one we have chosen to be with, but one whose uncanny closeness and simultaneous otherness most of all exemplifies the arbitrariness of being with others. Consanguinity turns out to be a figure of dislocation, not only self-sameness. To illuminate this, I cite two interrelated moments in the play that show Antigone's passage from the "benighted" category of blood to the universal site of the moral law: the first involves her distinction between the worlds above and below; the second, her distinction of civic affairs from what she calls "my own" (*A*, verse 54).

Confronting Creon, Antigone denies that the justice of the dead corresponds to that of the living. Where he sees a seamless continuity between the city and the earth below, she sees a sharp distinction. Seth Benardete writes: "The city must for him keep itself intact below. 'Below' . . . is only an extension in depth of Thebes. For Antigone, however, . . . that below means below the earth, burial means a removal from Thebes and its concerns. The city is restricted to the surface of the earth."[15] As a site of convention, the city posits arbitrary boundaries. What counteracts these boundaries is not their discursive extension or abolition, as Butler suggests; it is rather the earth below, oldest of the gods, and unperturbed by the machinations of man who tills her surface (*A*, verses 374–76). The earth, and not simply the land, refers to the chthonic principle of nature associated with blood and roots as the nondiscursive markers of human togetherness, for all humans are rooted in the earth.

Of course, the very mention of blood and earth cannot occur in modern discourse innocently, outside the fraught question of Blood and Soil and the sinister tradition upon which the modern nation-state has been built. However, without being able to do justice to this issue by presenting a thorough treatment of it in this particular context, I am compelled to point out at least summarily the fundamental differences of the play's understanding of blood and earth from their political appropriation. Firstly, unlike soil, which refers to the land—and is thus always reducible to a country—the chthonic refers to the earth below, transcending geopolitical specificity. In the play, Antigone's adherence to chthonic law, which dictates that all dead deserve a place under the earth as they deserve the love of those who bury them, is in direct opposition to Creon's concern for the safety of the land—namely, for the preservation of the city-state of Thebes, which he champions in his acceptance-of-the-throne speech. In this context, it is instructive to refer again to Loraux's work on tragic mourning as a fundamentally antipolitical mode of expression within the polis. Loraux elaborates on the sharp difference between the language of mourning, which communicates the truly universal experience of suffering, and that of the political assembly, which relies on the false universality of proclamations about a city-state's greatness, the immortality of its heroes, and so on—in other words, Creon's clichés. Loraux illustrates this separation literally in the urban landscape of ancient Athens, where the architectural space of the theater of Dionysus at the feet of the Acropolis is in contrast to the Assembly's placement at a higher point in the hill of the Pnyx (*MV*, 15–16). Secondly, in *Antigone*, blood functions as a figure of mortality, attesting to interrelatedness rather than exclusion. Haemon, whose name means blood, and who sheds his blood by Antigone's corpse, is exemplary of this relationality: despite the irresolvable demands made upon him, he manages to come off as a model citizen, a respectful son, and a devoted lover. It is Creon, the representative of civic duty, who, in disowning all blood relations, replaces human intimacy with the cold and calculative equity of state regulation.

Consequently, as *autochthon*,[16] the family is *of* the earth; it is different from any city built *on* the earth. While the chthonic is the condition of possibility of the polis, the reverse is not true. After birth, we are raised to be citizens of a state, but in death, we do not return to a state; we return to earth as men or women, persons once loved by their kin—not heroes or traitors. Family marks this suspended "state" out of which we emerge to partake in cultural convention, but to which we return by way of nature. The family, which in Butler's account forms a determinist and exclusive cultural construct, shows itself in its chthonic dimension to be inclusive and transposable.

The ethical centrality of the blood tie as *philia* is shown in Antigone's response to Ismene's charge that she will be guilty of disobeying Creon: how can she disobey civic law by attending to her own? As Gerald Else maintains, *philia* does not mean just friendship, but "it originally referred to *close blood relations,* and that sense is the only one Antigone ever employs. Kreon, on the other hand, consistently uses φίλος (*philos*) in the derived sense: 'friend.'"[17] Whether we deem Else's reading of Antigone's *philia* to be restrictive, it reveals the ethical importance of blood. Of course, the move from such narrow view of *philia* to the larger field of ethical relations can and must be made, but such move—though it may transcend—should not erase the ethical significance of blood. Indeed, Antigone's remarkable step, her ungraspable simplicity, is to move from kin to friend, from necessity to freedom, from chthonic duty to responsibility, without—however—refusing the friend's rootedness in the chthonic world.

But how does Antigone make this step? Benardete again offers a clue: "She will lie with those who love her through what she does for them. . . . She must first, to rejoin her own, acquire them as friends. Antigone proves her right to be by deed what she already is by birth. She reconstitutes the family as something into which one freely enters. The love of her own almost becomes a matter of choice. It is this to which Antigone partly owes her awesome uncanniness" (*ST*, 12–13). Unlike Ismene, Antigone does not take her kin for granted, assuming they would forgive her even if she does not act rightly just because she shares in blood. Instead, she who stands for the irrevocable blood tie gives herself the strangest test and passes it: before joining her relatives in the underworld, she proves herself worthy of their love as if this love could be revoked, the way one always risks it in friendship. This dislocating, ecstatic effect of blood kinship is, for Benardete, Antigone's uncanniness.

A parenthetical explanation is due here, since my espousal of the term "uncanniness" may be construed as a direct contradiction of my insistence on Antigone's elemental simplicity: while simplicity is often thought to signify something unary, the notion of the uncanny—whether in Freud, Heidegger, or even Benardete—involves a moment of doubleness.[18] In further clarifying some of my earlier remarks on the issue of the immediate and the elemental, I would like to emphasize that the immediacy, or simplicity, of which I speak is neither easily accessible nor one-sided. Firstly, insofar as the elementally simple is unbreakable, it resists all discursive attempts at analysis, and thus, at accessibility. Secondly, being unbreakable is not necessarily the same as being unary. Something is unbreakable when that which holds it together (and one-sidedness cannot be held together), the force that makes it exist, exceeds our analytic laws. However, this also does not mean that togetherness is the same as the complex, in the calculable sense of manifold—thus separable—layers, in which we think of the complex. After all, in this sense, no matter how complex an exigency, it would be eventually calculable and graspable. The immediate here occupies the realm of what is properly ungraspable, but to what one is inevitably exposed. Immediacy and simplicity are synonyms for the paradoxical intimacy of what appears at plain sight, yet makes visible only the invisible itself.

As such, Antigone's uncanniness, taken here to be a mode of her immediacy, is not exclusive of this double moment. Rather, her uncanniness consists in that she hides, or even invalidates, its doubleness. Consider, for instance, these paradoxes: Antigone's vitality stems from death; she privileges blood relations over civic ones, but her love for her relatives is mostly expressed through honoring them, and proving herself honorable in sharing their bloodline—a strangely civic, rather than familial, form of love. Thus, as Benardete shows, the essence of her uncanniness lies in the manner she turns this doubleness in a direction where it appears as always-already oneness. Antigone is at home in not being at home, yet we do not see her ever as not-being-at-home, since this is the only home she has and in which she remains firmly rooted.

Let us now briefly address the issue of incest. *Antigone* serves for Butler as a cautionary tale about the horrific ramifications of mistaking the arbitrary line of the incest taboo for a transcendental law of kinship, thus misrecognizing the social exclusion of the nonnormative family for an inevitable calamity. I suggest that the taboo figures most poignantly the necessity of *a* boundary. Such boundary separates first and foremost the mortal from the immortal spheres, since it is only in the realm of the gods, after all, that incest was not simply permitted but sanctioned. Incest is the exemplary modality of coupling and generation of the inhuman,[19] thus pointing to the inhuman origins from which and in contradistinction to which the human emerged. While it is fruitful to question the particular place where the limit is drawn, what remains out of the question is the necessity of positing it—a necessity imposed on the human, not by the human.

According to Butler, the play interrogates the taboo through the overdetermination of Polynices, whom Antigone addresses with the kinship term "brother," a term that can equally apply to her relationship with Oedipus. Antigone's devotion to Polynices and her death are for Butler effects of her incestuous desire that calls for this "transposability of the terms of kinship" (*AC*, 78). Despite Butler's force of argument in this quasi-literalized scene of incest, it is important to nuance the scene in view of the temporality of this "incest." Antigone's love for Polynices is heightened after his death. She loves him not just because he is dead, but because of the ordeal of his corpse. Polynices is more than a life not worth living; he is a man not worthy of death—the essence of the unlovable, of the one who deserves to be ritually dehumanized in death more than in life—a fate he shares neither with his incestuous parents, nor his equally accursed brother, Eteocles. What summons Antigone is the singular way in which the exposed body of Polynices, and his alone, stands for exposure in extremis.

Likewise, Creon does not legislate her mourning because of the impossibility of her incestuous desire; rather, his edict precipitates her love. Whatever Antigone's erotics might be, it is death she most longs for, and this is the only claim on which Antigone, Ismene, Creon, and the chorus, all agree. Creon gives her that "gift of death," so to speak. At the end, the play has little to do with binaries such as kinship versus state, or even man versus woman, and more with illuminating the rare desire of a human being to live toward its death, to incline toward it, and to claim it as its ownmost possibility. In this consists Antigone's uncanny simplicity: that she relates to death in a terrifying immediacy, with no need for evasions.

If this catastrophic stance—which dispels the political dream of immanence, where human law preempts tragedy—appears "theological" to Butler (*AC*, 75), I am hard-pressed to say it is social construction that runs the utopian/theological risk of slipping from emancipatory project to totalitarian nightmare. What state could be deadlier and more repugnant to Antigone than the one that would pretend to save her from her own death? Orwell had this in mind when he outlawed tragedy from his vision of the totalitarian state, precisely because tragedy is tied to the unlegislatable, because it marks the site where not everything in life is politically determinable. In the thoughts of his hero, "Tragedy . . . belonged to the ancient time, to a time when there were still privacy, love, and friendship, and when the members of a family stood by one another without needing to know the reason."[20]

Crystal (Un)Clear

The figure of Antigone demands less explanation and more admiration; maybe even reverence. If this sounds worrisome in its "religiosity," we should not forget that tragedy was sacred to the Greeks, witnessed not only by the mortal spectators but by the gods as well. Nietzsche recalled this sacred function,[21] and Sophocles's position as a high priest should only add credence to it.

But what exactly commands this reverence? It is not what Antigone represents, such as ethical conduct in extremis, personal responsibility, fearlessness, and generosity, but what she presents all too plainly: secret and withdrawal. For not only does Antigone keep several secrets: her silence about the origins of the civil war, the secret manner she performs Polynices's funeral rites and changes her hate of Ismene into compassion, and finally, the quiet step she takes to her own death. Beyond these thematic secrets, which remain detectable precisely in the telling silence of the text, there is another, prior withdrawal, which makes possible her mode of presentation. Her ethical resolve, her having always-already known what to do for which we admire her, is enabled by something that must remain hidden—not something she consciously hides to draw power from (that something could otherwise be divulged)—but something that must remain inviolable by representation in order to shine forth in her presence. It is toward this mysterious, recessive force that she approaches when she tells Creon that the order she obeys precedes the divine order itself, having been upheld from time immemorial.

Secrets, though, are neither concepts nor can we entrust them with political possibilities. This does not mean that secrets do not inform or even threaten political life; it means that they are reducible neither to philosophizing nor to politicizing. Of course, we can tailor philosophy and politics to account for a secret, and this may all be for the improvement of philosophy and politics, but it impoverishes still the experience of what remains unaccountable, the experience not simply of privacy, but of privation as well. This is why Antigone's secrecy cannot be thought from within the contemporary theoretical frame of "complexity." Belonging to the utilitarian and mechanistic vocabulary of networks and circuits, the obsession with complexity has nothing to do with the stony opacity of Antigone. The chorus is right that she is savage and raw like her father (*A*, verse 515), but she is neither complex nor convoluted like him. Unlike Oedipus, who provided the very definition of a complex, Antigone is traversed by a certain mysterious purity. What makes her infinitely opaque is in fact her transparency: a crystalline hardness, impenetrable but diaphanous. Benardete said it best when he wrote that, "[p]erhaps, then, the ultimate conflict does not consist in that between Antigone and Creon, or even between the family and the city, but between Antigone and Sophocles, of whom one is always what she shows herself to be, and the other is never what he shows himself to be" (*ST*, 21). It is Sophocles's subtlety in drawing such a transparently elemental character, among other things, that confuses us. Else too concurs, stating that Sophocles's "vision is ultimately mysterious and paradoxical. . . . Like the god of Delphoi in Herakleitos's phrase, Sophokles 'neither declares nor conceals, but gives a sign'" (*MA*, 8). His Sphinx-like sign is Antigone herself: the enigma of transparency, of rootedness even in the most extreme deracination—a problem that proves insurmountable for our optimistic, theoretical age of mediation.

Chapter 13

Metaphysical Topo*graphies* Re-Layered: Critique and the Feminine

Elena Tzelepis

In her book *This Sex Which Is Not One*, the feminist philosopher Luce Irigaray notes that Platonic mimesis is double: there is mimesis as *production*, which would lie more in the realm of music, and there is the mimesis that would be already caught up in a process of *initiation, specularization, adequation*, and *reproduction*. It is the latter form that is privileged throughout the history of philosophy, Irigaray remarks, whereas the former seems always to have been repressed. Yet, she argues, it is doubtless in the direction of, and on the basis of, that first mimesis that the possibility of women's writing may come about. (*THS*, 131). This is the kind of mimesis that Irigaray enacts in order to work out, through, and on sexual difference, in order to revisit the discursive and material sites where "woman" is essentialized or excluded. The mimetic mode of Irigaray's early period texts sets the stage here, as I am particularly interested in discussing mimesis in relation to the question of "woman": that polysemic other that resists definitions and appropriations invoked by the philosophical discourses; that indispensable aporetic other who remains unplaceable, eccentric, and inappropriate/d to the metaphysical closure.

The present chapter explores the philosophical, political, textual, and sexual aspects of Irigaray's particular mode of mimesis, which, as I suggest, is *performative* and *deconstructive*. More specifically, I attempt to elaborate how such a mimetic gesture transposes us into a fundamentally paradoxical and indeterminate mode of critique of metaphysics which, rather than holding to or being carried off by the truth of sameness, involves "touching" and being "touched" by—and implicated in—the object of critique, both at once, without subject or object.

Irigaray's textual mimesis involves a rewriting that bears traces of previous and inherited philosophical discourses while it also reinvents them, in a way that implicates all the involved texts, subtexts, and pretexts in perpetual movements of approximating, parting, and reconnecting: neither produced nor reproduced, but rather responsive to the archiving forces of the performative. Jacques Derrida's and Judith Butler's radicalization of J. L. Austin's theoretical formulations of the performative become critical for my consideration of the performative agency of Irigaray's mimesis: its capacity not merely to repeat, but rather to supplement, supplant, or subvert the regulatory norms of the philosophical tradition.

Both Derrida and Butler attribute the force of the performative to its potential of undoing the property and the propriety of convention.[1] In Derrida's theorization of citationality, the sign—either linguistic or nonlinguistic—*both* disengages from its context *and* engenders new contexts. A sign and its meanings can never be delimited by its original context, authorized convention, and authorial intention.[2] Derrida's notion of "performative powerlessness," which resonates with what Butler calls "performative vulnerability," refers to the disengagement of signs from their prior historical contexts and their radical reiteration in ways that inaugurate different contexts and potentially destabilize existing power structures. Derrida addresses the aporicity of performativity by positing performativity as that which *produces* events but also that which *neutralizes* the event. In other words, there is always in the performative a legitimizing and legitimized convention—a performative authority—that permits it to neutralize the happening, the eventness of the event. Derrida calls us to heed the singularity (of the event)—the otherness of the other—in the performative, by alerting us to the capacity of the performative to erase the event and the uniqueness of its arrival. Thus, the event emerges (or, irrupts) as the limit of/to the performative.[3]

Butler has written extensively and insightfully on subversive repetition, on the risks, the vulnerabilities, and the surprising possibilities of appropriation. In addressing the complex ways in which resignification works—what she calls "the expropriability of the authorized discourse"—Butler has politicized performativity.[4] Performativity is the discursive mode by which production happens through repetition and recitation: "the parodic repetition of 'the original' . . . reveals the original to be nothing other than a parody of the *idea* of the natural and original."[5] There is no subject who precedes the performative and operates according to an external power; rather, it is through the very processes of citationality that the citing/performing subject is temporarily produced and dissimulated as the fictive origin of the performative. For Butler, no performative can escape or fully own its authorial and authoritative histories; and no performative is completely circumscribed by these histories. It can only undermine or disrupt the lawfulness of the system from within by necessarily appropriating a system, which is not ours and yet it is within it that we become subjects.

As a philosophical critique and reinterpretation of Western metaphysics, Luce Irigaray's mimesis is read and appreciated—despite its own inevitable limits and unresolved paradoxes—as a performative provocation. Such notion of mimesis as critique does not presuppose a prior self-grounding and knowing subject; it rather addresses the limits of knowability and self-knowability in acknowledging reflexivity as a mode of subjectivation that takes place within the context of ontological and epistemological regimes of intelligibility that precede and exceed the reflexive subject.

As a mode of affirmative deconstruction, Irigaray's mimesis opens a way for rethinking and reworking the aporetic forces of discontinuous regularity and positioned eventuality that play out in the turbulent terrain of mimesis. The tactical, and also tactile (in Irigarayan terms), way of doing this, is essential to her peculiar genre of material deconstruction, which is characterized by an interplay of textuality and physicality (and, in particular, the forces of eventuality erupting from this interplay). In Irigaray's work, the performative and deconstructive forces of writing are instantiated in pursuing the goal of breaking out of the boundaries of the proper body. Writing of a sexuality that is not simply the inverse or the complement of male sexuality constitutes a challenge to the conventional understanding of sexual difference, whereby difference is reduced to phallic presence or absence. Thus the sexed body ceases to be secured, or securely contoured, within and through predetermined identificatory practices organized by regulatory codes of intelligibility. As a deconstructive gesture, Irigaray's mimesis obscures traditional distinctions between the philosophical method and literary devices. It is crucial to remember here Derrida's understanding of deconstruction as that "*other* writing" that breaks the distinction between reason and rhetoric, logos and mythos, philosophy and literature.[6] What interests me in Irigaray's mimetic writing is the exploration of mimesis as a critical engagement with the differing and deferring forces of philosophical tradition that does not merely and fatally renormalize this tradition but rather it points to its limits and its suppressed traces of alterity. What is at stake is difference within mimesis: the possibility of alteration emerging from the necessarily unstable logic of iteration. What I am ultimately proposing here is that a philosophy tainted with the critical force of mimesis becomes a conceptual, cultural, and political practice that puts the normative categories of signification and symbolic significance into crisis. In redoubling itself, philosophy is altered and resignified as a differential multiplicity of force relations. Beyond the known boundaries of convention and moral imagination, such a force of disruption within reiterative discourse—that is, such hiatus, spacing, or *différance*—has the potential of becoming a paradigm for the conceptualizations of the yet-unthought.

Mimesis

In her early period of deconstructive writing, Irigaray performs a strategy of producing, re-creating, and remetaphorizing difference by way of assuming the tactical technique of mimesis (*mimétisme*). Through a peculiar complex, critical, and ambivalent engagement with the texts of logocentrism, Irigaray restages and exposes the sexual economy of truth. In her entanglement with canonical texts that define the history of Western philosophy from Plato onward, she suggestively adopts—or, appropriates—the strategy of mimicry or mimesis, a gesture historically assigned to the feminine—i.e., woman's masquerade and woman's relegation to the realm of the copy—perceived as mere derivativeness and unoriginality.[7] This strategy of mimesis challenges both the notion of the copy and the notion of the original; most importantly, it disrupts the putatively antithetical connection between them.[8] Irigaray's work illustrates that such disruption of the relation between the antinomical terms through which mimesis has been traditionally construed, has profound gender/sexual implications.

In *This Sex Which Is Not One*, Irigaray identifies mimesis as one of the "paths" to be pursued in an affirmatively strategic way in the process of undercutting the phallogocentric structural assumptions of metaphysics. The adoption of the mimetic stance remains at the level of an "initial phase," as Irigaray clarifies, within the project of reopening and rewriting "the figures of philosophical discourse . . . in order to pry out of them what they have borrowed that is feminine" (*THS*, 74). Mimesis is then a necessary—albeit preliminary and speculative—performative strategy of subversive layering, bringing into question, and reclaiming the text of Western metaphysics, by means of identifying the forces that mark the repressed place of woman in the history of philosophy; it is a strategy of engaging with the intelligibility of metaphysics—even by assuming the voice of the masculine—in order to affirmatively reappropriate the feminine:

> There is, in an initial phase, perhaps one "path," the one historically assigned to the feminine: that of mimicry. One must assume the feminine role deliberately. Which means already to convert a form of subordination into an affirmation, and thus to begin to thwart it. Whereas a direct feminine challenge to this condition means demanding to speak as a (masculine) "subject," that is, it means to postulate a relation to the intelligible that would maintain sexual difference. (*THS*, 76)

Indeed, mimesis is one of the realms wherein one can trace Irigaray's relation—and perhaps, debt—to Derrida. Her thinking concerning the strategic gesture of mimesis invokes the displacement of mimesis, as is amply evident in Derrida's inversion and disruption of the putatively distinct constitutive terms of mimesis in "The Double Session," the second of the three essays that synthesize *Dissemination*. In this work, Derrida deconstructs the presuppositions concerning the unity of meaning that enable the problematics of presentation and representation of truth in the history of Western literature and philosophy. The language of literature and the language of philosophy, he argues, incorporate absence, the dissemination of their own meaning. "The Double Session" constitutes a critical commentary on the history of mimesis, a critique of the conventional duality between subject and object of mimesis, central to the classical ontological construal of mimesis since the Platonic hierarchy of mimesis (i.e., the example of the three beds in the *Republic*[9]). Derrida reads Platonic mimesis in conjuncture with Stéphane Mallarmé's "Mimique," where—in his reading—syntactical ambiguity signals the unstable and ambivalent articulation between subject and object of mimesis, an articulation of eternal undecidability.[10] Derrida argues that Mallarmé's text "mimes" these very articulations, in all their ambiguity and instability, and destabilizes the logocentric distinctions of form and content, idea and expression, materiality and meaning, as well as signifier and signified, which organize the conceptualizations of the acts of writing and reading within the bounds of Western metaphysics of presence. The mime Pierrot imitates the murder of his wife Columbine suggestively committed amidst the sheets of their conjugal bed (the pun between *le lit* [the bed] and *il lit* [he is reading] plays an obviously significant performative role here), Mallarmé imitates the flexible articulations of the terms of mimesis, and Derrida, in "miming" Mallarmé's writing strategies, mobilizes the slippages central to "Mimique": between the crime with the orgasm (it is worth recalling that the mime Pierrot kills

Columbine in/by tickling the soles of her feet), as well as between the victim and the perpetrator (Pierrot's mimetic gestures represent, or enact, both characters). In "The Double Session," the terms that synthesize the dialectical unity of the act of mimesis are reversed and displaced; the foundational hierarchical duality of mimesis is deinstituted and rewritten in a way that affirms that the imitated is produced or reproduced by and in the very praxis of imitation.[11] The Irigarayan text temporarily occupies, or provisionally overtakes, the representational economy of the logos in order to destabilize its postulated universality, whose "truth" is firmly ensconced in the fixed dialectical duality of originality and derivativeness. By way of textually reenacting a constitutive intertwining of critical performance, on the one hand, and the object of critique, on the other—of the read/criticized text and the very critical appropriation of the latter—Irigaray inevitably puts in question philosophy's will to truth, but also, concurrently, philosophy's way of speaking, philosophy's "style." Reading Irigaray's texts is unsettling to any pursuit of authorial authentication and apodictic adjudication; oscillating between adopting and questioning, rewriting and erasing, her texts are prone to induce a disquieting anxiety at times monumentalized in the question "Who is speaking?". Encountering Irigaray's texts, we encounter the uncertainty and the pleasure of reading not despite but rather by virtue of the textual modalities of decentering and dispersing the model of recognition: no quotation marks, no distinctive contours of direct and indirect speech, no fixed intersubjectivism of authorship and citation, no clear boundaries of attribution between "object" of critique and "subject" of commentary. It is certainly not accidental that it is sometimes hard to distinguish her own voice from the voice she reads, reworks, and rewrites. As Butler has aptly remarked: "How does the difference from the philosophical father resound in the mime that appears to replicate his strategy so faithfully? This is, clearly, no place between 'his' language and 'hers,' but only a disruptive movement that unsettles the topographical claim" (*B*, 36).

In Irigaray's work, the authorial subject—as the purported "ground" for truth—is never given, never grounded in the secure plane of self-presence, never trapped in the property and propriety of the fixed meaning. Encountering Irigaray's textual events, then, we find ourselves impelled to the "style" of deterritorializing the style of ontopological semiotics; we find ourselves, that is, impelled to the "style" of thinking and reading otherwise: "No clear nor univocal statement can, in fact, dissolve this mortgage, this obstacle, all of them being caught, trapped, in the same reign of credit. It is as yet better to speak only through equivocations, allusions, innuendos, parables. . . . Even if you are asked for some precisions."[12]

As a search for an alternative imaginary beyond the metaphysics of substance, Irigaray's radical mime exposes and reconstitutes the terms by which the economy of representation has been posed in Western metaphysics; it constitutes a performative strategy structured by reiteration and displacement, or, in Gilles Deleuze's terms, by the dynamics of repetition and difference, whereby repetition engenders difference, or repetition allows repressed difference to erupt in the alternative mode of an active process of becoming. The dominant model of representation, as Deleuze has shown, is characterized by its inability to conceive of difference in and for itself, without reducing it to the Same.[13] Deleuze's philosophical nomadology seeks to reverse the Platonic hierarchical and specular distinction between "origin" and "simulacra," between sameness and difference.[14] Irigaray's call for speaking through equivocations and allusions, beyond the signifying economy of clarity and precision, echoes Deleuze's critique of the logic of recognition as the rational orthodoxy of clarity and distinctness. Deleuze's critique of innateness in thought finds in Irigaray's strategy of mimetic becoming an apt responsive actualization. The project of philosophy, for Deleuze, is to break with the sovereign model of representation, recognition, and common sense (the dogmatic and moral "Image of Thought," the *Cogitatio Natura Universalis*), to overturn the postulates that define Representation, namely, identity, opposition, analogy, and resemblance, and to allow for the eruption of difference and newness in thought. The "rhizomatic" (that is, nonunitary and nonlinear) critique of the philosophy of representation involves shifting away from conventional conceptualizations of the distinction between "the model" qua originary superior identity and "the copy" qua causally derived resemblance. It also encompasses a critique of another, even more crucial distinction in Plato, namely, the one between two different kinds of copies: the good copies (icons), which resemble the original model, and the pernicious copies (phantasms or simulacra), which are stripped of resemblance. It is the latter that are to be reckoned with, harnessed, and banished in the Platonic world.

Difference, in the realm of Deleuze's transcendental empiricism, implies divergence and decentering, as much as repetition signals displacement. This Nietzschean eternal return that Deleuze appropriates as the infinite movement of the dissimilar and the disparate in his radical critique of the "Image of Thought," is, indeed, of critical significance in Irigaray's work. The philosophical text, Irigaray's work suggests, is an eventuality that conveys and mobilizes the already citational and equivocal nature of all writing. Words are not mere representations, reflections of the original, or shadowy instances of derivative materiality enframed in the dialectics of model-copy, matter-form, idea-expression, signifier-signified. Rather, the philosophical text is an eventuality which renders such distinctions and determinations impossible and untenable; it is, indeed, a set of disruptive differences that unsettle such topographical and causal polarities. In layering canonical philosophical texts with difference (*diaphora*), textual eventuality constitutes what Deleuze calls the *phantasteon*, "which is both that which can only be imagined and the empirically unimaginable" (*DR*, 144).

Irigaray's critical praxis of rewriting calls forth a multifaceted play of forces and voices, which are beyond the sovereign logic of univocity, representation, and recognition. Rather than closing the philosophical text of Western metaphysics, Irigaray layers it in order to deterritorialize and remap it, by igniting the interplay of forces and relations of difference within it. Echoing Deleuze, Irigaray's work teaches that difference is not to be relegated to the realm of negation. The *heteron* is not to be confused with—and reduced to—the *enantion*. In so doing, it opens up a field of proliferating and crisscrossed future possibilities of movement, questioning, and becoming. This is a practice of mimesis that safeguards the sign's future appropriations and significations from foreclosure.

Eirōneía

The disruptive difference, with which Irigaray layers and de-layers the philosophical tradition, astonishes the complacent seriousness that lies at the heart of the master narrative and has cast the feminine as the radical alterity of discourse. This ironic intervention works to expose the position of masquerade assigned to women by the solemn binaries of phallogocentrism. With irony, Irigaray playfully diverts and alters established philosophical meanings, thus echoing Socratic *eirōneía* as a rhetorical gesture of exposing preconceived claims of knowledge. Irigaray's "mimicry" of Socratic irony has its own limits and ambivalences, however: her mimetic irony works to deauthenticate and denormalize regimes of truth and not to exhort and reinstate truth as single and authentic the way the Socratic method of affected ignorance does.

While Irigaray's writing seems to be an ironic disruption of the philosophical tradition, it also ironically echoes a certain intimacy with it. Naomi Schor has rightly argued that Irigaray's mimesis enacts for us what Derrida has termed *paleonymy*, namely, "the occasional maintenance of an *old name* in order to launch a new concept."[15] This affected writing embodies a paradoxical relationship of desire and repulsion, reconciliation and disparity, recuperation and dissociation. It is a spatiotemporal threshold, a border space of partaking with, and partitioning from, the history of philosophy. It is not a question of exceeding or overcoming the limits of discourse but rather of ironically miming that discourse in ways that allow for acts of displacement, disarticulation, and disruptive inscription to occur. Such bodying-forth impels a remembrance of suppressing the other/s, whose parasitical and contaminating presence is incorporated within the deformed, uncanny text and its homely weirdness. The emergent and itinerant textual event figures a text-testimony: a textual testimony through which philosophy accounts for the erasures and displacements of other voices and modes of humanness. As a reemergence and reembodiment of these foreign and repudiated bodies, this rewriting emerges performatively as a rearchiving of both the past and the future.

To look at Irigaray's strategic use of mimesis is to look at the question of whether *eirōneía* can be redeemed within unanticipated and improper contexts to become what Naomi Schor calls "positive mimesis" (*TE*, 67–68) and Elizabeth Weed calls "radical citationality,"[16] that is, subversive discourse that vigilantly interrogates the terms of the intelligible itself without becoming fatally complicit to it. Does Irigaray's mimesis critically parody women's hysteric positions in phallocentric discourse or does it hysterically repeat its pretension to be self-constituting?[17] And, further, to recall Judith Butler's recurring key question: "What kind of subversive repetition might call into question the regulatory practice of identity itself?" (*GT*, 32). Irigaray strategically repossesses the "feminine" as a performative force that can disrupt the eternal return of the Same.[18] But here we need to ask: what does such *eirōneía* do to the house of metaphysics and its seriousness and proprieties? Where does it take place if not, inevitably, within discourse? In engaging the philosophical tradition is Irigaray dutifully echoing or is she usurping the solemn voice of the philosophical father? Is she seeking to find a place within his discourse, does she seek to take his place, or does she dis-place the very topoi—and topographical claims—of His Master's Voice?

"Woman"

The various attempts to rethink and retheorize the critical political deployments of mimesis have crucially given rise to the question of representation in its vexed relation to the question of essence. Indeed, in putting to question the model of representation, Irigaray's strategy of mimesis opens up a space for a different look at the problem of essence. This is by no means about a pursuit of essentialism versus antiessentialism, but rather about a breaking with and shifting beyond such polarity. Her project of citational reappropriation is to deconstruct and symbolically redistribute the terms of such polarity, to discursively imitate this putative antithesis, and to tactically assume the masculinist terms of the canon of monologic representation, in order to reallocate the essentialist language of logocentric metaphysics.

Irigaray's gesture of doubling both constructs and deconstructs essences (i.e., "woman") at the same time. Her mimetic repetition of the imaginary institution of the "feminine" emphasizes the inextricable entanglement of the two, one's investment in the other. As manifested in her own textual gestures of miming (i.e., her mimicry of the Platonic text in her *Speculum of the Other Woman*, or of the Nietzschean text in her *Marine Lover of Friedrich Nietzsche*), hers is neither a project of interpretative mastery of the text, nor a project of refusal, dismissal, or destructive mockery, despite the occasional acuteness and vehemence of her critical tone. It is rather a deconstructive strategy of drawing an alternative mapping of the masculine economy of Western onto-theology. As a discursive mode of intimate disrespect that goes beyond mere opposition or endorsement, her ambivalent lay(er)ing claim to "essence" is designed to be provisionally summoned as a *technē* of simultaneous reiterating and displacing. Indeed, her mimetic reassertion of sexual difference bears the marks of *technē*, that is, of revealing and bringing-forth (in Heidegger's sense): a performative strategy for bringing to light the tacit and unmarked masculine character of Western ontology and its presumptions of neutered universality; bringing to light the latent masculine economy of identity as an economy of exclusion and abjection; and bringing to light the repressed, eclipsed, and annihilated other of the masculine order, the function of the feminine as the constitutive alterity of the phallogocentric order. In this sense, her project of unveiling and revealing a new feminine specificity as multiplicity in opposition to rigid oneness is akin to a *poietic* pursuit of *alētheia*. Her endeavor is at once ethical and political: her

task is to resymbolize the symbolic in a way that suggests the repressed and censured element upon which phallogocentric metaphysics is predicated; in doing
so, she undeniably thematizes and rearticulates her own conceptual debt to the
object of her critique. Consider, for example, her reappropriation of Plato's metaphor of the cavern (the maternal, "the womb of the mother"), Nietzsche's images of mobility and fluidity (the "marine element" as a figure of feminine
jouissance), or, most importantly, Merleau-Ponty's tactile phenomenology (her
formulation of the figure of the "two touching lips" as a trope of nonphallic tactility and sensibility, provisionally deployed as an antidote to the ontological
primacy of the model of sight).

Irigaray's work echoes an intertwinement of debt and displacement: both
the displacement of debt and the debt of displacement. Her textual gesture is a
gesture of a troubled insistence on short-circuiting the fiction of the metaphysical polarities of language that have constructed the essence of woman, by way of
enacting this very language, its doxic presuppositions and determinations. Here
is how she emphasizes the strategic necessity of mimesis:

> To play with mimesis is thus, for a woman, to try to locate the place of her ex-
> ploitation by discourse, without allowing herself to be simply reduced to it. It
> means to resubmit herself—inasmuch as she is on the side of the "perceptible,"
> of "matter"—to "ideas," in particular to ideas about herself that are elaborated
> in/by a masculine logic, but so as to make "visible" by an effect of playful repe-
> tition, what was supposed to remain invisible: recovering a possible operation
> of the feminine in language. (*THS*, 76)

The accessible givenness of the so-called natural body is put into question,
supplanted by a fluid textual corporeality. Although Irigaray makes constant
reference to anatomical differences, her approach is being concerned primarily
with discourse, an approach seeking to revalue and decenter the ways in which
female embodiment is inscribed in language and in culture. A cautionary dis-
claimer is in order here: Irigaray's insistence on "nature"—the nature of the female body—has nothing to do with defining "woman." It should not be confused with an essentialist defining of woman through a metaphysics of
receptivity, weakness, and passivity, a metaphysics that prescribes what the single and unitary essence of woman is and should be.[19] In fact, it lays bare the
ethico-political investment of such defining of an imaginary morphology that is
commonly founded on an attribution of a fixed essence to women: "But there is
no essence without the will to force her back or reduce her to being the relation
to a unique mother-nature."[20]

Irigaray's insistent reference to the elemental economy of the female body
is designed to retheorize the specificity of the feminine. Her ultimate goal is to
reclaim sexual difference in such a way that would defamiliarize and rearticulate the proper-ty (the economy of possession and exchange) of "femininity": "Femininity is part and parcel of the patriarchal order. Woman is hidden in
the thought of the father" (*ML*, 96).[21] In Irigaray's particular materialist econo-

my of mimesis, the recurrent themes of flexibility, fluidity, and uncertainty play
a decisive role. Her endeavor to reclaim the elemental echoes Nietzsche's relation to the pre-Socratics' reflections on the elements—earth, fire, air, and water.
Irigaray's "economimesis"—to borrow Derrida's term—echoes pre-Socratic
elemental materialism, but it also resonates with the tropes of mobility and fluidity that Nietzsche deploys in offering his observations about "women" ("a spirit-
like intermediate being: quietly observing, gliding, floating"[22]). In engaging with
Nietzsche from the point of view of the fluid, Irigaray writes in *Marine Lover*:

> She does not set herself up as one, as a (single) female unit. She is not closed
> up or around one single truth or essence. The essence of a truth remains foreign
> to her. She neither has nor is a being. And she does not oppose a feminine truth
> to the masculine truth. Because this would once again amount to playing the—
> man's—game of castration. If the female sex takes place by embracing itself,
> by endlessly sharing and exchanging its lips, its edges, its borders, and their
> "content," as it ceaselessly becomes other, no stability of essence is proper to
> her. (*ML*, 86)[23]

What is "proper" to woman, then, is a perpetual becoming, an endless errancy. "Because she has no place in the time of essence, of durability, of self-
identity, the other errs: reverse of the sames" (*ML*, 88). In Irigaray's interrogation of the Nietzschean feminization of fluidity, depth, and abyssal wandering,
the trope of errancy is shown to be deployed as a signifier of the other of the
same, and, as such, by virtue of its force of alterity, is attributed to "woman." In
Irigaray, the feminization of depth and floating within the context of the ethico-
political order of patriarchy signifies the forced obscurity of the refusal and repression of the woman, an exemplary fugitive, the eternal other, both elusive
and repressed at once. "Woman" remains "buried in the deepest 'depths,' primi-
tively, in the swamps of oblivion" (*ML*, 94). She provocatively chooses to read
feminized depth as absence from herself, abyss as nothingness attributed to
women: "But so much is attributed to one who has nothing of her own" (*ML*,
110).

Interestingly enough, in *Speculum of the Other Woman*, Irigaray associates
castration with the death drives, absence, projection of lack onto the female
body, the "dark continent" of female sexuality in Freud. Woman is reduced to
the blank space of the "defective" or "castrated" other in the symbolic system of
castration, and, as such, she is excluded from the discourse of the Western metaphysics of presence. With her taking over of the image of the speculum, she
seeks to insinuate a nonphallomorphic sexual economy. Her own "play with
mimesis" involves a radical questioning of male specular logic of the same, the
scopic (or scopophilic) economy that sees women's bodies as lacking. Irigaray
explores the ways in which woman has been constructed within the terms of the
phallus as "other," and, at the same time, as mirror-image of man. Playing on the
idea of the mirror and Lacan's mirror stage, Irigarayan alternative morphology
of the sexed body exposes the phallomorphic status of the logic of identity and

challenges the idealized status of the phallus as the primary operator of difference in the ocularcentric sexual economy of Western culture. Reiterating the
phallogocentric metaphor of the cavity (i.e., the cavernous vagina) through
which woman has been represented, Irigaray counterposes the "speculum,"
which alludes to the mirror used by doctors for examining the internal cavities
of the female body. She takes on the word "speculum" in its multiplicity of
meanings—both the gynecological instrument and the mirror—in order to open
critically the scene of phallogocentric representation as it is structured by male
spectatorship and the specularization of woman. Her resignifying of the image
of the concave and reflecting speculum allows her to rearticulate a materialist
economy of feminine cavities, by introducing an economy of decentered touch,
exemplified by her metaphor/metonymy of the contact of the lips.[24] Such emphasis on tactility puts into question the privileging of the visual and the solidi-
fying effects of the gaze within Western metaphysics.[25]

Irigaray's rewriting of feminine morphology—through the metaphors of
multiplicity, plasticity, and tactility—is an engagement with the construction of
an imaginary body that empties and lays bare traditional discursive and disciplinary conceptions of women as receptacles for masculine completeness. The
question that emerges is: is this strategic use of essentialism about relapsing into
the topography of identity, or about instituting a new essentialist topography?
Does her deconstructive gesturing toward the "essence" of feminine specificity
leave the phallic field of ahistorical, apolitical, empiricist, and reductive essence
unaffected? To give women an essential topos of identification, Irigaray seems
to hold, will not leave the topos of subjectivity-as-saming in place; it will bring
about a change in what essence is, and will collapse the boundaries of universality, it will transform the very conditions of bounding and demarcating the
universal. The Irigarayan enterprise to reappropriate the feminine entails displacing, relocating, and relayering both essence and difference, as well as both
inside and outside the realm of phallogocentric intelligibility. Repeatedly in the
course of her exploring the possibilities of the feminine specificity, Irigaray insists not only on the plural and polysemic, but also on the "nonessential" of po-
sitionality within, outside of, or in regard to phallogocentrism: "There is no simple manageable way to leap to the outside of phallogocentrism, nor any possible
way to situate oneself there, that would result from the simple fact of being a
woman" (*THS*, 162).

Actio in distans

Irigaray explores woman's ambivalent relation, at once distant and intimate,
with the scene of representation. A propos of rewriting Nietzsche's becoming-
woman, Irigaray discusses distance and proximity in terms of doubling and oth-
ering. In his observations about women ("Women and Their Action at a Distance"), Nietzsche writes: "[t]he magic and the most powerful effect of women
is, in philosophical language, action at a distance, *actio in distans*; but this requires first of all and above all—distance" (*TGS*, 124). Irigaray discusses and re-

articulates "woman's" power to live and act at a distance as a possibility of disruption: "And as she is dis-tant—and in 'herself'—she threatens the stability of all values. In her there is always the possibility that truth, appearances, will, power, eternal recurrence . . . will collapse. By mimicking them all more or less adequately, that female other never holds firm to any of them univocally" (*ML*, 118). At the same time, she ironizes

> [t]his distant enchanting calm, whose happiness and retirement he longs for, is, it seems, associated with women. . . . Always at a distance. Out of reach but well in sight. Allowing the rhythm to pick up without missing a beat. From one hammering to the next, they remain there, calmly. Giving and taking back the dream of their supple spread of canvas. (*ML*, 104)

"Canvas" stands for the screen, the veil, the vacant blind and its duplicity into which woman is hypostasized, operating as at once the dressmaking of appearance and the screen of representation; the mask and the condition of acting, men's acting, that is: "The most powerful effect of women: to double for men, sublime souls" (*ML*, 109). "The mortal inertia of a double" to which woman is reduced "reproduces nothing that isn't masculine" (*ML*, 117). "She is—through her inexhaustible aptitude for mimicry—the living foundation for the whole staging of the world" (*ML*, 118). Irigaray claims that Nietzsche's becoming-woman—which is effected through his tropes of distancing and non-truth—betrays an intoxicated joy of being-beyond, which, nonetheless, remains firmly ensconced in the same logic of the truth of sameness. For Irigaray, such gestures are by no means taken to be unproblematic; rather, they are read as mastering moves trapped within the circle of merely reiterating the phallocentric order of things.

Now where does Irigaray's mimetic practice stand in regard to the question of distance, or, as she puts it, "the distancing in the nearing, or the opposite" (*ML*, 106)? Her mimesis encompasses both modalities of proximity and distancing at once. It could be said, even, that it is founded upon this simultaneity. Her critical intervention, taking the form of the bodily metaphor/metonymy of "the two lips," is one of unsettling the very antinomy between distancing and nearing. In rearticulating Nietzsche's trope of distancing, Irigaray writes: "dis-tance with no possible relations. No lips, since they too now, whether open or closed, beat the time, mark the tempo for distancing to take place" (*ML*, 110). She also signals woman's ambivalent relation, at once distant and intimate, with the performance of representation:

> She might act as prompter for the whole scene because she stays outside this way. In the wings. But also outside the scene of the action in a wider sense. Thus: she is disguised for the performance of representation, hidden in the wings—where she doubles up her own role as other, as well as same—, beyond all that is taking place. (*ML*, 83)

The rewriting of woman as a prompter, a hidden/distant but necessary condition for the play of representation itself, bespeaks her role of the phantasmatic constitutive outside of the phallogocentric play of presence and absence; a role that is radically ambivalent, both assigned and reworked. The image of woman as a figure residing in the dark and shadowy wings, recalls the depths of the Nietzschean abyss, but, in Irigaray's text, it does so otherwise, that is, by performing an (even more) defamiliarized version of difference. The realm of beyond (outside the stage set), where "she" is in full play, is what keeps "her," this errant shadow and distant double, from coming into the play of truth, from being subsumed into truth. The part that this outside plays in Irigaray remains radically ambivalent, indefinitely and undecidably oscillating between "moving beyond" and "falling short," as well as between "out of reach" and "well in sight." It is an out-of-place-ness that is double in itself: indeed, not merely a matter of her suffering a forced exile from discourse and representation, but also a matter of withholding herself from the economy of appearances to which she has been relegated and reduced.

To play with mimesis is, in Irigaray, crucially intertwined with resisting to the truth of mimesis: engaging with the playful language work of mimesis is, at the same time, "remaining elsewhere." This is about an appropriation that remains open to a (utopian) future and gestures toward a certain beyond-appropriation; one which does not uncritically replicate the logic of the proper, one which is not fatally circumscribed by relations of domination. This is, indeed, about an appropriation that bends itself or lends itself to what is to come, to the singularity—or, the event—of what lies beyond the signifying economy of the representable, the appropriable, and the anticipatable. This playing-with-mimesis-while-remaining-elsewhere figures a shift from the economy (the law of the *oikos*, the proper place, once again) of mimesis to the aneconomy of what does not allow itself to be subsumed under mimesis. Irigaray's mimesis returns us to the possibility of a theory of performativity which is reduced neither to a formal pragmatics that merely repeats and consolidates power structures nor to a facile pragmatics of subversion. Thus, it returns us to the question: is "subversive performative" an oxymoron?—a question that insists on the aporetics of a performative that is potentially recuperable and yet allows the incalculable possibility of challenging ontological and epistemological limits.

Philosophy's *eidōlon*

Taking up the case of Irigaray, I would like to cast into question the question: can such project of performative and deconstructive mimesis ever succeed? And furthermore, does Irigaray manage to move away from the language that she endeavors to expose and destabilize, does she eventually break with the binarisms that constitutively organize this very language? Instead of answering the question, I think it is important that we cast into question the linear, phallogocentric, liberalist, and religious undertones of such line of questioning. There is nothing redemptive, liberatory, or consummate about Irigaray's poetics. In fact, there is nothing corporate about Irigaray's corporeal poetics. It is important, I suggest, that we turn our attention and shift the perspective of questioning (it is important, in other words, that we go beyond such transcendental inquiry, such unidirectional topographical construal of "beyond" and "outside") and pose another question: do the texts remain the same after experiencing such provocation, or such provocative reading? Do they remain unlayered after having their own Irigaray, as it were? Even though Irigaray's project fails, and it was perhaps constitutively and inevitably bound to fail from the outset (for the violence of the signifier always and unavoidably returns), the fact that we can no longer read metaphysics without Irigaray's strategic layerings and mimetic revisitations bespeaks the consequential force of such textual performativity. For one, after her affirmative deconstruction of the feminine as a phantasmatic, mimetic, failed copy, the very notion of "failure" has changed.

Irigaray's mimesis as a performative disarticulates the economy of the unpresentability and refigures the figuration of the feminine in the textual register. From this gesture of intersecting philosophy and sexual difference, new modalities of critique emerge; we learn how to read the paternal language from the margins, how to engage textually with the canon of intelligibility from a position of the critically unintelligible. Sexual difference becomes in Derrida's words the "site or non-site (*non-lieu*) [from where] philosophy can as such appear to itself as other than itself, so that it can interrogate and reflect upon itself in an original manner."[26]

Epilogue

Layering Is Not

Christakis Chatzichristou

L000: In a different voice—MM, AL

As has often been acknowledged, the epilogue is what has always already been there at the beginning. It is the actual source of a series of discourses which, in their development, come to forget the pretext that has made them possible and opened up a space for them. Everything that precedes this epilogue (the introductions, the individual contributions, the 2007 IAPL conference) owes its existence to Christakis Chatzichristou's thinking on layering and his layered experimentations as an architect, a writer, and an artist. In this palimpsestic intervention we would like to add yet another layer of debt and gratitude which, though not always visible, remains in reality the vital node where all the ideas and philosophical debates mobilized in this volume return to and intersect.

L100: Paper number

Paper 1

L101: Title

Layering is not

L102: Keywords

Layering, drawing, painting, architectural theory, architectural technique, perception, philosophy

L103: Abstract for paper 1

This paper examines the concept of layering as this has so far developed through activities such as painting or architectural and urban design as well as through more theoretical investigations. The much more familiar concepts of collage and, more recently, of folding are used to clarify the characteristics of layering as a creative technique in design as well as a way of understanding everyday perception and conceptualization.

L104: A painting as a never-finished project

A work of art such as a painting is normally considered finished at one point or another. This does not seem to be the case with my work since, irrespective of an initial or earlier confidence that a specific piece is completed, I invariably tend to go back to it with the desire to keep working on it. Why that is and what implications does this practice have for the act of painting itself as well as its product.

L105: General intentions regarding the specific paper
This paper is intended to be neither exclusively theoretical, nor textual nor visual, while the format of the paper itself examines the concept of layering in the medium of writing.

L106: Why should the title be anything else than just another layer?
As with L0 (the alleged starting point of a series), the title of an article cannot claim any form of special status. It is indeed just another layer. Imagine if it is given in the middle or at the end, or at any other point in the body of the work. Its specific position of course influences the way it itself is received as well the way the rest of the material is comprehended. Still, does such a realization allow it to claim any privileged position? Doesn't any part of the work influence, admittedly in different ways, the other parts as well?

If placed at the beginning of the article, a title is clearly assigned a strong ideological role. It positions everything that follows according to itself. If placed at the end, it again serves a similar role, operating more like a conclusion. In both cases, it acts like the frame around a painting, the content of which is indeed organized in such a way that the boundary around it clearly influences its composition. Placed anywhere else, it may still be a sort of boundary but more like the frame in an action painting by Pollock since it does not really influence the composition of the painting.

One could argue that the title is the title precisely because it is placed at the beginning of a work. But, what if the work starts as follows?

> The title of this work can be found at the end. You thus have the choice of reading the whole work and then read the title, or go to the end, read the title and then come back to the beginning of the text and start reading.

Or it could start as follows:

> The title of the work is found somewhere within the body of the work. You thus have the choice of simply starting to read from the beginning and encounter the title in its place within the text, or search quickly for the title by scanning through the work, read it, and then start reading from the beginning of the work.

In both cases, as in the case where the title is at the beginning of the text, the work as well as the title is rendered different by their relative configuration. Still, the title remains a title and the text remains the text. In other words, the title is not necessarily rendered a title by its relative position in the text but more through the act of christening it as a title.
(What if there are many titles in the text?)

L107: Layering in architecture

Architecture is necessarily layered in form, space, and time, synchronically as well as diachronically. The easiest way to understand the above statement is to note the degree to which layers of different construction materials in both the horizontal as well as the vertical direction compose a wall or a floor. Similarly, any spatial configuration cannot but be perceived as a series of spaces, synchronically if they can be seen from one point, or diachronically if they are linked perceptually through memory when the subject travels through them. In the former case, transparency as well as the relationship between solids and voids influence the degree and nature of layering.

Then, of course, there is always the layering caused by the subject's previous experiences of a specific building or of other configurations of space and form, memories and impressions that are juxtaposed to the one presently experienced, whether consciously or not.

On a more theoretical level, the conceptual lenses offered by a number of architects are of relevance to the concept under investigation here. Jeffrey Kipnis's embracing of irrationality, ambivalence, multivocality, simultaneity, and the mystical,[1] and John Hejduk's description of "architectural tracings as apparitions, outlines, figments, ghosts, and tracings similar to X-Rays" could be seen as literal snapshots of a layered architectural composition.[2] Eisenman, who is seen as using mainly deconstruction and the concept of folding, explains that "two clarities equal a blur," and that "with this blur battle can be done with the good and common sense of prevailing aesthetico-architectural techniques."[3] He thus suggests another potential impact layering may have on the broader context within which it is purposefully applied by the architect.[4] Such may be the quite explicit use of layering present in Peter Cook's proposal for a Layered City, while it certainly is the case in Tschumi's work on La Vilette where he clearly layers horizontal planes not only to create the patterns on the ground but to also configure other more three-dimensional elements which delight while they confuse.

1. Jeffrey Kipnis, "Forms of Irrationality," in *Strategies in Architectural Thinking*, ed. John Whiteman and Jeffrey Kipnis (Cambridge, MA: Chicago Institute for Architecture and Urbanism, MIT Press, 1992), 148–65.
2. John Hejduk, "Thoughts of an Architect," in *Victims: A Work by John Hejduk* (London: Architectural Association, 1986), unpaged.
3. Peter Eisenman, "Processes of the Interstitial: Notes on Zaera-Polo's Idea of the Machinic," *El Croquis*, no. 83: "Peter Eisenman, 1990–1997," 26.
4. Hélène Frichot, "Stealing into Gilles Deleuze's Baroque House," in *Deleuze and Space*, ed. Ian Buchanan and Gregg Lambert (Edinburgh: Edinburgh University Press, 2005), 75.

L108: Layering and depth

Layering depends on a peculiar kind of "depth" due to the superposition of many layers. It tends to undermine perspectival vision. It has the depthless quality of the panoramic. The further away the subject moves from the object, the flatter this becomes. Its depth is latent. It is a potentiality; the closer the subject moves to the object, the more three-dimensional it gets.

Challenging the established human perception is a step toward creating potential for change. In *Downcast Eyes*, Martin Jay explains that perspective presents what could be taken as a "homogeneous, regularly ordered space, there to be duplicated by the extension of a gridlike network of coordinates." This is a "uniform, infinite, isotropic space that differentiated the dominant modern world view from its various predecessors, a notion of space congenial not only to modern science, but also, it has been widely argued, to the emerging economic system we call capitalism,"[1] since the "separation of the spaces of production and consumption permitted a radical disjunction between working the land and merely viewing it from afar, as an aesthetically pleasing prospect" (*DE*, 59). The Albertian "perspective is in this sense atemporal, decorporealized, and transcendental" (*DE*, 189).

Layering is a conceptual lens which attempts to challenge the, in many respects, still predominant perspectival space. Rather than positioning the subject at a point, a layered arrangement allows for depth as well as for "surface" navigation. Deleuze's concept of the "planomenon" might also be of relevance here:

> [W]hat needs to be thought is not this or that plane, nor this or that realized system of relations, but the potential to produce planes, the "planomenon," and our capacity to think or encounter that potential.[2]

Deleuze is here suggesting that planes, which he sees as systems of relations, can be encountered in a comparatively passive manner, but more significantly, they can be produced or thought of in a more active or creative manner.

On the other hand, layering may appear as two-dimensional or even epidermic, yet this occurs in such a pluralistic and dynamic manner that it at once undermines the notion of the surface. An extreme case of this is the surface of water which can absorb two or more wave forms traveling in different directions. Soundscapes are also layered in quite complex ways which, like a layered painting, may contain or portray more than one system of relations; the membrane of the ear receiving all the sounds present at any one point in time is simply a flat stretched surface, just like the canvas or the photographic film, yet what is actually perceived is a three-dimensional spatiotemporal entity.

1. Martin Jay, *Downcast Eyes: The Denigration of Vision in Twentieth-Century French Thought* (Berkeley, Los Angeles and London: University of California Press, 1993), 57. Henceforth cited as *DE*.
2. Claire Colebrook, "The Space of Man: On the Specificity of Affect in Deleuze and Guattari," in *Deleuze and Space*, 196. Henceforth cited as *SM*.

L109: Introduction for essay: Layering is not
Old and new paintings in my studio that seemed to be in need of further work encouraged the examination of the concept of erasure. It soon became clear that,

rather than erasing, what was actually happening was the creation of more relationships between existing and new elements in a sort of layered fashion, and that these concepts were also useful in an ongoing research in architecture and urban design.

Just like a city is never really "finished," so does a painting have the potential of always being modified, added on, layered. So, without underestimating the differences between painting and architecture or urban design, a more systematic examination of terms like collage, boundary, identity and the essence of the unit, the nature of pattern, and the meaning of *telos* in the sense of spatial and temporal completion, the simultaneous or synchronous and the *synchorous* began to contribute in the evolution of "layering" as a conceptual model.

It was also becoming clear that such a model could potentially be useful in other areas of interest such as my research dealing with the divided city of Nicosia, an urban entity with a walled core surrounded by a moat, a buffer zone running through its middle, and two halves growing to a large extent independently as two autonomous cities.

L110: Layering as more of a process than a product
The paralyzing effect of commitment accompanying the notion of finality or concreteness, is neutralized by the liberating promiscuity of layering; rather than laboring over any kind of work, whether this is a piece of architecture, a painting or a text, in order to clearly and for ever define it, the practice of layering allows for a shift of focus: from being concerned with fixing identities and products to being continuously creative with processes. In its refusal to stand still and reach a destination, layering is clearly much more of a process than a product.

L111: A painting

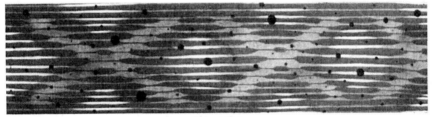

Figure E.1

(This, and all the artwork displayed in this chapter, is original.)

L112: Layering and intertextuality
Layering could be considered as a form of intertextuality since with layering no text is seen as a closed system. Furthermore, rather than a simple influence between more or less independent entities, it results not exactly in a "mosaic" or row of references or quotations from other texts, but in a pulsating situation where things are juxtaposed and seen simultaneously to different extents and in

varying degrees of transparency. Trains of words could be seen as layered: cho-ra-figure-matrix-*mitra*-mother-dead-grave-her grave-my grave-our house-father-other-Lacan-Pierce-indexicality. . .

The important thing to remember here is that any such train retains in layers all the "places" it travels through. It is as if the observer is not on the train but in a plane perpendicular and not parallel to the direction of travel.

L113: Layering and palimpsest

Similar to layering's relationship to intertextuality is its relationship to the no-tion of the palimpsest: each layer is neither eradicated completely, nor is it total-ly visible. Furthermore, the autonomy, and consequently the identity of each participating layer is challenged, blurred, or rendered apparently nonexistent.

L114: Folding in architecture

Peter Eisenman attempts to offer an alternative architectural discourse by aiming at disrupting the way space is rationalized and consequently understood by the subject. This is attempted by the use of the fold, a concept taken from Deleuze who sees folded space as a new articulation between vertical and horizontal, figure and ground, inside and outside.[1] Thus, if space is no longer translatable into the vision of the mind, then reason becomes detached from vision.

Greg Lynn posits that, "if there is a single effect produced in architecture by folding, it will be the ability to integrate unrelated elements within a new con-tinuous mixture."[2]

Folding, in this sense, depends on the existence of a single, continuous enti-ty. Still it does preserve the two faces of an opaque boundary. Layering reduces the boundary into one face but adds many single-faced layers of varying trans-parency.

1. Peter Eisenman, "Visions' Unfolding: Architecture in the Age of Electric Media," *Domus* 734 (January 1992), 144–49.
2. Greg Lynn, "Introduction" to *Folding in Architecture*, ed. Greg Lynn (New York: John Wiley & Son, 2004), 8.

L115: Layering and the notion of contamination

The notion of contamination is normally taken to involve an initially pure or clean entity which is entered or invaded by an unwanted element. What if the process is more of an osmosis, a flow which occurs across two sides of a bound-ary? Through enabling the dynamic interaction between layers, layering seems closer to osmosis than contamination.

L116: What if layers can. . .

The examination of different works from a variety of fields allows for a still far from comprehensive outline of the characteristics of layering:

— layers are separated by an in-between space which allows for their co-presence;

— each layer may be a pattern, or a composition made up of discrete entities;
— each layer potentially extends indefinitely in its plane;
— the sequence between layers is not fixed. The observer/creator of the setup can bring forth one layer and make others recede;
— not one layer is privileged in any absolute fashion by the setup. The observer/creator may use any hierarchical ordering system he/she desires at any specific moment;
— layers can be opaque, translucent, or transparent, or they may be rendered so as desired;
— the observer is not situated outside the setup but is immersed in it and is part of it. It could be said that the observer is part of the in-between space which partly defines spatially the foremost layer;
— time is part of the setup, not in any linear sense but in the sense that change is inherent in the setup. Traveling from one layer to another, or shifting positions while staying within the boundaries of the same layer cannot take place while fixed at the same point on the dimension of time;
— elements from one layer can "contaminate" the other;
— new layers can be created at will; and
— layering can be a physical arrangement available to vision, but is predominantly a conceptual frame of mind, an attitude. This explains why a literally two-dimensional entity may be perceived as layered while a clearly layered three-dimensional entity may be perceived as not-layered. The key player in both scenarios is the perceiving/creating subject.

L117: Second thoughts about the idea of having my written work composed of layers

Why on earth would I want to attempt this idea of layers in my written work? It may seem like a novel idea but it requires quite a commitment. . . Knowing myself I might as well give it up right now. . . But then again. . .

If my writing style regarding the whole body of an article or essay is seen diachronically, then the practice of putting together a group of layers may be seen as just one layer. If this "layer" is seen in isolation, then there is a danger of judging the practice itself as anti-layering since it implies a degree of commitment foreign to the idea of layering as a setup.

L118: Collage in art and architecture

Collage, a technique quite different from layering, is found in the discourses and practices of fields like art, architecture, and urban design. Versions of it appear in cubism, in Dada photomontages, in Surrealism's disruptive juxtaposition of more or less disparate realities, in the practice of "automatic writing," and in the work of decollage artists who used large-scale fragments detached or ripped from advertising billboards.

Within architectural discourse, one encounters a plethora of texts which, to a lesser or greater degree, use aspects of the technique of collage to build their proposal. Robert Venturi, Denise Scott Brown, and Steven Izenour, in *Learning from Las Vegas*, argue that "the iconography and mixed media of roadside commercial Architecture will point the way."[1] Venturi, in *Complexity and Contradiction* argues for an architecture which embraces contradiction as well as complexity, vitality as well as validity, preferring "both-and" to "either-or," embodying the difficult unity of inclusion rather that the easy unity of exclusion.[2] Elsewhere, he argues that "there is room in architecture for the fragment, for contradiction and improvisation and their attendant tensions."[3]

In *Collage City*, Colin Rowe and Fred Koetter suggest that:

[A] collage approach, an approach in which objects (and attitudes) are conscribed or seduced from their context is—at the present day—the only way of dealing with the ultimate problems of either or both Utopia and tradition. . . . Societies and persons assemble themselves according to their own interpretations of absolute reference and traditional value; and, up to a point, collage accommodates both hybrid display and the requirements of self-determination.[4]

And:

[B]ecause collage is a method deriving its virtue from its irony, because it seems to be a technique for using things and simultaneously disbelieving in them, it is also a strategy which can allow Utopia to be dealt with as image, to be dealt with in *fragments* without our having to accept it *in toto*, which is further to suggest that collage could even be a strategy which, by supporting the Utopian illusion of changelessness and finality, might even fuel a reality of change, motion, action, and history. (*COC*, 90)

Oswald Mathias Ungers believes that "all value judgments would be overturned if what is incomplete, or in other words the unresolved contradiction, was placed at the centre of the conception and of the plan and hence of architectural studies," observing that "the building as a fragment, as discontinuous object, composed of different unrelated parts, is not, if looked at historically, unusual."[5]

---

1. Robert Venturi, Denise Scott Brown, and Steven Izenour, *Learning from Las Vegas* (Cambridge, MA: MIT Press, 1977, revised edition), 131.
2. Robert Venturi, *Complexity and Contradiction in Architecture* (New York: The Museum of Modern Art, 1966).
3. Robert Venturi, "Complexity and Contradiction in Architecture: Selections from a Forthcoming Book," in *Theorizing a New Agenda for Architecture: an Anthology of Architectural Theory, 1965–1995*, ed. Kate Nesbitt (New York: Princenton Architectural Press, 1996), 75.
4. Colin Rowe and Fred Koetter, "Collage City," *Architectural Review* 158, no. 942 (August 1975), 88. Henceforth cited as *COC*.
5. Oswald Mathias Ungers, "Architettura con Tema/Architecture as Theme," in *Theories and Manifestoes of Contemporary Architecture*, ed. Charles Jenks and Karl Kropf (Chichester, West Sussex: Academy Editions, 1997), 95.

L119: A painting

Figure E.2

L120: Layering, collage, folding

Layering does not depend on fragments as collage does, nor does it use one continuous entity like a Mobius strip implied by the fold. It is rather in need of layers. Layering, collage, and folding are thus different. Still, a fold, even if it involves one continuous entity, superposes or layers, while a product of collage may be seen as layered if it is composed of pieces which overlap rather than form a mosaic.

L121: Lyotard's figure-matrix

Lyotard distinguishes among:

> "figure-images" which violate the perceptual recognition of objects' outlines (e.g., as in Cubist art), "figure-forms" which problematize the space of visibility itself in which outlines might appear (e.g., the abstract expressionism of a Jackson Pollock), and finally, "figure-matrices," which are simply invisible, although they somehow surge up into the realm of visibility as a principle of pure difference. (*DE*, 565)

With the idea of "figure-matrix" Lyotard attempts to conceptualize this

> third possibility, to describe a spatiality that is not consistent with the coordinates or external space, and from which the intervals and differences that make the external world recognizable and observable as objects are excluded. As with Freud's conception of the unconscious, the matrix contains incompatible figures that all occupy the same place at the same time, at war both with each other and with conscious experience. The matrix could, thus, be another avatar of George Bataille's concept of the Informe, or formless.[1]

The "figure-matrix" concept seems to be related to layering in the way it allows for *synchorization*, for the existence that is, of more than one entity in the same space. The idea of synchronization which involves the parameter of time has long been formulated and used either to model a thinking process or describe an existing phenomenon. This is not the case with Synchorization, the corresponding term involving the parameter of space this time. Such a term does not actually exist except, perhaps, in a theological sense in the Greek Orthodox faith where "sinchoro" means to create space for the "Other" so that copresence or coexistence may be possible—in other words, to forgive. It implies the existence of more than one entities without any of them loosing their identity.

1. Hal Foster, Rosalind Krauss, Yve-Alain Bois, and Benjamin H. D. Buchloh, *Art since 1900* (London: Thames & Hudson, 2004), 686.

L122: Bataille's informe

Bataille describes the "informe" as "a term working to undo/disturb/rearrange, demanding generally that each thing has its form/the form proper to it."[1] Referring to the Informe, Andrew Benjamin argues that

> attention should . . . be paid to the consequence of this process of "undoing," "moving" and "repositioning.". . . It results in a state of affairs in which the opposition between form and the formless (the latter as no more than that which could be counter-posed to form) is no longer appropriate as a way of accounting for form. The presence of form (or its opposite—the so called formless) is not central. The terms are not in strict opposition. What arises as the more demanding problem is accounting for the generation of form. . . . There is a move from what is—i.e., the givenness of a form—to what becomes or to what is generated. . . . [F]initude yields its place to a specific modality of becoming.[2]

A dynamic state of layering resembles the Informe's state of undoing, disturbing, and rearranging. It may also be helpful in avoiding the use of the duality form-formless by focusing more, as suggested above, on the becoming, which is an important aspect of a layered arrangement or configuration since any change anywhere cannot but influence everything else in the setup.

1. Georges Bataille, *Oeuvres Complètes*, vol. 1 (Paris: Gallimard, 1970), 217.
2. Andrew Benjamin, *Architectural Philosophy* (London and Brunswick, NJ: The Athlone Press, 2000), 31–32.

L123: The position of the subject in relation to the layered

Acknowledging the presence of layering is not an inevitable consequence of the way a work is presented. Layering is a creative process undertaken, consciously or otherwise, by the subject who perceives the layers.

Juxtaposition in layering does not have to be literal in a physical and/or temporal sense. It, actually, *always* takes place in the mind. Consequently, two or more works (paintings, pieces of music or works of literature) can be miles and decades apart and still be layers in a subject's mental composition. However, they cannot be involved in the same process of layering if they are not found within the same subjectivity. To experience or perceive layering is to perform layering. To layer is to get layered. We are all moving onion hearts. We are always in a layered environment which is either concentric with our own position as perceiving subjects, or allocentric, rendering us more as entities in a curved or spherical layer which has its center somewhere other than our position.

Layering implies a submersion of the observing subject within the setup. Unlike a geological or historical form of sedimentation or stratification, layering allows for the rearrangement of layers and a potential change in the relationship between the subject and the described setup. Consequently, real time is also implicated. Such a state resembles Deleuze's claim that in the "superfold," "each located observer is the opening of a fold, a world folded around its contemplations and rhythms."[1]

> There are as many spaces or folds as there are styles of perception. If a fold is the way perceptions "curve around" or are oriented according to an acting body, then the thought of these curves produces a life that can think not just its own human world—the space of man—but the sense of space as such. (*SM*, 190)

The subject itself is created and re-created with every act of layering. As with the framework through which the work *A Thousand Plateaus* presents itself, "the tripartite division of the spatial field normally associated with 'mental representation': the field of reality (the world), the field of representation (the book), the field of subjectivity" is here also replaced (*IDS*, 5).

Still, a valid question may be: schizo or layered? Clearly, answering such a question needs to be preceded by a discussion on whether the subject is indeed a discernible entity or a desiring machine which is always in the making.

1. Ian Buchanan and Gregg Lambert, "Introduction" to *Deleuze and Space*, 12. Henceforth cited as *IDS*.

L124: Plato's chora

Plato comes up with his concept of chora in his inquiry into the generation of forms. The main question is: what form does the space which generates all other forms take?

What if chora is not so much a space or a formal entity but more of a process? And what if such a process was more like the process of layering? Consistent with Plato's Theory of Forms, these are all taken to be preexisting and layered, emerging as entities through the different processes allowed by the layering setup itself.

L125: Eidos, theoria, form

Derrida argues that "all the concepts by which eidos or morphe could be translated and determined refer back to the theme of presence. Form is presence itself. Formality is what is presented, visible, and conceivable of the thing in general."[1] The emergence of form implies a distance between the form and its observer, the possibility of theoria. According to Martin Jay, for Heidegger "the tendency latent in Plato's doctrine of Being as Eidos became fully manifest in what he [Heidegger] called the modern 'age of the world picture,'" facilitating "the birth of the modern humanist subject, who stood apart from a world he [the human subject] surveyed and manipulated" (*DE*, 272). This position of the viewing subject is challenged in layering as is the idea of a stable form which is produced in any final way and then viewed: forms appear and disappear depending on the relationship of the subject with the setup.

1. Jacques Derrida, "Form and Meaning: A Note on the Phenomenology of Language," in *Speech and Phenomena*, trans. David Allison, ed. David Allison and Newton Garver (Evanston, IL: Northwestern University Press, 1973), 108.

L126: Layering, man and woman

It could be argued that, until recently, women have been seen as more "layered" than men. The more apparent layers may be those created by the comparatively more complex dependency on underwear, clothes, jewelry and other accessories, and makeup. The more subtle layers are those related to the female body and its functions, and to female psychology; observing herself being observed is in itself a layered situation, let alone the need to be "housed" in her parents' or husband's house, in a convent, or in a brothel. But it could be argued that this difference between the two sexes has changed; even the identification of body hair as a distinct male layer now depends on the way the male subject deals with or (re)presents himself.

L127: A painting

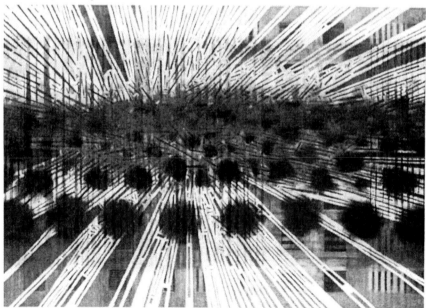

Figure E.3

L128: Film, layering, and blockage

Layering encourages the collection of what one could call viewpoints but it does not censor or attempt a final synthesis out of the material gathered. The presence of many images which can be viewed separately or simultaneously (layered), if desired, avoids "symbolic blockage," what "Bellour accuses film of; film contains the disruptive implications of language and yet produces narratives restoring equilibrium and reconciliation. It thus functions alongside of those other ideological apparatuses, schools, churches, newspapers, and so on, that Althusser saw as essential buttresses of the status quo" (*DE*, 476).

Yet, there is no claim to neutrality or innocence in layering. Simply, any new arrangement may potentially work for or against the ideological stance of the previous state. Thus, while each specific state is ideological in one way or another, the process itself is polemical by being against adhering to any one specific ideology.

L129: The in-between

According to architect Aldo Van Eyck, in an article written in 1962, it is essential for architecture to gain awareness of what he called the "in-between realm." To achieve this, he explains, one needs to be able to detect associative meanings simultaneously, an ability he found lacking from the mental equipment of architects.[1] The importance of the in-between or intermediate space is also identified by architect Kisho Kurokawa in 1987. Kurokawa has come up with the notion of a hybrid architecture which allows for symbiosis and in some cases triggers metamorphosis.[2]

Elizabeth Grosz finds that "the model of an in-betweenness, of an indeterminacy or undecidability, pervades the writings of contemporary philosophers, including Deleuze, Derrida, Serres, and Irigaray, where it goes under a number of different names: difference, repetition, iteration, the interval, among others" (*AO*, 93). She sees the in-between as the space of the bounding and undoing of the identities which constitute it.

> This in-between is the very site for the contestation of the many binaries and dualisms that dominate Western knowledge, for the very form of oppositional structure that has defined not only phallocentrism but also ethnocentrism and Eurocentrism, and the more general erasure of difference. The dualization of reality, the imposition of a representational structure that confirms the logic of self-identity—also known as the logic of the excluded middle—is one of the pre-eminent strategies in the propagation of power relations at the level of epistemology. (*AO*, 93)

The in-between in layering is not simply the "excluded-middle" between dualities, but a recurring entity between any two adjacent layers. This in-betweenness may be the very place one finds the observing subject in. If this is the case, and if the subject's very identity is influenced by its relationship with its context, then the existence of many in-betweens in any layered arrangement implies the possibility of a subject with an always "becoming" nature.

1. Aldo van Eyck, "Team 10 Primer." Pp. 20–23 in *Team 10 Primer*, ed. Alison Smithson (London: Studio Vista, 1968).
2. Kisho Kurokawa, *The Philosophy of Symbiosis* (London: Academy Editions, 1994).

L130: Redefining the concepts of ergon and parergon through layering

Derrida argues against the integrity of the work of art (the ergon), since this is always polluted by its framing contexts (the parergon) (*DE*, 516). The layered setup undermines the finality of each individual layer, making each the "parergon" of the other, creating the potential for dialogue, tension, or even conflict between them.

Regarding photography, Jean-Luc Nancy writes that it "is the act that obeys the sole necessity of exposing the limit: not the limit of communication, but the limit upon which communication takes place."[1] The above observation would equally hold if it was taken to refer to layering, reinforcing the notion of a fluid perception.

1. Jean-Luc Nancy, *The Inoperative Community*, trans. Peter Conor et al., ed. Peter Connor (Minneapolis: University of Minnesota Press, 1991), 66–67.

L131: Are there less layered areas or directions than others?

It all depends on who is looking, in the sense that layering can be considered as an activity involving degrees of agency and competency.

L132: Regarding extensive + intensive

If, as DeLanda argues, the extensive is "that which you can grasp, cut, twist, and turn," while the intensive is "that which affects you, but does not yield to your attempt to contain it . . . like the wind in your face" (*IDS*, 9), then layering could be seen as a process which continuously transforms the extensive into the intensive and vice versa. The superposition of layers which are allowed to influence, contaminate, enrich, or destroy each other allows for a Deleuzian state of "becoming."

One is here reminded of Kant's notion regarding the experience of beauty. According to him, this is created by the free play between understanding and imagination. The shifting relationship between the subject and his/her layered environment or context offers experiences which continually change, gradually or otherwise, from being aesthetic, to being virtual or actual.

L133: Layering as rhizomatic rather than arborified

If the arborified "imposes form or a correct structure from without or above, whereas the rhizomatic depends upon articulation from within,"[1] then layering is much closer to the rhizomatic rather than the arborified, since it is the always-already-layered perceiving subject rather than a transcendental signifier or an external logic which generate such a configurational setup.

1. Paul A. Harris, "To See with the Mind and Think through the Eye: Deleuze, Folding Architecture, and Simon Rodia's Watts Towers," in *Deleuze and Space*, 40.

L134: Layering Kapoor

I know where Anish Kapoor got his inspiration: by noticing his reflection on the shiny curved stainless steel bathroom fixtures while washing. Small body parts then may appear larger and thicker, or, alas, tinier and thinner.

L135: Abstraction and layering

John Rajchman's interpretation of Deleuze's definition of abstraction reveals similarities with layering since the relationship between layers can be "an impure mixing or mixing up" as discussed below:

> Deleuze advances another image of what abstraction means in philosophy: more "empiricist," more "immanentist," more "experimental"; at the same time, he sketches another view of what abstraction means in art: more "chaotic" or "formless," no longer defined in opposition to figure or image. These two kinds of abstraction intersect in many ways, forming part of a new way of doing art-connected philosophy. In both cases, we find a departure from the view of abstraction as a process of extracting pure or essential Forms, emptying a space of its concrete contents, towards another kind of abstraction, and another sense of "abstract": an abstraction that consists in an impure mixing and mixing up, prior to Forms, a reassemblage that moves towards an Outside, rather than a purification that turns up to essential Ideas, or in towards the constitutive "forms" of a medium.[1]

The constitutive "forms" of the medium of layering are the layers themselves and the potential relationships between them, allowing for this other type of abstraction to take place.

1. John Rajchman, "Another View of Abstraction," in *Abstraction, Journal of Philosophy and the Visual Arts* 5 (1995), 16.

L136: Layering as an ontological shift or an age-old practice?

Bergson believed cinematographic modes of thought antedated the invention of the moving picture (*DE*, 199). Similarly, the ability to deal with layered information must have antedated the invention of computer programs ranging from data spreadsheets to drafting and animation, that offer the possibility of working with different layers, cultivating further the ability of the human mind to deal with complex sets of information in a new fashion. What may have recently reinforced it though is "our newfound capacity to 'be there,' in many places at once, as we are when we speak on the phone or search the Internet," an ability which may be seen as constituting "a significant ontological shift."[1]

Elizabeth Grosz suggests that the city is in the subject as much as surrounding it, arguing that "the city has never been just anything but an ongoing site of virtuality" (*AO*, 17). In such a space the urban peripatetic "has the liberty to experiment" but "the price is one cannot keep what one gains. Emblematic of this space was the sidewalk, a space which brought together the passionate intensity of Benjamin's arcades and the chancy promiscuity of Simmel's strangers" (*IDS*, 3). Ian Buchanan comments on the ways in which our conception of space has had to alter in the face of the hyper-mobility of the postmodern subject (*IDS*, 7). The strengthening of this age-old ability to manipulate information in layers, spatial and temporal alike, can be seen as offering the potential for a new relationship between the body, space, and time.

1. Sulan Kolatan, "Blurring Perceptual Boundaries," in *The State of Architecture at the Beginning of the 21st Century*, ed. Bernard Tschumi and Irene Cheng (New York: The Monacelli Press, 2003), 116.

L137: Gestalt theory and layering

The gestaltists argue that a figure is distinguishable as an entity because it is rather neatly separated both from its neighbors as well as the space in which it exists. Layering upsets such a system by violating the clear distinction between figure and ground, and figure and figure, consequently creating bad-gestalt.

L138: Monuments and layering

Lefebvre argues that a monument either expresses or creates consensus in order to fulfill its purpose.[1] This can only happen not because it miraculously renders the same all those it is a monument for, nor due to its ability to, according to who they are, offer a different piece of itself to them. It is rather offered whole each time to each and every subject for whom it is a monument for. This can only happen if it is layered, giving the chance to each one to consume a whole yet different layer each time. Take a flag for example. Different groups take it to represent their ideology or even history by making some layers associated with it to recede or even disappear.

1. Henri Lefebvre, *The Production of Space*, trans. Donald Nicholson-Smith (Oxford and Cambridge, MA: Blackwell Publishers, 1991), 220.

L139: Thank God for layering

Imagine if no layering could take place. Then each moving shadow would require an exclusive space of its own at every moment, permanently and for ever changing everything it touches. That something can actually exist without claiming exclusive space for itself is what makes layering unique and potentially helpful in achieving synchorization.

L140: A project for Nicosia #2

A gate with a sign saying: "Welcome to the layered city of Nicosia, the last divided city of Europe." The same should be written on the other side of the sign. Nothing different is taking place on either side of the gate. This gate could be placed anywhere and at many points of the city at the same time. The reference to the fact that the city is partitioned into a north and a south half by a buffer zone, coupled with the fact that the same gate will be found in different locations on both sides as well as on the buffer zone itself confirms the view that the layering mentioned actually has nothing to do with the existence of a buffer zone.

L141: Is layering anti-architectural?

If architecture is taken to be the perceived solid uncompromising form then layering is anti-architectural. If it is taken to be the experience of the subject moving through it, then layering is architecture par excellence since images are continuously superimposed or layered in memory as well as literally. One simply needs to walk through a building and imagine taking snapshots every few seconds. Taking each snapshot to represent a layer may be a naïve start in beginning to understand the way layering works.

L142: A poem for my mother

How can lemon blossoms still smell
Now that you are dead?
What message of hope do they continue to give us?
The lamentations of Good Friday?
What did you long to steal from the wild lily?
Its beauty, its fragrance, or its promise for eternal rebirth?
And you fell.
Alas your name is not Persephone but Irinoulla
What on earth does Peace have to do with Life?
Not on earth.
Your mother's name is not Demeter but Ourania.

L143: Buyuk Hamam (St. George of Latin's Church)

What could be seen as historical layering is the following description of a building given in a booklet published by the Nicosia Master Plan, the bicommunal board responsible for forming a common planning policy for the walled city of Nicosia:

> Originally a Latin church built during the Lusignan period, the building was converted into a Turkish Bath (Hamam) during the Ottoman rule of Cyprus. It still retains its original ornamental stone-carved arched doorway, which is used today as the main entrance to the Baths.[1]

To enter, one needs to descend a number of steps since the street level has risen over the years. The street in front of the building allows for the movement of people and vehicles, spatially connecting the place with the rest of the city.

1. *Walled Nicosia: A Guide to Its Historical and Cultural Sites*, entry #18. Nicosia Master Plan.

L144: The sewage system of Nicosia
It was on that lower layer of the city that the two communities, the Turkish-Cypriots and the Greek-Cypriots managed to communicate after the events of 1974. On the ground level the whole island was divided into two.

L145: Is there room for everything?
There must be room for everything since, for anything to exist, it must already exist somewhere. The challenge is how one perceives his/her relationship with "everything." Indeed, layering is the kind of "filing" system that allows easy retrieval or storage of "everything."

L146: Layering Taj Mahal
After completing the tour of the monument during a visit in India in December 2004, the guide shared with us "a trick": he took us to a location where one could stand and pose in such a way so that a photo could be taken showing him holding with two fingers the whole building by the tip of the dome. This incident together with the experience of the truly panoramic, "cinematographic" view of the valley spreading below the building at the back, sandwiched the famous monument into a squeezed space in my memory.

L147: The story of the koupepia/mousaka
While a student at UT Austin I tried to cope with my nostalgia for my mother's cooking by attempting to prepare a Cypriot dish called koupepia. These are rolled up grape leaves filled with rice, minced meat, and herbs. Having spent half of Saturday to roll the koupepia, I decided to go from monads to layers; the koupepia took the form of mousaka. Apart from literally layering the filling between layers of grape leaves, I believe I have managed to layer the taste of koupepia with the form of mousaka.

L148: Triple X-X/2 by Xristakis Xatzi Xristou

Figure E.4

L149: A touch of Christmas throughout the year

The Christmas street decoration is always hanging up there. It is simply switched off except for the holiday season. The amazing thing is that one does not really notice it. It is practically invisible like so many other layers which, juxtaposed, make up the urban experience.

L150: Is space more promiscuous than form?

Wrong question; "Is space more layered than form?" may be more like it. Promiscuity and layering are related in the sense that both involve a reduced sense of commitment.

L151: The screwing of the unscrewable screw by the baker

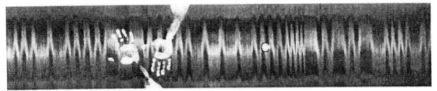

Figure E.5

L152: A story of layered sexualities

An interesting layer to the picture portraying prostitution in Cyprus until the 1980s was the practice of at least two men in the area who would disinfect any man who, after visiting a prostitute, wanted to decrease the chances of catching a venereal disease. A small entrance hall served as a waiting room, while a second space containing a washing basin was where the disinfection took place. The disinfectant was contained in a plastic bottle that was connected to a narrow hose which had an even narrower metal tip on its other end. The disinfectant was "pumped" into the man by positioning the bottle high and by inserting the metal tip into the man's penis. A short stool was used to allow the man to use the wash basin during the procedure which was repeated a number of times. In order to keep the man's clothes from getting dirty from splashing, paper sheets from magazines or newspapers were pierced to create a hole through which the penis could be conveniently exposed. On asked whether the procedure was painful, the interviewee who gave the above account described the sensation of the liquid gashing inside him as pleasurable and added that the hands of the man performing it were so soft that, sometimes, when he could not afford to actually visit a prostitute, he would settle for the much cheaper visit to the disinfection man.[1]

1. From Christakis Chatzichristou, "Prostitution Spatialized: Cyprians Then and Now," paper presented at the 6th International Space Syntax Symposium, 12–15 June 2007, ITU Faculty of Architecture, Istanbul, Turkey. http://www.spacesyntaxistanbul.itu.edu.tr/pa pers%5Cshortpapers%5C113%20-%20Hadjichristos.pdf (accessed June 15, 2013).

L153: Layered domesticities

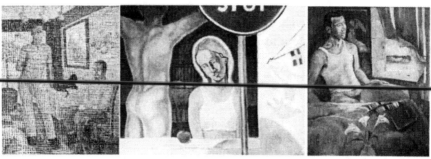

Figure E.6

L154: Disorienting before reorienting
The brief description given by the team of Christakis Chatzichristou (architect) and Dimitris Joannides (video and music artist) for their contribution to the Venice Architecture Biennale of 2006 was the following:

> The Minotaur knew no labyrinth; he recognized every corner, every wall by the blood marks he left after each of his encounters with Others. It has been said that, he was becoming more human whenever he got disoriented, lost.
>
> If change is indeed what is aimed at, the established relationships between the subject and the city of Nicosia need to be challenged. In other words, disorientation before reorientation.
>
> Since erasure is neither desired nor possible, the task is not attempted through collage, a technique which depends on fragments, but through layering, allowing for synchronicity, synchoricity, and choice.

A layer in the form of numbers on the street was proposed in order to disorient before reorienting the inhabitant of the city who is urged not to look at the walls but to focus his/her attention on the ground.

L155: Layering in architectural education and practice
First it was the tracing paper. Now, more and more, it is the layers in the different computer programs. Placing different sets of information in different layers has always been an important technique in the production of architecture. It is actually the very language used in the communication between the different agents involved in construction.

Still, layering's most crucial contribution in design is that it enables the designer to abstract and thus manage to deal with complexity. The recent tendency to work three-dimensionally from the start may prove disastrous if it reduces the designer's skill to consciously deal with sets of quite complex relationships. The ability of a student of architecture to produce complex-looking drawings with the help of the right software does not necessarily mean that the complexity of the situation or context has been dealt with accordingly.

L156: List of papers layered in the present one
Since this is the first paper written but the fourth to be published, no layers from other papers are found here, while layers from this paper are found in a number of other papers which were written later but published earlier. Such is Paper 2, "Layering in Software: Drawing, Thinking, Designing" (in *Teaching and Experimenting with Architectural Design: Advances in Technology and Changes in Pedagogy*, ENHSA-EAAE Architectural Design Teachers' Network Meeting, EAAE Transactions on Architectural Education, no. 35 (2007), 431–39) and Paper 4, *Be a Layer* (Syllabus for the Theory Course to be taught at Pratt Institute, Spring Semester, 2010).

L157: Layered angels

Figure E.7

L158: Layering is ubiquitous
- My God, you are everywhere!
- Are you talking to me or God?

L159: The nature of layers
In layering, each layer could be seen as a two-dimensional "container" with varying transparency, porosity, and memory. By varying its transparency it can be totally invisible or totally opaque. With varying porosity it can absorb or emit elements from and to other layers. With varying memory it can go back to an "original" state or agree to "temporarily forget" some of its elements or parts.

NOTES

General Introduction:
Textual Tradition, Body-Layering, and Nagiko's Seductions
Maria Margaroni

1. See the identity statement of the Society of Layerists in Multi-Media (SLMM), http://www.slmm.org (accessed July 23, 2011). For a brief reference to the diverse uses to which the term "layering" has been put, see also the following: Collins-Cope and Matthews, "A Reference Architecture for Component Based Development," http://www.markcollinscope.info/W9.html (accessed July 23, 2011); Hecht and Baldwin, "Layers and Holograms: A New Look at Prejudice," in *Communicating Prejudice*, ed. Michael L. Hecht (London: Sage, 1998), 57–86; "Causal Layered Analysis" in Wikipedia, http://en.wikipedia.org/wiki/Causal_layered_analysis (accessed July 23, 2011); Marcel Danesi, "Layering Theory and Human Abstract Thinking," *Cybernetics and Human Knowing* 8.3 (2001), 5–24, as well as his "Abstract Concept-Formation as Metaphorical Layering," *Studies in Communication Sciences* 2, no. 1 (winter 2002), 1–22; Paul Werth, "Extended Metaphor—a Text-World Account," *Language and Literature* 3, no. 2 (May 1994), 79–103; and Scott Samuelson, "Teaching and the Art of Layering," *Perspective: Expressing Mind & Spirit* 1, no. 2 (winter 2001), 10–19.

2. In "Freud and the Scene of Writing," Derrida discusses the "scene" as a site of representation, an illustration (visual depiction), a theatrical performance. More importantly, it is a machine of repetition/reproduction which displaces any metaphysical site of origin. Finally, it connotes a relation of "sociality," i.e., a necessary connection with "the stage of history and the play of the world." "Freud and the Scene of Writing," in *Writing and Difference*, trans. Alan Bass (London: Routledge, 1978), 227–28. Henceforth cited as *WD*.

3. François Cusset, *French Theory: How Foucault, Derrida, Deleuze & Co. Transformed the Intellectual Life of the United States*, trans. Jeff Fort with Josephine Berganza and Marion Jones (Minneapolis: Minnesota University Press, 2008), 338. Henceforth cited as *FT*.

4. Françoise Collin, "The Praxis of Difference: Notes on the Tragedy of the Subject," in *French Women Philosophers: A Contemporary Reader; Subjectivity, Identity, Alterity*, ed. Christina Howells (London and New York: Routledge, 2004), 11. Henceforth cited as *PD*.

5. Julia Kristeva, "The Novel as Polylogue," in *Desire in Language: A Semiotic Approach to Literature and Art*, trans. Thomas Gora, Alice Jardine and Leon S. Roudiez, ed. Leon S. Roudiez (New York: Columbia University Press, 1980), 168. *Desire in Language* henceforth cited as *DL*.

6. The bond is produced and cultivated by Nagiko's aunt who, on Nagiko's fourth birthday, tells her: "This is a book written a long time ago by a lady who has the same name as you. When you are 28 years old this book will be exactly a thousand years old. Think of that." Peter Greenaway, *The Pillow Book* (Paris: DIS VOIR, 1996), 34. Henceforth cited as *PB*.

7. One of her calligrapher/lovers tells Nagiko: "Text may look good on you—but it looks better in a book." In response to this comment, Nagiko replies: "We may not have books much longer. I am helping to keep a tradition alive" (*PB*, 53).

8. Greenaway comments at the end of the first birthday ceremony we witness: "The action, though innocent and ritualized and performed with domestic affection, is, nonetheless, a little odd, perhaps disturbing. The child is no more, for a moment, than some-

233

thing to write on. And the father's signing is a little too Godlike" (*PB*, 31).

9. By foregrounding the heroine's endeavor to connect two heterogeneous textual traditions (i.e., Shonagon's and her father's), my analysis of the film moves in the opposite direction to the one Paula Willoquet-Maricondi follows in her essay "Fleshing the Text: Greenaway's *Pillow Book* and the Erasure of the Body," in *Postmodern Culture* 9, no. 2 (1999), http://muse.jhu.edu/journals/postmodern_culture/v009/9.2willoquet.html (accessed February 28, 2011).

10. "I want to describe the Body as a Book | A Book as a Body," Nagiko writes in her first book inscribed on Jerome's body (*PB*, 102).

11. See Simon Critchley's discussion of "the gap between knowledge and wisdom" in *Continental Philosophy: A Very Short Introduction* (Oxford: Oxford University Press, 2001), 1–11. Henceforth cited as *CP*.

12. See Richard Ohmann's "The Function of English at the Present Time," in *Falling into Theory: Conflicting Views on Reading Literature*, ed. David H. Richter (Boston and New York: Bedford/St. Martin's, 2000), 89–95.

13. Greenaway fragments and layers the screen. He uses overlays and insets that complicate the reality the viewers are witnessing, confronting them with the parallel unfolding of different events or historically and geographically diverse contexts; a juxtaposition of past and present; the eruption of one surface (i.e., human skin) within another surface (the page of a book) or one form of writing (inscription on the body) within another form of writing (drawing lines or symbols on paper).

14. In the first book that Nagiko sends to the publisher she writes: "The second bulk of the book is in the belly, | Factory for the mixing of materials, | A laboratory of sorting and threading, | Retaining and Remaindering, | A publishing house in continual flux" (*PB*, 102).

15. In a 1997 interview with S. H. Abbot, Greenaway argues that "if the body makes the text," that is, if "the mind is influencing the arm and the arm is influencing the hand and the hand the pen and paper," then "the best place for that text is back on the body." Peter Greenaway, interview with S. H. Abbot (1997), http://users.skynet.be/chrisrenson-makemovies/Greenaw3.htm (accessed July 28, 2011). Henceforth cited as *PGI*.

16. The publisher (who bought her father's work in exchange of sexual favors and is currently Jerome's lover) rejects the first manuscript Nagiko submits for publication. In response, Nagiko and Jerome devise a plan to seduce him by sending him Nagiko's writing inscribed on Jerome's body. Greenaway describes the scene of his inscription as "an erotic ritual." He writes: "Jerome lies down on a white sheet on the dining-table. He resembles a sacrificial animal" (*PB*, 77).

17. "I'm not serious in that, it's metaphorical," Greenaway adds in the course of his exposition on the mutual indebtedness of body and text (*PGI*). The literal (i.e., nonmetaphorical) quality of the relation between body/book is again foregrounded when, after Jerome's death, the publisher has his body flayed and a pillow book made out of his lovingly inscribed skin.

18. In "The End of the Book and the Beginning of Writing," Jacques Derrida writes: "The idea of the book is the idea of a totality, finite or infinite, of the signifier; this totality of the signifier cannot be a totality, unless a totality constituted by the signified preexists it, supervises its inscriptions and its signs, and is independent of it in its ideality." Jacques Derrida, *Of Grammatology*, trans. Gayatri Chakravorty Spivak (Baltimore and London: The Johns Hopkins University Press, 1976), 18. Henceforth cited as *OG*. Similarly, in "The Book of the Dead," her thirteenth and last book, written on the body of a sumo wrestler, Nagiko writes: "The book to end all books. | The final book. | After this,

there is no more writing | no more publishing" (*PB*, 112). As I will argue, however, this does not foreclose the continuation of another kind of writing. This is what Nagiko herself suggests when she "acknowledges that she is now mature enough to have had sufficient experiences . . . to write her own PILLOW-BOOK—THE PILLOW-BOOK OF NAGIKO KIYOHARA" (*PB*, 101).

19. The risk of loss/misreading, betrayal and the possibility of a missed encounter are foregrounded on several occasions in the film. For example, the seventh book is seriously damaged by rain; the eighth book reaches the publisher only in the form of multiple Polaroid photographs; the tenth book is rejected by the publisher who fails to read the silent text inscribed on the tongue of Nagiko's messenger; the eleventh book is also spoiled, the script inscribed on the messenger's body smudged with blood-stains when he is knocked down by a van; finally, the messenger carrying the twelfth book only drives by the publisher's bookshop but does not stop.

20. It is "a thought," Derrida explains, because "a *thought* . . . escapes binarism and makes binarism possible on the basis of *nothing*" (*WD*, 230).

21. Notice how Greenaway visually erases the historical gap between the 10th and 20th centuries, thus emphasizing the bond between Nagiko and Sei Shonagon: "Nagiko's reflection in the window-pane fades, leaving the image of the winter landscape—a timeless image for both the present and Sei Shonagon's 10th century quotation" (*PB*, 36; see also 32, 34 and 39).

22. "This is where I begin to do the writing. I am now going to be the pen and not the paper," she tells Hoki (a photographer in love with her) after her first meeting with Jerome (*PB*, 71). While preparing her eighth book, "The Book of Youth," aimed to seduce the publisher, Nagiko reiterates her father's Godlike ritual blessing and adds: "Now you have been signed by me—you can go and do my business" (*PB*, 90).

23. He demands sexual favors from all the men who come to depend on his power (for the publication of their work, financial support or social status).

24. When her father is ill, the publisher attempts to appropriate the loving birthday ritual shared between father and daughter: "The publisher makes a gesture as though to write on Nagiko, who, alarmed, ducks out of his way" (*PB*, 39).

25. Interestingly, in Maxine Hong Kingston's rewriting of the legend, her parents carve their grievances on the female avenger's back. See *The Woman Warrior: Memoirs of a Girlhood among Ghosts* (London: Picador, 1977), 38–39.

26. After the first book inscribed on Jerome's body, Nagiko continues sending the publisher her embodied texts which aim at avenging her loved ones (i.e., her father and Jerome) by forcing the publisher to confront the consequences of and take responsibility for his actions.

27. Jerome's pillow book, now retrieved by Nagiko, is ritually buried in the soil beneath a Bonsai tree. Greenaway writes: "as we watch, in the growing half-dark, the Bonsai-bush flowers. On the black-and-white film, the thousands of flower-petals blush a deep red" (*PB*, 98). It is in this light, perhaps, that we need to interpret Nagiko's decision to give new life to her poem dedicated to Jerome by tattooing part of it on her body.

Notes to Part One

Chapter 1
Profane Mystical Practice: Resisting the Society of the Spectacle or the Society of the "As If"
Frances Restuccia

Epigraph: Giorgio Agamben, *Potentialities: Collected Essays in Philosophy*, trans. Daniel Heller-Roazen (Stanford: Stanford University Press, 1999), 148. Henceforth cited as *PO*.

Epigraph: Julia Kristeva, *Crisis of the ~~European~~ Subject*, trans. Susan Fairfield (New York: Other Press, 2000), 115. Henceforth cited as *CS*.

Epigraph: Giorgio Agamben, *Homo Sacer: Sovereign Power and Bare Life*, trans. Daniel Heller-Roazen (Stanford: Stanford University Press, 1998), 11. Henceforth cited as *HS*.

. Guy Debord, *The Society of the Spectacle*, trans. Donald Nicholson-Smith (New York: Zone Books, 2006). Henceforth cited as *SS*.

2. Julia Kristeva, *Intimate Revolt*, vol. 2 of *The Powers and Limits of Psychoanalysis*, trans. Jeanine Herman (New York: Columbia University Press, 2002), 12. Henceforth cited as *IR*.

3. Julia Kristeva, *The Sense and Non-Sense of Revolt*, vol. 1 of *The Powers and Limits of Psychoanalysis*, trans. Jeanine Herman (New York: Columbia University Press, 2000), 21. Henceforth cited as *SNS*.

4. Giorgio Agamben, *The Coming Community*, trans. Michael Hardt (Minneapolis: University of Minnesota Press, 1993), 15. Henceforth cited as *CC*.

5. Giorgio Agamben, *Profanations*, trans. Jeff Fort (New York: Zone Books, 2007), 10. Henceforth cited as *P*.

6. Giorgio Agamben, *Infancy and History: On the Destruction of Experience*, trans. Liz Heron (London and New York: Verso, 2007), 63. Henceforth cited as *IAH*.

7. Giorgio Agamben, *Means without End: Notes on Politics*, trans. Vincenzo Binetti and Cesare Casarino (Minneapolis: University of Minnesota Press, 2000), 82. Henceforth cited as *MWE*.

8. Catherine Clément and Julia Kristeva, *The Feminine and the Sacred*, trans. Jane Marie Todd (New York: Columbia University Press, 2001), 26. Henceforth cited as *FS*.

9. In a similar vein (and curiously, given his lack of interest in interiority), in *Profanations* Agamben advises us not to reject the timeless "impersonal" (one of his conceptions of "genius"), or it may "reappear in the form of symptoms and tics that are even more impersonal, or grimaces that are even more excessive" (*P*, 14).

10. Kristeva defines the sacred as feminine; yet she also ties the phallus itself to the sacred, taking it as a concept in which "physiology intersects symbolization" and drives join with meaning (*FS*, 59).

11. John Lechte and Maria Margaroni, *Julia Kristeva: Live Theory* (New York: Continuum, 2004), 26. Henceforth cited as *JK*.

12. Giorgio Agamben, *Homo Sacer* (Torino: Einaudi, 2005), 210.

13. Giorgio Agamben, *The Man without Content*, trans. Georgia Albert (Stanford: Stanford University Press, 1999), 58. Henceforth cited as *MWC*.

237

14. Giorgio Agamben, *The Open: Man and Animal*, trans. Kevin Attell (Stanford: Stanford University Press, 2004), 76–77. Henceforth cited as *O*.

15. I do not mean to give the impression that Agamben opposes pornography per se. The problem is its commodification. The apparatus of pornography has blocked and diverted any "profanatory intention." Were its profanability to be restored, pornography in fact, in Agamben's view, might enable "a new collective use of sexuality" (*P*, 91). Perhaps the idea here is (and I am guessing) that such profanability would turn pornography back into erotic representation or even erotic art.

16. Giorgio Agamben, *Remnants of Auschwitz: The Witness and the Archive*, trans. Daniel Heller-Roazen (New York: Zone Books, 1999), 106. Henceforth cited as *RA*.

17. Giorgio Agamben, *The Time That Remains: A Commentary on the Letter to the Romans*, trans. Patricia Dailey (Stanford: Stanford University Press, 2005), 62. Henceforth cited as *TR*.

18. For Agamben, the "Messiah is the figure in which the great monotheistic religions sought to master the problem of law." The arrival of the Messiah "signifies the fulfillment and complete consummation of the Law" (*HS*, 56). The messianic task is to make "the virtual state of exception real" by closing "the door of the Law" (*HS*, 57). Only after that door is shut will the Messiah be able to make an entrance. The Messiah is the power to subvert sovereignty predicated on the state of exception.

19. Catherine Mills, *The Philosophy of Agamben* (Stocksfield: Acumen, 2008), 77.

20. Giorgio Agamben, *Idea of Prose*, trans. Michael Sullivan and Sam Whitsitt (Albany: SUNY Press, 1995), 61. Henceforth cited as *IP*.

Chapter 2
Thinking the Image, Technics, and Embodiment:
Julia Kristeva's Challenge
John Lechte

1. Julia Kristeva, *Le temps sensible: Proust et l'expérience littéraire* (Paris: Gallimard, 1994), 239. Henceforth cited as *TS*. This, and all subsequent translations from cited French texts, are mine.

2. The point here is underlined by Kristeva's invocation of Merleau-Ponty's notion of chiasmus. So, just as the toucher may also be touched, so the writer is also a reader and the reader—as interpreter—also a writer (*TS*, 302).

3. Julia Kristeva, *Tales of Love*, trans. Leon S.Roudiez (New York: Columbia University Press, 1987), 103–5. Henceforth cited as *TL*.

4. "Transduction" derives from the work of Gilbert Simondon, *Du monde d'existence des objets techniques* (Paris: Aubier, 1989).

5. The fact that images are not simply representational could be observed in Kristeva's essay, first published in 1972, on color in Giotto, "Giotto's Joy" (*DL*, 210–36). Color is theorized there as essentially drive-based and is viewed as analogous to rhythm in language: "The chromatic apparatus, like rhythm for language, thus involves a shattering of meaning" (221). More importantly, color "translates an oversignifying logic in that it inscribes drive 'residues' that the subject has not symbolized at the level of understanding" (221; translation modified).

6. Julia Kristeva, *Revolution in Poetic Language*, trans. Margaret Waller (New York: Columbia University Press, 1984), 25. Henceforth cited as *RPL*.

7. Here it does not take much to understand the body as irreducible to its form, or to its conventional borders—which are entirely symbolic. Rather, the body would become a force of indeterminate content expressed perfectly by the notion of stases and their interruption. Such a notion brings Kristeva even closer than might be anticipated to work in the field of digital art and the body, as I will show with reference to Mark Hansen's work.

8. Bernard Stiegler, *La technique et le temps*, vol. 3: *Le temps du cinéma et la question du mal-être* (Paris: Galilée, 2001), 34. Henceforth cited as *TT3*.

9. Mark Hansen, "Time of Affect, or Bearing Witness to Life," *Critical Inquiry* 30 (spring 2004), 595. Henceforth cited as *TA*.

10. David Wills, "Techneology or the Discourse of Speed," in *The Prosthetic Impulse: From a Posthuman Present to a Biocultural Future*, ed. Marquand Smith and Joanne Morra (Cambridge, MA: MIT Press, 2006), 248 and 252.

11. Mark Hansen, "Media Theory," *Theory, Culture and Society* 23, no. 2–3 (May 2006), 303. Henceforth cited as *MT*.

12. Bernard Stiegler, *De la misère symbolique*, vol. 1: *L'époque hyperindustrielle* (Paris: Galilée, 2004); and vol. 2: *La catastrophe du sensible* (Paris: Galilée, 2005). Henceforth cited as *MS1* and *MS2*, respectively.

13. Gilles Deleuze, *Cinema 2: The Time Image*, trans. Hugh Tomlinson and Robert Galeta (Minneapolis: University of Minnesota Press, 1989), 82–83. Henceforth cited as *C*.

14. Bernard Stiegler, *La technique et le temps*, vol. 2: *La désorientation* (Paris: Galilée, 1996), 29. Henceforth cited as *TT2*.

15. Hansen's other points are: a) that Stiegler overgeneralizes about the effects of repeated perceptions of an orthographic object on the basis of a specific situation (melody and films as temporal objects) and thus makes inflated claims about the way that technics infiltrates perception; b) the shift from melody to cinema is problematic; 3) Stiegler's concern to valorize cinema as a temporal object (and as an instance of tertiary memory) leads him to neglect the extent to which primary retention itself is already infiltrated by history; 4) Stiegler neglects protension in his analysis (*TA*, 600–602).

16. Humberto Manturana and Francisco Varela, *Autopoiesis and Cognition* (Dordrecht: Reidel, 1980).

17. Walter Benjamin, "The Work of Art in the Age of Its Technological Reproducibility," trans. Edmund Jephcott and Harry Zohn, in *Walter Benjamin: Selected Writings*, vol. 3, ed. Howard Eiland and Gary Smith (Cambridge MA, London: The Belknap Press of Harvard University Press, 2002), 117–18.

18. Cf. "The semiotic can thus be understood as pre-thetic, preceding the positing of the subject" (*RPL*, 37).

19. Lest it should be thought that the symbolic in Kristeva's theory would translate into a Cartesian mind in relation to a material body, it should be recalled that the symbolic and the semiotic only exist separately in an analytical sense. In reality, we have only a single entity, what I have called elsewhere the "sembolic." Moreover, it is made quite clear in *Revolution in Poetic Language* that the Kristevan subject is not at all transcendental, nor, as a result, in any way Cartesian.

20. In addition, see supra, note 5, on Kristeva's theorization of the relationship between the drives and color. Also, in *Revolution in Poetic Language*, Kristeva writes that in art, "signification is pulverized because the drive charge has always pre-altered representation and language (a painting by Giotto or, even more so, one by Rothko represents, if anything, a *practice*, more than it represents *objectivity*)" (*RPL*, 103).

21. In English in the original.

22. Julia Kristeva, "L'expérience littéraire est-elle encore possible? Entretien: Julia Kristeva, Danièlle Sallenave 1994–1995," *L'Infini* 53 (spring 1996), 20.

23. Plato, *Timaeus*, trans. Benjamin Jowett, in *The Collected Dialogues of Plato*, ed. Edith Hamilton and Huntington Cairns (Princeton: Princeton University Press, 1980).

24. Jean-Paul Sartre, *The Imaginary: A Phenomenological Psychology of the Imagination*, trans. Jonathan Webber (London and New York: Routledge, 2004). Henceforth cited as *I*.

25. See Julia Kristeva, *New Maladies of the Soul*, trans. Ross Guberman (New York, and Chichester, West Sussex: Columbia University Press, 1995), 42–44.

26. Julia Kristeva, *La révolte intime*, vol. 2 of *Pouvoirs et limites de la psychanalyse* (Paris: Fayard, 1997), 230. Henceforth cited as *RI*.

27. Jean-Paul Sartre, *L'imagination* (Paris: Presses Universitaires de France, 1989), 4.

28. To be noted here is the fact that Kristeva does not refer at all to the earlier work of Sartre on imagination.

29. See supra, note 5.

30. In this regard, note Brian Massumi's observation that "[s]omething that happens too quickly to have happened, actually, is *virtual*. The body is as immediately virtual as it is actual." Brian Massumi, *Parables of the Virtual* (Durham and London: Duke University Press, 2002), 30.

Chapter 3
The Layered Being of Merleau-Ponty and the Being Layered of Deleuze: A Comparison of Two Conceptions of Immanentism on the Basis of the Notion "Fold"
Judith Wambacq

1. Gilles Deleuze and Felix Guattari, *Qu'est-ce que la philosophie?* (Paris: Les Editions de Minuit, 2000), 48. Henceforth cited as *QP*.

2. Maurice Merleau-Ponty, *Phenomenology of Perception*, trans. Colin Smith (London and New York: Routledge, 1996), 182. Henceforth cited as *PP*.

3. In "Le langage indirect et les voix du silence," Merleau-Ponty also reverses this relation: words are not only gestures; gestures are also words, or more specifically creative expression. In what way? Just as a creative expression is an operation in which the sense of a sign is produced by the configuration of all other signs that surround it in such a way that the sense transcends the pure materiality of the sign, the meaning of a gesture arises from the context of the gesture in such a way that it is not reducible to the physicality of the gesture. *Signes* (Paris: Gallimard, 1960), 83–84. Henceforth cited as *S*.

4. This view clearly differs from a rationalist account in which speaking is explained as the verbalization of the intellectual synthesis of a word that is stored in our memory. The empirical account of speaking refers to the reactivation of auditive-perceptual circuits that are carved in the brain.

5. Frank Baeyens, *De ongrijpbaarheid der dingen. Over de vervlechting van taal en waarneming bij M. Merleau-Ponty* (Leuven: Universitaire Pers Leuven, 2004), 23.

6. "La signification sans aucun signe, la chose même—ce comble de clarté serait l'évanouissement de toute clarté" (*S*, 103).

7. "[L]a parole joue toujours sur fond de parole, elle n'est jamais qu'un pli dans

l'immense tissu de parler" (*S*, 53). And: "Son opacité, son obstinée référence [du langage] à lui-même, ses retours et ses replis sur lui-même sont justement ce qui fait de lui un pouvoir spirituel : car il devient à son tour quelque chose comme un univers" (*S*, 54).

8. "[L]'idée d'une expression *complète* fait non-sens" (*S*, 54); "la genèse du sens n'est jamais achevée" (*S*, 52).

9. Maurice Merleau-Ponty, *Le visible et l'invisible, suivi de notes de travail*, ed. Claude Lefort (Paris: Gallimard, 1971), 194, 201, 244, 251, 255, 270, 311, and 326. Henceforth cited as *VI*.

10. "Ce qu'il [Hegel, with whom Merleau-Ponty agrees with respect to this subject] a en vue, lui, c'est le moment où l'intérieur se fait extérieur, le virage ou le virement par lequel nous passons en autrui et dans le monde comme le monde et autrui en nous" (*S*, 90).

11. When I produce a singular expression, a personal style of relating to the world, this is understandable for others because it is grounded on a universal being in the world and a tradition of language (or linguistically relating to this world). Hence the singularity presupposes the universality. On the other hand, this universal being in the world is also shaped by the different personal expressions of this being, which reverses the relation and makes the contribution of singularity and universality undeterminable.

12. "Inséparablement *le sens est l'exprimable ou l'exprimé de la proposition, et l'attribut de l'état de choses*." *Logique du sens* (Paris: Les Editions de Minuit, 2002), 34. Henceforth cited as *LS*. The last part of this sentence can also be shortened as follows: "Le sens . . . il est attribut de la chose" (33).

13. "Le sens est la même chose que l'événement, mais cette fois rapporté aux propositions" (*LS*, 195).

14. *LS*, 14. Deleuze considers a battle as a typical event (*LS*, 122–23): on the battlefield there is nothing but bodies that are attacking and stabbing each other, but the battle does not happen; the battle is always someplace else. The battle emanates from the bodies; it is produced by the bodies as an effect and at the same time it precedes them as the condition of their possible meetings. See also Ronald Bogue, *Deleuze on Literature* (London and New York: Routledge, 2003), 24.

15. "On ne peut pas dire qu'ils [les événements] existent, mais plutôt qu'ils subsistent ou insistent, ayant ce minimum d'être qui convient à ce qui n'est pas une chose, entité non existante" (*LS*, 13).

16. *Le pli: Leibniz et le baroque* (Paris: Les Editions de Minuit, 1988).

17. *Différence et répétition* (Paris: Presses Universitaires de France, 1993), 89–91 and 278. Henceforth cited as *DER*.

18. *Proust et les signes* (Paris: Quadrige/Presses Universitaires de France, 1998), 39–40. Henceforth cited as *PS*.

19. *Spinoza et le problème de l'expression* (Paris: Les Editions de Minuit, 2002), 153–69.

20. "Un Dehors, plus lointain que tout extérieur, 'se tord,' 'se plie,' 'se double' d'un Dedans, plus profond que tout intérieur, et rend seul possible le rapport dérivé de l'intérieur avec l'extérieur." Gilles Deleuze, *Foucault* (Paris: Les Editions de Minuit, 2004), 117. Henceforth cited as *F*.

21. "Ce qui définit le mouvement infini [le mouvement du plan d'immanence], c'est un aller et retour, parce qu'il ne va pas vers une destination sans déjà revenir sur soi" (*QP*, 40).

22. Richard de Brabander, "Foucault," in *Deleuze Compendium*, ed. Ed Romein, Marc Schuilenburg and Sjoerd van Tuinen (Amsterdam: Boom, 2009), 147–60.

23. "[L]e pli ne constituera pas le se-voyant de la vue sans constituer aussi le se-parlant du langage, au point que c'est le même monde qui se parle dans le langage et qui se voyait dans la vue" (*F*, 118–19).

24. Judith Wambacq, "Het differentiële gehalte van Merleau-Ponty's ontologie," *Tijdschrift voor Filosofie* 70, no. 3 (September 2008), 479–508.

25. "[L]a phénoménologie est trop pacifiante, elle a béni trop de choses" (*F*, 120).

Chapter 4
The / Turn and the " " Pause:
Agamben, Derrida, and the Stratification of Poetry
William Watkin

1. Mikhail M. Bakhtin, *Dialogic Imagination: Four Essays*, trans. Caryl Emerson (Austin: University of Texas Press, 1982), 264. Henceforth cited as *DI*.

2. You can trace the lineage of stratification as a metaphor for prosaic multiplicity, as I have done, through Bakhtin, Sartre, and Merleau-Ponty specifically. See William Watkin, "The Materialization of Prose: Poiesis versus Dianoia in the Work of Godzich & Kittay, Schklovsky, Silliman, and Agamben," *Paragraph* 31, no. 3 (2008), 344–64. That said, the influence of the idea that prose gives special access to multiple social layers emanates from the very origins of the modern novel in the bedrock of eighteenth-century narratives, and the rich seam of aesthetic gold that was unearthed across Europe all through the nineteenth century, these days located underneath terms such as realism and naturalism. By the time Bakhtin gave voice to it, heteroglossia was already seen as facilitated by prose as a medium. This is primarily due, according to Godzich and Kittay, to prose's deictic abilities which always seem to mark a passage from language to the world beyond. See Wlad Godzich and Jeffrey Kittay, *The Emergence of Prose: An Essay in Prosaics* (Minneapolis: University of Minnesota Press, 1987). Again, by the time Bakhtin is bewailing the closed nature of poetic unity, the social experiments of Romanticism had long been superseded by what was seen by many, Heidegger being foremost, as the constructive solipsism of the modern lyric typified, of course, by the rise of the lyric over narrative poetry during European modernism.

3. Maurice Merleau-Ponty, *The Prose of the World*, trans. John O'Neill (Evanston, IL: Northwestern University Press, 1973), 13. Henceforth cited as *POW*.

4. Martin Heidegger, *On the Way to Language*, trans. Peter D. Hertz (San Francisco: Harper Collins, 1971), 70 and 89.

5. It is apparent here therefore that first singularity does not indicate unity, anything but. As Derrida tirelessly reveals, singularity is the moment of rupture within any totalized, self-present textual entity. Second that the "closed" nature of singularity does not preclude stratification. In Nancy's work for example singularity is the precondition for all multiplicities as is also the case in Deleuze of course. And finally that descriptions of modern poetry as univocal, closed, hermetic and seamless are willful misreadings as my brief history of modern poetic stratification shows.

6. See Martin Heidegger, *Poetry, Language, Thought*, trans. Albert Hofstadter (New York: Harper & Row, 1971), 95, and Alain Badiou, *Handbook of Inaesthetics*, trans. Alberto Toscano (Stanford: Stanford University Press, 2005), 19–20.

7. I am thinking here, in no particular order, of Badiou, Agamben, Gadamer, Nancy, Lacoue-Labarthe, and Derrida, all of whom in the latter part of last century and into the

earliest lap of this one have developed a, shall we call it, Heideggerian critical appropriation of poetic singularity influenced by a core of European modern poets, most notably Mallarmé and Celan. This does not suggest that any of them accept Heideggerian singularity, that their different accounts sit together easily, or indeed that all present the same idea of singularity, but one can see, for example, in recent work by Derek Attridge and Timothy Clark, how the conceptualization and assumption of poetic singularity has come to form a semi-coherent modality of approaching the literary text.

8. Giorgio Agamben, *The End of the Poem*, trans. Daniel Heller-Roazen (Stanford: Stanford University Press, 1999), 77. Henceforth cited as *EP*.

9. To trace the argumentation of this intention here would be impossible as the relation of Agamben's work to the term life encapsulates and incorporates the totality of this thinking on aesthetics, politics, and metaphysics which, I contend, represents the totality of his thought to date. For a detailed consideration of these issues see William Watkin, *The Literary Agamben: Adventures in Logopoiesis* (London: Continuum, 2010), especially the opening remarks 4–40, and later developments 123–24 and 169–71. Henceforth cited as *LA*. That said, one pertinent comment can be made here as concerns the relation between the term life and that of caesura in Agamben. In *The Open* Agamben uses caesura to describe the crucial history of the development of the term "life" in terms of an obsessive division of life into human and animal. In particular he attacks the Heideggerian Dasein as being anthropocentric and overly dependent on a presupposition of human difference based on the appropriation of and division from the term animal. Rather than defining self-consciously finite (human) life as in contradistinction to oblivious animal life, as Heidegger ends up doing, Agamben defines life not due to a caesura between one category and another but as "*what cannot be defined, yet, precisely for this reason, must be ceaselessly articulated and divided*" (*O*, 13). Thus the caesura does not facilitate a theory of life but constitutes the process of life.

10. Agamben uses the term boustrophedonic to describe the folded-backwards nature of enjambment as an experience of reading. For a full consideration see *LA*, 139–44.

11. Susan Howe, *Singularities* (Hanover, NH: Wesleyan University Press, 1990), 41. Henceforth cited as *SI*.

12. Loath as I am to repeatedly cite my own work again, the easiest point of reference for a full consideration of Agamben's use of these terms is *LA*, 26–32.

13. For the full range of these considerations of structure in Agamben's work see *MWC*, 94–103; *Language and Death: The Place of Negativity*, trans. Karen E. Pinkus with Michael Hardt (Minneapolis: University of Minnesota Press, 1991), 84–98; and *TR*, 59–87.

14. The semiotic in Agamben's work is not to be taken to mean the science of signifying systems. Rather the semiotic is the raw fact of material signification as such. It is nonsignifying signification or the potential to signify without signifying anything in particular. In Agamben's work the semiotic takes three key forms. The first, found in *Infancy and History*, is language as such in its infancy or the fact that there is language prior to or separated from the metaphysical insistence on language signifying some thing. The second, again in *Infancy and History* and later developed in *Remnants of Auschwitz*, is inherited from the French linguist Benveniste, whose theory of the semiotic in relation to indicative forms such as deixis presents a language which both draws attention to itself as pure medium, and which presents, through shifting, one of the few instances where one can move across the imposed division between the semiotic and the semantic. Finally in relation to poetry it is the basis of his conception in *The End of the Poem* of the definition of poetry as prolonged hesitation between sound and sense, as well as being the key term

in poetry's ability, through the predominance of the semiotic, to actually suspend the false division/relation between semiotic and semantic.

15. Jacques Derrida, *Dissemination*, trans. Barbara Johnson (London: Athlone Press, 1981), 208. Henceforth cited as *D*.

16. Derrida's remarkable consideration of parerga, in painting in fact but of clear and direct relevance to the formation of the poetic body, is to be found in the essay "Parergon" in *The Truth in Painting*, trans. Geoff Bennington and Ian McLeod (Chicago: Chicago University Press, 1987), 15–148.

17. In the opening comments of Derrida's essay "Khōra," he traces its use in Plato's *Timaeus* as naming an element of philosophy that succumbs to contradiction, a logic he explains citing Plato "other than that of the logic of the *logos*. The *khōra*, which is neither 'sensible' nor 'intelligible,' belongs to a 'third genus' (*triton genos*, 48a–52a)." Jacques Derrida, *On the Name*, trans. David Wood, John P. Leavey Jr., and Ian McLeod (Stanford: Stanford University Press, 1995), 89. Henceforth cited as *ON*. This undecidability within the *khōra*, translatable although never entirely successfully as place and/or receptacle, results in an oscillation between "the logic of exclusion and that of participation" (*ON*, 89). This combination of receptive space or region and oscillation clearly recommends it to the Derridean conception of hymen, an entente finally sealed where one notes that *khôra* is also often taken to mean womb. It is worth noting that Agamben too, through his conception of the stanza as potential term for immediate mediation in *Stanzas*, picks up on the troubadour association of the stanza to "receptive 'womb.'" Giorgio Agamben, *Stanzas: Word and Phantasm in Western Culture*, trans. Ronald L. Martinez (Minneapolis: University of Minnesota Press, 1993), xvi.

18. The fold is in fact not a break as such but the production of a sharp point that sticks into space. Thus Derrida also uses the metaphor of the hinge or *le brisure* (*OG*, 65–72), and, less famously, Agamben speaks of the "corn" or unrelated rhyme in troubadour poetry which also means tip, corner, or angle (*EP*, 23–42). There is no space to follow up on this as the issues in play are so complex it would require a whole other essay but to clarify, enjambment is a break-presenting fold facilitated by flow just as obversely caesura is a flow-presenting break facilitated by a pause.

19. See *TR*, 68.

20. Jacques Derrida, *Sovereignties in Question*, ed. Thomas Dutoit and Outi Pasanen (New York: Fordham University Press, 2005), 3. Henceforth cited as *SQ*.

Notes to Part Two

Chapter 5
Layering and Extending:
Architecture's Traumatic Work of Mourning
Michael Beehler

1. Elizabeth Grosz, *Architecture from the Outside: Essays on Virtual and Real Space* (Boston: MIT Press, 2001), 88. Henceforth cited as *AO*.

2. Jean-Luc Marion, *In Excess: Studies of Saturated Phenomena* (New York: Fordham University Press, 2002), 79. Henceforth cited as *IE*.

3. Daniel Libeskind, *The Space of Encounter* (New York: Universe Publishing, 2000), 148. Henceforth cited as *SE*.

4. Nicosia, site of the 2007 IAPL conference at which this paper was first given.

5. Robyn Horner, *Rethinking God as Gift: Marion, Derrida, and the Limits of Phenomenology* (New York: Fordham University Press, 2001), 163.

6. The story of the tower of Babel is, of course, exemplary in this regard.

7. Edith Wyschogrod, "Eating the Text, Defiling the Hands: Specters in Arnold Schoenberg's Opera *Moses and Aaron*," in *God, the Gift, and Postmodernism*, ed. John D. Caputo and Michael J. Scanlon (Bloomington: Indiana University Press, 1999), 245–46. Henceforth cited as *ET*.

8. Jacques Derrida, "Archive Fever: A Freudian Impression," trans. Eric Prenowitz, *Diacritics* 25, no. 2 (summer 1995), 52. Henceforth cited as *AF*.

9. Daniel Libeskind, *Breaking Ground: Adventures in Life and Architecture* (New York: Riverhead Books, 2004), 107. Henceforth cited as *BG*.

10. Jacques Derrida, *Points. . . : Interviews, 1974–1994*, trans. Peggy Kamuf et al., ed. Elisabeth Weber (Stanford: Stanford University Press, 1995), 321. Henceforth cited as *PI*.

11. Daniel Libeskind, *radix-matrix* (Munich: Prestel Verlag, 1997), 114. Henceforth cited as *RM*.

Chapter 6
The "Forgotten" as Epic Vorwelt
Brendan Moran

Epigraph: Friedrich Nietzsche, *Werke*, ed. Giorgio Colli and Mazzino Montinari, vol. 8, tome 3: *Nachgelassene Fragmente. Anfang 1888 bis Anfang Januar 1889* (Berlin: Walter de Gruyter, 1972), 23.

1. Walter Benjamin, *Gesammelte Schriften*, ed. R. Tiedemann et al. (Frankfurt: Suhrkamp, 1974–1999), vol. 2, tome 3, 1198. Henceforth cited as *GS*, and the abbreviation will be followed by a Roman numeral indicating the volume number, and an Arabic numeral indicating the tome number. Further abbreviations: *CWB* = *The Correspondence of Walter Benjamin*, trans. Manfred R. Jacobson and Evelyn M. Jacobson, ed. Gershom Scholem and Theodor Adorno (Chicago: University of Chicago Press, 1994); *GB* = Benjamin, *Gesammelte Briefe*, 6 vols., ed. C. Gödde and H. Lonitz (Frankfurt: Suhrkamp,

1995–2000); *OGD* = Benjamin, *The Origin of German Tragic Drama*, trans. John Osborne (London: Verso Books, 1998); *SW* = Benjamin, *Selected Writings*, 4 vols., ed. M. W. Jennings et al. (Cambridge, MA: The Belknap Press of Harvard University Press, 1996–2003).

2. Bernd Müller, *"Denn ist noch nichts geschehen." Walter Benjamins Kafka-Deutung* (Cologne: Böhlau, 1996), 101. Henceforth cited as *KD*. The translation of this and of all German and French texts is mine, unless an existing English translation is cited.

3. Beatrice Hanssen, *Walter Benjamin's Other History: Of Stones, Animals, Human Beings, and Angels* (Berkeley: University of California Press, 1998), 143.

4. Michael Jennings, "Introduction" to Walter Benjamin, *The Writer of Modern Life. Essays on Charles Baudelaire* (Cambridge, MA: Harvard University Press, 2006), 7.

5. Marc Sagnol, "Archaïsme et Modernité: Benjamin, Kafka et la Loi," *Les Temps Modernes* 618 (2002), 92; see also 93–95 and 98.

6. Marc Sagnol, "Le bourbier et la cigale. Sur Benjamin et Bachofen," *Walter Benjamin. Critique philosophique de l'art*, ed. R. Rochlitz and P. Rusch (Paris: Presses Universitaires de France, 2005), 59.

7. For an analysis, see Marc Sagnol's "Le bourbier et la cigale," especially 52–56. For Benjamin's own Bachofen essay and materials related to it, see *SW*3, 11–24/*GS*II:1, 219–33 and *GS*II:3, 963–69. Also see *GS*III, 88–89. Benjamin was especially familiar with the collection of Bachofen's writings edited by Bernoulli (Johann Jakob Bachofen, *Urreligion und antike Symbole*, 3 vols., ed. Carl Albrecht Bernoulli [Leipzig: Verlag von Philipp Reclam jun., 1926]). It is from the latter collection that Benjamin quotes in his 1934 essay on Kafka (e.g., *SW* 2, 809/*GS*II:2, 429). For Benjamin's review of Bernoulli's own study of Bachofen, which appeared in 1924, see *SW*1, 426–27/*GS*III, 43–45.

8. Rodolphe Gasché, "Kafka's Law: In the Field of Forces Between Judaism and Hellenism," *MLN* 117, no. 5 (2002), 986. Henceforth cited as *KL*.

9. Elaboration of this distinction of mythic muteness and namelessness from non-mythic muteness and namelessness may be found in Monad Rrenban, *Wild, Unforgettable Philosophy* (Lanham, MD: Lexington, 2005), especially 22–24, 28–29, 32, 40, 57–58, 79, 134, 156, 178–79, 221–33. Henceforth cited as *WUP*. For a reading of Benjamin's Kafka texts with regard to the non-mythic notion of namelessness, see Werner Hamacher, "The Gesture in the Name," *Premises*, trans. P. Fenves (Stanford: Stanford University Press, 1999), especially 301, 328–29.

10. See Kafka, "The Silence of the Sirens," in *Kafka's Selected Stories*, trans. and ed. S. Corngold (New York: W.W. Norton and Company, 2007), 127–28; *Kafka's Selected Stories* will henceforth be cited as *KS*; "Das Schweigen der Sirenen," in *Nachgelassene Schriften und Fragmente*, vol. 2, ed. Jost Schillemeit (Frankfurt: Fischer Verlag, 2002), 40–42.

11. On Bachofen's tendency to regard myth as all-pervasive, see *GS*II:3, 967–68. Concerning Ludwig Klages's transformation of Bachofen's views into a "philosophy" or "neo-paganism" that intertwines the forgotten with mythic substances of "primal images [*Urbilder*]," see *SW*3, 18–19, 21/*GS*II:1, 229–30, 232. On the relevance between Benjamin's reflections on Bachofen and his work on Kafka, see Sigrid Weigel, "Johann Jakob Bachofen," in *Benjamin-Handbuch*, ed. Burkhardt Lindner (Stuttgart: Verlag J.B. Metzler, 2006), 540.

12. For an attempt to analyze shame in Benjamin's Kafka writings, see Brendan Moran, "An Inhumanly Wise Shame," *The European Legacy* 14, no. 5 (August 2009), 573–85. Henceforth cited as *IWS*.

13. With the expression "infinite amount of hope," Benjamin is quoting a remark by Kafka that is cited in Max Brod, "Der Dichter Franz Kafka," *Die neue Rundschau* 11 (November 1921), 1213.

14. See the very similar formulation in *SW*2, 808–9/*GS*II:2, 428.

15. For an alternative reading, see *WUP*, 226.

16. See Kafka "The Worry of the Father of Family," in *KS*, 72–73/"Die Sorge des Hausvaters," *Drucke zu Lebzeiten* (Frankfurt: Fischer Verlag, 2002), 282–84.

17. The two sentences (from the 1934 essay) concerning Kafka's world (*SW*2, 799/*GS*II.2, 415) have been discussed carefully here, partly because the reading given (which is fairly close to the translation by Harry Zohn that is available in *SW*) does differ from the reading (and the translation) given in Gasché's article on Benjamin's writings on Kafka. For Gasché's interpretation, which—as mentioned—is not the reading followed in this article, the contention that it is not possible ("ist hier nicht möglich") to speak of orders or hierarchies ("[v]on Ordnungen und Hierarchien zu sprechen") is made by the world of myth ("[d]ie Welt des Mythos, die das nahelegt"); Kafka's world is identified with the world of myth that promises redemption (paradoxically, to or from Kafka's world), and the world of myth comes to mind, is conveyed, as "a world lacking all order and hierarchies," as a world of "the oppressive and gloomy nature of the law that reigns over Kafka's world" (*KL*, 992). For a reading somewhat closer to the one proposed in this chapter, see Winfried Menninghaus, *Schwellenkunde: Walter Benjamins Passage des Mythos* (Frankfurt: Suhrkamp, 1986), 89–90.

18. For some of Scholem's relevant comments, see *GS*II:3, 1155–56 and Walter Benjamin and Gershom Scholem, *Briefwechsel, 1933–1940*, ed. G. Scholem (Frankfurt: Suhrkamp, 1980), 154, 157–58, 174–75, 281–86. For some of Benjamin's relevant remarks, see: *SW*2, 815/*GS*II:2, 437; *GS*II:3, 1172, 1192, 1216, 1245–46 and 1250; and *CWB*, 448–50 and 453/*GB*4, 459–60, 479/*Briefwechsel*, 159–60, 166–67.

19. Also see Werner Kraft, "Gott," in *Franz Kafka: Durchdringung und Geheimnis* (Frankfurt: Suhrkamp, 1968), 74.

20. See Réda Bensmaïa, in the foreword to Deleuze and Guattari, *Kafka: Towards a Minor Literature*, trans. D. Polan (Minneapolis: University of Minnesota Press, 1986), xiii, xvii, xix, xxi. In contrast, Bruno Tackels contends that theology in Benjamin's readings of Kafka is in "un *mode mineur*," is "toujours mineure" ("Les Kafkas de Benjamin," in *Walter Benjamin. Critique philosophique de l'art*, ed. Rainer Rochlitz and Pierre Rusch [Paris: Presses Universitaires de France, 2005], 73).

21. This has often been suggested. See, for instance, Jean-Michel Palmier, *Walter Benjamin. Le chiffonnier, l'Ange et le Petit Bossu* (Paris: Klincksieck, 2006), 626, n.8 and Uwe Steiner, *Walter Benjamin* (Stuttgart: Verlag J. B. Metzler, 2004), 133–45, especially 135–38.

22. Concerning Brecht, see the remarks in the first paragraph of this chapter. Concerning Oskar Maria Graf, see *GS*III, 309–10. Noteworthy too are Benjamin's comments on Alfred Döblin's *Berlin Alexanderplatz*, although those comments are also quite critical (*SW* 2, 299–304/*GS*III, 230–36).

23. Also see notes written toward this letter: *GS*II:3, 1246 (especially point 10).

24. See the "Storyteller" essay (*SW* 3, 147/*GS*II:2, 444, and as discussed above).

25. Daniel Weidner, "Jüdisches Gedächtnis, mystische Tradition und moderne Literatur. Walter Benjamin und Gershom Scholem deuten Kafka," *Weimarer Beiträge* 46, no. 2 (2000), 243.

26. As noted above (n. 13), Benjamin is quoting Max Brod.

27. Benjamin is quoting Haas, *Gestalten der Zeit* (Berlin: Kiepenheuer, 1930), 195.

28. Again, quoting Haas, 195.

29. Also see: *GS*II:3, 1192, 1207, 1210, 1213–14, 1237 and 1269.

30. For an attempt to analyze this, see Brendan Moran, "Foolish Wisdom in Benjamin's Kafka," in *Laughter in Eastern and Western Philosophies*, ed. Hans-Georg Moeller and Günter Wohlfart (Freiburg and Munich: Verlag Karl Alber, 2010), 175–92. For some pertinent remarks, see *SW*3, 327/*GB*6, 113 as well as the following: *GS*II:3, 1212; *SW*2, 798, 813 and 816/*GS*II:2, 414, 434 and 438.

31. Concerning Odradek, see n. 16 above. Concerning Gregor Samsa, see *The Metamorphosis*, trans. S. Corngold (New York: W.W. Norton and Company, 1996), 1–60/"Die Verwandlung," in *Drucke zu Lebzeiten*, 113–200. Concerning the half-kitten, half-lamb, see "A Crossbreed," in *KS*, 125–27/"Die Kreuzung," in *Nachgelassene Schriften und Fragmente*, vol. 1, ed. Malcolm Pasley (Frankfurt: Fischer Verlag, 2002), 372–74.

32. Concerning Leni, see *The Trial*, trans. B. Mitchell (New York: Schocken Books, 1999), 108/*Der Proceß*, ed. Malcolm Pasley (Frankfurt: Fischer Verlag, 2002), 145. From Bachofen, Benjamin is quoting *Urreligion und antike Symbole*, vol. 1, 386. Mentioning "Leni and her web [*Schwimmhaut*]," Benjamin refers to "[t]he world of monsters" and wonders: "Perhaps an allusion to her swamp- or water-origin" (*GS*II:3, 1201).

33. Also see *SW*2, 798–99/*GS*II:2, 414–15; and further remarks in *GS*II:3, 1212.

34. For further such references to *Schoß*, for which the term "womb" seems the appropriate translation, see *SW*2, 798–99 and 809/*GS*II:2, 414–15 and 429, as well as *GS*II:3, 1212, 1222, 1225 and 1248.

35. The bird-like clerk appears in *The Trial*, 102/*Der Proceß*, 137.

36. See *IWS*, 581–82.

37. Eric L. Santner, "Miracles Happen: Benjamin, Rosenzweig, Freud, and the Matter of the Neighbor," in Slavoj Žižek, Eric L. Santner, and Kenneth Reinhard, *The Neighbor: Three Inquiries in Political Theology* (Chicago: University of Chicago Press, 2005), 94.

38. Very brief replies to such objections may be found in *WUP*, 57, 96, 311 n.105, 313 n.18, 321 n.73, 322 n.78, 370 n.119.

39. Emmanuel Levinas, *Totality and Infinity: An Essay on Exteriority*, trans. Alphonso Lingis (Pittsburgh, PA: Duquesne University Press, 1969), 79/*Totalité et Infini. Essai sur l'extériorité* (The Hague: Martinus Nijhoff, 1961), 78.

40. Walter Benjamin, *Oeuvres*, vol. 2, trans. M. de Gandillac (Paris: Denoël, 1971), 67. See *GS*II:2, 412 and Bruno Tackels, *Walter Benjamin: Une vie dans les textes* (Arles: Actes Sud, 2009), 732.

41. Quoting "The Worry of the Father of the Family," in *KS*, 73/"Die Sorge des Hausvaters," in *Drucke zu Lebzeiten*, 284. Also see Benjamin's comments in *SW*2, 811/*GS*II:2, 431, as well as *GS*II:3, 1240.

42. Cf. Eric Santner, *On Creaturely Life: Rilke, Benjamin, Sebald* (Chicago: University of Chicago Press, 2006), 24.

43. In addition to this note of 1931, see *GS*II:3, 1201 (from some time up to 1931).

44. Also see *GS*II:3, 1243.

45. Also see *GS*II:3, 1198–99 and 1205.

46. Also see *GS*II:3, 1270.

47. See Kafka, "The Hunter Gracchus," in *KS*, 112/"Der Jäger Grachus," in *Nachgelassene Schriften und Fragmente*, vol. 1, 311.

48. The quotation from Plutarch's *Isis and Osiris* is cited from a text by Bachofen (*Urreligion und antike Symbole*, vol. 1, 253). See Plutarch, *Moralia*, vol. 5, trans. Frank

Cole Babbitt, Loeb Classical Library 197 (Cambridge, MA: Harvard University Press, 1927), 111.

49. This reading contrasts with that given by Santner, *On Creaturely Life*, 92–95.

50. See, for instance, Hans Mayer, "Walter Benjamin und Franz Kafka. Bericht über eine Konstellation," *Aufklärung Heute. Reden und Vorträge. 1978–1984* (Frankfurt: Suhrkamp, 1985), 60–61.

Chapter 7
Halal History and Existential Meaning in Salman Rushdie's Early Fiction
Adnan Mahmutovic

1. Daniel Pipes, *The Rushdie Affair: The Novel, the Ayatollah, and the West* (London: Transaction Publishers, 1990).

2. Salman Rushdie, *The Satanic Verses* (London: Vintage, 1998). Henceforth cited as *SV*.

3. Qur'an, 6:108.

4. Salman Rushdie, *Imaginary Homelands* (London: Penguin Books, 1991), 408. Henceforth cited as *IH*.

5. Salman Rushdie, *The Jaguar Smile* (London: Vintage, 2000).

6. Homi K. Bhabha, *The Location of Culture* (London: Routledge Classics, 2004), xvii–xviii. Henceforth cited as *LC*.

7. Salman Rushdie, *Midnight's Children* (London: Vintage, 1995), 9. Henceforth cited as *MC*. Copyright © 1980 by Salman Rushdie, used by permission of The Wylie Agency LLC and reprinted by permission of The Random House Group Ltd.

8. As Henry Schwarz claims, "whenever definitions of identity and belonging, inclusion and exclusion, rights and entitlements are posited, they are done for specific, contingent and situational reasons. . . . [T]he world is an integrated ensemble of historical and regional processes. . . . [P]articular times and places can rarely be separated out from larger patterns if we are to make interpretations capable of producing change. The reverse is also true: large historical patterns only take on meaning when they can be shown at work in specific contexts." Henry Schwarz, "Mission Impossible: Introducing Postcolonial Studies in the US Academy," in *A Companion to Postcolonial Studies*, ed. Henry Schwarz and Sangeeta Ray (Malden, MA: Blackwell Publishers, 2000).

9. Jean-Paul Sartre, *Critique of Dialectical Reason*, vol. 1: *Theory of Practice of Ensembles*, trans. Alan Sheridan Smith (London: New Left Books, 1976), 36.

10. To use Sartre again: "*several* collectivities, *several* societies, and *one* history—realities, that is, which impose themselves on individuals; but at the same time it must be woven out of millions of individual actions" (*Critique of Dialectical Reason*, 36).

11. Timothy Brennan, *Salman Rushdie and the Third World: Myths of the Nation* (London: Macmillan, 1989), 7.

12. Lloyd Spencer, "Allegory in the World of Commodity: The Importance of *Central Park*," *New German Critique* 34 (1985), 63. In addition, it could be argued that allegory is grounded in the removal of elements from their organic context and giving them another meaning. For Peter Bürger "The allegorist pulls one element out of the totality of the life context, isolating it, depriving it of its function. . . . The allegorist joins the isolated reality fragments and thereby creates meaning. This is posited meaning; it does not derive from the original context of the fragments." Peter Bürger, *Theory of the Avant-Garde* (Minneapolis: University of Minnesota Press, 1984), 69. In my view, Saleem's

play with allegory shows that there is no "organic" context.

13. Friedrich Nietzsche, *Collected Works*, vol. 2, trans. and ed. Oscar Levy (London: T. L. Foulis, 1911), 180. Following Nietzsche, David Campbell claims, there cannot "be a self that does not make sense to itself." David Campbell, "Nietzsche, Heidegger, and Meaning," *Journal of Nietzsche Studies* 26 (autumn 2003), 28. In fact, "one is constrained by a need for order and meaning to interpret the world in ways that others may share" (30). Indeed "what gives meaning and value to one's life is a feeling of vitality both strong enough to meet its contingency, disorder, and pain and stable enough to persist if it recurred numberless times" (32).

14. For instance, Saleem evokes Bombay cinema. In other cases he uses English fiction, which Neil ten Kortenaar shows is out of character and makes readers aware of a third writer, that is Rushdie. Neil ten Kortenaar, *Self, Nation, Text in Salman Rushdie's "Midnight's Children"* (Montreal: McGill-Queen's University Press, 2004), 244–49. Henceforth cited as *SNT*. Saleem is furthermore in "terror at finding himself written and thus read" (248).

15. To "swallow" is indeed a sedimented metaphor for "accepting an argument or claims." At one level the idea of edible lives and histories is a parody of Western consumerism of the exotic. When he demands that the reader consume everything, he implies not just the exotic, not just the juicy, but also the undesirable truth.

16. Joseph Heller's *God Knows* contains a strikingly similar passage: "Chronicles . . . that's a prissy whitewash in which the juiciest parts of my life are discarded as unimportant or unworthy. Therefore, I hate Chronicles. In Chronicles I am a pious bore." Joseph Heller, *God Knows* (New York: Knopf, 1984), 4.

17. Hans Wehr, *A Dictionary of Modern Written Arabic*, ed. J. M. Cowan. (Ithaca, NY: Spoken Language Services, 1979). The verb *halal* means to untie, unbind, unfasten, unravel, solve, decipher. For other prescriptions of *halal* and *haram*, see Qur'an 5:5, and 2:177 in which it is forbidden to refuse help to poor and orphans as well as to have premarital sex and marry polytheists.

18. Claude Lévi-Strauss, *The Savage Mind*, trans. John Weightman and Doreen Weightman (London: Weidenfeld & Nicolson, 1966), 257.

19. The "body of history" and the cracking "body politic" are both his own body (*MC*, 245).

20. Saleem also alludes to the first revealed verse of the Qur'an: "Recite, in the name of the Lord thy Creator, who created man from clots of blood" (*MC*, 10), where he attempts to show the connection between recitation (narrative), Divine creation, and blood in the inceptive moment of the Islamic message.

21. As Chakrabarty has argued, the discovery of the "pleasures of privacy" is what grounds the modern, bourgeois individual, who is "in fact, a deferred 'public' self . . . 'always already oriented to an audience (*Publicum*).'" Dipesh Chakrabarty, *Provincializing Europe: Postcolonial Thought and Historical Difference* (Princeton: Princeton University Press, 2000), 35. Henceforth cited as *PE*. William Connolly makes a distinction between public/political life in citizenship and the private self that often expresses itself through diaries, letters, autobiographies, and novels. William Connolly, *Political Theory and Modernity* (Oxford: Blackwell, 1989).

22. Dipesh Chakrabarty, *Habitations of Modernity* (Chicago and London: The University of Chicago Press, 2002), 94. Henceforth cited as *HM*.

23. Linda Hutcheon, *A Poetics of Postmodernism: History, Theory, Fiction* (New York: Routledge, 1988), 190. Henceforth cited as *POP*.

24. Salman Rushdie, *Shame* (London: Vintage, 1995), 28. Henceforth cited as *SH*.

25. Sabrina Hassumani, *Salman Rushdie: A Postmodern Reading of His Major Works* (Madison: Farleigh Dickinson University Press, 2002).

26. Mieke Bal, *Loving Yusuf: Conceptual Travels from Present to Past* (Chicago:

University of Chicago Press, 2008), passim.

27. Michael Reder, *Conversations with Salman Rushdie* (Jackson: University Press of Mississippi, 2000), viii. Henceforth cited as *CSR*.

28. Erik Strand, "Gandhian Communalism and the *Midnight Children's* Conference," *ELH* 72 (2005), 981–82.

29. As Chakrabarty claims, when "we think of the world as disenchanted . . . we set limits to the ways the past can be narrated" (*PE*, 89).

30. Nandini Bhattacharya, "Portrait of a Fascist in the Novels of Salman Rushdie," in *Salman Rushdie: Critical Essays*, Vol. 1, ed. Mohit K. Ray and Rama Kundu (New Delhi: Atlantic Publishers and Distributors, 2006), 7.

31. These novels set up the opposition and entangle the opposed terms without unraveling and solving the discovered paradoxes (*POP*, 106). They go against the epistemological demand to a final solution and thus do something "haram." One of the meanings of the verb "halal" was "to unravel," "solve," or "decipher."

32. According to Kortenaar, the detached, "outside perspective on the state is something new, even in Indian literature written in English, which, before Rushdie, concentrated on the local and the domestic" (*SNT*, 8).

33. Apologetically speaking, if Islamic history was focused on being *halal*, *The Satanic Verses* would lack the basic premise. For Rushdie, this incident only strengthens Muhammad's own insistence on his humanity (*IH*, 408). He does not, however, allow for the possibility of it being the product of propaganda. An unorthodox critic, Massimo Campanini maintains this event would be a sign of the openness of Muhammad's private life to public scrutiny. Not even such a supposedly incriminating datum was erased in a period when recording was not an easy enterprise. Would the beginning of Islamic history be *haram* in Saleem's sense? Massimo Campanini, *The Qur'an*, trans. Oliver Leaman (New York: Routledge, 2007), 63–64.

34. Hutcheon quotes Doctorow as claiming that history and fiction mediate "the world for the purpose of introducing meaning" (*POP*, 112).

35. Erik L. Berlatsky, *Fact, Fiction, and Fabrication: History, Narrative, and the Postmodern Real from Woolf to Rushdie*, PhD diss., University of Maryland, 2003. Henceforth cited as *FFF*.

36. John J. Su, "Epic of Failure: Disappointment as Utopian Fantasy in *Midnight's Children*," *Twentieth Century Literature: A Scholarly and Critical Journal* 47, no. 4 (2001), 546.

37. Martin Heidegger, *Poetry, Language, Thought*, trans. Albert Hofstadter (New York: Harper & Row, 1975), 19.

38. In *Shame*, Rani Harappa, wife of the ruler of Pakistan, makes eighteen allegorical shawls that "say unspeakable things which nobody wanted to hear" (*SH*, 191).

39. The publishing of the cartoons did not only cause public riots and burnings of flags, but economic sanctions, the use of (Muslim) purchase power to stifle Danish economy, in particular hurting the dairy producer Arla.

Chapter 8
Tactical Reason: Philosophy and the Colonial Question
Marios Constantinou

Epigraph: William Shakespeare, *King Richard II*, act II, scene 3, lines 89–99, in *William Shakespeare: The Complete Works* (New York: Barnes & Noble Books, 1994), p. 371.

Epigraph: William Shakespeare, *King Richard II*, act IV, scene 1, lines 107–13, in

William Shakespeare: The Complete Works, 379.

Epigraph: William Wordsworth, *The Prelude*, lines 206–9, in *The Norton Anthology of English Literature*, vol. 2, ed. M. H. Abrams (New York: W. W. Norton & Company, 1979), 298.

1. Alain Badiou, *Polemics*, trans. Steven Corcoran (London: Verso, 2006), 85.

2. Alexis de Tocqueville, *Democracy in America*, trans. George Lawrence, ed. J. P. Meyer (New York: Perennial Library, 1988), 638.

3. Alain Badiou, *Metapolitics*, trans. Jason Barker (London: Verso, 2005), 127. Henceforth cited as *M*.

4. This apt comparison is also made by Andrew Cutrofello, who provides bright insights on the issue in *Continental Philosophy* (New York: Routledge, 2005), 217–18. Nonetheless, Hannah Arendt reminds us of Kant's profound confusion of revolution with a coup d'état. In other words, Kant, Arendt argues, "conceives action only as acts of the powers-that-be. Any action from the side of the subjects could consist only in conspiratorial activity, the acts and plots of secret societies." Hannah Arendt, *Lectures on Kant's Political Philosophy*, ed. Ronald Beiner (Chicago: University of Chicago Press, 1982), 60. Henceforth cited as *LK*. Shakespeare's play reflects this reduction of revolt to a coup d'état.

5. Immanuel Kant, *Political Writings*, trans. H. B. Nisbet, ed. H. S. Reiss (Cambridge: Cambridge University Press, 1970), 81. Henceforth cited as *PW*.

6. Clément Rosset, *Le réel et son double. Essai sur l'illusion* (Paris: Gallimard, 1984), 176.

7. Carl Schmitt, *The Nomos of the Earth in the International Law of the Jus Publicum Europaeum*, trans. G. L. Ulmen (New York: Telos Press, 2003). Henceforth cited as *NE*.

8. For an opposing view which considers the Enlightenment as an anti-imperialist movement without, however, coping with the contradictions and inconsistencies of Kant which make allowances for exceptions to the rule of justice, see Sankar Muthu, *Enlightenment against Empire* (Princeton: Princeton University Press, 2003).

9. Immanuel Kant, *The Metaphysics of Morals*, trans. Mary Gregor (Cambridge: Cambridge University Press, 1991), 155, paragraph 60. Henceforth cited as *MM*.

10. My hypothesis here about a "pastoral logic" of imperialism elaborates on Foucault's understanding of the state "as a modern matrix of individualization," i.e., as a source of pastoral care, protection and security against accidents, natural disasters, epidemics, revolutions, etc. Michel Foucault, "The Subject and Power," trans. Leslie Sawyer, afterword to Dreyfus Hubert and Paul Rabinow, *Michel Foucault: Beyond Structuralism and Hermeneutics* (Chicago: University of Chicago Press, 1982), 215. This pastoral logic of imperial power is precisely what weighs on the Enlightenment's quest for reason, maturity, etc. Foucault's insights into the pastoral operations of power anticipate in general terms the present state of biopolitical imperialism. What I am rethinking here is Foucault's critique of a kind of Comtean humanism cum positive religion of man as an axiomatic principle for a critique of deterritorialized imperialism in the present. Pastoral power in this perspective is an ingenious concept, as it shifts the emphasis from technics of territorial control to the "government of souls," i.e., the biopolitical alignment of populations (collectively) and inhabitants (individually). What this practically means is the progressive substitution of nations, tribes, recalcitrant identities, etc., with benevolent communities and malleable population flows. The tragic irony with Foucault's bright insight is the implication of pastoral power within the production of countermemory, dubiously projected as the ideal state of freedom in the present age of biopolitical reason. Insofar as memory, according to Foucault, designates a condition of captivity that restricts freedom and binds us to the ontological obligation of identity, the dissociation of the self from this confinement through the creation of a countermemory may be "a sign

of superior culture," liberating "countless spirits." In fact, Foucault argues, "the purpose of history, guided by genealogy, is not to discover the roots of our identity but to commit itself to its dissipation." *Language, Counter-Memory, Practice: Selected Essays and Interviews*, trans. Donald F. Bouchard and Sherry Simon, ed. Donald F. Bouchard (Ithaca, NY: Cornell University Press, 1977), 161–62. Foucault does, of course, provide a necessary caveat: "Nietzsche reproached critical history for detaching us from every real source and for sacrificing the very movement of life to the exclusive concern for truth" (164). This is well taken, yet it is insufficient, in my view, to presently counteract the Empire's diabolical implication within the massive production of countermemory as the privileged trope of biopolitical domination in the postcolonies.

11. The expulsion of Greek-Cypriots by the invading Turkish troops in 1974, the expropriation of property and its subsequent appropriation by mainland Turkish settlers present a Kantian case whereby the current users of the occupied Northern territory of Cyprus enjoy unlimited use and continual performance without ownership of the land. Could this business of state-sponsored usurpation of occupied land elevate the current user to the status of a joint owner? How then could the Kantian hypothesis concerning the universal disposition of mankind for constitutional self-founding through revolution (*PW*, 182) be justified on the contradictory ground of territorial usurpation as the material basis of imperial pacifism?

12. My concept of apparatus is drawn from Foucault, but relies also on Agamben's current retrieval of this notion. Giorgio Agamben, *What Is an Apparatus?, and Other Essays*, trans. David Kishik and Stefan Pedatella (Stanford: Stanford University Press, 2009). Certainly, Agamben is not engaging imperial apparatuses in his discussion. Nonetheless, he deduces the Foucaultian notion of governmentality from the divine economy of providential sovereignty which operates as an apparatus that assigns duties and strategic functions of incarnation, redemption, salvation, etc. Agamben perceptively names the functions of such divine economy "positivities" and intersects them etymologically with "dispositions" or *dispositif* which is Foucault's term for apparatus. I, therefore, extend his analysis of the concept of apparatus in the direction of an imperial economy whose spatial logic designates positivities by disposing protectorates. The imperialist function of the biopolitical apparatus as discussed in this essay is, in fact, implied in the Latin term *dispositio* which denotes operations of placement, arrangement, management, ordering and direction. Its meaning ranges from the arranging of everyday affairs to the distribution of a body of men and the setting up of a military guard, including functions of forming, fashioning and setting in order.

13. For insightful and masterly accounts on this issue see Hannah Arendt, *On Revolution* (New York: Penguin Books, 1977), and *Lectures on Kant's Political Philosophy*; Michel Foucault, "The Art of Telling the Truth," trans. Alan Sheridan, in *Politics, Philosophy, Culture: Interviews and Other Writings, 1977–1984*, ed. Lawrence D. Kritzman (London and New York: Routledge, 1988); Dick Howard, *From Kant to Marx* (New York: SUNY Press, 1985), and *The Politics of Critique* (Minneapolis: University of Minnesota Press, 1988); and Dieter Henrich, "On the Meaning of Rational Action in the State," in *Kant and Political Philosophy: The Contemporary Legacy*, ed. Ronald Beiner and W. J. Booth (New Haven: Yale University Press, 1993); henceforth cited as *MRA*.

14. The English translation is by R. G. Bury, from the Loeb edition of Plato's works.

15. See endnote 12.

16. For a more sympathetic view which explains Kant's excessive prudence by stressing extenuating circumstances such as the paternalistic surveillance and the enlightened despotism of Frederick the Great, see Dana Villa, *Public Freedom* (Princeton: Princeton University Press, 2008), 130. This apologetic view, however, fails to explain Kant's admittedly self-contradictory defense of the will to Revolution as a universal sign of mankind's openness and inclination to constitutional self-founding. For an exemplary

elaboration of this view see Foucault, "The Art of Telling the Truth." In other words, Dana Villa wards off the paramount Kantian question, namely, how to make "political domination rational within the framework of a philosophy of history." Ironically, this entailed the necessity to terminate public inquiry by irrational means. On this issue see Jürgen Habermas, *The Structural Transformation of the Public Sphere: An Inquiry into a Category of Bourgeois Society*, trans. Thomas Burger (Cambridge, MA: MIT Press, 1989), 130.

17. Immanuel Kant, *Critique of Judgment*, trans. Werner S. Pluhar (Indianapolis: Hackett Publishing, 1987), 132. Henceforth cited as *CJ*.

18. William Sewell, *Logics of History: Social Theory and Social Transformation* (Chicago: University of Chicago Press, 2005), 263. Henceforth cited as *LH*.

19. Alain Badiou, *Ethics*, trans. Peter Hallward (London: Verso, 2001), 43.

20. On this issue see Peter Hallward, *Badiou: A Subject to Truth* (Minneapolis: University of Minnesota Press, 2003), 213.

21. See *LH*, 91; also Charles Tilly, *The Vendée: A Sociological Analysis of the Counter-Revolution of 1793* (Harvard: Harvard University Press, 1964), 160, and *The Contentious French: Four Centuries of Popular Struggle* (Harvard: Harvard University Press, 1986), 287–88.

22. Le Roy Ladurie is one of the prominent exponents of a neo-Malthusian analysis of long-term historical evolution grounded axiomatically on demographic determinism. His method foregrounds statistical patterns of demographic expansion and settlement, depopulation and pauperization. It focuses on the impact of famines, contraception techniques, war as well as biological factors such as epidemics. Le Roy Ladurie postulates a homeostatic ecosystem with a built-in mechanism of self-correction that restores the balance between population and resources. Although his neo-Malthusian methodology obscures class antagonism, implying social durability and political inertia, it may, in my view, also supplement conflictual logics of change.

23. Emmanuel Le Roy Ladurie, "The 'Event' and the 'Long Term' in Social History: The Case of Chouan Uprising," in *The Territory of the Historian*, trans. Ben Reynolds and Sîan Reynolds (Chicago: University of Chicago Press, 1979), 115; my emphasis.

24. Certainly, Le Roy Ladurie considers all the above only as preliminary precautions. In the long run "there will always come a moment when the historian, having worked out a solid conceptual basis, will need to start counting . . . frequencies . . . repetitions . . . percentages" (*LH*, 15). Because only this tedious, validating task can establish what is anecdotal or paradigmatic: "history that is not quantifiable cannot claim to be scientific" (15). Similarly, Sewell at the end reclaims quantitative reasoning, beyond the epistemological divide between interpretivism and positivism, on the ground of a common ontology which he calls "hermeneutical quantification" (369–72). This, however, appears more suggestive than settled and conclusive. For instance, it may enhance our understanding of logics of spatial fixing and material instantiation in African-American neighborhoods, but it certainly cannot account for the aleatoric encounter between event and structure. Nonetheless, Sewell's sociology of the event is not simply a landmark curiosity but a valuable fragment in the revolt against the positivist Thermidor in the social sciences.

25. Michel Foucault, "Truth and Power," interview by Alessandro Fontana and Pasquale Pasquino, trans. Colin Gordon et al., in *Power/Knowledge: Selected Interviews and Other Writings, 1972–77*, ed. Colin Gordon (New York: Pantheon Books, 1980), 114–15.

26. See *The Old Regime and the French Revolution*, trans. Stuart Gilbert (New York: Anchor Books, 1955), chapters 6–9.

27. Michael Hereth, *Alexis de Tocqueville: Threats to Freedom in Democracy*, trans. George Bogardus (Durham, NC: Duke University Press, 1986), 111–18. Henceforth cited

as *AT*.

28. Quoted in *AT*, 120.

29. Quoted in Melvin Richter, "Tocqueville on Algeria," *The Review of Politics* 25, no. 3 (July 1963), 395.

30. For an updated, comparative and even-handed account of this dimension in Tocqueville's engagement with the colonial question see Jennifer Pitts, *A Turn to Empire: The Rise of Imperial Liberalism in Britain and France* (Princeton: Princeton University Press, 2005), the comprehensive chapter 7. Earlier, pioneering statements on this issue include Melvin Richter's "Tocqueville on Algeria" as well as Michael Hereth's *Alexis de Tocqueville*. It should be noticed that this critical dimension concerning Tocqueville in his capacity as an imperialist is glaringly missing from Raymond Aron's otherwise authoritative assessment of Tocqueville as a sociologist, *Main Currents in Sociological Thought*, vol. 1: *Montesquieu, Comte, Marx, Tocqueville, and the Sociologists and the Revolution of 1848*, trans. Richard Howard and Helen Weaver (New York: Anchor Books, 1968).

31. Max Weber's "Sociology of Law" still remains a classical account of lawfinding by the folk assembly. "Economy and Law (The Sociology of Law)," trans. Edward Shils and Max Rheinstein, in *Economy and Society*, vol. 2, ed. Guenther Roth and Claus Wittich (Berkeley and Los Angeles: University of California Press, 1978), esp. 768–74. It is also noteworthy that Foucault himself has dedicated considerable time of research on the discursive controversy over this imperial form of right examined in conjunction with the Frankish culture of invasion. See especially lectures six and seven in *Society Must Be Defended: Lectures at the Collège de France, 1975–76*, trans. David Macey, ed. Mauro Bertani and Alessandro Fontana (New York: Picador, 2003), 115–66. Louis Althusser provides an excellent synopsis of the genealogical self-understanding of feudal nobility in chapter six of his outstanding book on Montesquieu who is a cunning and tenacious Germanist. *Politics and History: Montesquieu, Rousseau, Marx*, trans. Ben Brewster (London: Verso, 2007). What is missing in contemporary bibliography, in my view, is precisely a retracing of Tocqueville's engagement with the colonial question in terms of great power policy and national honor back to the Germanist tradition of a noble-minded and "impartial imperialism," i.e., an imperialism which combined the enduring liberty of the nobility qua assembled monarchy (personified, for instance, by Charlemagne) and *the right of conquest*. This prerogative of conquest is also absent from contemporary accounts which record some kind of association or influence by Montesquieu on Tocqueville. See, for instance, George Kelly Armstrong, *The Humane Comedy: Constant, Tocqueville, and French Liberalism* (Cambridge: Cambridge University Press, 1992) and Sheldon Wolin, *Tocqueville between Two Worlds: The Making of a Political and Theoretical Life* (Princeton: Princeton University Press, 2001).

32. See Tacitus, "The Germania," in *"The Agricola" and "The Germania,"* trans. Harold Mattingly (London: Penguin, 1970), chapters 7 and 11.

33. See Harold Mattingly's introduction to Tacitus's *Germania*, 42–43.

34. Perry Anderson, *Passages from Antiquity to Feudalism* (London: Verso, 1978), 130–31. Henceforth cited as *PA*.

35. For an instructively focused and updated account of the medieval imperialist energy in association with the Frankish *élan vital* "which changed the rules and expectations of warfare," see Robert Bartlett, *The Making of Europe: Conquest, Colonization and Cultural Change, 950–1350* (London: Penguin, 1994). Henceforth cited as *ME*. For an earlier pioneering account of the atavistic "will to conquest" in terms of a sociology of imperialisms see Joseph Schumpeter, *Imperialism and Social Classes*, trans. Heinz Norden, ed. Paul M. Sweezy (Philadelphia: Orion Editions, 1951).

36. Alexis de Tocqueville, *Writings on Empire and Slavery*, trans. and ed. Jennifer Pitts (Baltimore: Johns Hopkins University Press, 2001), 91. Henceforth cited as *W*.

37. See Pierre Bourdieu, *Sociology in Question*, trans. Richard Nice (London: Sage Publications, 1993), 50–51. Henceforth cited as *SIQ*.

38. See the prolific introduction by Jennifer Pitts in *W*, xii.

39. On the conceptual difference between *apparatus* and *field* see *SIQ*, 88. The appearances of the state as an apparatus, however, mask a field of antagonisms and tensions which may or may not be successfully exploited for its own stabilization.

40. For the context of Tocqueville's moral logistics see "The Emancipation of Slaves" (*W*, 221–24). My view here is consistent with Samir Amin's insight that capitalism not only integrates but also creates archaic, i.e., pre-capitalist, modes of exploitation of labor. Samir Amin, *Delinking: Towards a Polycentric World*, trans. Michael Wolfers (London: Zed Books, 1990). I even go further in the development of this pivotal idea by arguing that modern imperialism not only integrates but also creates new biopolitical forms of pre-capitalist states and politics. The integration of Cyprus in the legal apparatus of imperialism as a protectorate is one such case.

41. Amazingly, the ex-UN Secretary General Kofi Annan in 2004, acting in concert with the local collaborationist elites, Turkey, and Greece, subjected the population of Cyprus to a compulsory referendum in which he proposed a constitutional scheme with similar provisions that imposed restrictions on fundamental freedoms of residence, settlement, movement, etc., to the benefit of the Turkish settler population and the occupying armed forces. Greek-Cypriots rejected it by 76% branding it as constitutional legitimation of a new form of slavery.

Notes to Part Three

Introduction
Apostolos Lampropoulos

1. This is the title of an article available on *Eurozine* (http://www.eurozine.com/pdf/2008-09-24-dely-en.pdf; accessed August 29, 2013).

Chapter 9
Kristeva's Revolt, Illusion, and the Feminine
Gertrude Postl

1. Julia Kristeva, *Revolt She Said*, trans. Brian O'Keeffe (Los Angeles and New York: Semiotext(e), 2002), 39. Henceforth cited as *RS*.
2. In a shortened version she mentions psychoanalysis, "a certain literature," and "the combinatory or the game" (*SNS*, 29).
3. Ewa Płonowska Ziarek, "Kristeva and Fanon: Revolutionary Violence and Ironic Articulation," in *Revolt, Affect, Collectivity: The Unstable Boundaries of Kristeva's Polis*, ed. Tina Chanter and Ewa Płonowska Ziarek (Albany: SUNY Press, 2005), 72. Henceforth cited as *KF*.
4. Luce Irigaray, *This Sex Which Is Not One*, trans. Catherine Porter with Carolyn Burke (Ithaca, NY: Cornell University Press, 1985), 76. Henceforth cited as *THS*.
5. Judith Butler, *Gender Trouble. Feminism and the Subversion of Identity* (New York and London: Routledge, 1990). Henceforth cited as *GT*.

Chapter 10
The Layering of Abjection in Relation to Fetish: Reading Kristevan Abjection as the Unthought Ground of Fetishism
Tina Chanter

1. Julia Kristeva, *Powers of Horror: An Essay on Abjection*, trans. Leon S. Roudiez (New York: Columbia University Press, 1982), 6. Henceforth cited as *PH*.
2. See Anannya Bhattacharjee, "The Public/Private Mirage: Mapping Homes and Undomesticating Violence Work in the South Asian Immigrant Community," in *Feminist Genealogies, Colonial Legacies, Democratic Futures*, ed. M. Jacqui Alexander and Chandra Talpade Mohanty (New York: Routledge, 1997). Henceforth cited as *PPM*. See also Patricia Hill Collins, *Black Feminist Thought: Knowledge, Consciousness, and the Politics of Empowerment* (New York: Routledge, 1990); Hazel V. Carby, "White Woman Listen! Black Feminism and the Boundaries of Sisterhood," in *Theories of Race and Racism*, ed. Les Back and John Solomos (London: Routledge, 2000); and Chandra Talpade Mohanty, "Under Western Eyes: Feminist Scholarship and Colonial Discourses," in *Third World Women and the Politics of Feminism*, ed. Chandra Talpade Mohanty, Ann Russo, and Lourdes Torres (Bloomington: Indiana University Press, 1997).
3. Marie Anna Jaimes Guerrero, "Civil Rights versus Sovereignty: Native American

Women in Life and Land Struggles," in *Feminist Genealogies, Colonial Legacies and Democratic Futures*.

4. Civil rights have operated in largely liberatory ways for white, Western women, and in this Foucaultian sense power is not merely to be opposed but that to which we seek access. Yet power has operated in negative and repressive ways for native American women, whose forced assimilation to American, individualist, capitalist, and colonialist practices has all but obliterated the collective, tribal, traditional ways of life that existed prior to colonization. The effects of power tend to be variegated, often along racialized lines, so that both the Hegelian/Marxist model and the Foucaultian model are in operation at the same time for different groups. The classical model of the state as oppressive has more pertinence than Foucault's, depending on the color of your skin.

5. See *PPM*.

6. This point echoes, to some extent, Kelly Oliver's observations about recognition. She says, "[j]ust as money has been the hard currency for which women and slaves have been exchanged (directly and indirectly), recognition is the soft currency with which oppressed people are exchanged within the global economy. In this way, recognition, like capital, is essential to the economy of domination, which is not to say that oppressed people should not fight for both capital and recognition." Kelly Oliver, *Witnessing: Beyond Recognition* (Minneapolis: University of Minnesota Press, 2001), 23. Oliver is absolutely right to point out that "[t]he internalization of stereotypes of inferiority and superiority leave the oppressed with the sense that they are lacking something that only their *superior* dominators have or can give them. The very notion of recognition as it is deployed in various contemporary theoretical contexts is, then, a symptom of the pathology of oppression itself. Implied in this diagnosis is the conclusion that struggles for recognition and theories that embrace those struggles may indeed presuppose and thereby perpetuate the very hierarchies, domination, and injustice that they attempt to overcome" (9). Oliver goes on, "[a]n effective aspect of the pathology of oppression is that those who are dominant have the power to create, confer, or withhold recognition, which operates as cultural currency" (26). The logic of disavowal circulates in a way that enables even those who use it to illuminate the conditions of oppression to benefit from its transference across discourses, so that its circulation either continues to abject the dejects of psychoanalytic or Marxist theory, or invents new dejects. Oliver says, "[e]ven if oppressed people are making demands for recognition, insofar as those who are dominant are empowered to confer it, we are thrown back into the hierarchy of domination. This is to say that if the operations of recognition require a recognizer and a recognizee, then we have done no more than replicate the master-slave, subject-other/object hierarchy in this new form" (9). I agree, but by taking seriously the way in which the discourses of feminism and race theory, for example, create their own abjects, I also want to insist that this recognition is labile. That is, we create new hierarchies of domination, which have new imaginary configurations. Oliver is closer to this in one of her more recent books, coauthored with Trigo, where they say, "[t]he fear of, or desire for, racial difference can be displaced onto a fear of, or desire for, sexual difference. The fear of maternal sexuality can be displaced onto or condensed into the threat of racial difference"—and so on. Kelly Oliver and Benigno Trigo, *Noir Anxiety* (Minnesota: University of Minnesota Press, 2003), xix. Here she reads "the free-floating existential anxiety of film noir" as a "screen for concrete anxieties over arbitrary and blurred boundaries of racial, sexual, and national identity" (xv), and goes on to use abjection to illuminate the "lost boundaries of noir" (xxix).

7. Joan Brandt, "Julia Kristeva and the Revolutionary Politics of *Tel Quel*," in *Revolt, Affect, Collectivity: The Unstable Boundaries of Kristeva's Polis*, ed. Tina Chanter

and Ewa Płonowska Ziarek (Albany, NY: SUNY Press, 2005), 26. Henceforth cited as *TQ*.

8. See Freud, "The Ego and the Id," in *The Standard Edition of the Complete Psychological Works*, vol. 19, trans. and ed. James Strachey (London: Hogarth Press and the Institute of Psycho-analysis, 1953), 26.

9. Sigmund Freud, "Negation," in *The Standard Edition of the Complete Works*, trans. and ed. James Strachey, vol. 19 (London: Hogarth Press and the Institute of Psycho-analysis, 1961).

10. Frantz Fanon, *Black Skin, White Masks*, trans. Charles Lam Markmann (New York: Grove Press, 1967).

11. For various feminist responses to Fanon see Rey Chow, "The Politics of Admittance: Female Sexual Agency, Miscegenation, and the Formation of Community in Frantz Fanon," in *Frantz Fanon: Critical Perspectives*, ed. Anthony C. Alessandrini (New York: Routledge, 1999), 45; Kaja Silverman, *The Threshold of the Visible World* (New York: Routledge, 1996), 30–31; and Mary Ann Doane, *Femmes Fatales: Feminism, Film Theory, Psychoanalysis* (New York: Routledge, 1991), 225; henceforth cited as *FF*.

12. See for example Robyn Ferrell's interesting discussion of *terra nullius* in the context of art. The judgment that the land was *terra nullius* (an empty one), Ferrell argues, "did not say that it saw *nobody*, only that it did not see *law*." She goes on to ask: "What sort of blindness was this principle of settlement? It was aesthetically blind, in the most general sense, in that it didn't see what there was to see *as law, as order*." Robyn Ferrell, "Untitled: Art as Law," *Studies in Practical Philosophy: A Journal of Ethical and Political Thought* 3, no. 1 (2003), 42.

13. Antonio Gramsci suggests that "subaltern groups are always subject to the activity of ruling groups, even when they rebel and rise up; only 'permanent' victory breaks their subordination, and that not immediately." *Selections from Prison Notebooks*, trans. and ed. Quinton Hoare and Geoffrey Nowell Smith (New York: International Publishers, 1971), 55.

14. As Raymond Williams puts it, hegemony "is not to be understood at the level of mere opinion or mere manipulation. It is a whole body of practices and expectations; our assignments or energy, our ordinary understanding of the nature of man and of his world. It is a set of meanings and values which as they are experienced as practices appear as reciprocally confirming. It thus constitutes a sense of reality for most people in society." *Problems in Materialism and Culture: Selected Essays* (New York: Verso, 1997), 38.

15. I owe a debt of gratitude to Mary Beth Mader, whose response to my paper at the Central APA in December 2003 helped me clarify this logic.

16. I thank Rachel Jones, whose observations and conversation at a feminist conference at Basel University, *Phenomenological Reflections in Ethics*, in June, 2003 helped me think about the mobility of this constitutive gesture.

17. As Mary Ann Doane puts it, "the logical consequence of the Lacanian alignment of the phallus with the symbolic order and the field of language is the exclusion of the woman or, at the very least, the assumption of her different or deficient relation to language and its assurance of subjectivity." *The Desire to Desire: The Woman's Film of the 1940s* (Bloomington and Indianapolis: Indiana University Press, 1987), 10.

18. Doane says: "Fetishism has been particularly important in the theorization of the film-spectator relation because its scenario turns on the 'glance' and on a reading of the image of the castrated woman. In the cinema, spectatorial fetishism is evidenced as a

process of balancing knowledge and belief in relation to the reality status of the image. While the spectator knows that the image is merely an image and not the real (similarly, the fetishist knows that the fetish object is simply a substitute for the woman's lack), he simultaneously believes in the impression of reality produced by that image in order to follow the story (the fetishist believes in the substitute maternal phallus in order to attain sexual pleasure). Because it is so intimately articulated with castration anxiety and the desire to preserve the phallus, because it relies on the image of the mutilated female body, fetishism is not available to the woman—for she has nothing to lose" (*The Desire to Desire*, 15).

19. See, for example, Mary Douglas, *Purity and Danger: An Analysis of the Concepts of Pollution and Taboo* (New York: Routledge, 2003), 148.

Chapter 11
Reviving Oedipus: Oedipus, Anti-Oedipus, and the Nomadic Body in Kristeva
S. K. Keltner

1. See, for example, Gilles Deleuze and Félix Guattari, *Anti-Oedipus*, vol. 1 of *Capitalism and Schizophrenia*, trans. Robert Hurley, Mark Seem, and Helen R. Lane (Minneapolis: University of Minnesota Press, 1983); Judith Butler, *Antigone's Claim: Kinship between Life and Death* (New York: Columbia University Press, 2000), henceforth cited as *AC*; and Slavoj Žižek, *The Ticklish Subject: The Absent Centre of Political Ontology* (New York: Verso, 1999).

2. Julia Kristeva, *New Maladies of the Soul*, trans. Ross Guberman (New York: Columbia University Press, 1995), 177–78. Henceforth cited as *NM*.

3. Julia Kristeva, *La haine et le pardon*, vol. 3 of *Pouvoirs et limites de la psychanalyse* (Paris: Fayard, 2005). Henceforth cited as *HP*. The translation of all the quoted material from this book is mine, although an English translation has been published after the submission of this essay: Julia Kristeva, *Hatred and Forgiveness*, vol. 3 of *The Powers and Limits of Psychoanalysis*, trans. Jeanine Herman (New York: Columbia University Press, 2010).

4. Julia Kristeva, "Feminism and Psychoanalysis," interview by Elaine Hoffman Baruch, in *Julia Kristeva: Interviews*, ed. Ross Mitchell Guberman (New York: Columbia University Press, 1996). Henceforth cited as *FP*.

5. In *Powers of Horror*, particularly with reference to Freud's analysis and treatment of Little Hans, Kristeva suggests alternative "cures" within symbolic activity that bypass the phallic reference of the Oedipal triangle. See chapter two especially.

6. Jean-Pierre Vernant and Pierre Vidal-Naquet, *Myth and Tragedy in Ancient Greece*, trans. Janet Lloyd (Cambridge, MA: Zone Books, 1990). Henceforth cited as *MTG*.

7. See footnotes to chapter 3, numbers 35 and 36.

8. Sophocles, *Oedipus at Colonus*, trans. David Grene, in *Sophocles*, vol. 1, ed. David Grene and Richmond Lattimore (Chicago: The University of Chicago Press, 1991). Henceforth cited as *OC*.

9. Kristeva takes the term "temporalizing" from Heidegger in order to indicate that time is "always already there."

10. In *Powers of Horror*, Antigone represents "another logic" (see section above). In

The Sense and Non-Sense of Revolt, Kristeva identifies a "female Oedipus" who is structured within an "interminable phallic revolt" (*SNS*, 103). In *The Feminine and the Sacred*, Kristeva names this female Oedipus Antigone (*FS*, 60). In the present volume, see Gertrude Postl's "Kristeva's Revolt, Illusion, and the Feminine."

11. Kristeva's analysis of the "two great categories," I would argue, should be read against the background of her interrogation of nationalism in *Strangers to Ourselves*. Julia Kristeva, *Strangers to Ourselves*, trans. Leon S. Roudiez (New York: Columbia University Press, 1991).

Chapter 12
Tragedy as De-Layering: The Opaque Immediacy of Antigone
Kalliopi Nikolopoulou

1. To simply give a list of texts that, according to my opinion, fetishize complexity would be inappropriate for many reasons, not least of which would be the legitimate critical objection that such a list is too arbitrary because too subjective. Instead, by way of illustrating my claim, I will cite a couple of exemplary instances within the postwar critical and philosophical scene, in which renowned thinkers have engaged in this debate on difficulty at times by even accusing each other of the "sin" they themselves might have committed. Take, for example, Theodor Adorno, the very proponent of all things difficult, particularly when it comes to works of art, as his *Aesthetic Theory* indicates. One of Adorno's major accusations against Heidegger—an accusation that is not independent of their sharp political differences—is that Heidegger resorts to a dangerous kind of obscurantism and jargonism. *The Jargon of Authenticity* shows in its very title Adorno's view of Heidegger's language. In another example, John Searle bolsters his critique of deconstruction by citing a conversation he had with Michel Foucault, during which the latter criticized Jacques Derrida's writing practice as "*obscurantisme terroriste*" (quoted in Dermot Moran, *Introduction to Phenomenology* [London and New York: Routledge, 2000], 442). At any rate, my remark on the fetishization of complexity should not be read as a mindless support of easiness, since I do not disagree with the fact that some ideas, which are intrinsically difficult, demand a requisite degree of linguistic difficulty to be expressed. Rather, I remain skeptical of the hypostatization of "complexity" as the only worthy way of approaching all philosophical issues—a tendency largely coincident with the "linguistic turn" in the humanities. The problem is that complex-sounding language does not always correspond to genuinely difficult ideas. Fetishization signifies the moment where difficult language is used not to disclose something difficult, but rather to conceal (often unwittingly) an unoriginal, if not also interpretatively dubious, idea. Indeed, clarity has been underestimated in contemporary theoretical discourses, which, however tacitly, equate it with conceptual naïveté, if not downright ignorance.

2. The adjective "elemental" serves as a corrective version of "elementary," which, regrettably, is often mistaken for the simplistic, perhaps even the idiotic. However, the simplicity of the elementary *qua* basic, primary, and indivisible constitutes also its real difficulty: simple things are often the hardest to grasp because they cannot be broken down further. When the ancient natural philosophers thought of the world elementally (as fire, air, earth, or water), they too evoked this primordially indivisible character of these substances—though later, of course, science discovered them to be compounds or mixtures. I should add that this intrinsic relation that the elemental (and elementary) bears to

nature will be very important in my reading of Antigone, whose ethical stance proceeds from her adherence to nature rather than to civic conventions.

3. From now onward, all parenthetical citations of the play refer to the Chicago translation of the text: Sophocles, *Antigone*, trans. David Grene, in *Greek Tragedies*, vol. 1, ed. David Grene and Richmond Lattimore (Chicago: University of Chicago Press, 1991). Henceforth cited as *A*. For the original Greek I consulted the Loeb edition.

4. I am in complete agreement with Nietzsche's diagnosis of the modern theoretical age as optimistic, in that it relies on the power of reason to explain away everything reflexively. This is correct even in theoretical critiques of reason, which abound today, since the only way in which they launch their respective critiques is exactly that: theoretical! In this sense, despite whatever dark themes post-Hegelian theory has chosen for its musings (melancholia, mourning, death, negativity, and so on), its underlying principle remains that of radicalization and supersession, thus following along a line of progress toward absolute knowledge.

5. Martha Nussbaum, "Sophocles' *Antigone*: Conflict, Vision, and Simplification," in *The Fragility of Goodness: Luck and Ethics in Greek Tragedy and Philosophy* (Cambridge: Cambridge University Press, 1986), 51.

6. Friedrich Nietzsche, *The Birth of Tragedy and the Case of Wagner*, trans. Walter Kaufmann (New York: Vintage, 1967), 72. Henceforth cited as *BT*. Nietzsche uses this formula to encapsulate the duality of Aeschylus's Prometheus as a Dionysian and Apollonian figure at the same time. Prometheus transgresses boundaries on the one hand, yet he seeks justice on the other—justice that, in order to be delivered, must assume some form of boundary. The paradoxical formula of course applies to all tragedy.

7. It has been the work of "sacred sociology," particularly that of Georges Bataille, to critique such understanding of the world as project, and to show that our attachment to taking actions and to doing things—discursivity being a dominant form of such doing in modern thought—is in fact a veneer, a layer, intending to distract us from direct exposure to the limit. Although I refer only once explicitly to Bataille's work in this piece, the spirit behind the essay is indebted to Bataille's call for a rethinking of the sacred in political thought. I am grateful to my friend and copanelist, Jason Winfree, whose work on Bataille and nondetermination has opened unexpected paths in my engagement with tragedy.

8. Jacques Lacan, "The Essence of Tragedy: A Commentary on Sophocles's *Antigone*," in *Seminar VII: The Ethics of Psychoanalysis*, trans. Dennis Porter, ed. Jacques-Alain Miller (New York: Norton, 1992), 252.

9. Butler admits that she is not interested in *Antigone* as a classicist, but as a humanist. See *AC*, 2.

10. See *The Mourning Voice: An Essay on Greek Tragedy*, trans. Elizabeth Trapnell Rawlings (Ithaca, NY: Cornell University Press, 2002), especially the chapter entitled "Tragedy and the Antipolitical," 26–41. Henceforth cited as *MV*.

11. Georg Wilhelm Friedrich Hegel, *Phenomenology of Spirit*, trans. A. V. Miller (Oxford: Oxford University Press, 1977), 288.

12. Martin Heidegger, *Introduction to Metaphysics*, trans. Gregory Fried and Richard Polt (New Haven: Yale University Press, 2000).

13. Carol Jacobs presents this argument in relation to the tracelessness of Antigone's acts. Contrary to man's building enterprises, which furnish the theme of the second choral ode, Antigone's burial mound for Polynices is swept away like dust. Carol Jacobs, "Dusting Antigone," *MLN* 111, no. 5 (1996), 890–917.

14. See Bataille's "The Sovereign," in *The Unfinished System of Nonknowledge*,

trans. Michelle Kendall and Stuart Kendall, ed. Stuart Kendall (Minneapolis: University of Minnesota Press, 2001).

15. Seth Benardete, *Sacred Transgressions: A Reading of Sophocles' "Antigone"* (South Bend, IN: St. Augustine's Press, 1999), 5. Henceforth cited as *ST*.

16. For a critical view of autochthony as an Athenian myth serving claims of citizenship (thus, in different context from the one I am discussing here), see also Loraux's *The Children of Athena: Athenian Ideas about Citizenship and the Division between the Sexes*, trans. Caroline Levine (Princeton: Princeton University Press, 1993).

17. Gerald F. Else, *The Madness of Antigone* (Heidelberg: Carl Winter Universitätsverlag, 1976), 30. Henceforth cited as *MA*.

18. I am grateful to Tina Chanter for alerting me to this potential inconsistency with her question during the roundtable, and for her general input in our follow-up correspondence.

19. Benardete makes this point in "Sophocles' *Oedipus Tyrannus*," in *The Argument of the Action: Essays on Greek Poetry and Philosophy*, ed. Ronna Burger and Michael Davis (Chicago: University of Chicago Press, 2000).

20. George Orwell, *1984* (New York: Harcourt, Brace and Jovanovich, 1977), 31.

21. See especially Nietzsche's discussion of the chorus in Section 7 of the *Birth of Tragedy*.

Chapter 13
Metaphysical Topo*graphies* Re-Layered:
Critique and the Feminine
Elena Tzelepis

1. This undecidable suspension of the performative between being implicated in the convention that authorizes it and yet undermining the operations of authorial and authoritative conventionality resonates with the ethics and politics of affirmative deconstruction. In *Of Grammatology*, Derrida articulates the aporia that founds all deconstruction thus: "The movements of deconstruction do not destroy structures from the outside. They are not possible and effective, nor can they take active aim, except by inhabiting those structures. Inhabiting them in a certain way, because one always inhabits, and all the more when one does not suspect it. Operating necessarily from the inside, borrowing all the strategic and economic resources of subversion from the old structure, borrowing them structurally, that is to say without being able to isolate their elements and atoms, the enterprise of deconstruction always in a certain way falls prey to its own work" (*OG*, 24).

2. On iterability, see Jacques Derrida, "Signature Event Context" (1–23) and "Limited Inc a b c . . . " (29–110), trans. Samuel Weber, in *Limited Inc* (Evaston, IL: Northwestern University Press, 1988).

3. One might contest that Derrida's claim to the "brute eventness of the arrivant" is premised upon a messianic conception of the new—the pure singularity of the event: but is the performative not unforeseeably and incalculably open to newness and the forces of *différance*? See Jacques Derrida, "Performative Powerlessness. A Response to Simon Critchley," trans. by James Ingram, *Constellations* 7, no. 4 (December 2000), 467.

4. Judith Butler, *Excitable Speech: A Politics of the Performative* (New York: Routledge, 1997), 157.

5. Judith Butler, *Bodies That Matter: On the Discursive Limits of "Sex"* (New York:

Routledge, 1993), 41. Henceforth cited as *B*.

6. "In particular, the issue is to deconstruct practically the *philosophical* opposition between philosophy and myth, between *logos* and *mythos*. Practically, I insist, this can only be done textually, along the lines of an *other* writing, with all the implied risks. And I fear that these risks will grow greater still." Jacques Derrida, *Positions*, trans. Alan Bass (London: Continuum, 2008), 47.

7. It is worth noting at this juncture that in Plato's *Republic*, mimesis is cast in terms of a metaphor of intercourse and biological reproduction (the sequence between intercourse and procreation is taken to be direct and uninterrupted in the Platonic text). Mimesis is presented as the inferior, the counterfeit, fake, or vulgar one (*faulē*), who, coupling (*ksyggignomenē*) with a partner of a similar quality (*faulo*), begets equally inferior and fake offspring (*faula*): "Imitation, therefore, an ordinary thing having intercourse with what is ordinary, produces ordinary offspring" (603b). The English translation I am using here and in consequent references is from *The Republic of Plato*, trans. Alan Bloom (New York: Basic Books, 1991).

It is of particular significance that mimesis is linked with a problematic of reproduction, whereby the principles of origination and generationality are at stake. But not less importantly, in the Platonic scene of mimesis's profane intercourse and ensuing reproduction, mimesis is unequivocally gendered as female; the feminine principle is directly associated with the principle of reproductive origin. One could remark that this metaphoric configuration of the *matrix*—as both origin and womb—inaugurates a long tradition of construing and theorizing mimesis as "woman" within Western metaphysics.

8. The reference here is to the Platonic distinction between the original and the copy. In his discussion of representation in the *Republic*—the process of creating fictive signs that resemble/imitate the "reality" they represent—Plato introduces a dichotomous structure of mimesis consisting on one hand of the original, the *archē*—which is essential, mental, absent, same, identical—and on the other hand the copy, the reproduction—which is (or, appears to be) unessential, material, present, other, different. Plato does not only differentiate these two components, but he also morally judges them. The original is primary, authentic, true, and real, whereas the copy is secondary, deficient, artificial, and unreal.

9. In the *Republic*, Plato offers the distinction between benign and pernicious mimesis or, to put it differently, the distinction between icons and phantasms. In the suggestive scene of the three kinds of beds and the differences among them, one is created by the god, and it is thus original and unique in nature, the second is crafted by a carpenter (icon), and the third one is a painted bed, produced by a painter who has imitated the work of the craftsman (phantasm): "Therefore, imitation is surely far from the truth; and as it seems, it is due to this that it produces everything—because it lays hold of a certain small part of each thing, and that part is itself only a phantom. For example, the painter, we say, will paint for us a shoemaker, a carpenter, and the other craftsmen, although he doesn't understand the arts of anyone of them. But, nevertheless, if he is a good painter, by painting a carpenter and displaying him from far off, he would deceive children and foolish human beings into thinking that it is truly a carpenter" (597b–598c). It is by no means accidental that Plato's example falls into these particular three agents of imitation: the god, the craftsman, and the painter; this division bespeaks the common connotations of mimesis, namely: creation, construction, and art. In this model, Plato draws the borders between the authorial self-identical subject of mimesis and its (imitated) objects.

10. However, even Plato remarks a particular kind of mimesis that the distinction between its subject and object is not clear. In the course of the examination of poetry in

Book III in *Republic*, such mimesis is discredited. That is the mimesis as a reproduction of likeness that involves a certain confusion of voices, a confusion between the subject and object of mimesis. According to Plato, this pernicious mimesis occurs when the voice of the poet and the voices of the poetic characters become confused, when the poet does not speak of himself but rather speaks of someone else in the voice of someone else. When the poet speaks in the voice of someone else, then his own voice is invaded by the voice of the other, this intrusive agent of mimesis that takes over and annihilates the "I," the ego of the poet. The poet is self-subtracted and dissolved and what emerges from the lack of the poet is an anarchic crowd of characters. So, this dangerous mimesis has to do with a becoming absent of the poet that is caused by direct speech; a certain obscuring, hiding, and disappearance, even lack, of the poet: "If the poet nowhere hid himself, his poetic work and narrative as a whole would have taken place without imitation" (393c). Imitation is a cryptic gesture, Plato contends; what is disconcerting about it is its veiling operation: mimesis involves a certain hiding of the authorial "I," ensuing the improper closeness in the relationship between the authorial ego and the others.

11. "The Double Session" ("La Double Séance") is one of the three essays that constitute Derrida's *Dissemination*. The other two are "Plato's Pharmacy" ("La Pharmacie de Platon") and "Dissemination" ("La Dissémination"). In each of these essays, Derrida chooses a text as a central site of reference: Plato's *Phaedrus* in "Plato's Pharmacy," Mallarmé's "Mimique" in the "The Double Session," and Philippe Sollers's *Nombres* in "Dissemination."

12. Luce Irigaray, *Speculum of the Other Woman*, trans. Gillian Gill (Ithaca, NY: Cornell University Press, 1985), 178. Henceforth cited as *SOW*. Irigaray's *Speculum*, originally published as *Spéculum de l' autre femme*, was her doctoral thesis, which led to her expulsion from Lacan's *École Freudienne* at Vincennes.

13. Gilles Deleuze, *Difference and Repetition*, trans. Paul Patton (New York: Columbia University Press, 1994). Henceforth cited as *DR*.

14. Importantly, in order to expose the impulse in Western metaphysics to subject difference and heterogeneity to resemblance and identity, or to relegate difference to the status of pernicious parasiticity, Deleuze uses an example from linguistics: "Why does Saussure, at the very moment when he discovers that 'in language there are only differences,' add that these differences are 'without positive terms' and 'eternally negative'?" (*DR*, 204).

15. Naomi Schor, "This Essentialism Which Is Not One: Coming to Grips with Irigaray," in *Engaging with Irigaray: Feminist Philosophy and Modern European Thought*, ed. Carolyn Burke, Naomi Schor, and Margaret Whitford (New York: Columbia University Press, 1994), 67. Henceforth cited as *TE*. Derrida introduces the concept of *paleonymy* in *Positions*, 71.

16. Elizabeth Weed, "The Question of Style," in *Engaging with Irigaray: Feminist Philosophy and Modern European Thought*, 83.

17. Importantly, Derrida has written that in order to avoid and resist the fatal endless repetition of the law, one has to take up a feminine position—that is, a position of hysterical displacement. See Jacques Derrida, *The Postcard: From Socrates to Freud and Beyond*, trans. Alan Bass (Chicago: University of Chicago Press, 1987).

18. Rosi Braidotti, *Nomadic Subjects: Embodiment and Sexual Difference in Contemporary Feminist Theory* (New York: Columbia University Press, 1994), 74.

19. In Plato's *Republic*, the metaphysics of weakness and passivity is one of the devices through which "woman" is construed and represented: "Everything in common. . . .

Except that we use the females as weaker and the males as stronger" (451e). "But lighter parts of these tasks must be given to the women than the men because of the weakness of the class" (457a).

20. Luce Irigaray, *Marine Lover of Friedrich Nietzsche*, trans. Gillian C. Gill (New York: Columbia University Press, 1991), 116. Henceforth cited as *ML*.

21. In the early phase of Irigaray's writing that I am focusing on in this essay, sexual difference relies on the feminine as opposed to her later phase where sexual difference is attached to the couple of the two irreducibly different sexuate beings.

22. Friedrich Nietzsche, *The Gay Science*, trans. Walter Kaufmann (New York: Vintage Books, 1974), 123. Henceforth cited as *TGS*.

23. Irigaray's rewriting of Nietzsche recalls Derrida's reading of Nietzsche: "There is no woman, a truth of woman as such." See Jacques Derrida, *Spurs: Nietzsche's Styles*, trans. Barbara Harlow (Chicago: Chicago University Press, 1978), 100.

24. An insightful reading of this figure has been proposed by Diana Fuss in her perceptive conception of the "two lips" as "a metaphor for *metonymy*" (Diana Fuss, *Essentially Speaking: Feminism, Nature, and Difference* [New York: Routledge, 1989], 72) in response to Margaret Whitford's construal of "the two lips" as a figure for metonymy (Margaret Whitford, *Luce Irigaray: Philosophy in the Feminine* [New York: Routledge, 1991], 177). Writes Irigaray: "A woman 'touches herself' constantly without anyone being able to forbid her to do so, for her sex is composed of two lips which embrace continually. Thus, within herself she is already two—but not divisible into ones—who stimulate each other" (*THS*, 24).

25. Irigaray's sustained focus on this trope of tactility as an antidote to the primacy of specularity is largely indebted to Merleau-Ponty's phenomenological critique of the dominance of the model of vision in Western theories of human knowledge. See Maurice Merleau-Ponty, *The Visible and the Invisible*, trans. Alphonso Lingis (Chicago: Northwestern University Press, 1969). For Irigaray's development of her mimetic critique of Merleau-Ponty, see Luce Irigaray, *An Ethics of Sexual Difference*, trans. Carolyn Burke and Gillian C. Gill (Ithaca, NY: Cornell University Press, 1993). Other feminist theorists such as Christine Delphy and Monique Wittig, however, have argued that Irigaray's formulation of the anatomical specificity of "the two touching lips" replicates uncritically the hegemonic essentialist discourse that derives the meaning of the feminine from its biological facticity and corporeality.

26. Jacques Derrida, "Deconstruction and the Other: Interview with Richard Kearney," in *Dialogues with Contemporary Thinkers*, ed. Richard Kearney (Manchester: Manchester University Press, 1984), 107.

Bibliography

Adorno, Theodor W. *Aesthetic Theory*, translated and edited by Robert Hullot-Kentor. Minneapolis: University of Minnesota Press, 1997.

———. *The Jargon of Authenticity*, translated by Knut Tarnowski and Frederic Will. Evanston, IL: Northwestern University Press, 1979.

Agamben, Giorgio. *Homo Sacer: Sovereign Power and Bare Life*, translated by Daniel Heller-Roazen. Stanford: Stanford University Press, 1998. Originally published as *Homo Sacer*. Torino: Einaudi, 2005.

———. *Idea of Prose*, translated by Michael Sullivan and Sam Whitsitt. Albany: SUNY Press, 1995.

———. *Infancy and History: On the Destruction of Experience*, translated by Liz Heron. London and New York: Verso, 2007.

———. *Language and Death: The Place of Negativity*, translated by Karen E. Pinkus with Michael Hardt. Minneapolis: University of Minnesota Press, 1991.

———. *Means without End: Notes on Politics*, translated by Vincenzo Binetti and Cesare Casarino. Minneapolis: University of Minnesota Press, 2000.

———. *Potentialities: Collected Essays in Philosophy*, translated by Daniel Heller-Roazen. Stanford: Stanford University Press, 1999.

———. *Profanations*, translated by Jeff Fort. New York: Zone Books, 2007.

———. *Remnants of Auschwitz: The Witness and the Archive*, translated by Daniel Heller-Roazen. New York: Zone Books, 1999.

———. *Stanzas: Word and Phantasm in Western Culture*, translated by Ronald L. Martinez. Minneapolis: University of Minnesota Press, 1993.

———. *The Coming Community*, translated by Michael Hardt. Minneapolis: University of Minnesota Press, 1993.

———. *The End of the Poem*, translated by Daniel Heller-Roazen. Stanford: Stanford University Press, 1999.

———. *The Man without Content*, translated by Georgia Albert. Stanford: Stanford University Press, 1999.

———. *The Open: Man and Animal*, translated by Kevin Attell. Stanford: Stanford University Press, 2004.

———. *The Time That Remains: A Commentary on the Letter to the Romans*, translated by Patricia Dailey. Stanford: Stanford University Press, 2005.

———. *What Is an Apparatus?, and Other Essays*, translated by David Kishik and Stefan Pedatella. Stanford: Stanford University Press, 2009.

Althusser, Louis. *Politics and History: Montesquieu, Rousseau, Marx*, translated by Ben Brewster. London: Verso, 2007.

Amin, Samir. *Delinking: Towards a Polycentric World*, translated by Michael Wolfers. London: Zed Books, 1990.

Anderson, Perry. *Passages from Antiquity to Feudalism*. London: Verso, 1978.

Arendt, Hannah. *Lectures on Kant's Political Philosophy*, edited by Ronald Beiner. Chicago: University of Chicago Press, 1982.

————. *On Revolution*. New York: Penguin Books, 1977.

Armstrong, George Kelly. *The Humane Comedy: Constant, Tocqueville, and French Liberalism*. Cambridge: Cambridge University Press, 1992.

Aron, Raymond. *Main Currents in Sociological Thought*. Vol. 1, *Montesquieu, Comte, Marx, Tocqueville, and the Sociologists and the Revolution of 1848*, translated by Richard Howard and Helen Weaver. New York: Anchor Books, 1968.

Bachofen, Johann Jakob. *Urreligion und antike Symbole*, 3 vols., edited by Carl Albrecht Bernoulli. Leipzig: Verlag von Philipp Reclam jun., 1926.

Badiou, Alain. *Ethics*, translated by Peter Hallward. London: Verso, 2001.

————. *Handbook of Inaesthetics*, translated by Alberto Toscano. Stanford: Stanford University Press, 2005.

————. *Metapolitics*, translated by Jason Barker. London: Verso, 2005.

————. *Polemics*, translated by Steven Corcoran. London: Verso, 2006.

Baeyens, Frank. *De ongrijpbaarheid der dingen. Over de vervlechting van taal en waarneming bij M. Merleau-Ponty*. Leuven: Universitaire Pers Leuven, 2004.

Bakhtin, Mikhail M. *Dialogic Imagination: Four Essays*, translated by Caryl Emerson. Austin: University of Texas Press, 1982.

Bal, Mieke. *Loving Yusuf: Conceptual Travels from Present to Past*. Chicago: University of Chicago Press, 2008.

Bartlett, Robert. *The Making of Europe: Conquest, Colonization, and Cultural Change, 950–1350*. London: Penguin, 1994.

Bataille, Georges. "The Sovereign." Pp. 185–95 in *The Unfinished System of Nonknowledge*, translated by Michelle Kendall and Stuart Kendall, edited by Stuart Kendall. Minneapolis: University of Minnesota Press, 2001.

————. *Oeuvres Complètes*, vol. 1. Paris: Gallimard, 1970.

Benardete, Seth. *Sacred Transgressions: A Reading of Sophocles' "Antigone."* South Bend, IN: St. Augustine's Press, 1999.

————. "Sophocles' *Oedipus Tyrannus*." Pp. 71–83 in *The Argument of the Action: Essays on Greek Poetry and Philosophy*, edited by Ronna Burger and Michael Davis. Chicago: University of Chicago Press, 2000.

Benjamin, Andrew. *Architectural Philosophy*. London and Brunswick, NJ: The Athlone Press, 2000.

Benjamin, Walter. *Gesammelte Briefe*, 6 vols., edited by C. Gödde and H. Lonitz. Frankfurt: Suhrkamp, 1995–2000.

————. *Gesammelte Schriften*, 14 vols., edited by R. Tiedemann et al. Frankfurt: Suhrkamp, 1974–1999.

————. *Oeuvres*, vol. 2, translated by M. de Gandillac. Paris: Denoël, 1971.

————. *Selected Writings*, 4 vols., edited by M. W. Jennings et al. Cambridge, MA: The Belknap Press of Harvard University Press, 1996–2003.

————. *The Correspondence of Walter Benjamin*, translated by Manfred R. Jacobson and Evelyn M. Jacobson, edited by Gershom Scholem and Theodor Adorno. Chicago: University of Chicago Press, 1994.

————. *The Origin of German Tragic Drama*, translated by John Osborne.

London: Verso Books, 1998.

————. "The Work of Art in the Age of Its Technological Reproducibility," translated by Edmund Jephcott and Harry Zohn. Pp. 101–33 in *Walter Benjamin: Selected Writings*, vol. 3, edited by Howard Eiland and Gary Smith. Cambridge, MA and London: The Belknap Press of Harvard University Press, 2002.

Benjamin, Walter, and Gershom Scholem. *Briefwechsel, 1933–40*, edited by Gershom Scholem. Frankfurt: Suhrkamp, 1980.

Bensmaïa, Réda. "The Kafka Effect," translated by Terry Cochran. Pp. ix–xxi in Gilles Deleuze and Félix Guattari. *Kafka: Towards a Minor Literature*, translated by D. Polan. Minneapolis: University of Minnesota Press, 1986.

Berlatsky, Erik L. *Fact, Fiction, and Fabrication: History, Narrative, and the Postmodern Real from Woolf to Rushdie*. PhD diss., University of Maryland, 2003.

Bhabha, Homi K. *The Location of Culture*. London: Routledge Classics, 2004.

Bhattacharjee, Anannya. "The Public/Private Mirage: Mapping Homes and Undomesticating Violence Work in the South Asian Immigrant Community." Pp. 353–403 in *Feminist Genealogies, Colonial Legacies, Democratic Futures*, edited by M. Jacqui Alexander and Chandra Talpade Mohanty. New York: Routledge, 1997.

Bhattacharya, Nandini. "Portrait of a Fascist in the Novels of Salman Rushdie." Pp. 1–11 in *Salman Rushdie: Critical Essays*, vol. 1, edited by Mohit K. Ray and Rama Kundu. New Delhi: Atlantic Publishers and Distributors, 2006.

Bogue, Ronald. *Deleuze on Literature*. London and New York: Routledge, 2003.

Bourdieu, Pierre. *Sociology in Question*, translated by Richard Nice. London: Sage Publications, 1993.

Brabander, Richard de. "Foucault." Pp. 147–60 in *Deleuze Compendium*, edited by Ed Romein, Marc Schuilenburg, and Sjoerd van Tuinen. Amsterdam: Boom, 2009.

Braidotti, Rosi. *Nomadic Subjects: Embodiment and Sexual Difference in Contemporary Feminist Theory*. New York: Columbia University Press, 1994.

Brandt, Joan. "Julia Kristeva and the Revolutionary Politics of *Tel Quel*." Pp. 21–36 in *Revolt, Affect, Collectivity: The Unstable Boundaries of Kristeva's Polis*, edited by Tina Chanter and Ewa Płonowska Ziarek. Albany, NY: SUNY Press, 2005.

Brennan, Timothy. *Salman Rushdie and the Third World: Myths of the Nation*. London: Macmillan, 1989.

Buchanan, Ian, and Gregg Lambert. "Introduction." Pp. 1–15 in *Deleuze and Space*, edited by Ian Buchanan and Gregg Lambert. Edinburgh: Edinburgh University Press, 2005.

Burger, Peter. *Theory of the Avant-Garde*. Minneapolis: University of Minnesota Press, 1984.

Butler, Judith. *Antigone's Claim: Kinship between Life and Death*. New York:

Columbia University Press, 2000.

———. *Bodies That Matter: On the Discursive Limits of "Sex."* New York: Routledge, 1993.

———. *Excitable Speech: A Politics of the Performative.* New York: Routledge, 1997.

———. *Gender Trouble: Feminism and the Subversion of Identity.* New York and London: Routledge, 1990.

Campanini, Massimo. *The Qur'an*, translated by Oliver Leaman. New York: Routledge, 2007.

Campbell, David. "Nietzsche, Heidegger, and Meaning." *Journal of Nietzsche Studies* 26 (autumn 2003), 25–54.

Carby, Hazel V. "White Woman Listen! Black Feminism and the Boundaries of Sisterhood." Pp. 389–402 in *Theories of Race and Racism*, edited by Les Back and John Solomos. London: Routledge, 2000.

Chakrabarty, Dipesh. *Habitations of Modernity.* Chicago and London: The University of Chicago Press, 2002.

———. *Provincializing Europe: Postcolonial Thought and Historical Difference.* Princeton: Princeton University Press, 2000.

Chanter, Tina. *The Picture of Abjection: Film, Fetish, and the Nature of Difference.* Bloomington: Indiana University Press, 2008.

Chatzichristou, Christakis. "Prostitution Spatialized: Cyprians Then and Now," paper presented at the 6th International Space Syntax Symposium, 12–15 June 2007, ITU Faculty of Architecture, Istanbul, Turkey. http://www.spacesyntaxistanbul.itu.edu.tr/papers%5Cshortpapers%5C113% 20-%20Hadjichristos.pdf (accessed June 15, 2013).

Chow, Rey. "The Politics of Admittance: Female Sexual Agency, Miscegenation, and the Formation of Community in Frantz Fanon." Pp. 34–56 in *Frantz Fanon: Critical Perspectives*, edited by Anthony C. Alessandrini. New York: Routledge, 1999.

Clément, Catherine, and Julia Kristeva. *The Feminine and the Sacred*, translated by Jane Marie Todd. New York: Columbia University Press, 2003.

Colebrook, Claire. "The Space of Man: On the Specificity of Affect in Deleuze and Guattari." Pp. 189–206 in *Deleuze and Space*, edited by Ian Buchanan and Gregg Lambert. Edinburgh: Edinburgh University Press, 2005.

Collin, Françoise. "The Praxis of Difference: Notes on the Tragedy of the Subject." Pp. 8–23 in *French Women Philosophers: A Contemporary Reader; Subjectivity, Identity, Alterity*, edited by Christina Howells. London and New York: Routledge, 2004.

Collins, Patricia Hill. *Black Feminist Thought: Knowledge, Consciousness, and the Politics of Empowerment.* New York: Routledge, 1990.

Collins-Cope, Mark, and Hubert Matthews. "A Reference Architecture for Component Based Development." http://www.markcollinscope.info/W9 .html (accessed July 23, 2011).

Connolly, William. *Political Theory and Modernity.* Oxford: Blackwell, 1989.

Critchley, Simon. *Continental Philosophy: A Very Short Introduction.* Oxford:

Oxford University Press, 2001.

Cusset, François. *French Theory: How Foucault, Derrida, Deleuze & Co. Transformed the Intellectual Life of the United States*, translated by Jeff Fort with Josephine Berganza and Marion Jones. Minneapolis: Minnesota University Press, 2008.

Cutrofello, Andrew. *Continental Philosophy*. New York: Routledge, 2005.

Danesi, Marcel. "Abstract Concept-Formation as Metaphorical Layering." *Studies in Communication Sciences* 2, no. 1 (winter 2002), 1–22.

——. "Layering Theory and Human Abstract Thinking." *Cybernetics and Human Knowing* 8, no. 3 (2001), 5–24.

Debord, Guy. *The Society of the Spectacle*, translated by Donald Nicholson-Smith. New York: Zone Books, 2006.

Deleuze, Gilles. *Cinema 2: The Time Image*, translated by Hugh Tomlinson and Robert Galeta. Minneapolis: University of Minnesota Press, 1989.

——. *Difference and Repetition*, translated by Paul Patton. New York: Columbia University Press, 1994. Originally published as *Différence et Répétition*. Paris: Presses Universitaires de France, 1993.

——. *Foucault*. Paris, Les Editions de Minuit, 2004.

——. *Le pli: Leibniz et le baroque*. Paris, Les Editions de Minuit, 1988.

——. *Logique du sens*. Paris: Les Editions de Minuit, 2002.

——. *Proust et les signes*. Paris: Quadrige/Presses Universitaires de France, 1998.

——. *Spinoza et le problème de l'expression*. Paris: Les Editions de Minuit, 2002.

Deleuze, Gilles, and Félix Guattari. *Anti-Oedipus*. Vol. 1 of *Capitalism and Schizophrenia*, translated by Robert Hurley, Mark Seem, and Helen R. Lane. Minneapolis: University of Minnesota Press, 1983.

——. *Kafka: Towards a Minor Literature*, translated by D. Polan. Minneapolis: University of Minnesota Press, 1986.

——. *Qu'est-ce que la philosophie?* Paris: Les Editions de Minuit, 2000.

Dely, Carole. "Jacques Derrida: The Perchance of a Coming of the Otherwoman," translated by Wilson Baldridge. *Eurozine*. http://www.eurozine .com/pdf/2008-09-24-dely-en .pdf (accessed August 29, 2013).

Derrida, Jacques. "Archive Fever: A Freudian Impression," translated by Eric Prenowitz. *Diacritics* 25, no. 2 (summer 1995), 9–63.

——. "Deconstruction and the Other: Interview with Richard Kearney." Pp. 105–26 in *Dialogues with Contemporary Thinkers*, edited by Richard Kearney. Manchester: Manchester University Press, 1984.

——. *Dissemination*, translated by by Barbara Johnson. Chicago: University of Chicago Press, 1983.

——. "Form and Meaning: A Note on the Phenomenology of Language." Pp. 107–28 in *Speech and Phenomena, and Other Essays on Husserl's Theory of Signs*, translated by David Allison, edited by David Allison and Newton Garver. Evanston, IL: Northwestern University Press, 1973.

——. "Freud and the Scene of Writing." Pp. 196–231 in *Writing and Differ-*

ence, translated by Alan Bass. London: Routledge, 1978.

———. "Limited Inc a b c . . . ," translated by Samuel Weber. Pp. 29–110 in *Limited Inc*. Evaston, IL: Northwestern University Press, 1988.

———. *Of Grammatology*, translated by Gayatri Chakravorty Spivak. Baltimore and London: Johns Hopkins University Press, 1976.

———. *On the Name*, translated by David Wood, John P. Leavey Jr., and Ian McLeod. Stanford: Stanford University Press, 1995.

———. "Parergon." Pp. 15–148 in *The Truth in Painting*, translated by Geoff Bennington and Ian McLeod. Chicago: Chicago University Press, 1987.

———. "Performative Powerlessness: A Response to Simon Critchley." *Constellations* 7, no. 4 (December 2000), 466–68.

———. *Points . . . : Interviews, 1974–1994*, translated by Peggy Kamuf et al., edited by Elisabeth Weber. Stanford: Stanford University Press, 1995.

———. *Positions*, translated by Alan Bass. London: Continuum, 2008.

———. "Signature Event Context," translated by Alan Bass. Pp. 1–23 in *Limited Inc*. Evaston, IL: Northwestern University Press, 1988.

———. *Sovereignties in Question*, edited by Thomas Dutoit and Outi Pasanen. New York: Fordham University Press, 2005.

———. *Spurs: Nietzsche's Styles*, translated by Barbara Harlow. Chicago: Chicago University Press, 1978.

———. *The Postcard: From Socrates to Freud and Beyond*, translated by Alan Bass. Chicago: University of Chicago Press, 1987.

Doane, Mary Ann. *Femmes Fatales: Feminism, Film Theory, Psychoanalysis*. New York: Routledge, 1991.

———. *The Desire to Desire: The Woman's Film of the 1940s*. Bloomington and Indianapolis: Indiana University Press, 1987.

Douglas, Mary. *Purity and Danger: An Analysis of the Concepts of Pollution and Taboo*. New York: Routledge, 2003.

Eisenman, Peter. "Processes of the Interstitial: Notes on Zaera-Polo's Idea of the Machinic." *El Croquis*, no. 83: "Peter Eisenman, 1990–1997," 21–35.

———. "Visions' Unfolding: Architecture in the Age of Electric Media." *Domus* 734 (January 1992), 144–49.

Else, Gerald F. *The Madness of Antigone*. Heidelberg: Carl Winter Universitätsverlag, 1976.

Eyck, Aldo van, "Team 10 Primer." Pp. 20–23 in *Team 10 Primer*, edited by Alison Smithson. London: Studio Vista, 1968.

Fanon, Frantz. *Black Skin, White Masks*, translated by Charles Lam Markmann. New York: Grove Press, 1967.

Ferrell, Robyn. "Untitled: Art as Law." *Studies in Practical Philosophy: A Journal of Ethical and Political Thought* 3, no. 1 (2003), 38–52.

Foster, Hal, Rosalind Krauss, Yve-Alain Bois, and Benjamin H. D. Buchloh. *Art since 1900*. London: Thames & Hudson, 2004.

Foucault, Michel. *Language, Counter-Memory, Practice: Selected Essays and Interviews*, translated by Donald F. Bouchard and Sherry Simon, edited by Donald F. Bouchard. Ithaca, NY: Cornell University Press, 1977.

————. *Society Must Be Defended: Lectures at the Collège de France, 1975–76,* translated by David Macey, edited by Mauro Bertani and Alessandro Fontana. New York: Picador, 2003.

————. "The Art of Telling the Truth," translated by Alan Sheridan. Pp. 86–95 in *Politics, Philosophy, Culture: Interviews and Other Writings, 1977–1984,* edited by Lawrence D. Kritzman. London and New York: Routledge, 1988.

————. The Subject and Power," translated by Leslie Sawyer. Pp. 208–26 in Dreyfus Hubert and Paul Rabinow, *Michel Foucault: Beyond Structuralism and Hermeneutics.* Chicago: University of Chicago Press, 1982.

————. "Truth and Power," interview by Alessandro Fontana and Pasquale Pasquino, translated by Colin Gordon et al. Pp. 109–33 in *Power/Knowledge: Selected Interviews and Other Writings, 1972–77,* edited by Colin Gordon. New York: Pantheon Books, 1980.

Freud, Sigmund. "Negation." Pp. 232–39 in *The Standard Edition of the Complete Works,* translated and edited by James Strachey, vol. 19. London: Hogarth Press and the Institute of Psychoanalysis, 1961.

————. "The Ego and the Id." Pp. 19–27 in *The Standard Edition of the Complete Psychological Works,* vol. 19, translated and edited by James Strachey. London: Hogarth Press and the Institute of Psycho-analysis, 1953.

Frichot, Hélène. "Stealing into Gilles Deleuze's Baroque House." Pp. 61–79 in *Deleuze and Space,* edited by Ian Buchanan and Gregg Lambert. Edinburgh: Edinburgh University Press, 2005.

Fuss, Diana. *Essentially Speaking: Feminism, Nature, and Difference.* New York: Routledge, 1989.

Gasché, Rodolphe. "Kafka's Law: In the Field of Forces Between Judaism and Hellenism." *MLN* 117, no. 5 (December 2002), 971–1002.

Godzich, Wlad, and Jeffrey Kittay. *The Emergence of Prose: An Essay in Prosaics.* Minneapolis: University of Minnesota Press, 1987.

Gramsci, Antonio. *Selections from Prison Notebooks,* translated and edited by Quinton Hoare and Geoffrey Nowell Smith. New York: International Publishers, 1971.

Greenaway, Peter. *The Pillow Book.* Paris: DIS VOIR, 1996.

————. Interview with S. H. Abbot (1997). http://users.skynet.be/chrisrenson-makemovies/Greenaw3.htm (accessed July 28, 2011).

Grosz, Elizabeth. *Architecture from the Outside: Essays on Virtual and Real Space.* Boston: MIT Press, 2001.

Guerrero, Marie Anna Jaimes. "Civil Rights versus Sovereignty: Native American Women in Life and Land Struggles." Pp. 101–21 in *Feminist Genealogies, Colonial Legacies, Democratic Futures,* edited by M. Jacqui Alexander and Chandra Talpade Mohanty. New York: Routledge, 1997.

Habermas, Jürgen. *The Structural Transformation of the Public Sphere: An Inquiry into a Category of Bourgeois Society,* translated by Thomas Burger. Cambridge, MA: MIT Press, 1989.

Hallward, Peter. *Badiou: A Subject to Truth.* Minneapolis: University of Minnesota Press, 2003.

Hamacher, Werner. *Premises*, translated by P. Fenves. Stanford: Stanford University Press, 1999.

Hansen, Mark. "Media Theory." *Theory, Culture and Society* 23, no. 2–3 (May 2006), 297–306.

———. "Time of Affect, or Bearing Witness to Life." *Critical Inquiry* 30 (spring 2004), 584–626.

Hanssen, Beatrice. *Walter Benjamin's Other History: Of Stones, Animals, Human Beings, and Angels*. Berkeley: University of California Press, 1998.

Harris, Paul A. "To See with the Mind and Think through the Eye: Deleuze, Folding Architecture, and Simon Rodia's Watts Towers." Pp. 36–60 in *Deleuze and Space*, edited by Ian Buchanan and Gregg Lambert. Edinburgh: Edinburgh University Press, 2005.

Hassumani, Sabrina. *Salman Rushdie: A Postmodern Reading of His Major Works*. Madison: Farleigh Dickinson University Press, 2002.

Hecht, Michael L., and John R. Baldwin. "Layers and Holograms: A New Look at Prejudice." Pp. 57–86 in *Communicating Prejudice*, edited by Michael L. Hecht. London: Sage, 1998.

Hegel, Georg Wilhelm Friedrich. *Phenomenology of Spirit*, translated by A. V. Miller. Oxford: Oxford University Press, 1977.

Heidegger, Martin. *Introduction to Metaphysics*, translated by Gregory Fried and Richard Polt. New Haven: Yale University Press, 2000.

———. *On the Way to Language*, translated by Peter D. Hertz. San Francisco: Harper Collins, 1971.

———. *Poetry, Language, Thought*, translated by Albert Hofstadter. New York: Harper & Row, 1975.

Hejduk, John. "Thoughts of an Architect." Unpaged in *Victims: A Work by John Hejduk*. London: Architectural Association, 1986.

Heller, Joseph. *God Knows*. New York: Knopf, 1984.

Henrich, Dieter. "On the Meaning of Rational Action in the State." Pp. 97–116 in *Kant and Political Philosophy: The Contemporary Legacy*, edited by Ronald Beiner and W. J. Booth. New Haven: Yale University Press, 1993.

Hereth, Michael. *Alexis de Tocqueville: Threats to Freedom in Democracy*, translated by George Bogardus. Durham, NC: Duke University Press, 1986.

Horner, Robyn. *Rethinking God as Gift: Marion, Derrida, and the Limits of Phenomenology*. New York: Fordham University Press, 2001.

Howard, Dick. *From Kant to Marx*. New York: SUNY Press, 1985.

———. *The Politics of Critique*. Minneapolis: University of Minnesota Press, 1988.

Howe, Susan. *Singularities*. Hanover, NH: Wesleyan University Press, 1990.

Hutcheon, Linda. *A Poetics of Postmodernism: History, Theory, Fiction*. New York: Routledge, 1988.

Irigaray, Luce. *An Ethics of Sexual Difference*, translated by Carolyn Burke and Gillian C. Gill. Ithaca, NY: Cornell University Press, 1993.

———. *Marine Lover of Friedrich Nietzsche*, translated by Gillian C. Gill. New

York: Columbia University Press, 1991.

──────. *Speculum of the Other Woman*, translated by Gillian C. Gill. Ithaca, NY: Cornell University Press, 1985.

──────. *This Sex Which Is Not One*, translated by Catherine Porter with Carolyn Burke. Ithaca, NY: Cornell University Press, 1985.

Jacobs, Carol. "Dusting Antigone." *MLN* 111, no. 5 (1996), 890–917.

Jay, Martin. *Downcast Eyes: The Denigration of Vision in Twentieth-Century French Thought.* Berkeley, Los Angeles, and London: University of California Press, 1993.

Jennings, Michael. "Introduction." Pp. 1–20 in Walter Benjamin, *The Writer of Modern Life: Essays on Charles Baudelaire*. Cambridge, MA: Harvard University Press, 2006.

Kafka, Franz. "The Silence of the Sirens." Pp. 127–28 in *Kafka's Selected Stories*, translated and edited by Stanley Corngold. New York: W.W. Norton and Company, 2007. Originally published as "Das Schweigen der Sirenen." Pp. 40–42 in *Nachgelassene Schriften und Fragmente*, vol. 2, edited by Jost Schillemeit. Frankfurt: Fischer Verlag, 2002.

──────. "The Hunter Gracchus." P. 112 in *Kafka's Selected Stories*, translated and edited by Stanley Corngold. New York: W.W. Norton and Company, 2007. Originally published as "Der Jäger Grachus." P. 311 in *Nachgelassene Schriften und Fragmente*, vol. 1, edited by Malcolm Pasley. Frankfurt: Fischer Verlag, 2002.

──────. "A Crossbreed." Pp. 125–27 in *Kafka's Selected Stories*, translated and edited by Stanley Corngold. New York: W.W. Norton and Company, 2007. Originally published as "Die Kreuzung." Pp. 372–74 in *Nachgelassene Schriften und Fragmente*, vol. 1, edited by Malcolm Pasley. Frankfurt: Fischer Verlag, 2002.

──────. "The Worry of the Father of Family." Pp. 72–73 in *Kafka's Selected Stories*, translated and edited by Stanley Corngold. New York: W.W. Norton and Company, 2007. Originally published as "Die Sorge des Hausvaters." Pp. 282–84 in *Drucke zu Lebzeiten*. Frankfurt: Fischer Verlag, 2002.

──────. "The Metamorphosis." Pp. 1–60 in *Kafka's Selected Stories*, translated and edited by Stanley Corngold. New York: W.W. Norton and Company, 2007. Originally published as "Die Verwandlung." Pp. 113–200 in *Drucke zu Lebzeiten*, Frankfurt: Fischer Verlag, 2002.

──────. *The Trial*, translated by B. Mitchell. New York: Schocken Books, 1999. Originally published as *Der Proceß*. Frankfurt: Fischer Verlag, 2002.

Kant, Immanuel. *Critique of Judgment*, translated by Werner S. Pluhar. Indianapolis: Hackett Publishing, 1987.

──────. *Political Writings*, translated by H. B. Nisbet, edited by H. S. Reiss. Cambridge: Cambridge University Press, 1970.

──────. *The Metaphysics of Morals*, translated by Mary Gregor. Cambridge: Cambridge University Press, 1991.

Kingston, Maxine Hong. *The Woman Warrior: Memoirs of a Girlhood among Ghosts*. London: Picador, 1977.

Kipnis, Jeffrey. "Forms of Irrationality." Pp. 148–65 in *Strategies in Architectural Thinking*, edited by John Whiteman and Jeffrey Kipnis. Cambridge, MA: Chicago Institute for Architecture and Urbanism, MIT Press, 1992.

Kolatan, Sulan. "Blurring Perceptual Boundaries." Pp. 116–7 in *The State of Architecture at the Beginning of the 21st Century*, edited by Bernard Tschumi and Irene Cheng. New York: The Monacelli Press, 2003.

~~Kortenaar, Neil ten. *Self, Nation, Text in Salman Rushdie's "Midnight's Children."*~~ Montreal: McGill-Queen's University Press, 2004.

Kraft, Werner. *Franz Kafka: Durchdringung und Geheimnis*. Frankfurt: Suhrkamp, 1968.

Kristeva, Julia. *Crisis of the ~~European~~ Subject*, translated by Susan Fairfield. New York: Other Press, 2000.

————. *Desire in Language: A Semiotic Approach to Literature and Art*, translated by Thomas Gora, Alice Jardine, and Leon S. Roudiez, edited by Leon S. Roudiez. New York: Columbia UP, 1980.

————. "Feminism and Psychoanalysis," interview by Elaine Hoffman Baruch. Pp. 113–21 in *Julia Kristeva: Interviews*, edited by Ross Mitchell Guberman. New York: Columbia University Press, 1996.

————. *Hatred and Forgiveness*. Vol. 3 of *The Powers and Limits of Psychoanalysis*, translated by Jeanine Herman. New York: Columbia University Press, 2010. Originally published as *La haine et le pardon*. Vol. 3 of *Pouvoirs et limites de la psychanalyse*, Paris: Fayard, 2005.

————. *Intimate Revolt*. Vol. 2 of *The Powers and Limits of Psychoanalysis*, translated by Jeanine Herman. New York: Columbia University Press, 2002. Originally published as *La révolte intime*. Vol. 2 of *Pouvoirs et limites de la psychanalyse*. Paris: Fayard, 1997.

————. "L'expérience littéraire est-elle encore possible? Entretien: Julia Kristeva, Danièlle Sallenave 1994–1995." *L'Infini* 53 (spring 1996), 20–46.

————. *Le temps sensible: Proust et l'expérience littéraire*. Paris: Gallimard, 1994.

————. *New Maladies of the Soul*, translated by Ross Guberman. New York: Columbia University Press, 1995.

————. *Powers of Horror: An Essay on Abjection*, translated by Leon S. Roudiez. New York: Columbia University Press, 1982.

————. *Revolt She Said*, translated by Brian O'Keeffe. Los Angeles and New York: Semiotext(e), 2002.

————. *Revolution in Poetic Language*, translated by Margaret Waller. New York: Columbia University Press, 1984.

————. *Strangers to Ourselves*, translated by Leon S. Roudiez. New York: Columbia University Press, 1991.

————. *Tales of Love*, translated by Leon S. Roudiez. New York: Columbia University Press, 1987.

————. *The Sense and Non-Sense of Revolt*. Vol. 1 of *The Powers and Limits of Psychoanalysis*, translated by Jeanine Herman. New York: Columbia University Press, 2000.

Kurokawa, Kisho. *The Philosophy of Symbiosis*. London: Academy Editions, 1994.

Lacan, Jacques. "The Essence of Tragedy: A Commentary on Sophocles's *Antigone.*" Pp. 243–83 in *Seminar VII: The Ethics of Psychoanalysis*, translated by Dennis Porter, edited by Jacques-Alain Miller. New York: Norton, 1992.

Le Roy Ladurie, Emmanuel. *The Territory of the Historian*, translated by Ben Reynolds and Sian Reynolds. Chicago: The University of Chicago Press, 1979.

Lechte, John, and Maria Margaroni. *Julia Kristeva: Live Theory*. New York: Continuum, 2004.

Lefebvre, Henri. *The Production of Space*, translated by Donald Nicholson-Smith. Oxford and Cambridge, MA: Blackwell Publishers, 1991.

Levinas, Emmanuel. *Totality and Infinity: An Essay on Exteriority*, translated by Alphonso Lingis. Pittsburgh, PA: Duquesne University Press, 1969. Originally published as *Totalité et Infini: Essai sur l'extériorité*. The Hague: Martinus Nijhoff, 1961.

Lévi-Strauss, Claude. *The Savage Mind*, translated by John Weightman and Doreen Weightman. London: Weidenfeld & Nicolson, 1966.

Libeskind, Daniel. *Breaking Ground: Adventures in Life and Architecture*. New York: Riverhead Books, 2004.

———. *radix-matrix*. Munich: Prestel Verlag, 1997.

———. *The Space of Encounter*. New York: Universe Publishing, 2000.

Loraux, Nicole. *The Children of Athena: Athenian Ideas about Citizenship and the Division between the Sexes*, translated by Caroline Levine. Princeton: Princeton University Press, 1993.

———. *The Mourning Voice: An Essay on Greek Tragedy*, translated by Elizabeth Trapnell Rawlings. Ithaca, NY: Cornell University Press, 2002.

Lynn, Greg. "Introduction." Pp. 8–13 in *Folding in Architecture*, edited by Greg Lynn. New York: John Wiley & Son, 2004.

Manturana, Humberto, and Francisco Varela. *Autopoiesis and Cognition*. Dordrecht: Reidel, 1980.

Marion, Jean-Luc. *In Excess: Studies of Saturated Phenomena*. New York: Fordham University Press, 2002.

Massumi, Brian. *Parables of the Virtual*. Durham and London: Duke University Press, 2002.

Mayer, Hans. *Aufklärung Heute: Reden und Vorträge, 1978–1984*. Frankfurt: Suhrkamp, 1985.

Menninghaus, Winfried. *Schwellenkunde: Walter Benjamins Passage des Mythos*. Frankfurt: Suhrkamp, 1986.

Merleau-Ponty, Maurice. *Phenomenology of Perception*, translated by Colin Smith. London and New York: Routledge, 1996.

———. *Signes*. Paris: Gallimard, 1960.

———. *The Prose of the World*, translated by John O'Neill. Evanston, IL: Northwestern University Press, 1973.

278   Bibliography

————. *The Visible and the Invisible*, translated by Alphonso Lingis. Chicago: Northwestern University Press, 1969. Originally published as *Le visible et l'invisible, suivi de notes de travail*, edited by Claude Lefort. Paris: Gallimard, 1971.

Mills, Catherine. *The Philosophy of Agamben*. Stocksfield: Acumen, 2008.

Mohanty, Chandra Talpade. "Under Western Eyes: Feminist Scholarship and Colonial Discourses." Pp. 51–80 in *Third World Women and the Politics of Feminism*, edited by Chandra Talpade Mohanty, Ann Russo, and Lourdes Torres. Bloomington: Indiana University Press, 1997.

Moran, Brendan. "An Inhumanly Wise Shame." *The European Legacy* 14, no. 5 (August 2009), 573–85.

————. "Foolish Wisdom in Benjamin's Kafka." Pp. 175–92 in *Laughter in Eastern and Western Philosophies*, edited by Hans-Georg Moeller and Günter Wohlfart. Freiburg and Munich: Verlag Karl Alber, 2010.

Moran, Dermot. *Introduction to Phenomenology*. London and New York: Routledge, 2000.

Müller, Bernd. *"Denn ist noch nichts geschehen." Walter Benjamins Kafka-Deutung*. Cologne: Böhlau, 1996.

Muthu, Sankar. *Enlightenment against Empire*. Princeton: Princeton University Press, 2003.

Nancy, Jean-Luc. *The Inoperative Community*, translated by Peter Conor et al., edited by Peter Connor. Minneapolis: University of Minnesota Press, 1991.

Nietzsche, Friedrich. *Collected Works*, vol. 2, translated and edited by Oscar Levy. London: T. L. Foulis, 1911.

————. *Nachgelassene Fragmente. Anfang 1888 bis Anfang Januar 1889*. Vol. 8, tome 3 of *Werke*, edited by Giorgio Colli and Mazzino Montinari. Berlin: Walter de Gruyter, 1972.

————. *The Birth of Tragedy and the Case of Wagner*, translated by Walter Kaufmann. New York: Vintage, 1967.

————. *The Gay Science*, translated by Walter Kaufmann. New York: Vintage Books, 1974.

Nikolopoulou, Kalliope. "Rhiza Aimatoessa: On *Antigone*." *Intertexts* 11, no. 1 (spring 2007), 1–23.

Nussbaum, Martha. "Sophocles' *Antigone*: Conflict, Vision, and Simplification." Pp. 51–82 in *The Fragility of Goodness: Luck and Ethics in Greek Tragedy and Philosophy*. Cambridge: Cambridge University Press, 1986.

Ohmann, Richard. "The Function of English at the Present Time." Pp. 89–95 in *Falling into Theory: Conflicting Views on Reading Literature*, edited by David H. Richter. Boston and New York: Bedford/St. Martin's, 2000, second edition.

Oliver, Kelly, and Benigno Trigo. *Noir Anxiety*. Minnesota: University of Minnesota Press, 2003.

Oliver, Kelly. *Witnessing: Beyond Recognition*. Minneapolis: University of Minnesota Press, 2001.

Orwell, George. *1984*. New York: Harcourt, Brace, Jovanovich, 1977.

Palmier, Jean-Michel. *Walter Benjamin. Le chiffonnier, l'Ange et le Petit Bossu.* Paris: Klincksieck, 2006.

Pipes, Daniel. *The Rushdie Affair: The Novel, the Ayatollah, and the West.* London: Transaction Publishers, 1990.

Pitts, Jennifer. *A Turn to Empire: The Rise of Imperial Liberalism in Britain and France.* Princeton: Princeton University Press, 2005.

Plato. *Laws, Books 1–6*, translated by R. G Bury, Loeb Classical Library 187. Cambridge, MA: Harvard University Press, 2001.

———. *Laws, Books 7–12*, translated by R. G. Bury, Loeb Classical Library 192. Cambridge, MA: Harvard University Press, 1961.

———. *The Republic of Plato*, translated by Alan Bloom. New York: Basic Books, 1991.

———. *Timaeus*, translated by Benjamin Jowett. Pp. 1151–211 in *The Collected Dialogues of Plato*, edited by Edith Hamilton and Huntington Cairns. Princeton: Princeton University Press, 1980.

———. *Timaeus, Critias, Cleitophon, Menexenus, Epistles*, translated by. R. G. Bury, Loeb Classical Library 234. Cambridge, MA: Harvard University Press, 2005.

Plutarch. *Moralia*, vol. 5, translated by Frank Cole Babbitt, Loeb Classical Library 197. Cambridge, MA: Harvard University Press, 1927.

Rajchman, John. "Another View of Abstraction." *Abstraction, Journal of Philosophy and the Visual Arts* 5 (1995), 16–24.

Reder, Michael. *Conversations with Salman Rushdie.* Jackson: University Press of Mississippi, 2000.

Richter, Melvin. "Tocqueville on Algeria." *The Review of Politics* 25, no. 3 (July 1963), 362–98.

Rosset, Clément. *Le réel et son double. Essai sur l'illusion.* Paris: Gallimard, 1984.

Rowe, Colin, and Fred Koetter. "Collage City." *Architectural Review* 158, no. 942 (August 1975), 66–90.

Rrenban, Monad. *Wild, Unforgettable Philosophy.* Lanham, MD: Lexington, 2005.

Rushdie, Salman. *Imaginary Homelands.* London: Penguin Books, 1991.

———. *Midnight's Children.* London: Vintage, 1995.

———. *Shame.* London: Vintage, 1995.

———. *The Jaguar Smile.* London: Vintage, 2000.

———. *The Satanic Verses.* London: Vintage, 1998.

Sagnol, Marc. "Archaïsme et Modernité: Benjamin, Kafka et la Loi." *Les Temps Modernes* 618 (spring 2002), 90–104.

———. "Le bourbier et la cigale. Sur Benjamin et Bachofen." Pp. 47–70 in *Walter Benjamin: Critique philosophique de l'art*, edited by Rainer Rochlitz and Pierre Rusch. Paris: Presses Universitaires de France, 2005.

Samuelson, Scott. "Teaching and the Art of Layering." *Perspective: Expressing Mind & Spirit* 1, no. 2 (winter 2001), 10–19.

Santner, Eric L. "Miracles Happen: Benjamin, Rosenzweig, Freud, and the Matter of the Neighbor." Pp. 76–132 in Slavoj Žižek, Eric L. Santner, and Kenneth Reinhard, *The Neighbor: Three Inquiries in Political Theology*. Chicago: University of Chicago Press, 2005.

———. *On Creaturely Life: Rilke/Benjamin/Sebald*. Chicago: University of Chicago Press, 2006.

Sartre, Jean-Paul. *Critique of Dialectical Reason*. Vol. 1, *Theory of Practice of Ensembles*, translated by Alan Sheridan-Smith. London: New Left Books, 1976.

———. *L'imagination*. Paris: Presses Universitaires de France, 1989.

———. *The Imaginary: A Phenomenological Psychology of the Imagination*, translated by Jonathan Webber. London and New York: Routledge, 2004.

Schmitt, Carl. *The Nomos of the Earth in the International Law of the Jus Publicum Europaeum*, translated by G. L. Ulmen. New York: Telos Press, 2003.

Schor, Naomi. "This Essentialism Which Is Not One: Coming to Grips with Irigaray." Pp. 57–78 in *Engaging with Irigaray: Feminist Philosophy and Modern European Thought*, edited by Carolyn Burke, Naomi Schor, and Margaret Whitford. New York: Columbia University Press, 1994.

Schumpeter, Joseph. *Imperialism and Social Classes*, translated by Heinz Norden, edited by Paul M. Sweezy. Philadelphia: Orion Editions, 1951.

Schwarz, Henry. "Mission Impossible: Introducing Postcolonial Studies in the US Academy." Pp. 1–20 in *A Companion to Postcolonial Studies*, edited by Henry Schwarz and Sangeeta Ray. Malden, MA: Blackwell Publishers, 2000.

Sewell, William. *Logics of History: Social Theory and Social Transformation*. Chicago: University of Chicago Press, 2005.

Shakespeare, William. *King Richard II*. Pp. 359–83 in *William Shakespeare: The Complete Works*, edited by Arthur Henry Bullen. New York: Barnes & Noble Books, 1994.

Silverman, Kaja. *The Threshold of the Visible World*. New York: Routledge, 1996.

Simondon, Gilbert. *Du monde d'existence des objets techniques*. Paris: Aubier, 1989.

Society of Layerists in Multi-Media (SLMM). http://www.slmm.org (accessed July 23, 2011).

Sophocles. *Antigone*, translated by David Grene. Pp. 177–232 in *Greek Tragedies*, vol. 1, edited by David Grene and Richmond Lattimore. Chicago: University of Chicago Press, 1991.

———. *Antigone*. Pp. 1–127 in *Sophocles*, vol. 2, translated and edited by Hugh Lloyd-Jones, Loeb Classical Library 21. Cambridge, MA: Harvard University Press, 1994.

———. *Oedipus at Colonus*, translated by David Grene. Pp. 77–157 in *Sophocles*, vol. 1, edited by David Grene and Richmond Lattimore. Chicago: The University of Chicago Press, 1991.

Spencer, Lloyd. "Allegory in the World of Commodity: The Importance of *Central Park*." *New German Critique* 34 (winter 1985), 59–77.

Steiner, Uwe. *Walter Benjamin*. Stuttgart: Verlag J. B. Metzler, 2004.

Stiegler, Bernard. *De la misère symbolique*. Vol. 1, *L'époque hyperindustrielle*. Paris: Galilée, 2004.

———. *De la misère symbolique*. Vol. 2, *La catastrophe du sensible*. Paris: Galilée, 2005.

———. *La technique et le temps*. Vol. 2, *La désorientation*. Paris: Galilée, 1996.

———. *La technique et le temps*. Vol. 3, *Le temps du cinéma et la question du mal-être*. Paris: Galilée, 2001.

Strand, Erik. "Gandhian Communalism and the *Midnight Children's* Conference." *ELH* 72 (2005), 975–1016.

Su, John J. "Epic of Failure: Disappointment as Utopian Fantasy in *Midnight's Children*." *Twentieth Century Literature: A Scholarly and Critical Journal* 47, no. 4 (winter 2001), 545–68.

Tacitus, Cornelius Gaius. *"The Agricola" and "The Germania,"* translated by Harold Mattingly. London: Penguin, 1970.

Tackels, Bruno. "Les Kafkas de Benjamin." Pp. 71–89 in *Walter Benjamin: Critique philosophique de l'art*, edited by Rainer Rochlitz and Pierre Rusch. Paris: Presses Universitaires de France, 2005.

———. *Walter Benjamin: Une vie dans les textes*. Arles: Actes Sud, 2009.

Tilly, Charles. *The Contentious French: Four Centuries of Popular Struggle*. Harvard: Harvard University Press, 1986.

———. *The Vendée: A Sociological Analysis of the Counter-Revolution of 1793*. Harvard: Harvard University Press, 1964.

Tocqueville, Alexis de. *Democracy in America*, translated by George Lawrence, edited by J. P. Meyer. New York: Perennial Library, 1988.

———. *The Old Regime and the French Revolution*, translated by Stuart Gilbert. New York: Anchor Books, 1955.

———. *Writings on Empire and Slavery*, translated and edited by Jennifer Pitts. Baltimore: Johns Hopkins University Press, 2001.

Ungers, Oswald Mathias. "Architettura con Tema/Architecture as Theme." Pp. 94–96 in *Theories and Manifestoes of Contemporary Architecture*, edited by Charles Jenks and Karl Kropf. Chichester, West Sussex: Academy Editions, 1997.

Venturi, Robert. *Complexity and Contradiction in Architecture*. New York: The Museum of Modern Art, 1966.

———. "Complexity and Contradiction in Architecture: Selections from a Forthcoming Book." Pp. 72–77 in *Theorizing a New Agenda for Architecture: An Anthology of Architectural Theory, 1965–1995*, edited by Kate Nesbitt. New York: Princenton Architectural Press, 1996.

Venturi, Robert, Denise Scott Brown, and Steven Izenour. *Learning from Las Vegas*. Cambridge, MA: MIT Press, 1977, revised edition.

Vernant, Jean-Pierre, and Pierre Vidal-Naquet. *Myth and Tragedy in Ancient Greece*, translated by Janet Lloyd. Cambridge, MA: Zone Books, 1990.

Villa, Dana. *Public Freedom*. Princeton: Princeton University Press, 2008.

Wambacq, Judith. "Het differentiële gehalte van Merleau-Ponty's ontologie." *Tijdschrift voor Filosofie* 70, no. 3 (September 2008), 479–508.

Watkin, William. *The Literary Agamben: Adventures in Logopoiesis.* London: Continumm, 2010.

———. "The Materialization of Prose: Poiesis versus Dianoia in the work of Godzich & Kittay, Schklovsky, Silliman, and Agamben." *Paragraph* 31, no. 3 (2008), 344–64.

Weber, Max. *Economy and Society*, vol. 2, translated by Ephraim Fischoff et al., edited by Guenther Roth and Claus Wittich. Berkeley and Los Angeles: University of California Press, 1978.

Weed, Elizabeth. "The Question of Style." Pp. 79–110 in *Engaging with Irigaray: Feminist Philosophy and Modern European Thought*, edited by Carolyn Burke, Naomi Schor, and Margaret Whitford. New York: Columbia University Press, 1994.

Wehr, Hans. *A Dictionary of Modern Written Arabic*, edited by J. M. Cowan. Ithaca, NY: Spoken Language Services, 1979.

Weidner, Daniel. "Jüdisches Gedächtnis, mystische Tradition und moderne Literatur. Walter Benjamin und Gershom Scholem deuten Kafka." *Weimarer Beiträge* 46, no. 2 (2000), 234–49.

Weigel, Sigrid. "Johann Jakob Bachofen." Pp. 539–42 in *Benjamin-Handbuch*, edited by Burkhardt Lindner. Stuttgart: Verlag J. B. Metzler, 2006.

Werth, Paul. "Extended Metaphor—a Text-World Account." *Language and Literature* 3, no. 2 (May 1994), 79–103.

Whitford, Margaret. *Luce Irigaray: Philosophy in the Feminine.* New York: Routledge, 1991.

Wikipedia contributors. "Causal Layered Analysis." *Wikipedia, The Free Encyclopedia.* http://en.wikipedia.org/wiki/Causal_layered_analysis (accessed July 23, 2011).

Williams, Raymond. *Problems in Materialism and Culture: Selected Essays.* New York: Verso, 1997.

Willoquet-Maricondi, Paula. "Fleshing the Text: Greenaway's *Pillow Book* and the Erasure of the Body." *Postmodern Culture* 9, no. 2 (1999). http://muse.jhu.edu/journals/postmodern_culture/v009/9.2willoquet.html (accessed February 28, 2011).

Wills, David. "Techneology or the Discourse of Speed." Pp. 237–65 in *The Prosthetic Impulse: From a Posthuman Present to a Biocultural Future*, edited by Marquand Smith and Joanne Morra. Cambridge, MA: MIT Press, 2006.

Wolin, Sheldon. *Tocqueville between Two Worlds: The Making of a Political and Theoretical Life.* Princeton: Princeton University Press, 2001.

Wordsworth, William. *The Prelude.* Pp. 230–313 in *The Norton Anthology of English Literature*, vol. 2, fourth edition, edited by M. H. Abrams. New York: W. W. Norton & Company, 1979.

Wyschogrod, Edith. "Eating the Text, Defiling the Hands: Specters in Arnold Schoenberg's Opera *Moses and Aron*." Pp. 245–59 in *God, the Gift, and*

Postmodernism, edited by John D. Caputo and Michael J. Scanlon. Bloomington: Indiana University Press, 1999.

Ziarek, Ewa Płonowska. "Kristeva and Fanon: Revolutionary Violence and Ironic Articulation." Pp. 57–75 in *Revolt, Affect, Collectivity: The Unstable Boundaries of Kristeva's Polis*, edited by Tina Chanter and Ewa Płonowska Ziarek. Albany: SUNY Press, 2005.

Žižek, Slavoj. *The Ticklish Subject: The Absent Centre of Political Ontology.* New York: Verso, 1999.

Contributors

MICHAEL BEEHLER is professor emeritus of English at Montana State University and a longtime contributor to IAPL. He has published widely on literary theory, modern American poetry, and architectural theory and practice. His recent works include essays on the architecture of Frank Lloyd Wright, the poetry of Wallace Stevens, and the intersections of theory and architecture in Jacques Derrida and Daniel Libeskind.

TINA CHANTER is professor of philosophy and gender at Kingston University, London. She is the author of *Whose Antigone? The Tragic Marginalization of Slavery* (SUNY Press, 2011), *The Picture of Abjection: Film, Fetish, and the Nature of Difference* (Indiana University Press, 2008), *Gender* (Continuum, 2006), *Time, Death and the Feminine: Levinas with Heidegger* (Stanford University Press, 2001), and *Ethics of Eros: Irigaray's Re-writing of the Philosophers* (Routledge, 1995). She is also the editor of *Feminist Interpretations of Emmanuel Levinas* (Penn State University Press, 2001), and coeditor of *Revolt, Affect, Collectivity: The Unstable Boundaries of Kristeva's Polis* (SUNY Press, 2005), *Sarah Kofman's Corpus* (SUNY Press, 2008), and *The Returns of Antigone: Interdisciplinary Essays* (SUNY Press, 2014). In addition, she edits the Gender Theory series at SUNY Press. Her book tentatively titled *Rancière, Art, and Politics: Broken Perceptions* will appear shortly with Bloomsbury Press.

MARIOS CONSTANTINOU was born in Cyprus, semioccupied by Turkish troops. He holds a PhD from the New School for Social Research. Until recently he held a post at the University of Cyprus, from which he resigned in protest against corruption, censorship, and the increasing NGOization of academic life. He is the editor of *Badiou and the Political Condition* (Edinburgh University Press, 2014). His publications on and reviews of Badiou's work reclaim it in an anti-imperialist direction as the only available alternative to the postcolonial impasse of foreign dependence and local corruption. Current publications on these issues have appeared in *Parallax, Third Text, Parrhēsia* and *The Year's Work in Critical and Cultural Theory*. He has translated Jodi Dean's *Publicity's Secret* in Greek and is currently working on a monograph on the political economy of the Internet.

STACY KELTNER is associate professor of gender and women's studies at Kennesaw State University in Kennesaw, GA. She is author of *Kristeva: Thresholds* (Polity, 2011) and coeditor, with Kelly Oliver, of *Psychoanalysis, Aesthetics, and Politics in the Work of Kristeva* (SUNY Press, 2009).

JOHN LECHTE is emeritus professor in sociology at Macquarie University in Sydney. His most recent book, published with Saul Newman, is *Agamben and the Politics of Human Rights: Statelessness, Images, Violence* (Edinburgh University Press, 2013). His book *The Human: Bare Life and Ways of Life* is due to be published by Bloomsbury in 2017. He has published widely in European philosophy and theory, especially on the work of Arendt, Bataille, Derrida, Kristeva, and Levinas.

ADNAN MAHMUTOVIC is lecturer in English literature and creative writing at Stockholm University. His work includes *Ways of Being Free* (Rodopi, 2012), *Thinner than a Hair* (Cinnamon Press, 2010), and *How to Fare Well and Stay Fair* (Salt Publishing, 2012). He has coedited *Worlds of Grant Morrison* with Frank Bramlett and Francesco-Alessio Ursini (special issue of *Image-TexT*, 2015), and *How Is Future Portrayed in Comics* (MacFarland Press, 2017).

BRENDAN MORAN is associate professor of philosophy and affiliate associate professor of German at the University of Calgary, Canada. He has published a book titled *Wild, Unforgettable Philosophy in Early Works of Walter Benjamin* (Lexington Books, 2005), and articles on Benjamin, Agamben, Kafka, Salomo Friedlaender, and others. With Carlo Salzani, he has edited *Philosophy and Kafka*, and *Towards the Critique of Violence: Walter Benjamin and Giorgio Agamben*.

KALLIOPI NIKOLOPOULOU is associate professor of comparative literature at the University at Buffalo. She works on philosophical approaches to literature and, particularly, on the relationship of ancients to moderns. Her book *Tragically Speaking: On the Use and Abuse of Theory for Life* (University of Nebraska Press, 2013) focuses on the philosophical impact of Greek tragedy on modern thought.

GERTRUDE POSTL is professor of philosophy and women's and gender Studies at Suffolk County Community College, Selden, NY, USA. Her research focus is on feminist philosophy, in particular authors such as Luce Irigaray, Julia Kristeva, Hélène Cixous, and Judith Butler. She currently works on the interrelation between body and language in feminist theory and the political implications of reading/writing. Publications include: *Weibliches Sprechen. Feministische Entwürfe zu Sprache und Geschlecht* (Passagen, 1991), *Contemporary Feminist Philosophy in German* (special issue editor of *Hypatia: A Journal of Feminist Philosophy*, 2005), and *Hélène Cixous. Das Lachen der Medusa zusammen mit aktuellen Beiträgen* (coeditor with Esther Hutfless and Elisabeth Schäfer, Passagen, 2013).

FRANCES L. RESTUCCIA is professor of English at Boston College, where she teaches contemporary theory, modernism, and the world novel. She cochairs the "Psychoanalytic Practices" seminar at Harvard's Mahindra Humanities Center. She is the author of *James Joyce and the Law of the Father* (Yale University Press, 1989), *Melancholics in Love: Representing Women's Depression and*

Domestic Abuse (Rowman & Littlefield, 2000), *Amorous Acts: Lacanian Ethics in Modernism, Film, and Queer Theory* (Stanford University Press, 2006), and *The Blue Box: Kristevan/Lacanian Readings of Contemporary Film* (Continuum, 2012). She has published articles in journals such as *Raritan, Contemporary Literature, Novel, Genre, Genders, American Imago, Lacanian Ink, Film-Philosophy,* and *Semplokē.* She has a chapter in *Revolt, Affect, Collectivity: The Unstable Boundaries of Kristeva's Polis* (edited by Ewa Ziarek and Tina Chanter, SUNY Press, 2005) and another piece in *Psychoanalysis, Aesthetics, and Politics in the Work of Kristeva* (edited by Kelly Oliver and S. K. Keltner, SUNY Press, 2009). A chapter titled "Sebastian's Skull: Establishing 'the Society of the Icon'" is part of *Kristeva's Fiction* (edited by Benigno Trigo, SUNY Press, 2013). Two of her essays on Agamben have appeared in *Philosophy Today* (2012, 2015). She is currently writing a book on Agamben's notion of the messianic, especially as it is manifested in literature.

ELENA TZELEPIS teaches at the University of Athens. She completed her doctoral studies in philosophy at the New School for Social Research, New York. She has taught at Columbia University and has been a fellow at the Center for the Study of Social Difference, Columbia University, and at the Birkbeck Institute for the Humanities, University of London. She works on the intersections of politics and art, on critique and social change, and on the politics of difference. Among her publications are the coedited volume *Rewriting Difference: Luce Irigaray and "the Greeks"* (SUNY Press, 2010) and the edited volume *Antigone's Antinomies: Critical Readings of the Political* (in Greek, Ekkremes, 2014).

JUDITH WAMBACQ is a philosopher teaching at the School of Art in Ghent, Belgium. She publishes on French philosophy (phenomenology and poststructuralism), aesthetics, contemporary dance, and theater. She is the author of *Thinking between Merleau-Ponty and Deleuze* (Ohio University Press, 2017). Together with Bart Buseyne and Liesbet Samyn, she has translated Stiegler's *Passer à l'acte* into Dutch (*Als een vliegende vis,* Garant, 2007) and is currently translating a Dutch novel on Marcel Duchamp (K. A. Schippers, *De Bruid van Marcel Duchamp*) into French.

WILLIAM WATKIN is professor of contemporary literature and philosophy at Brunel University, West London. He is the author of *In the Process of Poetry: The New York School and the Avant-Garde* (Bucknell, 2001), *On Mourning: Theories of Loss in Modern Literature* (Edinburgh University Press, 2004) and *The Literary Agamben: Adventures on Logopoiesis* (Continuum, 2010). He has just completed his fourth monograph, *Agamben and Indifference,* and is currently finishing the final draft of a fifth, *Deleuze and the Consistency of Indifference.*

Editors

CHRISTAKIS CHATZICHRISTOU is associate professor of architecture at the University of Cyprus. He received his first degree in architectural engineering in 1986 and a master in architecture in 1991 from the University of Texas at Austin, and was awarded a PhD in architecture from the Bartlett School of Graduate Studies at the University College London in 2002. He taught at Pratt in New York (visiting professor, spring 2010), the American University of Beirut, and the Lebanese American University (2002–2003).

Through his designs, paintings and short videos he examines issues in visual perception, which are central to architectural debates as well. Such is the relationship between figure and form or syntax and semiotics, subtraction or erasure, abstraction and layering, synchronicity and "synchoricity." Central to this research is the concept of sacrifice in architectural and urban space.

He has received a number of awards in architectural competitions, participated in the Venice Biennale for Cyprus in 2006 and 2008, while in 2010 he was appointed as the curator of the Cyprus pavilion for the same exhibition.

APOSTOLOS LAMPROPOULOS is professor of comparative literature at the University Bordeaux Montaigne. He has also taught at the University of Cyprus (2002–2014), as well as at the University Paris Ouest Nanterre La Défense, at the University of Patras and at the Free University of Berlin. He has published a monograph entitled *Le Pari de la description: l'effet d'une figure déjà lue* (L'Har-mattan, 2002), coedited the volumes *States of Theory: History and Geography of Critical Narratives* (with Antonis Balasopoulos, Metaichmio, 2010) and *AutoBioPhagies* (with May Chehab, Peter Lang, 2011), as well as the thematic issue "Configurations of Cultural Amnesia" of the journal *Synthesis* (with Vassiliki Markidou, 2011). He has also translated into Greek Antoine Compagnon's *Le Démon de la théorie. Littérature et sens commun* (Metaichmio, 2003) and Jonathan Culler's *On Deconstruction: Theory and Criticism after Structuralism* (Metaichmio, 2006).

MARIA MARGARONI is associate professor in literary theory and feminist thought at the University of Cyprus. She has held visiting fellowships at the Institute for Advanced Studies in the Humanities (University of Edinburgh) and the Centre for Cultural Analysis, Theory and History (University of Leeds). Her publications include: *Julia Kristeva: Live Theory* (with John Lechte, Continuum, 2004), *Metaphoricity and the Politics of Mobility* (with Effie Yiannopoulou, Rodopi, 2006), *Intimate Transfers* (with Effie Yiannopoulou, special issue of the *European Journal of English Studies*, 2005) and *Violence and the Sacred*, special issue of *Philosophy Today*, 2012. She is currently working on a monograph focusing on the thought of Julia Kristeva.

Index of Names

Index of Topics